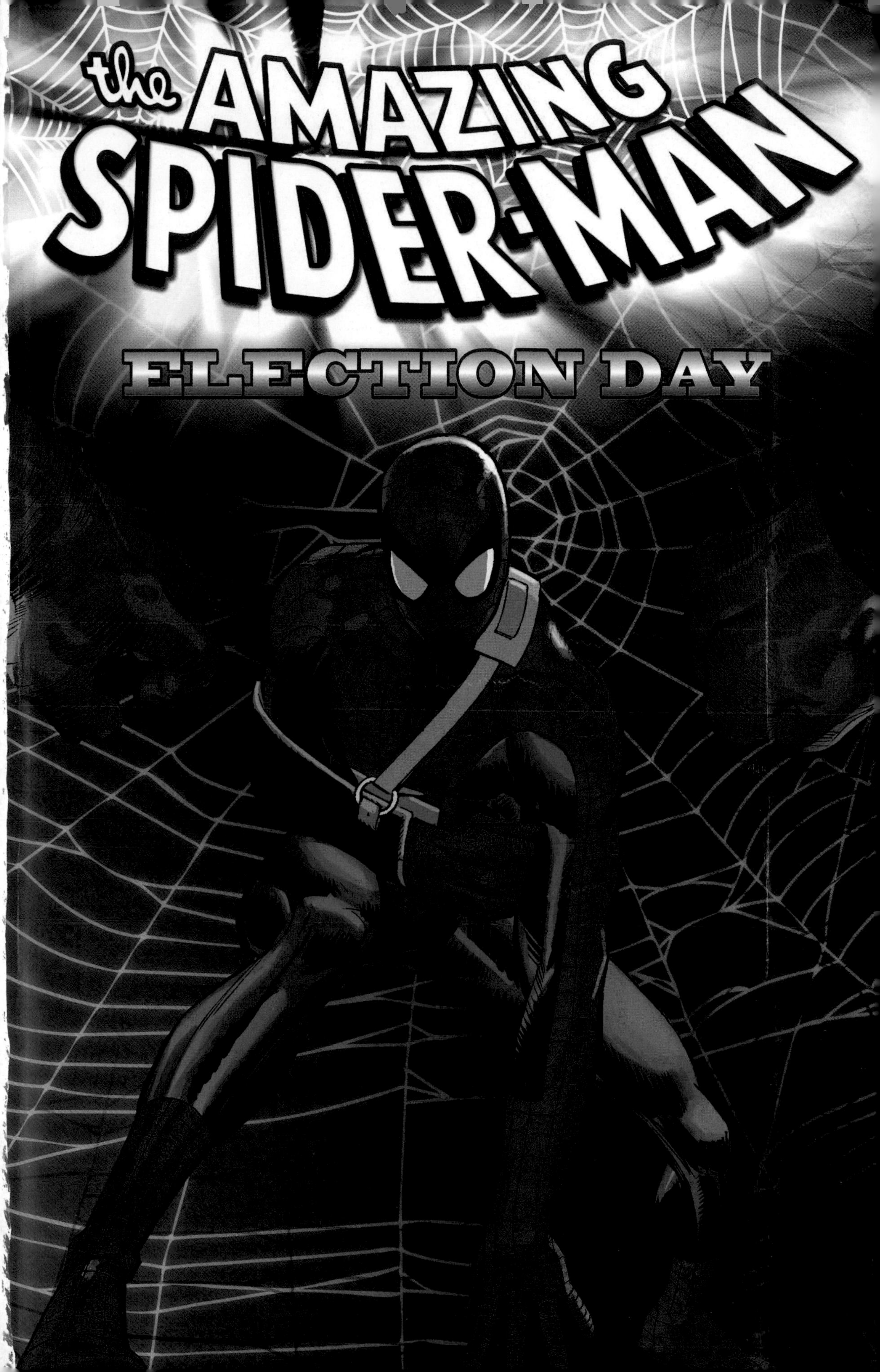
the AMAZING SPIDER-MAN
ELECTION DAY

the AMAZING SPIDER-MAN
ELECTION DAY

ISSUES #584-588
Writer: **MARC GUGGENHEIM**
Pencilers: **JOHN ROMITA JR.**
WITH **BARRY KITSON (ISSUE #586)**
Inkers: **KLAUS JANSON**
    WITH **KARL KESEL (ISSUE #586)**
    & **TOM PALMER (ISSUE #588)**
Colorists: **DEAN WHITE**
    WITH **ANDRES MOSSA (ISSUE #586)**
Letterer: **VIRTUAL CALLIGRAPHY'S CORY PETIT**
Covers: **JOHN ROMITA JR., KLAUS JANSON**
& **DEAN WHITE**

"WITH GREAT RESPONSIBILITY COMES GREAT POWER"
Writer: **MARC GUGGENHEIM**
Pencilers: **FABRIZIO FIORENTINO**
    & **PATRICK OLLIFFE**
Inkers: **KRIS JUSTICE, LIVESAY**
    & **SERGE LAPOINTE**
Colorists: **CHRIS CHUCKRY** & **ALLEN PASSALAQUA**
Letterer: **VIRTUAL CALIGRAPHY'S RUS WOOTON**
Cover: **TOMM COKER**

"THE SPARTACUS GAMBIT"
Writer: **MARC GUGGENHEIM**
Art: **MARCOS MARTIN**
Colorist: **JAVIER RODRIGUEZ**
Letterer: **VIRTUAL CALLIGRAPHY'S CORY PETIT**
Cover: **GREG LAND, JAY LEISTEN**
& **FRANK D'ARMATA**

"SPIDEY MEETS THE PRESIDENT"
Writer: **ZEB WELLS**
Art: **TODD NAUCK**
Colorist: **FRANK D'ARMATA**
Letterer: **JARED K. FLETCHER**
Cover: **PHIL JIMENEZ**

"GETTYSBURG DISTRESS"
Writer: **MATT FRACTION**
Art: **ANDY MACDONALD**
Colorist: **NICK FILARDI**
Letterer: **CHRIS ELIOPOULOS**
Cover: **PAOLO RIVERA**

Spidey's Braintrust: **BOB GALE, MARC GUGGENHEIM & DAN SLOTT**
Assistant Editor: **THOMAS BRENNAN** • Editor: **STEPHEN WACKER** • Executive Editor: **TOM BREVOORT**

Collection Editor: **JENNIFER GRÜNWALD** • Editorial Assistant: **ALEX STARBUCK**
Assistant Editors: **CORY LEVINE & JOHN DENNING** • Editor, Special Projects: **MARK D. BEAZLEY**
Senior Editor, Special Projects: **JEFF YOUNGQUIST** • Senior Vice President of Sales: **DAVID GABRIEL**

Editor in Chief: **JOE QUESADA** • Publisher: **DAN BUCKLEY** • Executive Producer: **ALAN FINE**

SPIDER-MAN: ELECTION DAY. Contains material originally published in magazine form as AMAZING SPIDER-MAN #583-588, and AMAZING SPIDER-MAN: EXTRA! #1 and #3. First printing 2009. ISBN# 978-0-7851-4131-0. Published by MARVEL PUBLISHING, INC., a subsidiary of MARVEL ENTERTAINMENT, INC. OFFICE OF PUBLICATION: 417 5th Avenue, New York, NY 10016. Copyright © 2009 Marvel Characters, Inc. All rights reserved. $29.99 per copy in the U.S. (GST #R127032852). Canadian Agreement #40668537. All characters featured in this issue and the distinctive names and likenesses thereof, and all related indicia are trademarks of Marvel Characters, Inc. No similarity between any of the names, characters, persons, and/or institutions in this magazine with those of any living or dead person or institution is intended, and any such similarity which may exist is purely coincidental. **Printed in the U.S.A.** ALAN FINE, CEO Marvel Publishing Division and EVP & CMO Marvel Characters B.V.; DAN BUCKLEY, President of Publishing - Print & Digital Media; JIM SOKOLOWSKI, Chief Operating Officer; DAVID GABRIEL, SVP of Publishing Sales & Circulation; DAVID BOGART, SVP of Business Affairs & Talent Management; MICHAEL PASCIULLO, VP Merchandising & Communications; JIM O'KEEFE, VP of Operations & Logistics; DAN CARR, Executive Director of Publishing Technology; JUSTIN F. GABRIE, Director of Publishing & Editorial Operations; SUSAN CRESPI, Editorial Operations Manager; ALEX MORALES, Publishing Operations Manager; STAN LEE, Chairman Emeritus. For information regarding advertising in Marvel Comics or on Marvel.com, please contact Mitch Dane, Advertising Director, at mdane@marvel.com. For Marvel subscription inquiries, please call 800-217-9158.
10 9 8 7 6 5 4 3 2 1

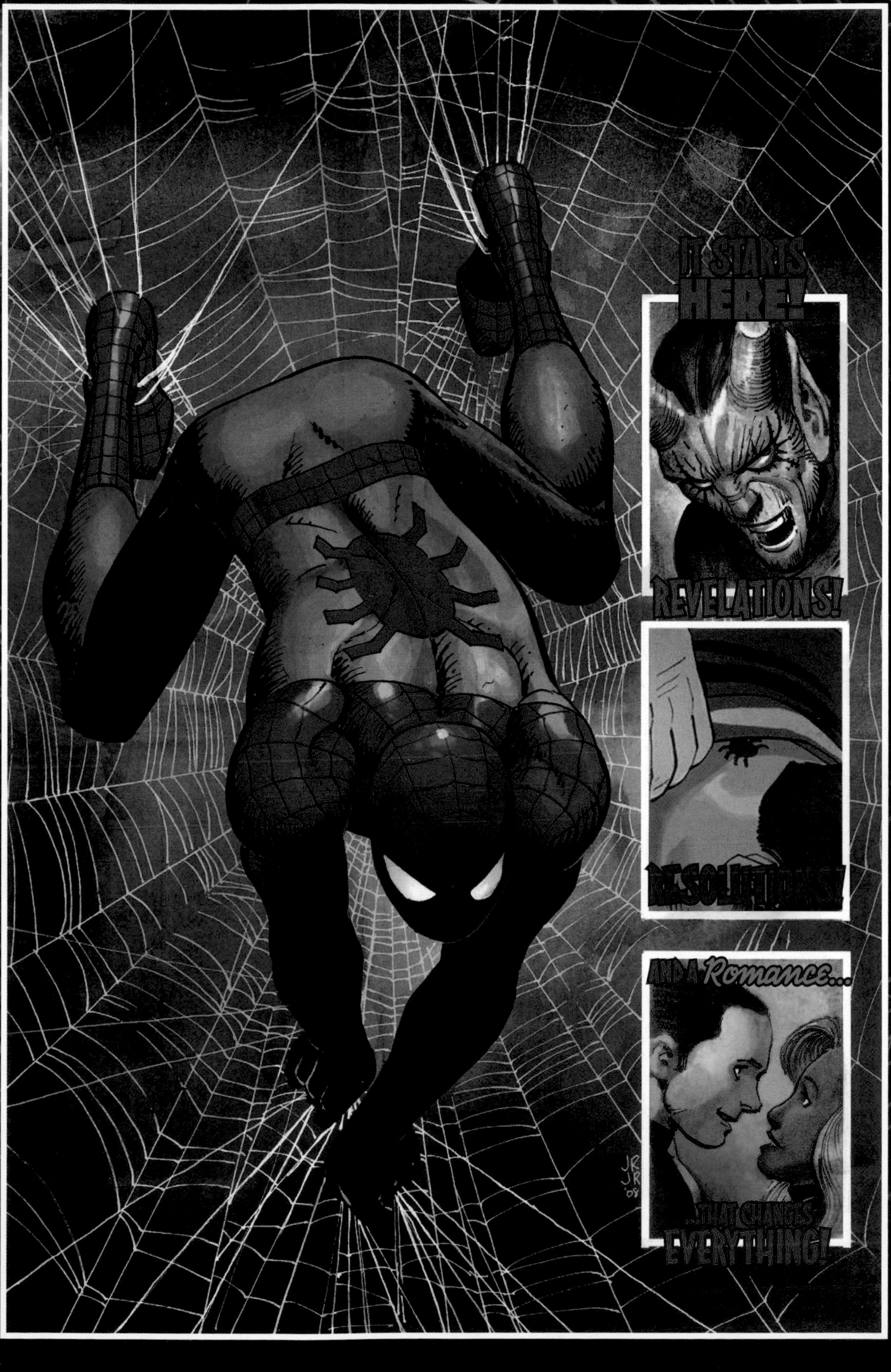

IT STARTS HERE!
REVELATIONS!
RESOLUTIONS!
AND A Romance...
...THAT CHANGES EVERYTHING!

AMAZING SPIDER-MAN #584

THE DB! FOR EVERY BRAND *NEWS* DAY!

THE DB

ELECTION DAY TUESDAY! POLS FIGHTIN' AS POLLS TIGHTEN CROWNE TO DO FIVE BOROUGH SWEEP WHILE HOLLISTER "WORKS AT A SOUP KITCHEN" IN CROWN HEIGHTS (NICE NAME, HUH?!) MORE COVERAGE ON PAGE Y13!

JANUARY 21, 2009 • WEDNESDAY

WHO IS MENACE?

BILL HOLLISTER | RANDALL CROWNE | JACKPOT | CARLIE COOPER

VIN GONZALES | DEXTER BENNETT | LILY HOLLISTER | HARRY OSBORN

The question has plagued Spider-Man since this gray goblin first entered his life, killing Mayoral Candidate Lisa Parfrey. Who is this twisted freak? And why is he so invested in the mayor's race? At first he seemed to target anyone running against Randall Crowne, a billionaire real estate developer backed by Dexter Bennett, publisher of The DB! – a newspaper whose sales have skyrocketed thanks to Menace's machinations. His primary target has been straight-arrow Councilman Bill Hollister, father of the beautiful Lily Hollister, Harry Osborn's girlfriend. But in a recent attack on Hollister in his home, Menace implied he was actually out to help the Hollister campaign. Whose side is he really on? One thing's for certain – Menace isn't done yet.

HUNT FOR SPIDER-TRACER KILLER HEATS UP

By Betty Brant

The hunt for accused serial killer and illegal vigilante Spider-Man is on, according to Detective Quentin Palone, lead investigator of the so-called "Spider-Tracer" murders. The seemingly random killings share only one common trait – each victim has one of Spider-Man's famed "Spider-Tracers." The first victim was a John Doe pulled from the East River, but Palone's men, officers Alan O'Neil and Vin Gonzales, spotted Spider-Man over the second victim, Sean Boyle, a wanted felon…

(Continued on Page L19)

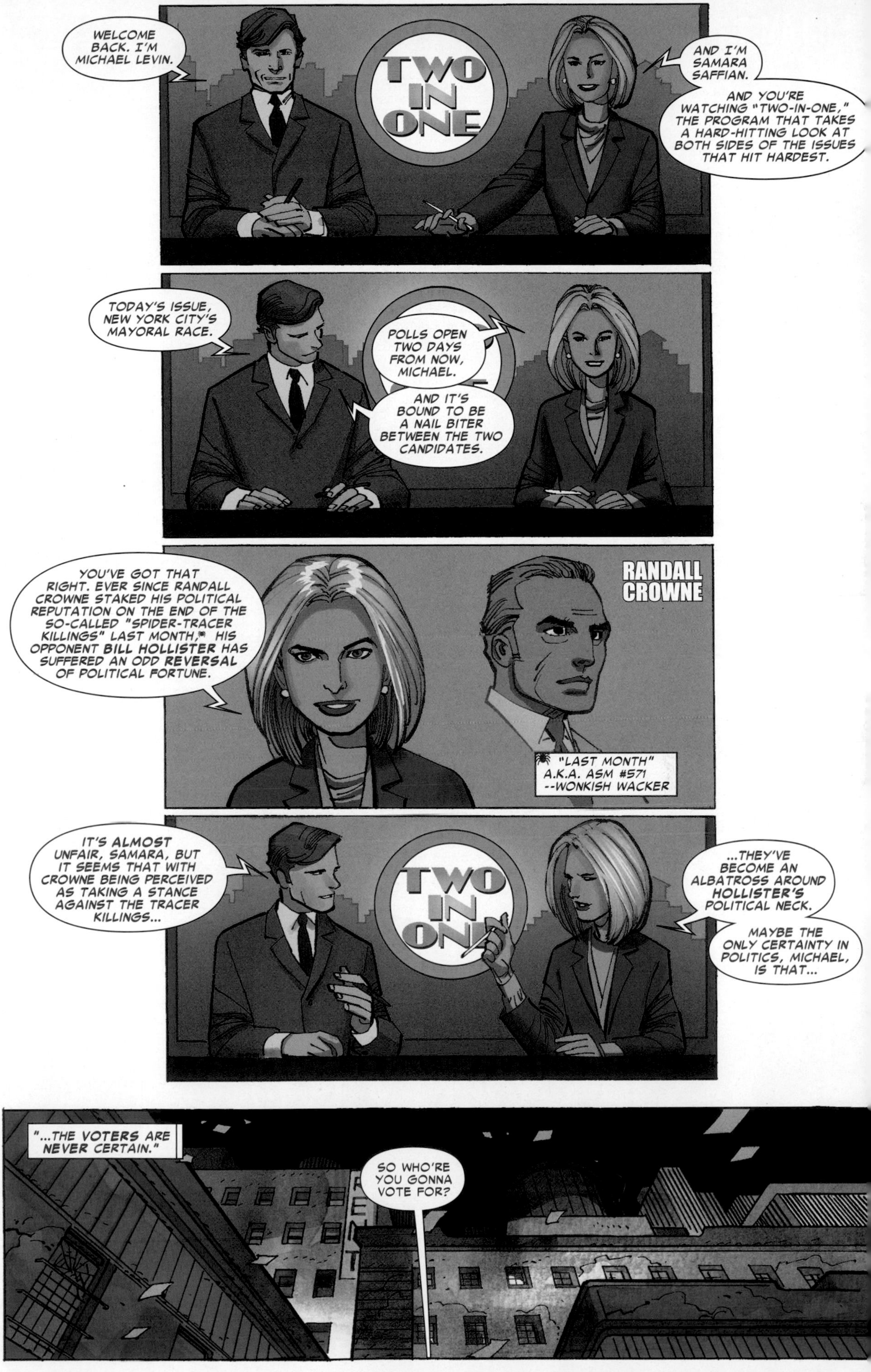
WELCOME BACK. I'M MICHAEL LEVIN.
TWO IN ONE
AND I'M SAMARA SAFFIAN.
AND YOU'RE WATCHING "TWO-IN-ONE," THE PROGRAM THAT TAKES A HARD-HITTING LOOK AT BOTH SIDES OF THE ISSUES THAT HIT HARDEST.
TODAY'S ISSUE, NEW YORK CITY'S MAYORAL RACE.
POLLS OPEN TWO DAYS FROM NOW, MICHAEL.
AND IT'S BOUND TO BE A NAIL BITER BETWEEN THE TWO CANDIDATES.
YOU'VE GOT THAT RIGHT. EVER SINCE RANDALL CROWNE STAKED HIS POLITICAL REPUTATION ON THE END OF THE SO-CALLED "SPIDER-TRACER KILLINGS" LAST MONTH,* HIS OPPONENT BILL HOLLISTER HAS SUFFERED AN ODD REVERSAL OF POLITICAL FORTUNE.
RANDALL CROWNE
* "LAST MONTH" A.K.A. ASM #571 --WONKISH WACKER
IT'S ALMOST UNFAIR, SAMARA, BUT IT SEEMS THAT WITH CROWNE BEING PERCEIVED AS TAKING A STANCE AGAINST THE TRACER KILLINGS...
TWO IN ONE
...THEY'VE BECOME AN ALBATROSS AROUND HOLLISTER'S POLITICAL NECK.
MAYBE THE ONLY CERTAINTY IN POLITICS, MICHAEL, IS THAT...
"...THE VOTERS ARE NEVER CERTAIN."
SO WHO'RE YOU GONNA VOTE FOR?

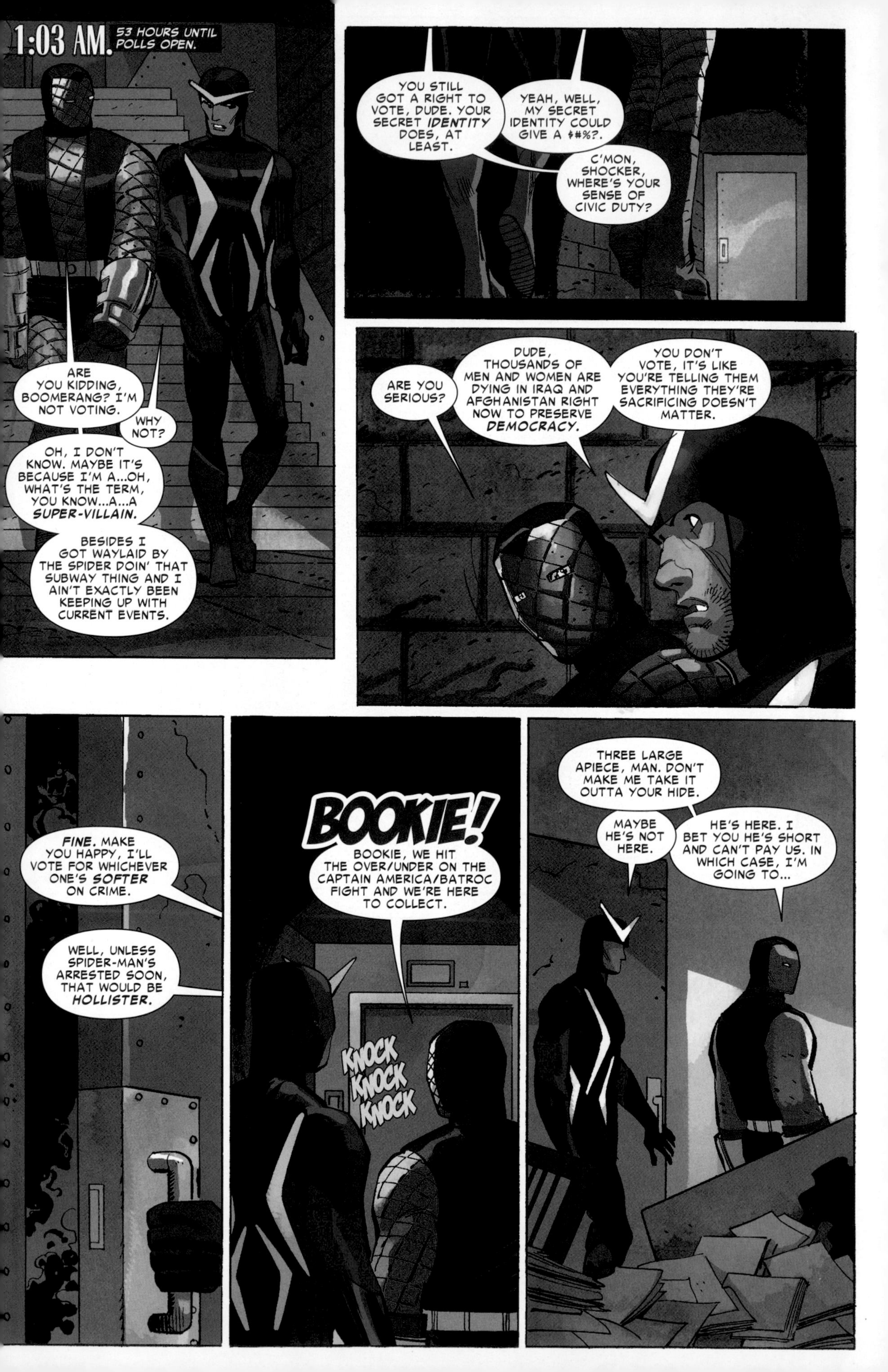
1:03 AM. 53 HOURS UNTIL POLLS OPEN.
ARE YOU KIDDING, BOOMERANG? I'M NOT VOTING.
WHY NOT?
OH, I DON'T KNOW. MAYBE IT'S BECAUSE I'M A...OH, WHAT'S THE TERM, YOU KNOW...A...A SUPER-VILLAIN.
BESIDES I GOT WAYLAID BY THE SPIDER DOIN' THAT SUBWAY THING AND I AIN'T EXACTLY BEEN KEEPING UP WITH CURRENT EVENTS.
YOU STILL GOT A RIGHT TO VOTE, DUDE. YOUR SECRET IDENTITY DOES, AT LEAST.
YEAH, WELL, MY SECRET IDENTITY COULD GIVE A $#%?.
C'MON, SHOCKER, WHERE'S YOUR SENSE OF CIVIC DUTY?
ARE YOU SERIOUS?
DUDE, THOUSANDS OF MEN AND WOMEN ARE DYING IN IRAQ AND AFGHANISTAN RIGHT NOW TO PRESERVE DEMOCRACY.
YOU DON'T VOTE, IT'S LIKE YOU'RE TELLING THEM EVERYTHING THEY'RE SACRIFICING DOESN'T MATTER.
FINE. MAKE YOU HAPPY, I'LL VOTE FOR WHICHEVER ONE'S SOFTER ON CRIME.
WELL, UNLESS SPIDER-MAN'S ARRESTED SOON, THAT WOULD BE HOLLISTER.
BOOKIE!
BOOKIE, WE HIT THE OVER/UNDER ON THE CAPTAIN AMERICA/BATROC FIGHT AND WE'RE HERE TO COLLECT.
KNOCK KNOCK KNOCK
THREE LARGE APIECE, MAN. DON'T MAKE ME TAKE IT OUTTA YOUR HIDE.
MAYBE HE'S NOT HERE.
HE'S HERE. I BET YOU HE'S SHORT AND CAN'T PAY US. IN WHICH CASE, I'M GOING TO...

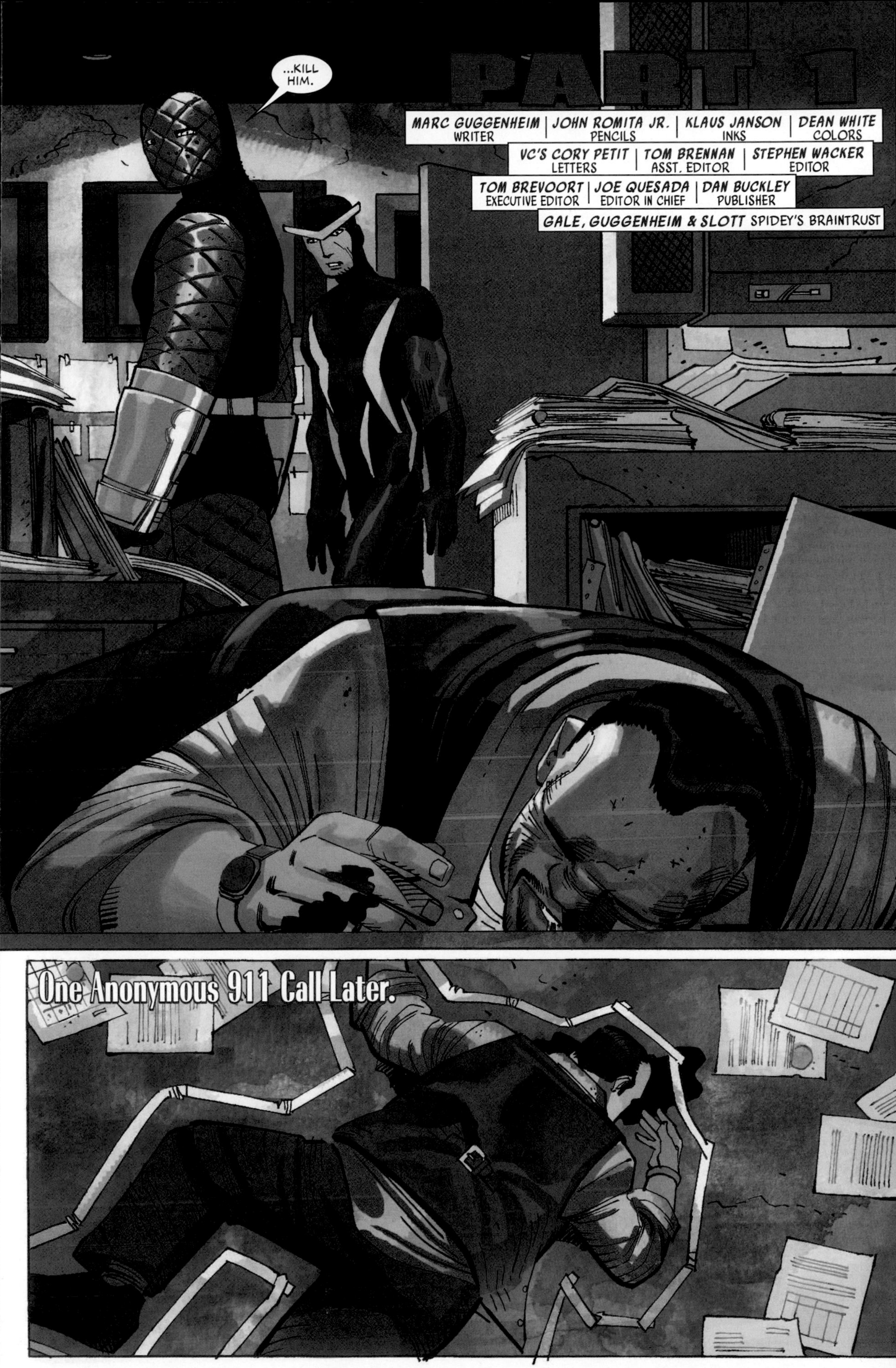

...KILL HIM.
PART 1
MARC GUGGENHEIM WRITER | JOHN ROMITA JR. PENCILS | KLAUS JANSON INKS | DEAN WHITE COLORS
VC'S CORY PETIT LETTERS | TOM BRENNAN ASST. EDITOR | STEPHEN WACKER EDITOR
TOM BREVOORT EXECUTIVE EDITOR | JOE QUESADA EDITOR IN CHIEF | DAN BUCKLEY PUBLISHER
GALE, GUGGENHEIM & SLOTT SPIDEY'S BRAINTRUST
One Anonymous 911 Call Later.

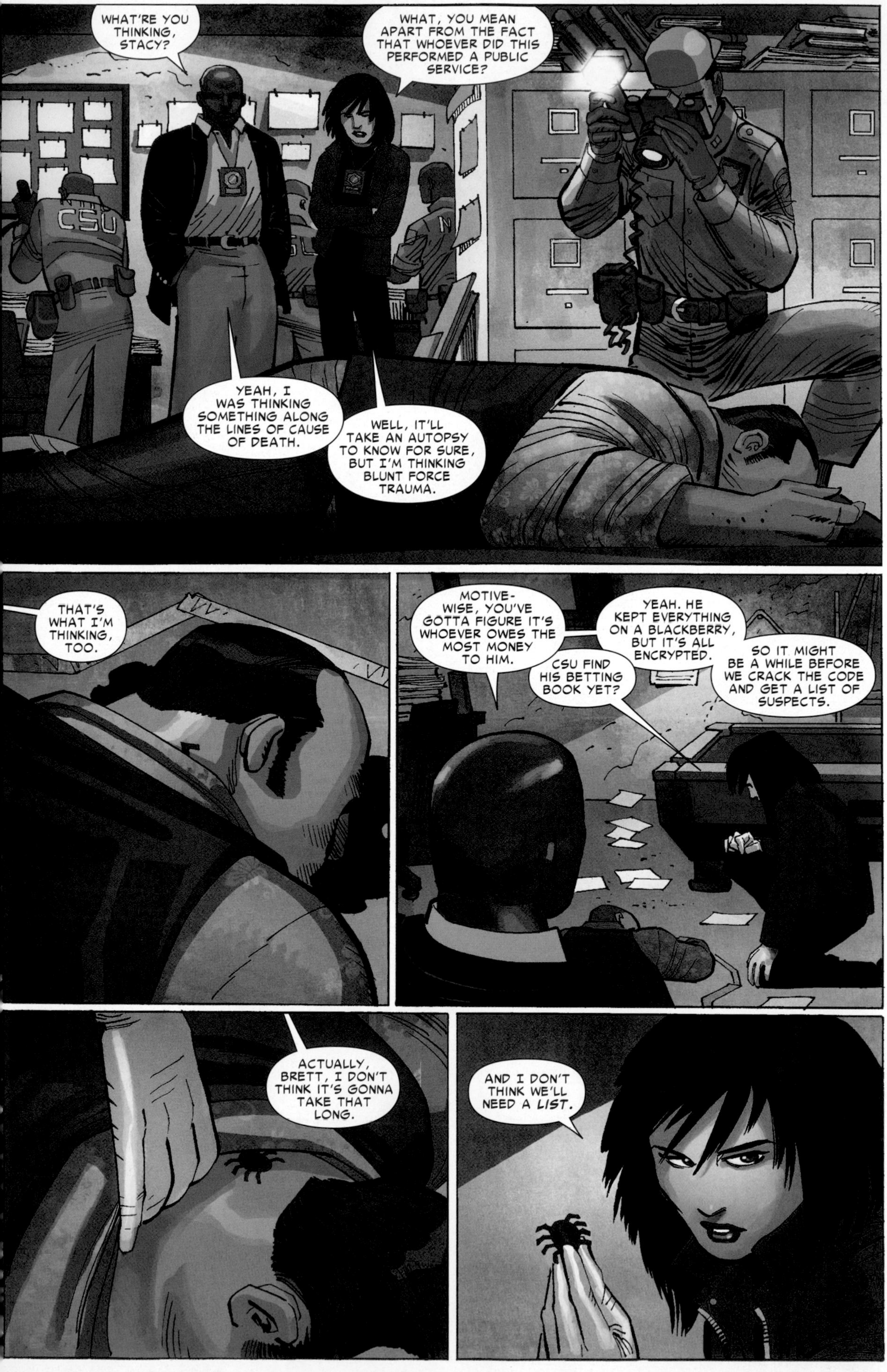
WHAT'RE YOU THINKING, STACY?
WHAT, YOU MEAN APART FROM THE FACT THAT WHOEVER DID THIS PERFORMED A PUBLIC SERVICE?
YEAH, I WAS THINKING SOMETHING ALONG THE LINES OF CAUSE OF DEATH.
WELL, IT'LL TAKE AN AUTOPSY TO KNOW FOR SURE, BUT I'M THINKING BLUNT FORCE TRAUMA.
CSU
THAT'S WHAT I'M THINKING, TOO.
MOTIVE-WISE, YOU'VE GOTTA FIGURE IT'S WHOEVER OWES THE MOST MONEY TO HIM.
CSU FIND HIS BETTING BOOK YET?
YEAH. HE KEPT EVERYTHING ON A BLACKBERRY, BUT IT'S ALL ENCRYPTED.
SO IT MIGHT BE A WHILE BEFORE WE CRACK THE CODE AND GET A LIST OF SUSPECTS.
ACTUALLY, BRETT, I DON'T THINK IT'S GONNA TAKE THAT LONG.
AND I DON'T THINK WE'LL NEED A *LIST*.

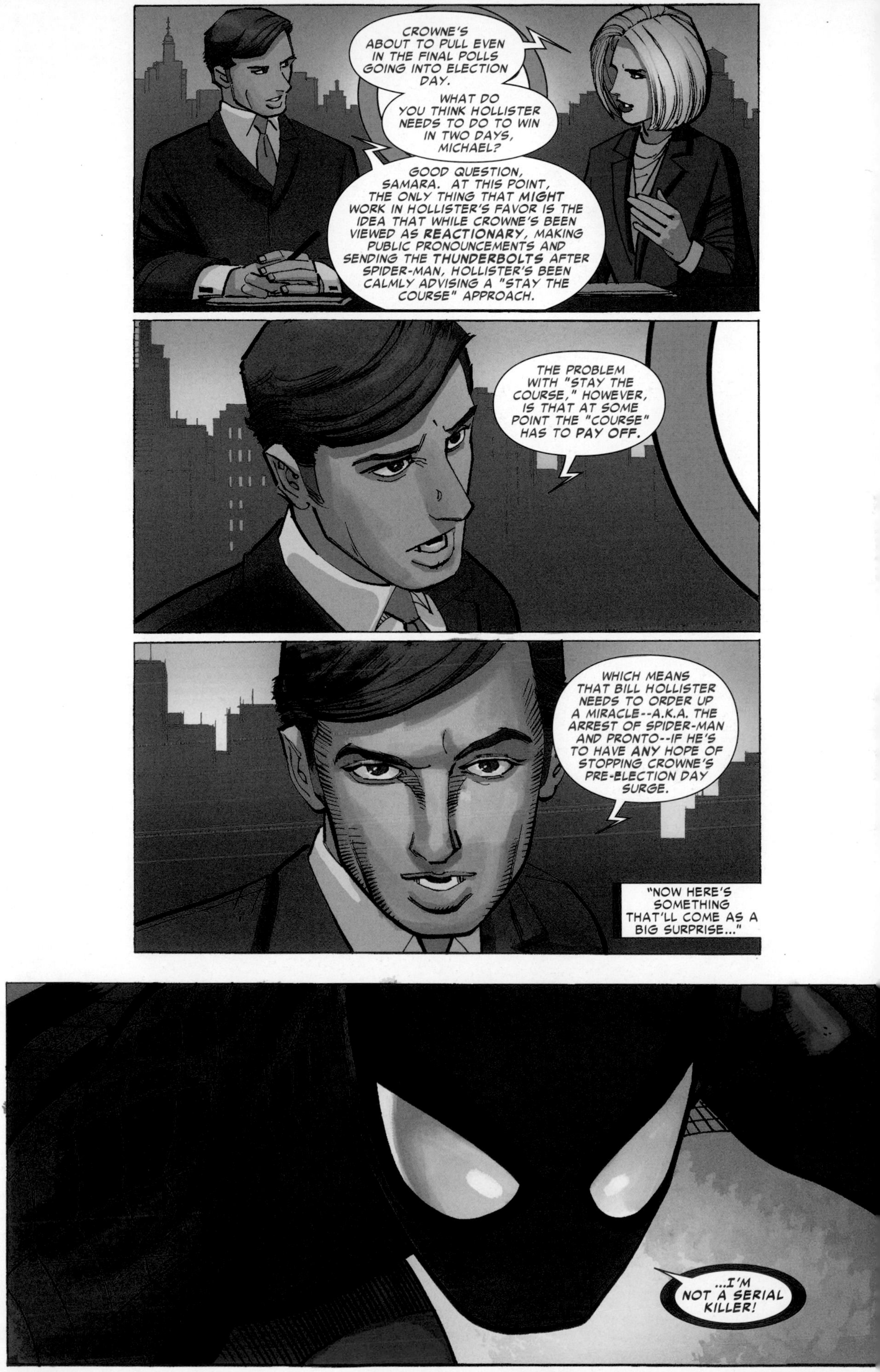
CROWNE'S ABOUT TO PULL EVEN IN THE FINAL POLLS GOING INTO ELECTION DAY.
WHAT DO YOU THINK HOLLISTER NEEDS TO DO TO WIN IN TWO DAYS, MICHAEL?
GOOD QUESTION, SAMARA. AT THIS POINT, THE ONLY THING THAT MIGHT WORK IN HOLLISTER'S FAVOR IS THE IDEA THAT WHILE CROWNE'S BEEN VIEWED AS REACTIONARY, MAKING PUBLIC PRONOUNCEMENTS AND SENDING THE THUNDERBOLTS AFTER SPIDER-MAN, HOLLISTER'S BEEN CALMLY ADVISING A "STAY THE COURSE" APPROACH.
THE PROBLEM WITH "STAY THE COURSE," HOWEVER, IS THAT AT SOME POINT THE "COURSE" HAS TO PAY OFF.
WHICH MEANS THAT BILL HOLLISTER NEEDS TO ORDER UP A MIRACLE--A.K.A. THE ARREST OF SPIDER-MAN AND PRONTO--IF HE'S TO HAVE ANY HOPE OF STOPPING CROWNE'S PRE-ELECTION DAY SURGE.
"NOW HERE'S SOMETHING THAT'LL COME AS A BIG SURPRISE..."
...I'M NOT A SERIAL KILLER!

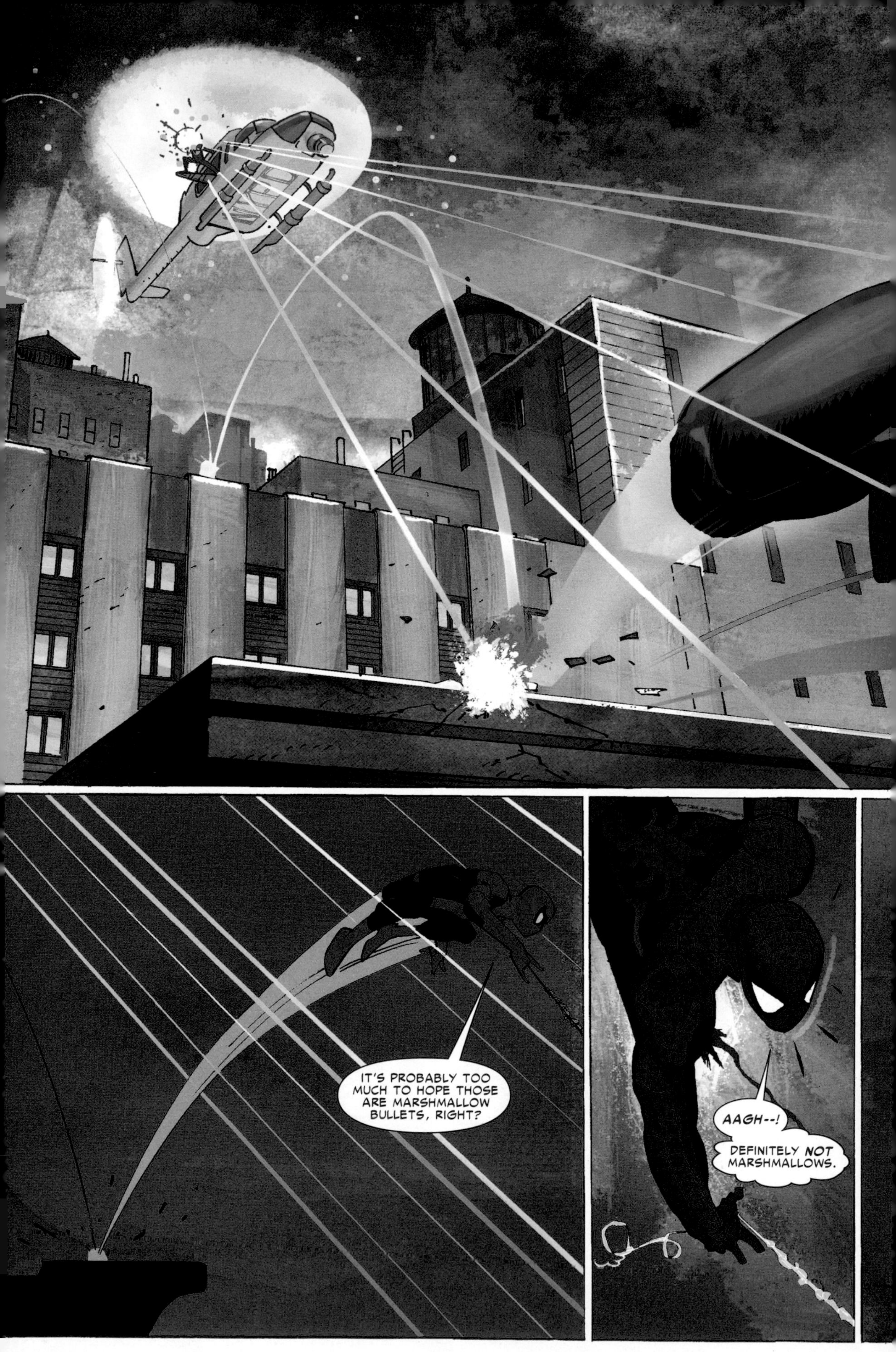
IT'S PROBABLY TOO MUCH TO HOPE THOSE ARE MARSHMALLOW BULLETS, RIGHT?
AAGH--!
DEFINITELY NOT MARSHMALLOWS.

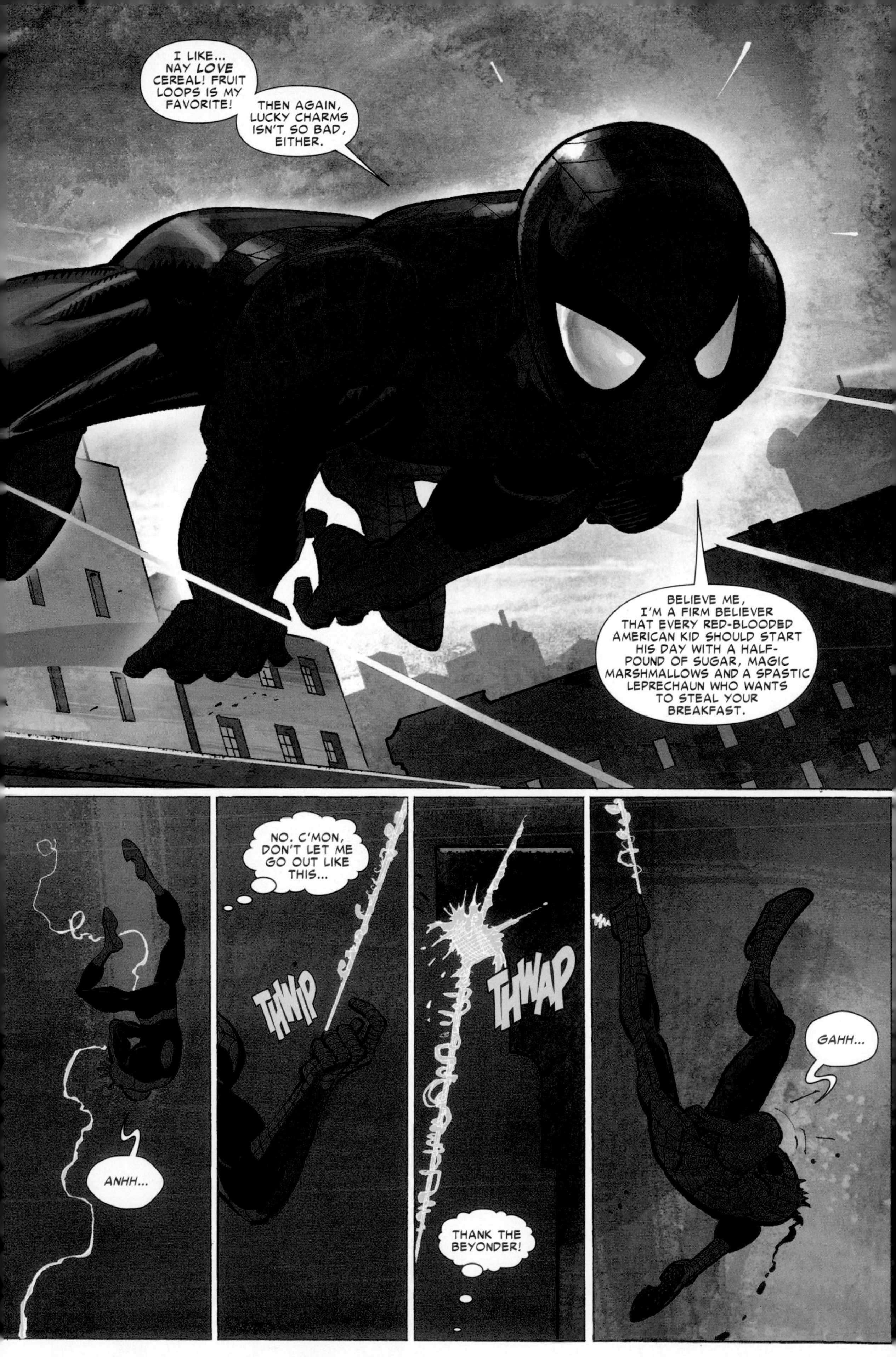
I LIKE... NAY *LOVE* CEREAL! FRUIT LOOPS IS MY FAVORITE!
THEN AGAIN, LUCKY CHARMS ISN'T SO BAD, EITHER.
BELIEVE ME, I'M A FIRM BELIEVER THAT EVERY RED-BLOODED AMERICAN KID SHOULD START HIS DAY WITH A HALF-POUND OF SUGAR, MAGIC MARSHMALLOWS AND A SPASTIC LEPRECHAUN WHO WANTS TO STEAL YOUR BREAKFAST.
ANHH...
NO. C'MON, DON'T LET ME GO OUT LIKE THIS...
THWIP
THWAP
THANK THE BEYONDER!
GAHH...

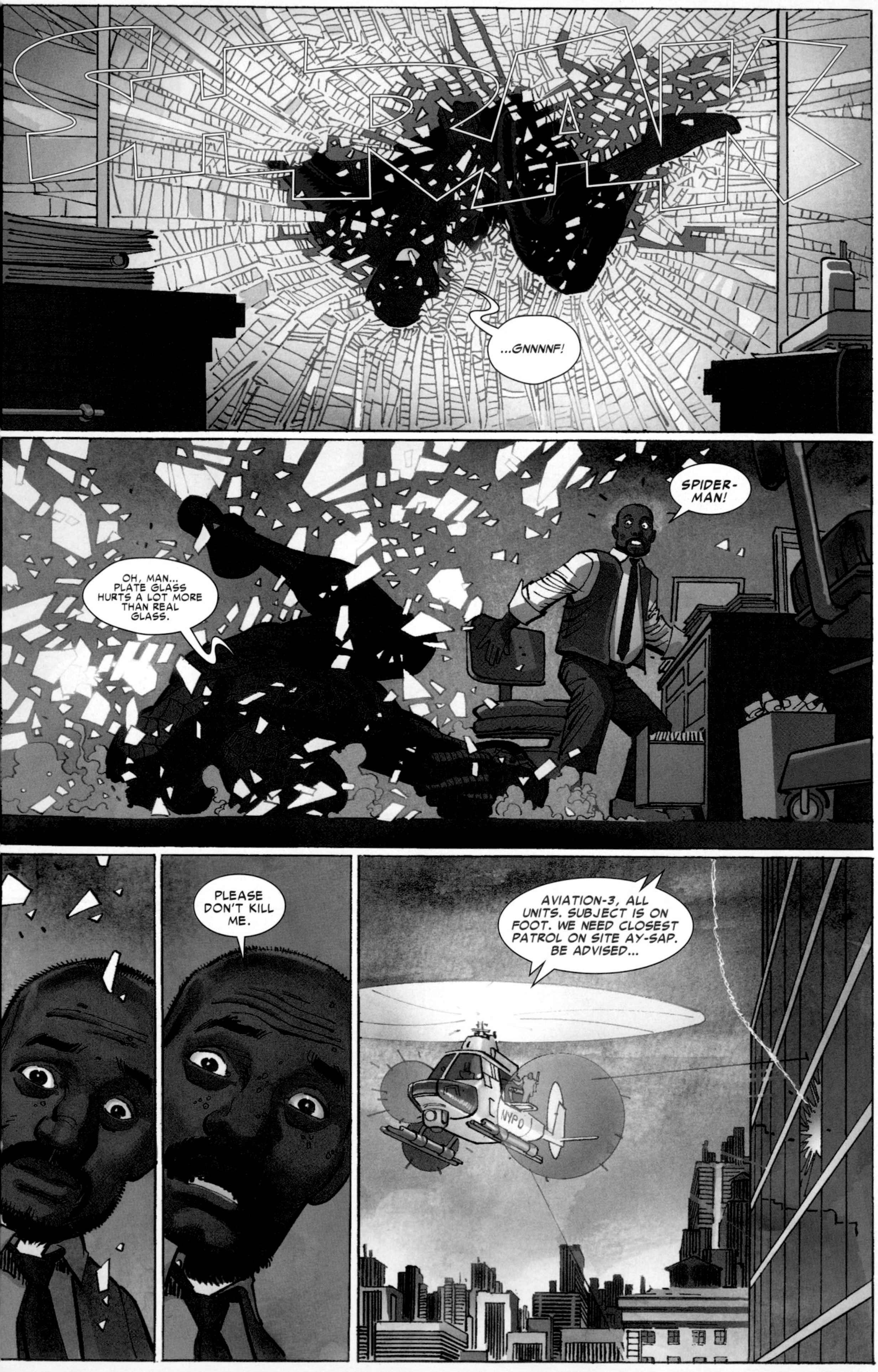
...GNNNNF!
SPIDER-MAN!
OH, MAN... PLATE GLASS HURTS A LOT MORE THAN REAL GLASS.
PLEASE DON'T KILL ME.
AVIATION-3, ALL UNITS. SUBJECT IS ON FOOT. WE NEED CLOSEST PATROL ON SITE AY-SAP. BE ADVISED...
NYPD

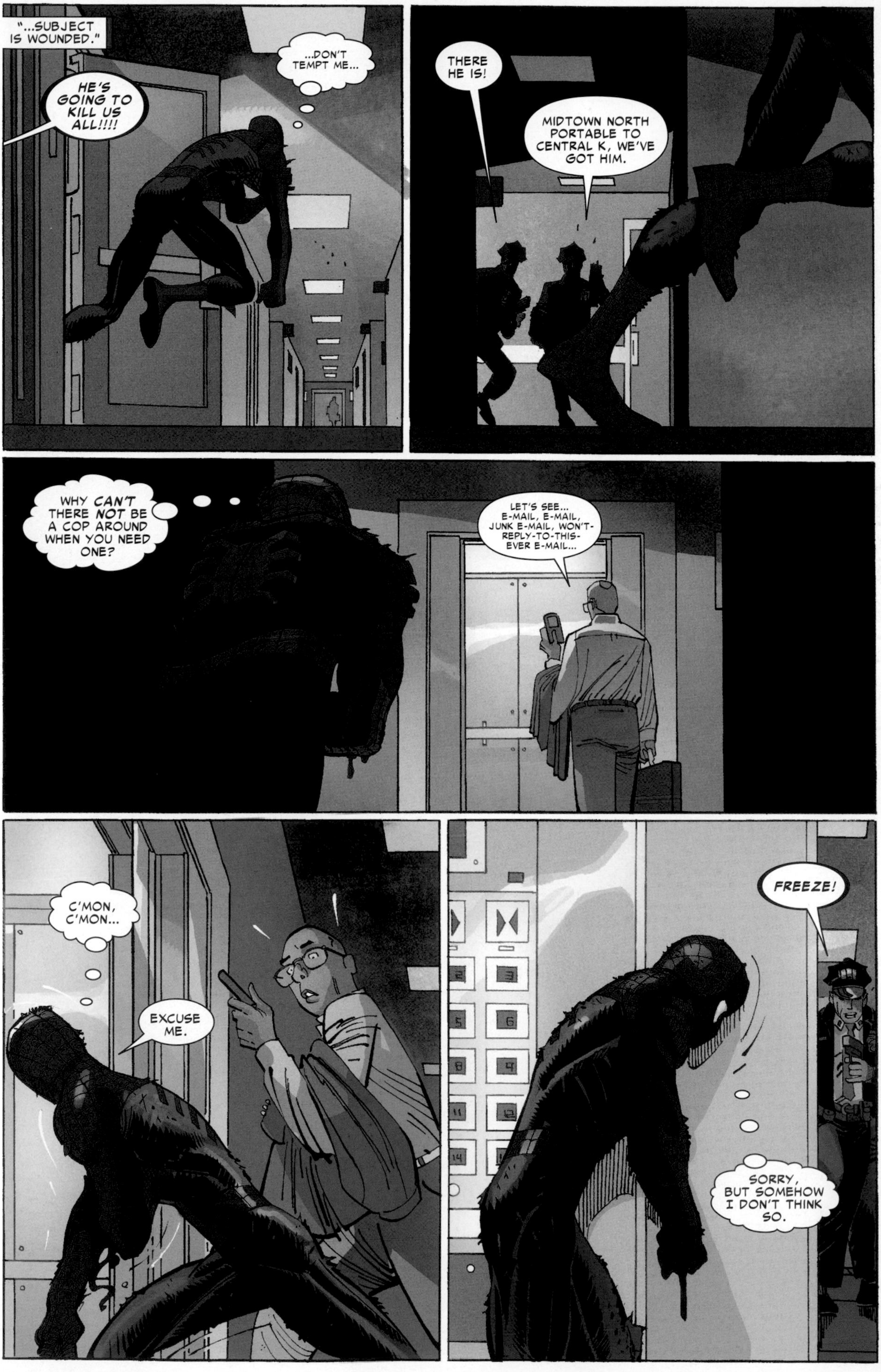
"...SUBJECT IS WOUNDED."
HE'S GOING TO KILL US ALL!!!!
...DON'T TEMPT ME...
THERE HE IS!
MIDTOWN NORTH PORTABLE TO CENTRAL K, WE'VE GOT HIM.
WHY CAN'T THERE NOT BE A COP AROUND WHEN YOU NEED ONE?
LET'S SEE... E-MAIL, E-MAIL, JUNK E-MAIL, WON'T-REPLY-TO-THIS-EVER E-MAIL...
C'MON, C'MON...
EXCUSE ME.
FREEZE!
SORRY, BUT SOMEHOW I DON'T THINK SO.

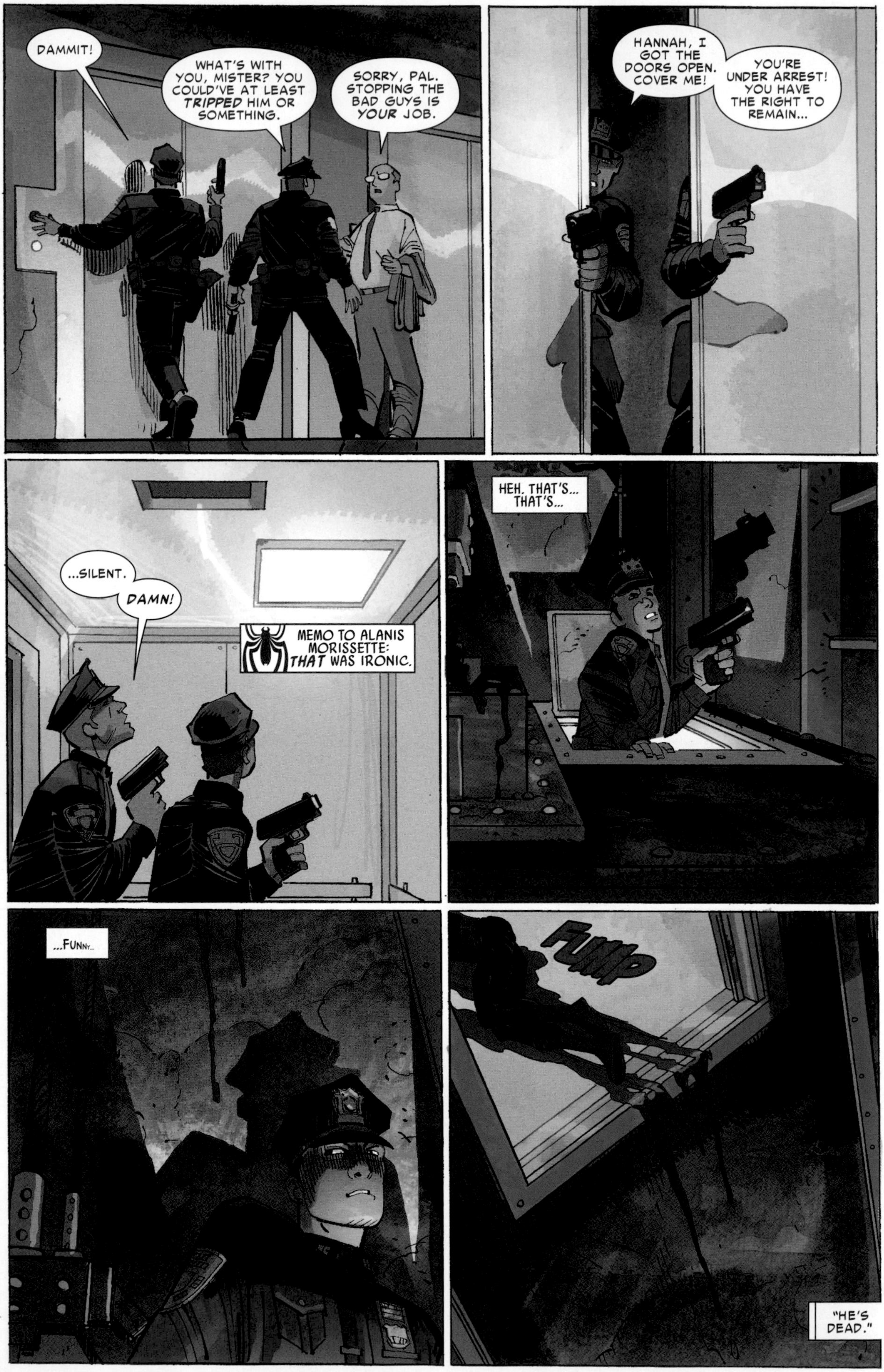
DAMMIT!
WHAT'S WITH YOU, MISTER? YOU COULD'VE AT LEAST *TRIPPED* HIM OR SOMETHING.
SORRY, PAL. STOPPING THE BAD GUYS IS *YOUR* JOB.
HANNAH, I GOT THE DOORS OPEN. COVER ME!
YOU'RE UNDER ARREST! YOU HAVE THE RIGHT TO REMAIN...
...SILENT.
DAMN!
MEMO TO ALANIS MORISSETTE: *THAT* WAS IRONIC.
HEH. THAT'S... THAT'S...
...FUNNY...
FUMP
"HE'S DEAD."

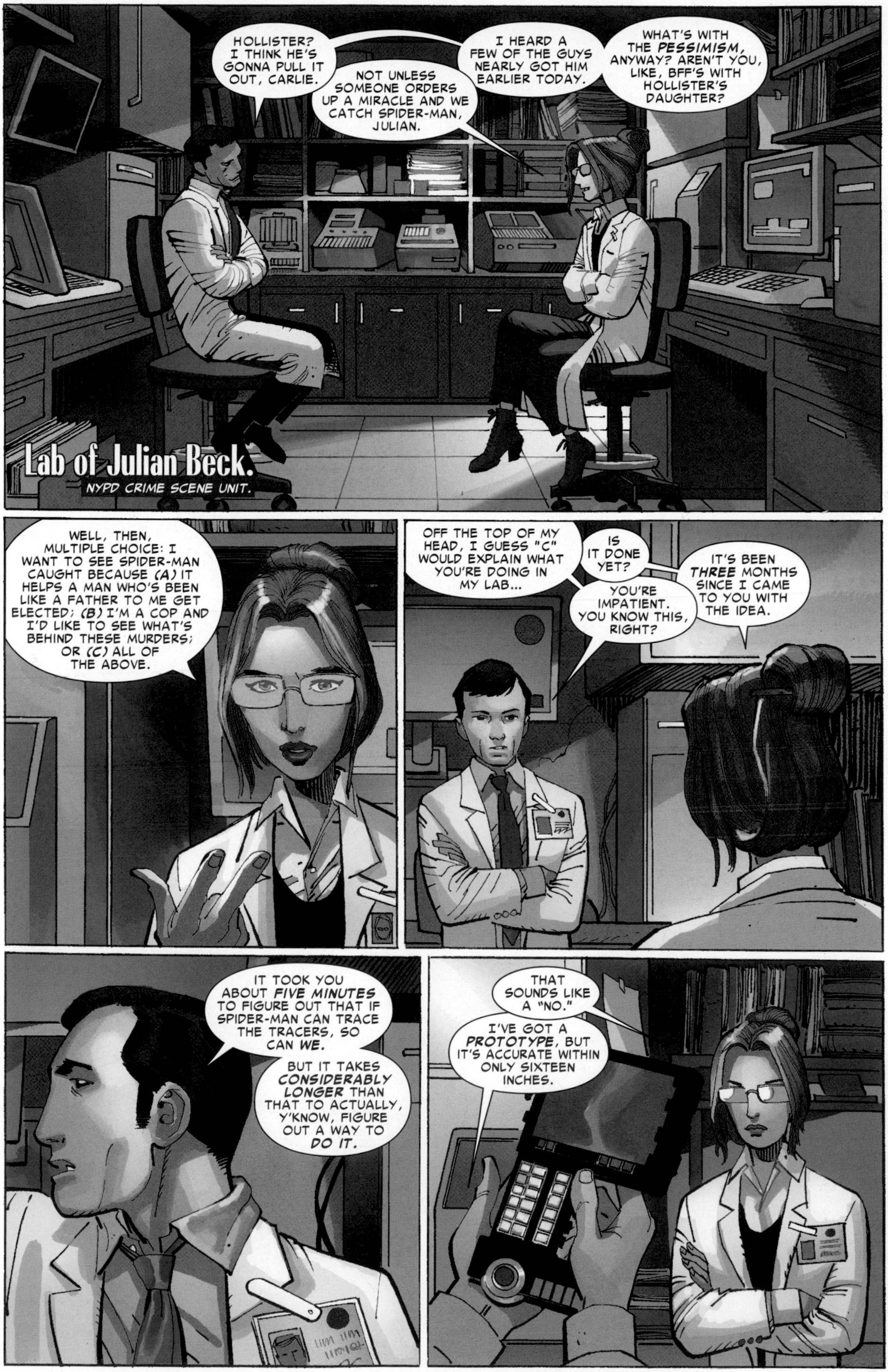
HOLLISTER? I THINK HE'S GONNA PULL IT OUT, CARLIE.
I HEARD A FEW OF THE GUYS NEARLY GOT HIM EARLIER TODAY.
NOT UNLESS SOMEONE ORDERS UP A MIRACLE AND WE CATCH SPIDER-MAN, JULIAN.
WHAT'S WITH THE PESSIMISM, ANYWAY? AREN'T YOU, LIKE, BFF'S WITH HOLLISTER'S DAUGHTER?
Lab of Julian Beck.
NYPD CRIME SCENE UNIT.
WELL, THEN, MULTIPLE CHOICE: I WANT TO SEE SPIDER-MAN CAUGHT BECAUSE (A) IT HELPS A MAN WHO'S BEEN LIKE A FATHER TO ME GET ELECTED; (B) I'M A COP AND I'D LIKE TO SEE WHAT'S BEHIND THESE MURDERS; OR (C) ALL OF THE ABOVE.
OFF THE TOP OF MY HEAD, I GUESS "C" WOULD EXPLAIN WHAT YOU'RE DOING IN MY LAB...
IS IT DONE YET?
YOU'RE IMPATIENT. YOU KNOW THIS, RIGHT?
IT'S BEEN THREE MONTHS SINCE I CAME TO YOU WITH THE IDEA.
IT TOOK YOU ABOUT FIVE MINUTES TO FIGURE OUT THAT IF SPIDER-MAN CAN TRACE THE TRACERS, SO CAN WE.
BUT IT TAKES CONSIDERABLY LONGER THAN THAT TO ACTUALLY, Y'KNOW, FIGURE OUT A WAY TO DO IT.
THAT SOUNDS LIKE A "NO."
I'VE GOT A PROTOTYPE, BUT IT'S ACCURATE WITHIN ONLY SIXTEEN INCHES.

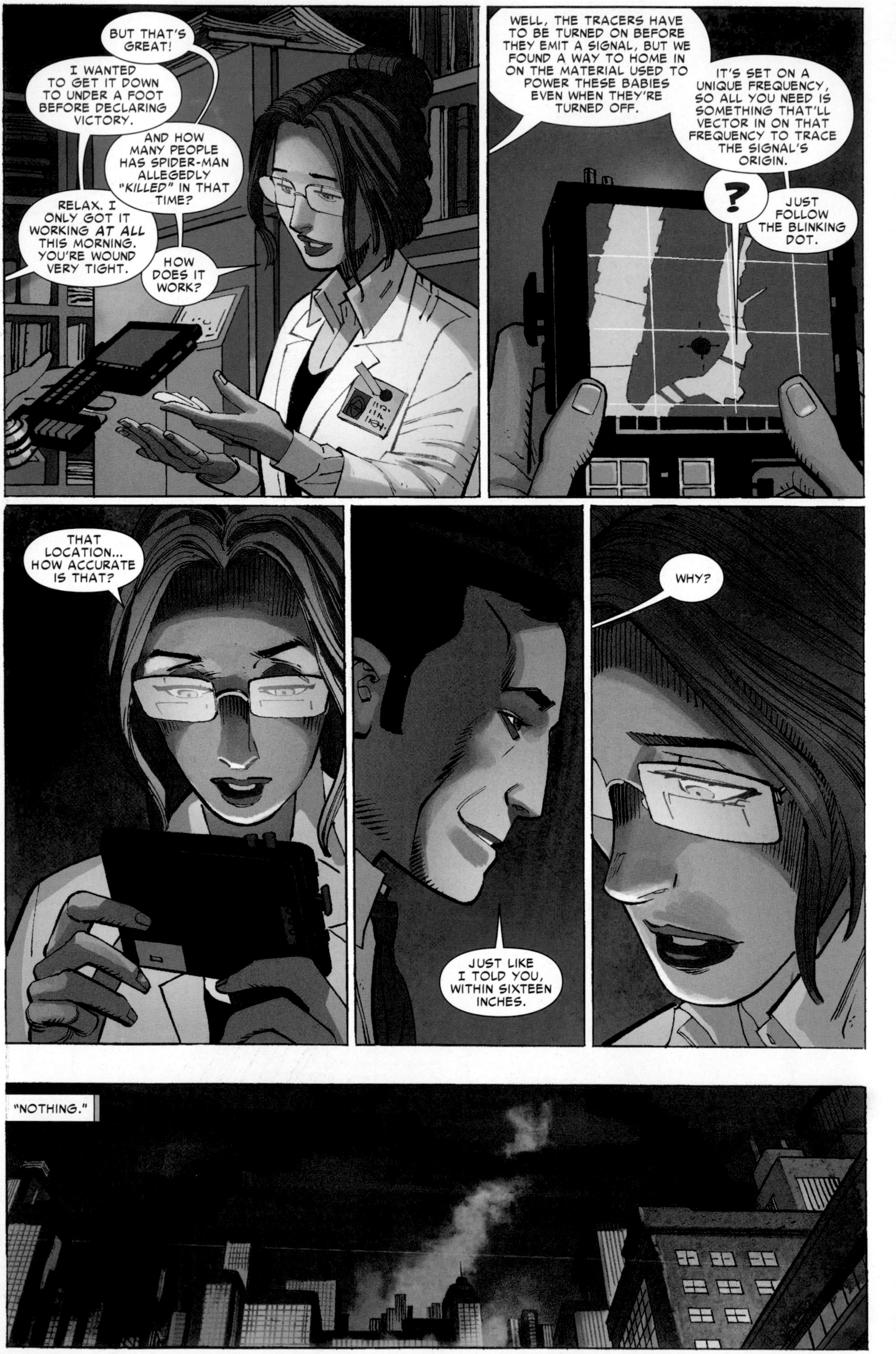

BUT THAT'S GREAT!
I WANTED TO GET IT DOWN TO UNDER A FOOT BEFORE DECLARING VICTORY.
AND HOW MANY PEOPLE HAS SPIDER-MAN ALLEGEDLY "KILLED" IN THAT TIME?
RELAX. I ONLY GOT IT WORKING AT ALL THIS MORNING. YOU'RE WOUND VERY TIGHT.
HOW DOES IT WORK?
WELL, THE TRACERS HAVE TO BE TURNED ON BEFORE THEY EMIT A SIGNAL, BUT WE FOUND A WAY TO HOME IN ON THE MATERIAL USED TO POWER THESE BABIES EVEN WHEN THEY'RE TURNED OFF.
IT'S SET ON A UNIQUE FREQUENCY, SO ALL YOU NEED IS SOMETHING THAT'LL VECTOR IN ON THAT FREQUENCY TO TRACE THE SIGNAL'S ORIGIN.
?
JUST FOLLOW THE BLINKING DOT.
THAT LOCATION... HOW ACCURATE IS THAT?
JUST LIKE I TOLD YOU, WITHIN SIXTEEN INCHES.
WHY?
"NOTHING."

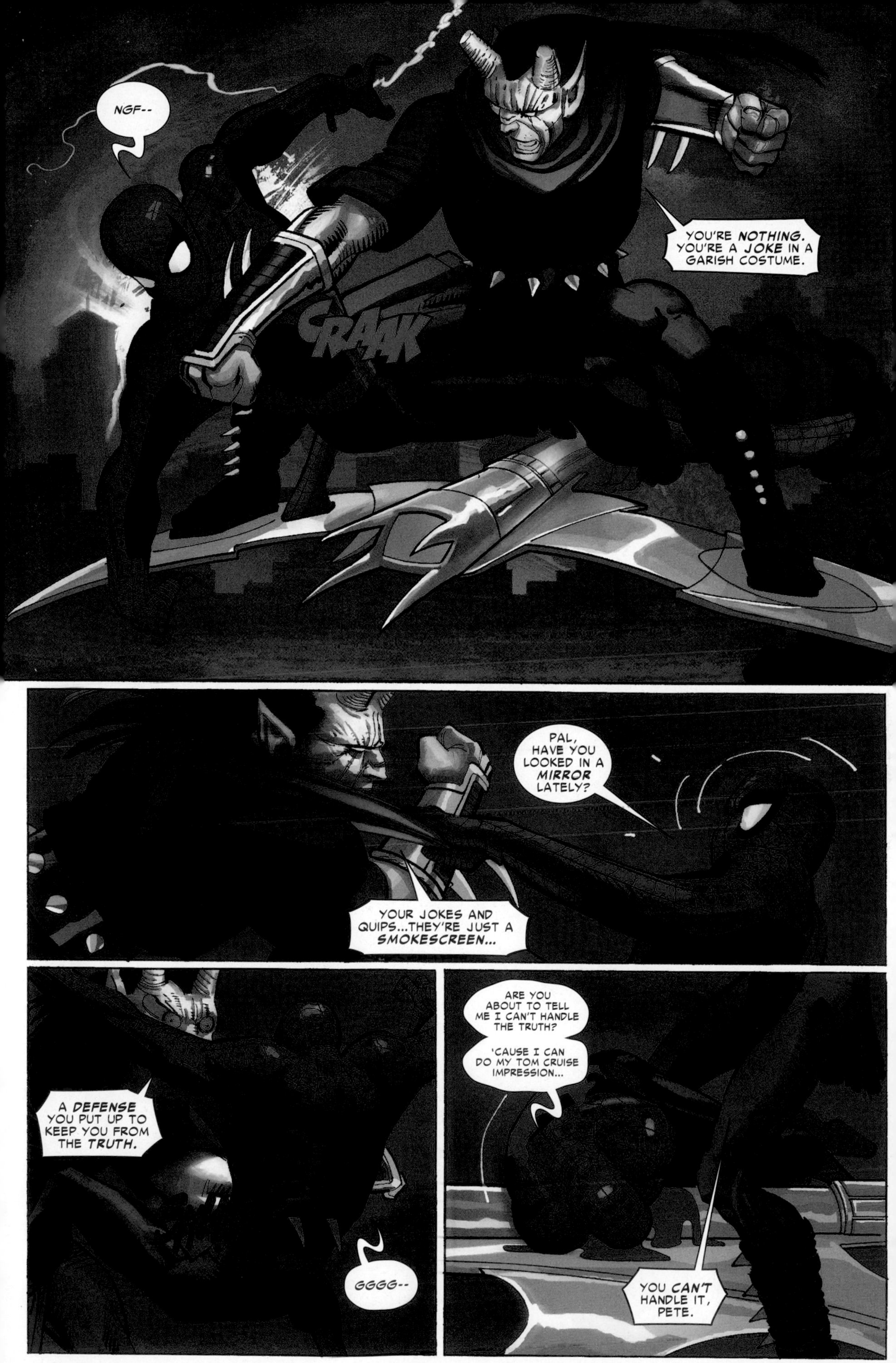
NGF--
YOU'RE NOTHING. YOU'RE A JOKE IN A GARISH COSTUME.
CRAAK
PAL, HAVE YOU LOOKED IN A MIRROR LATELY?
YOUR JOKES AND QUIPS...THEY'RE JUST A SMOKESCREEN...
A DEFENSE YOU PUT UP TO KEEP YOU FROM THE TRUTH.
GGGG--
ARE YOU ABOUT TO TELL ME I CAN'T HANDLE THE TRUTH?
'CAUSE I CAN DO MY TOM CRUISE IMPRESSION...
YOU CAN'T HANDLE IT, PETE.

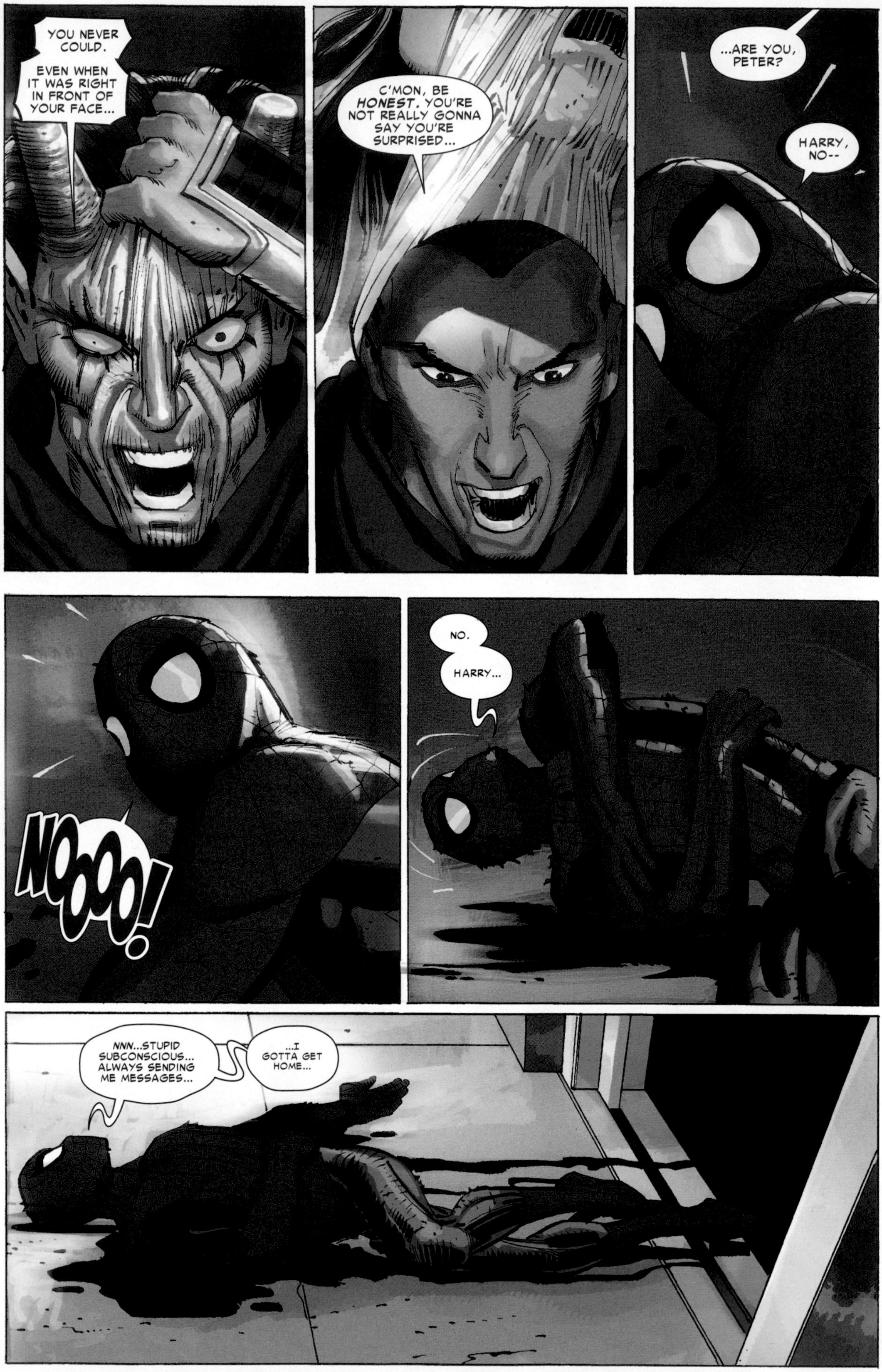
YOU NEVER COULD.
EVEN WHEN IT WAS RIGHT IN FRONT OF YOUR FACE...
C'MON, BE *HONEST*. YOU'RE NOT REALLY GONNA SAY YOU'RE SURPRISED...
...ARE YOU, PETER?
HARRY, NO--
NOOOO!
NO.
HARRY...
NNN...STUPID SUBCONSCIOUS... ALWAYS SENDING ME MESSAGES...
...I GOTTA GET HOME...

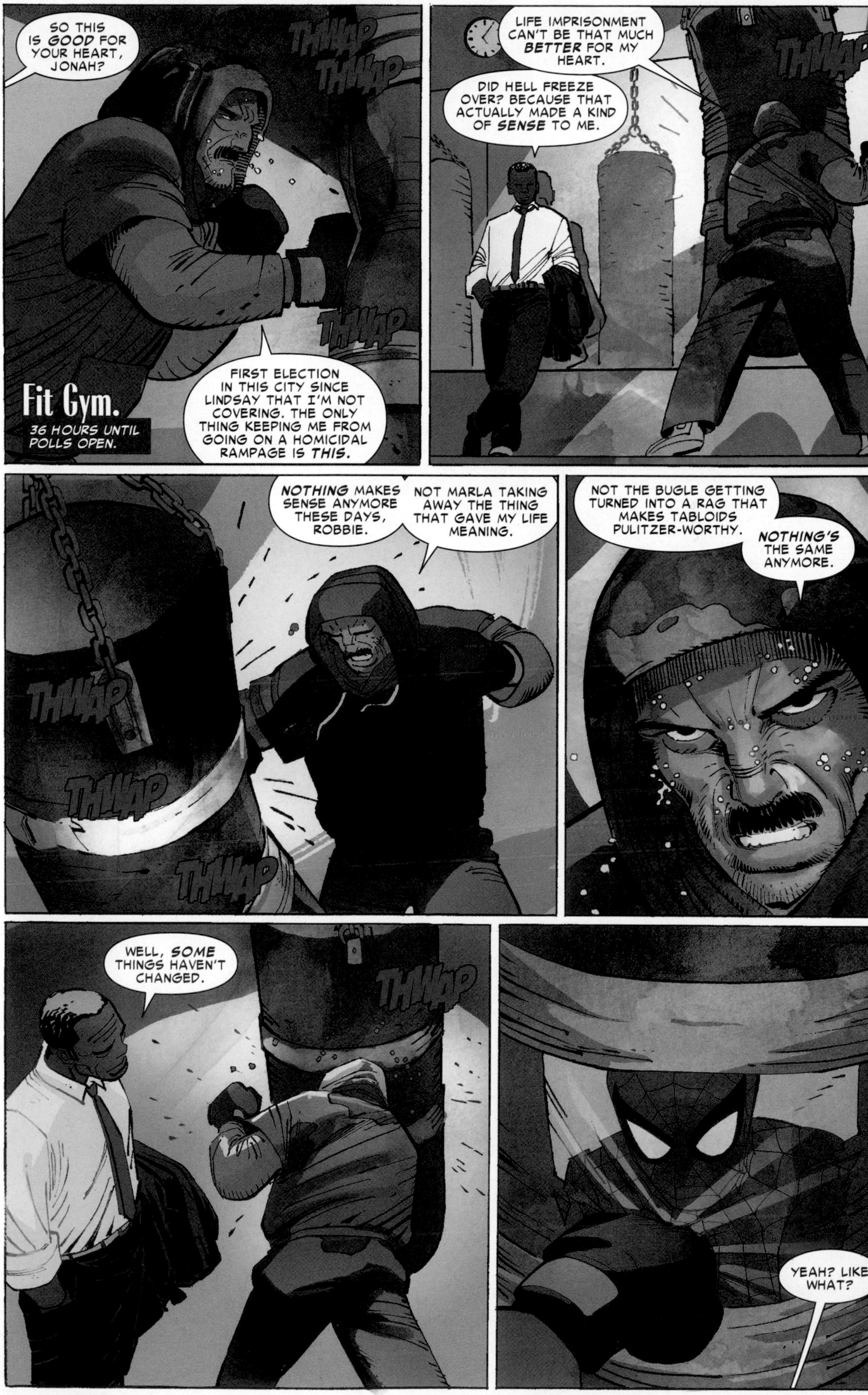
SO THIS IS GOOD FOR YOUR HEART, JONAH?
THWAP
THWAP
THWAP
Fit Gym.
36 HOURS UNTIL POLLS OPEN.
FIRST ELECTION IN THIS CITY SINCE LINDSAY THAT I'M NOT COVERING. THE ONLY THING KEEPING ME FROM GOING ON A HOMICIDAL RAMPAGE IS THIS.
LIFE IMPRISONMENT CAN'T BE THAT MUCH BETTER FOR MY HEART.
THWAP
DID HELL FREEZE OVER? BECAUSE THAT ACTUALLY MADE A KIND OF SENSE TO ME.
NOTHING MAKES SENSE ANYMORE THESE DAYS, ROBBIE.
NOT MARLA TAKING AWAY THE THING THAT GAVE MY LIFE MEANING.
THWAP
THWAP
THWAP
NOT THE BUGLE GETTING TURNED INTO A RAG THAT MAKES TABLOIDS PULITZER-WORTHY.
NOTHING'S THE SAME ANYMORE.
WELL, SOME THINGS HAVEN'T CHANGED.
THWAP
YEAH? LIKE WHAT?

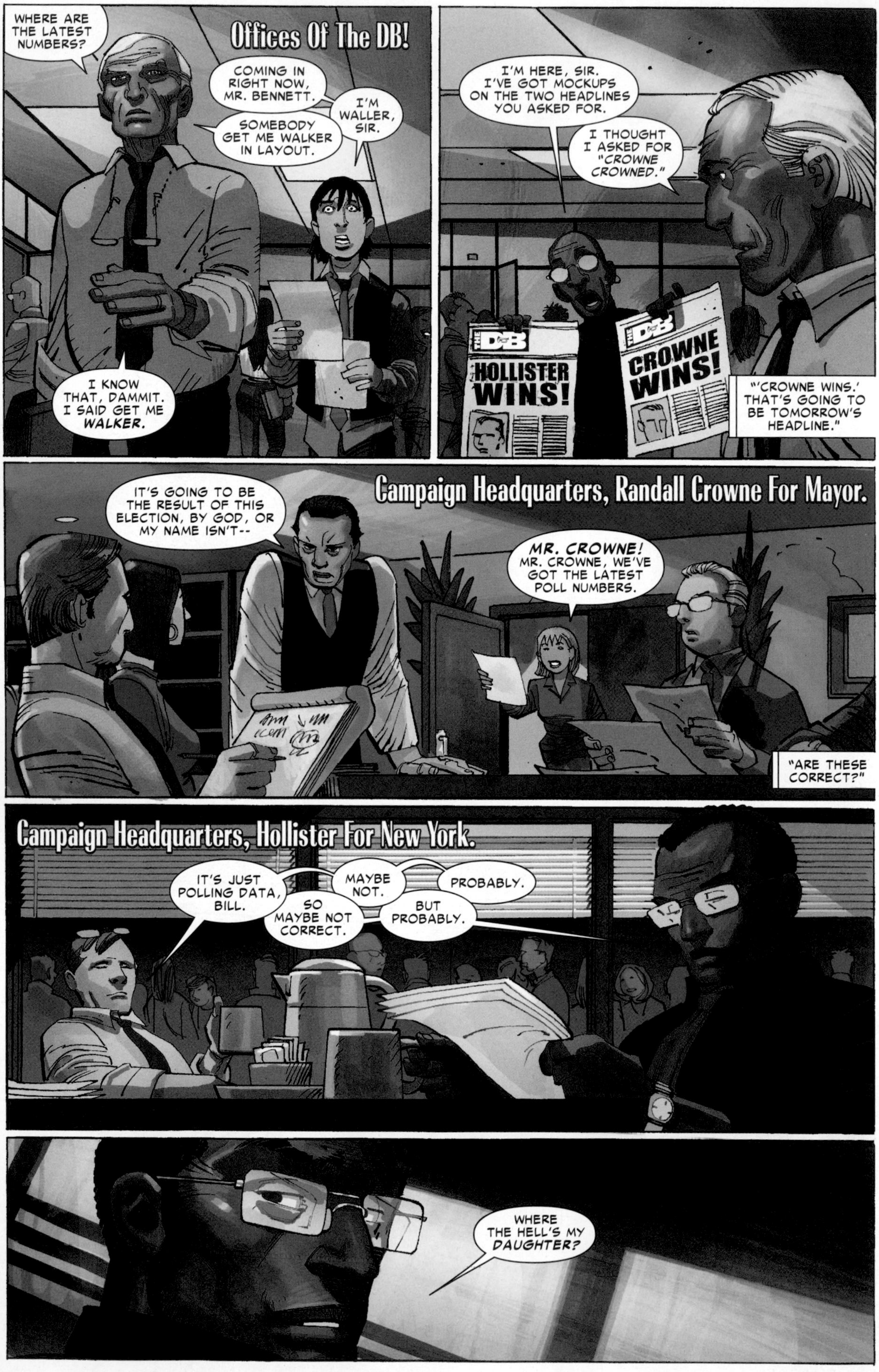
Offices Of The DB!
WHERE ARE THE LATEST NUMBERS?
COMING IN RIGHT NOW, MR. BENNETT.
SOMEBODY GET ME WALKER IN LAYOUT.
I'M WALLER, SIR.
I KNOW THAT, DAMMIT. I SAID GET ME WALKER.
I'M HERE, SIR. I'VE GOT MOCKUPS ON THE TWO HEADLINES YOU ASKED FOR.
I THOUGHT I ASKED FOR "CROWNE CROWNED."
THE DB
HOLLISTER WINS!
THE DB
CROWNE WINS!
"'CROWNE WINS.' THAT'S GOING TO BE TOMORROW'S HEADLINE."
Campaign Headquarters, Randall Crowne For Mayor.
IT'S GOING TO BE THE RESULT OF THIS ELECTION, BY GOD, OR MY NAME ISN'T--
MR. CROWNE! MR. CROWNE, WE'VE GOT THE LATEST POLL NUMBERS.
"ARE THESE CORRECT?"
Campaign Headquarters, Hollister For New York.
IT'S JUST POLLING DATA, BILL.
MAYBE NOT.
PROBABLY.
SO MAYBE NOT CORRECT.
BUT PROBABLY.
WHERE THE HELL'S MY DAUGHTER?

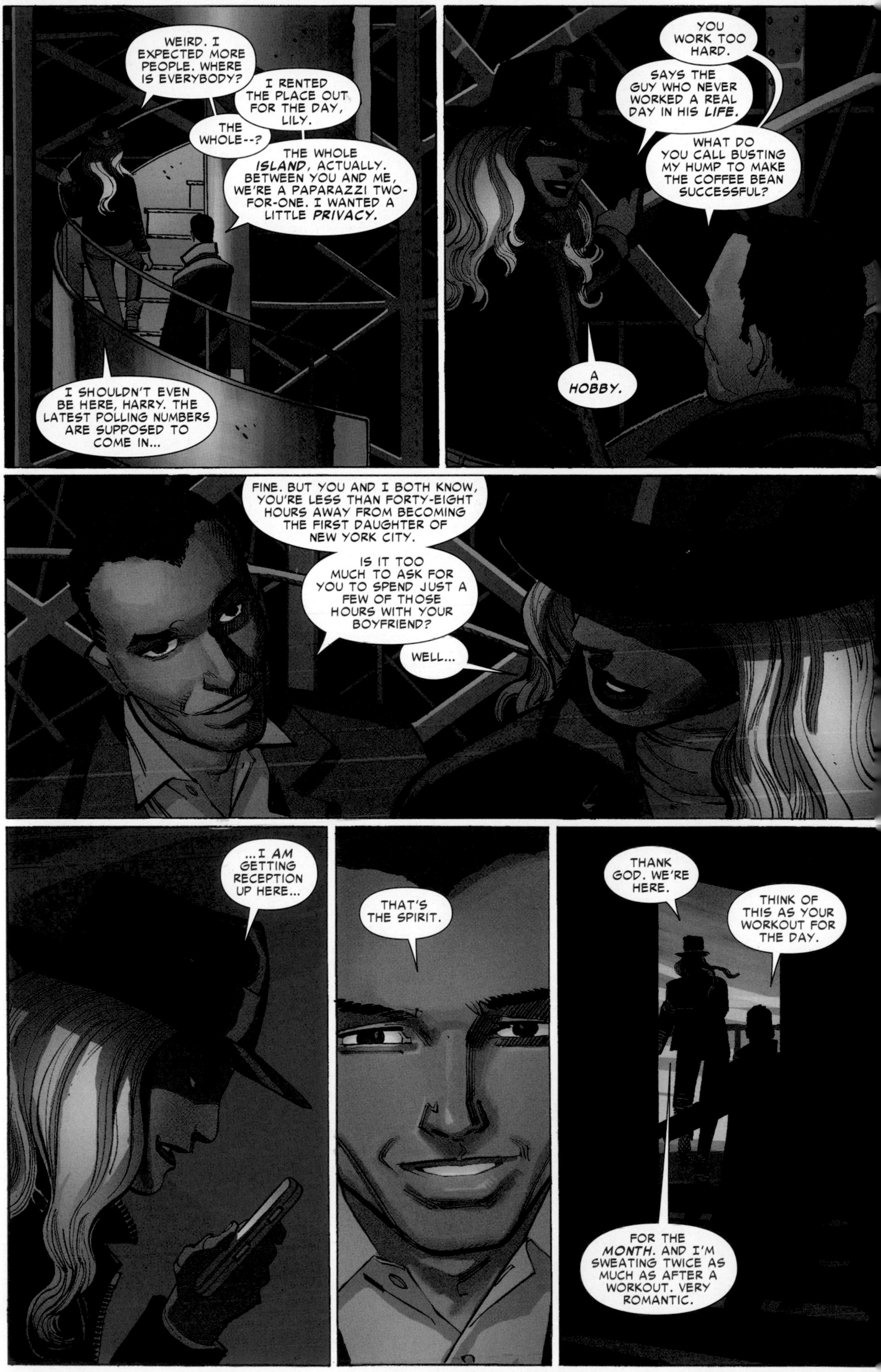

WEIRD. I EXPECTED MORE PEOPLE. WHERE IS EVERYBODY?
I RENTED THE PLACE OUT FOR THE DAY, LILY.
THE WHOLE--?
THE WHOLE ISLAND, ACTUALLY. BETWEEN YOU AND ME, WE'RE A PAPARAZZI TWO-FOR-ONE. I WANTED A LITTLE PRIVACY.
I SHOULDN'T EVEN BE HERE, HARRY. THE LATEST POLLING NUMBERS ARE SUPPOSED TO COME IN...
YOU WORK TOO HARD.
SAYS THE GUY WHO NEVER WORKED A REAL DAY IN HIS LIFE.
WHAT DO YOU CALL BUSTING MY HUMP TO MAKE THE COFFEE BEAN SUCCESSFUL?
A HOBBY.
FINE. BUT YOU AND I BOTH KNOW, YOU'RE LESS THAN FORTY-EIGHT HOURS AWAY FROM BECOMING THE FIRST DAUGHTER OF NEW YORK CITY.
IS IT TOO MUCH TO ASK FOR YOU TO SPEND JUST A FEW OF THOSE HOURS WITH YOUR BOYFRIEND?
WELL...
...I AM GETTING RECEPTION UP HERE...
THAT'S THE SPIRIT.
THANK GOD. WE'RE HERE.
THINK OF THIS AS YOUR WORKOUT FOR THE DAY.
FOR THE MONTH. AND I'M SWEATING TWICE AS MUCH AS AFTER A WORKOUT. VERY ROMANTIC.

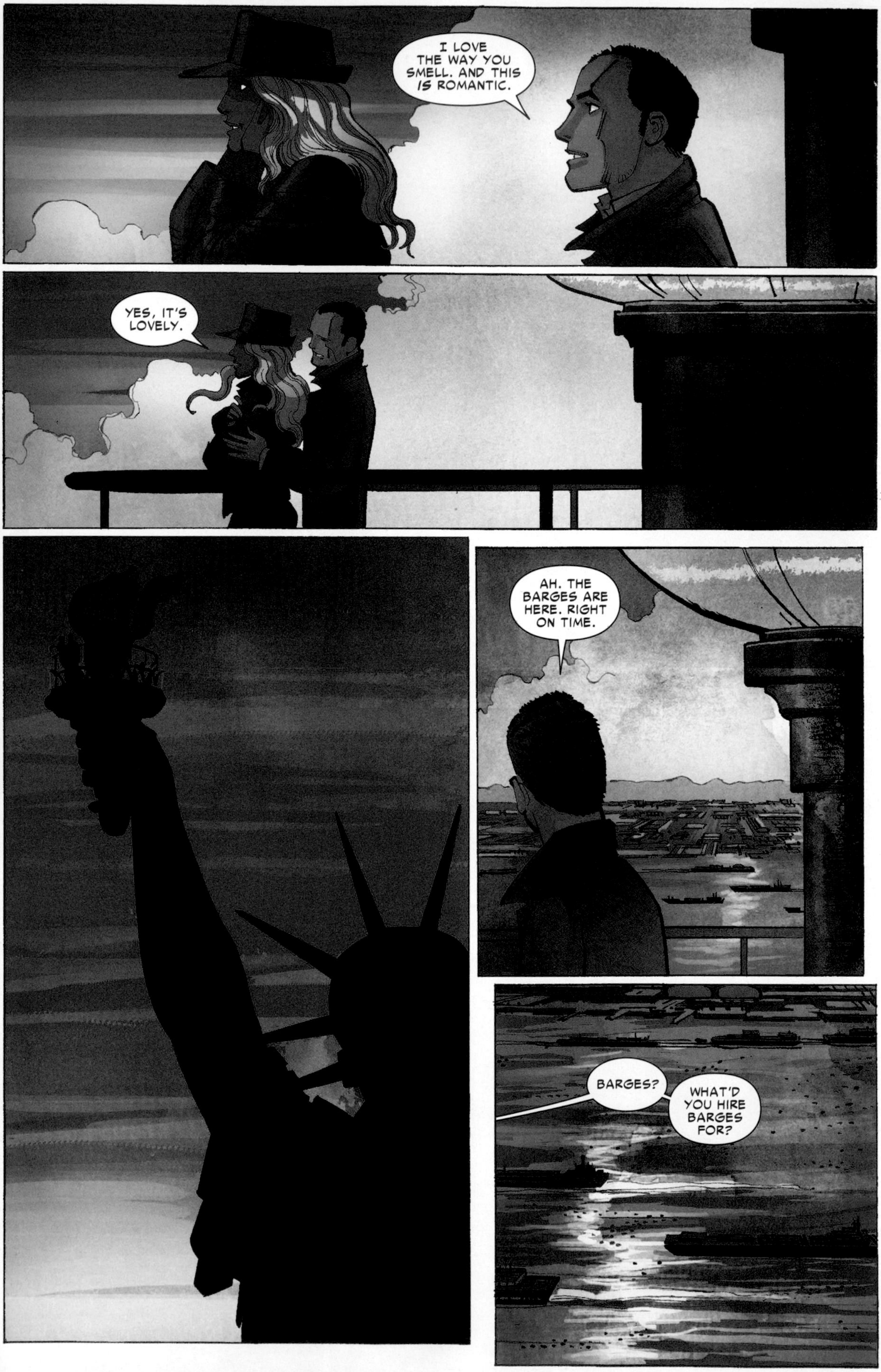
I LOVE THE WAY YOU SMELL. AND THIS *IS* ROMANTIC.
YES, IT'S LOVELY.
AH. THE BARGES ARE HERE. RIGHT ON TIME.
BARGES?
WHAT'D YOU HIRE BARGES FOR?

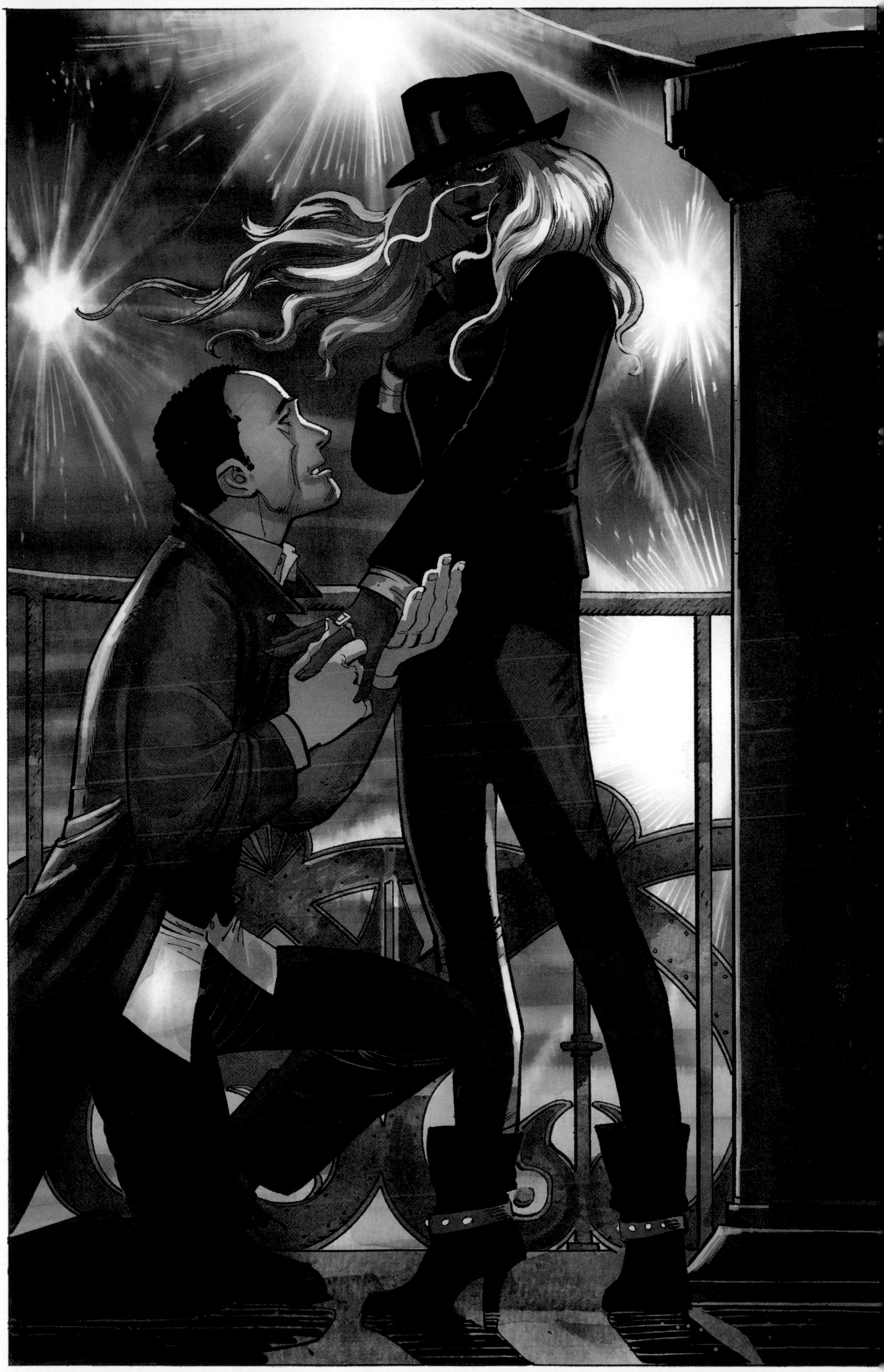

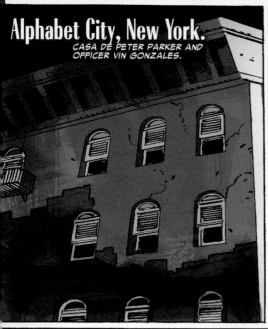

Alphabet City, New York.

CASA DE PETER PARKER AND OFFICER VIN GONZALES.

--JUST SAYING, I DIDN'T SIGN ON FOR *THAT.*

DAMN STRAIGHT WE'RE GONNA *TALK* ABOUT IT.

YEAH, I'M HEADED TO THE HOUSE NOW...

THANKS, I REALLY DIDN'T KNOW WHEN THE EIGHT-TO-EIGHT SHIFT *STARTED.*

I SAID WE WERE GONNA TALK, DIDN'T I?

I'LL SEE YOU IN TWENTY MINUTES.

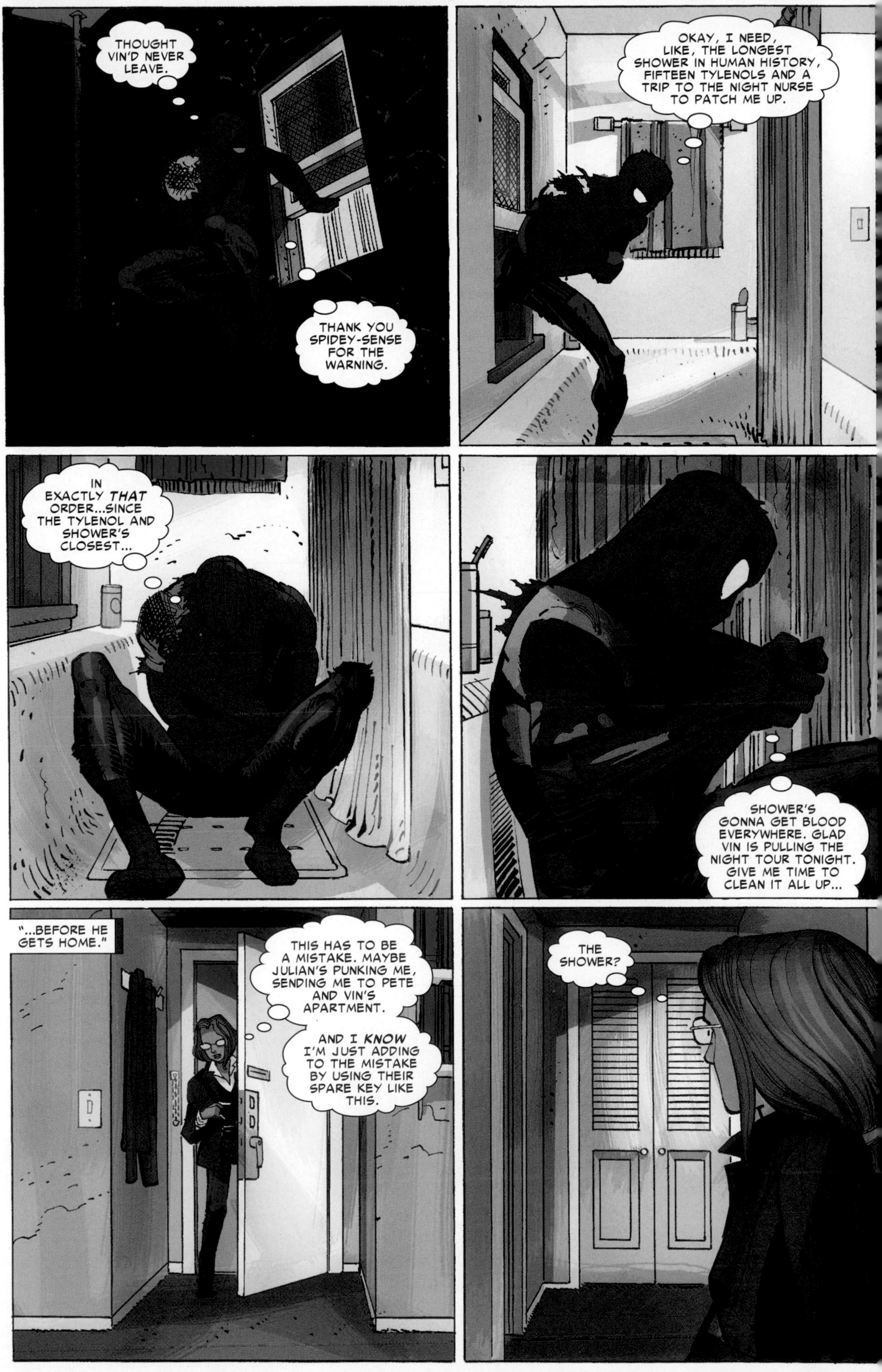
THOUGHT VIN'D NEVER LEAVE.
THANK YOU SPIDEY-SENSE FOR THE WARNING.
OKAY, I NEED, LIKE, THE LONGEST SHOWER IN HUMAN HISTORY, FIFTEEN TYLENOLS AND A TRIP TO THE NIGHT NURSE TO PATCH ME UP.
IN EXACTLY *THAT* ORDER...SINCE THE TYLENOL AND SHOWER'S CLOSEST...
SHOWER'S GONNA GET BLOOD EVERYWHERE. GLAD VIN IS PULLING THE NIGHT TOUR TONIGHT. GIVE ME TIME TO CLEAN IT ALL UP...
"...BEFORE HE GETS HOME."
THIS HAS TO BE A MISTAKE. MAYBE JULIAN'S PUNKING ME, SENDING ME TO PETE AND VIN'S APARTMENT.
AND I *KNOW* I'M JUST ADDING TO THE MISTAKE BY USING THEIR SPARE KEY LIKE THIS.
THE SHOWER?

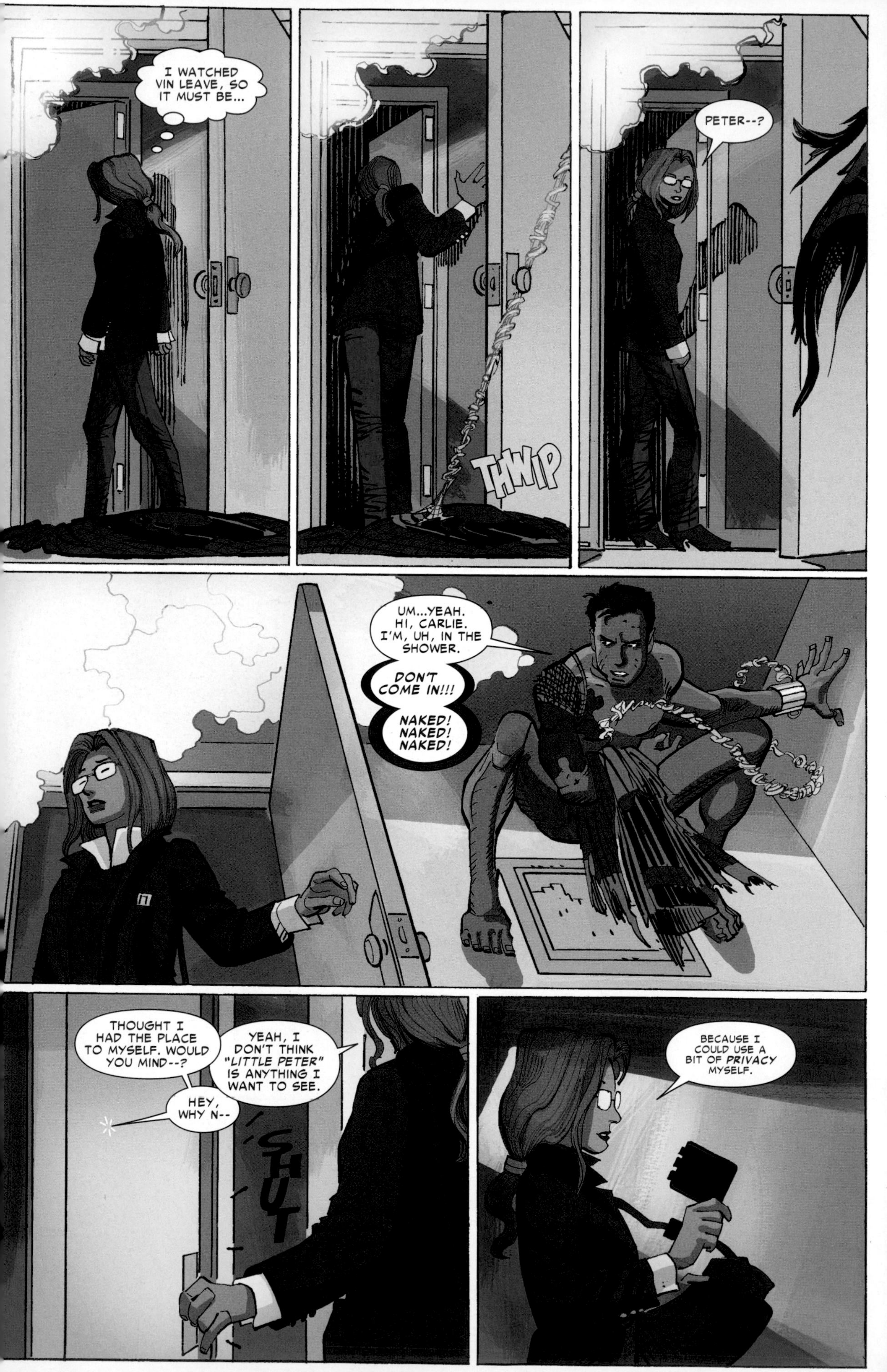
I WATCHED VIN LEAVE, SO IT MUST BE...
THWIP
PETER--?
UM...YEAH. HI, CARLIE. I'M, UH, IN THE SHOWER.
DON'T COME IN!!!
NAKED! NAKED! NAKED!
THOUGHT I HAD THE PLACE TO MYSELF. WOULD YOU MIND--?
YEAH, I DON'T THINK "LITTLE PETER" IS ANYTHING I WANT TO SEE.
HEY, WHY N--
SHUT
BECAUSE I COULD USE A BIT OF PRIVACY MYSELF.

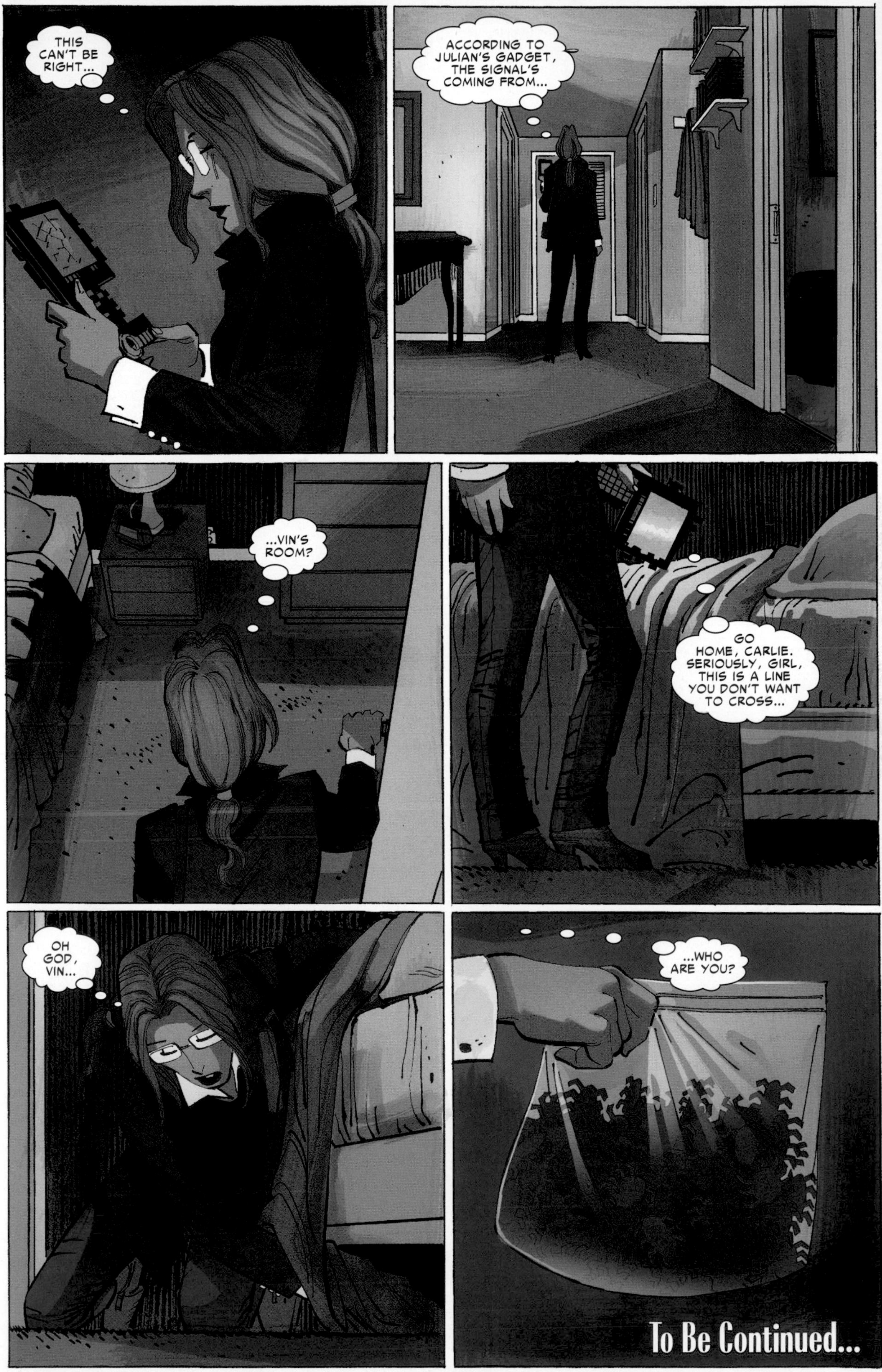
THIS CAN'T BE RIGHT...
ACCORDING TO JULIAN'S GADGET, THE SIGNAL'S COMING FROM...
...VIN'S ROOM?
GO HOME, CARLIE. SERIOUSLY, GIRL, THIS IS A LINE YOU DON'T WANT TO CROSS...
OH GOD, VIN...
...WHO ARE YOU?
To Be Continued...

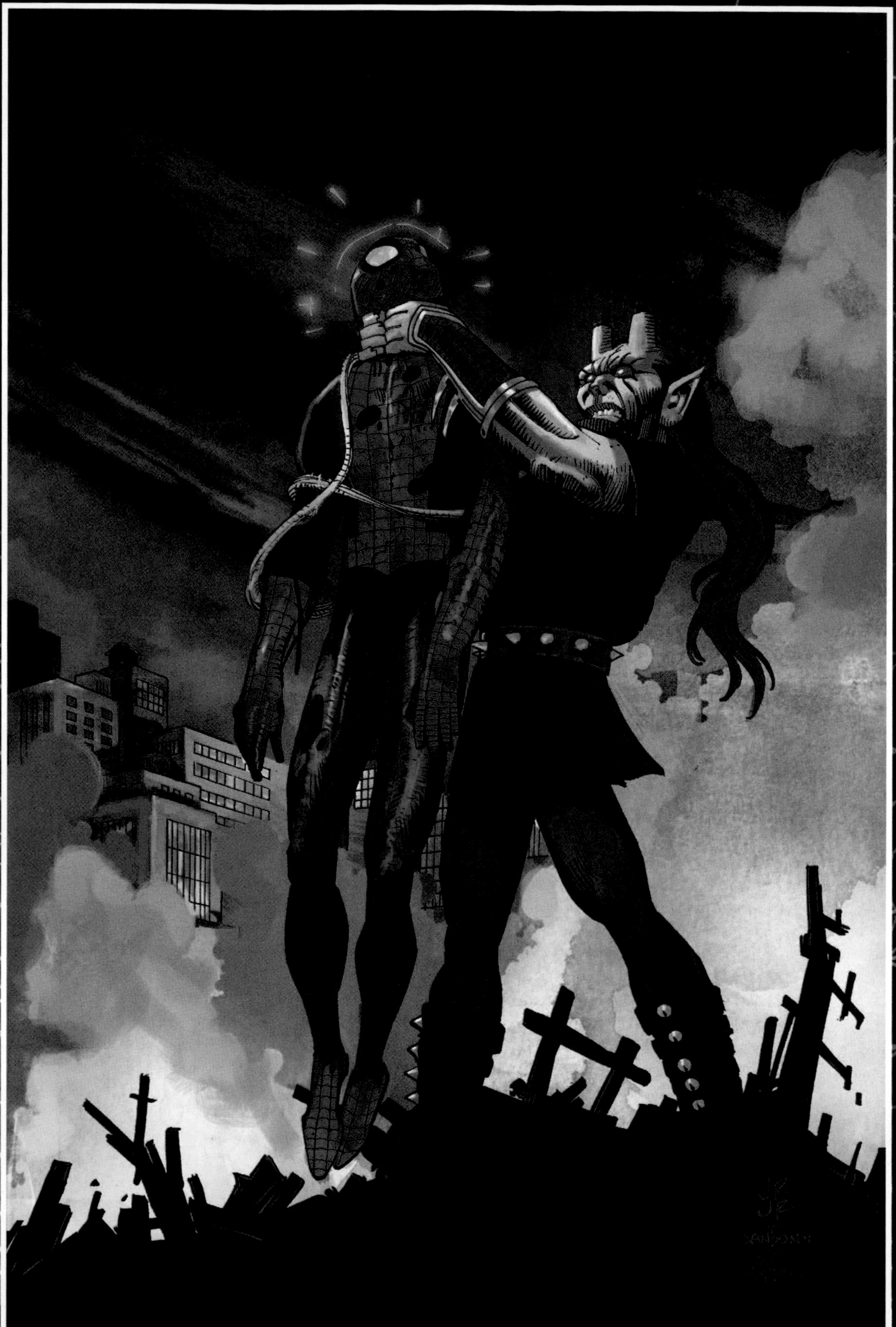

AMAZING SPIDER-MAN #585

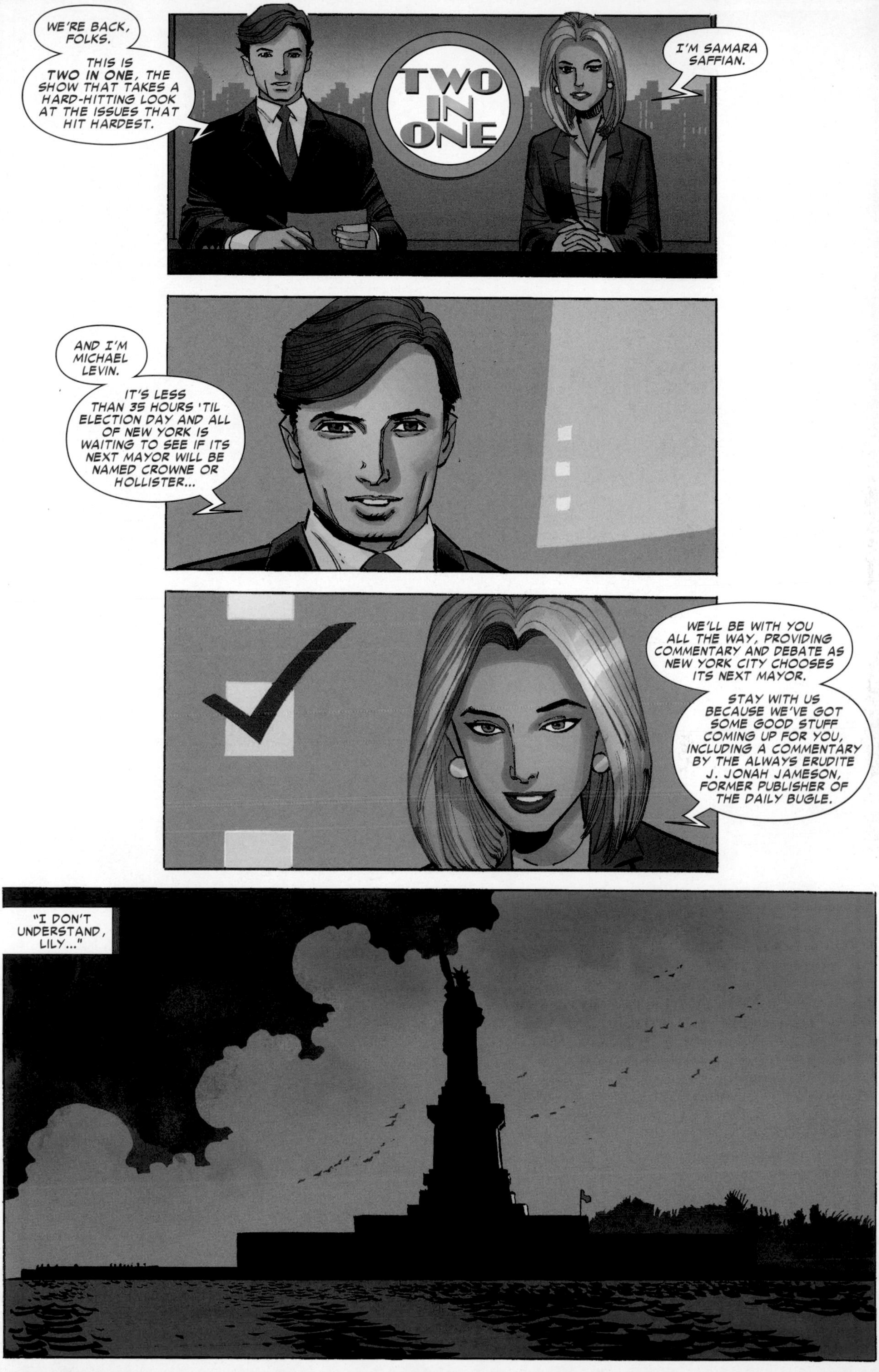
WE'RE BACK, FOLKS.
THIS IS TWO IN ONE, THE SHOW THAT TAKES A HARD-HITTING LOOK AT THE ISSUES THAT HIT HARDEST.
TWO IN ONE
I'M SAMARA SAFFIAN.
AND I'M MICHAEL LEVIN.
IT'S LESS THAN 35 HOURS 'TIL ELECTION DAY AND ALL OF NEW YORK IS WAITING TO SEE IF ITS NEXT MAYOR WILL BE NAMED CROWNE OR HOLLISTER...
WE'LL BE WITH YOU ALL THE WAY, PROVIDING COMMENTARY AND DEBATE AS NEW YORK CITY CHOOSES ITS NEXT MAYOR.
STAY WITH US BECAUSE WE'VE GOT SOME GOOD STUFF COMING UP FOR YOU, INCLUDING A COMMENTARY BY THE ALWAYS ERUDITE J. JONAH JAMESON, FORMER PUBLISHER OF THE DAILY BUGLE.
"I DON'T UNDERSTAND, LILY..."

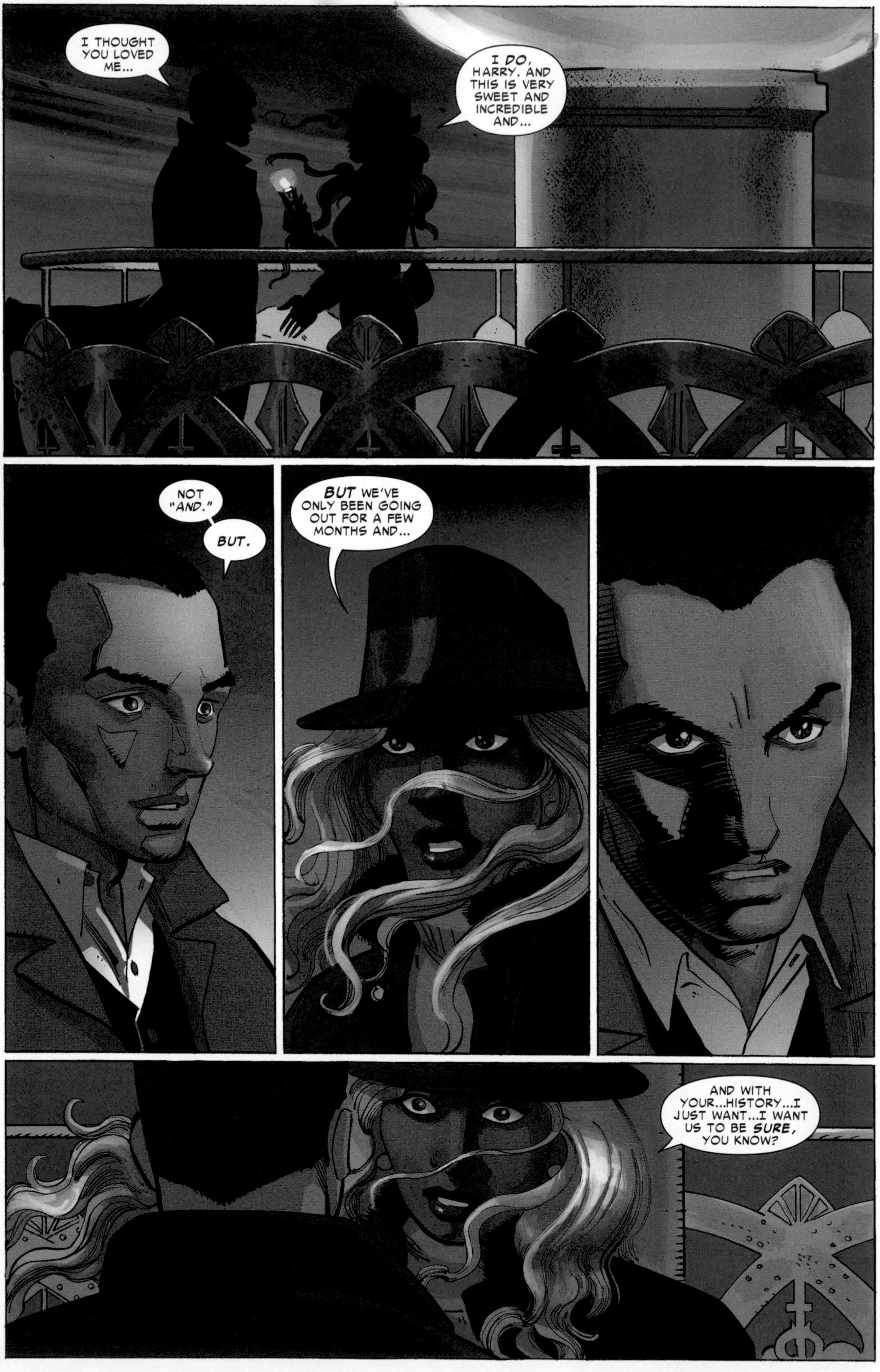
I THOUGHT YOU LOVED ME...
I DO, HARRY. AND THIS IS VERY SWEET AND INCREDIBLE AND...
NOT "AND."
BUT.
BUT WE'VE ONLY BEEN GOING OUT FOR A FEW MONTHS AND...
AND WITH YOUR...HISTORY...I JUST WANT...I WANT US TO BE SURE, YOU KNOW?

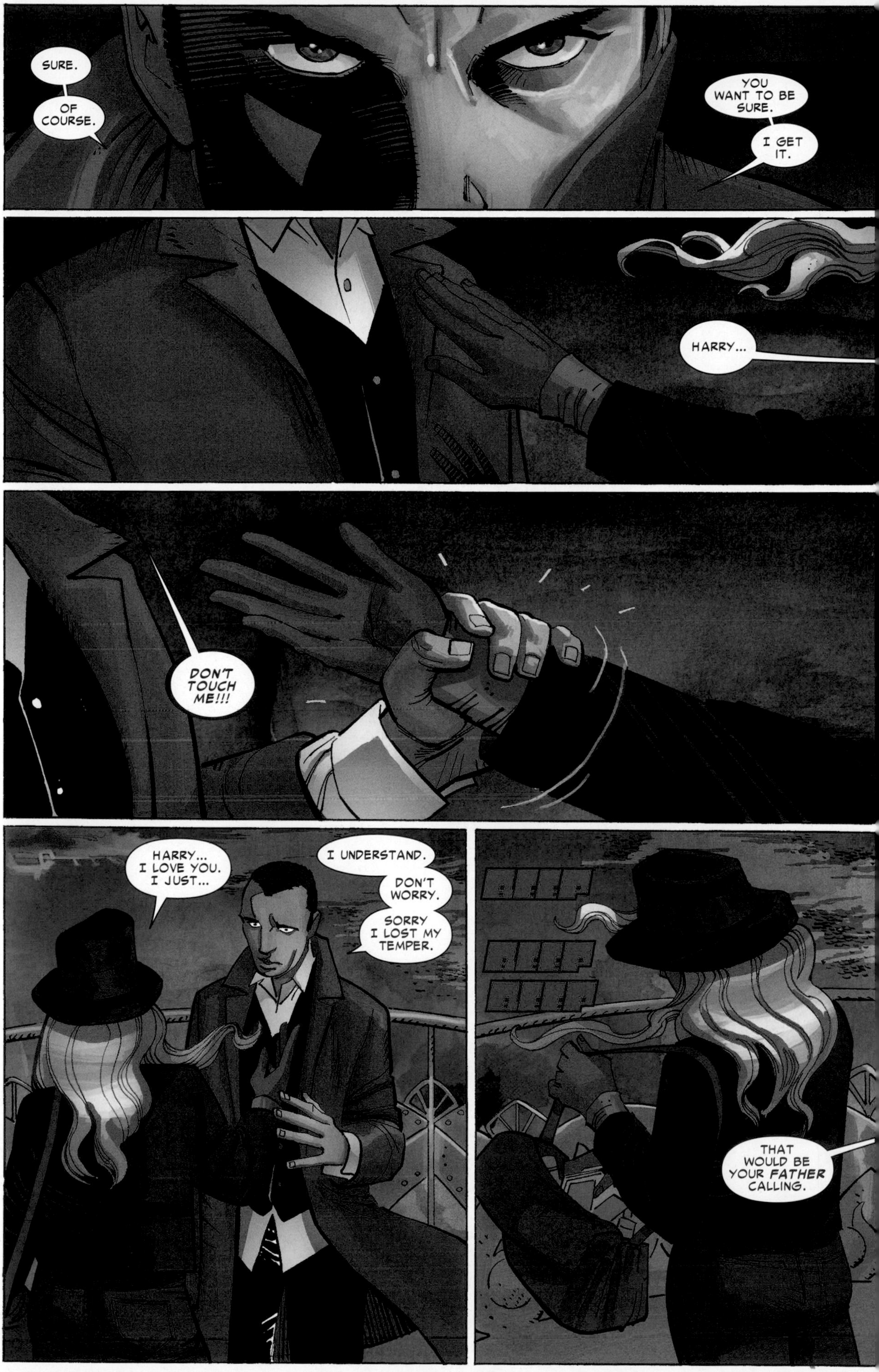
SURE.
OF COURSE.
YOU WANT TO BE SURE.
I GET IT.
HARRY...
DON'T TOUCH ME!!!
HARRY... I LOVE YOU. I JUST...
I UNDERSTAND.
DON'T WORRY.
SORRY I LOST MY TEMPER.
BEEP
BEEP
BEEP
THAT WOULD BE YOUR *FATHER* CALLING.

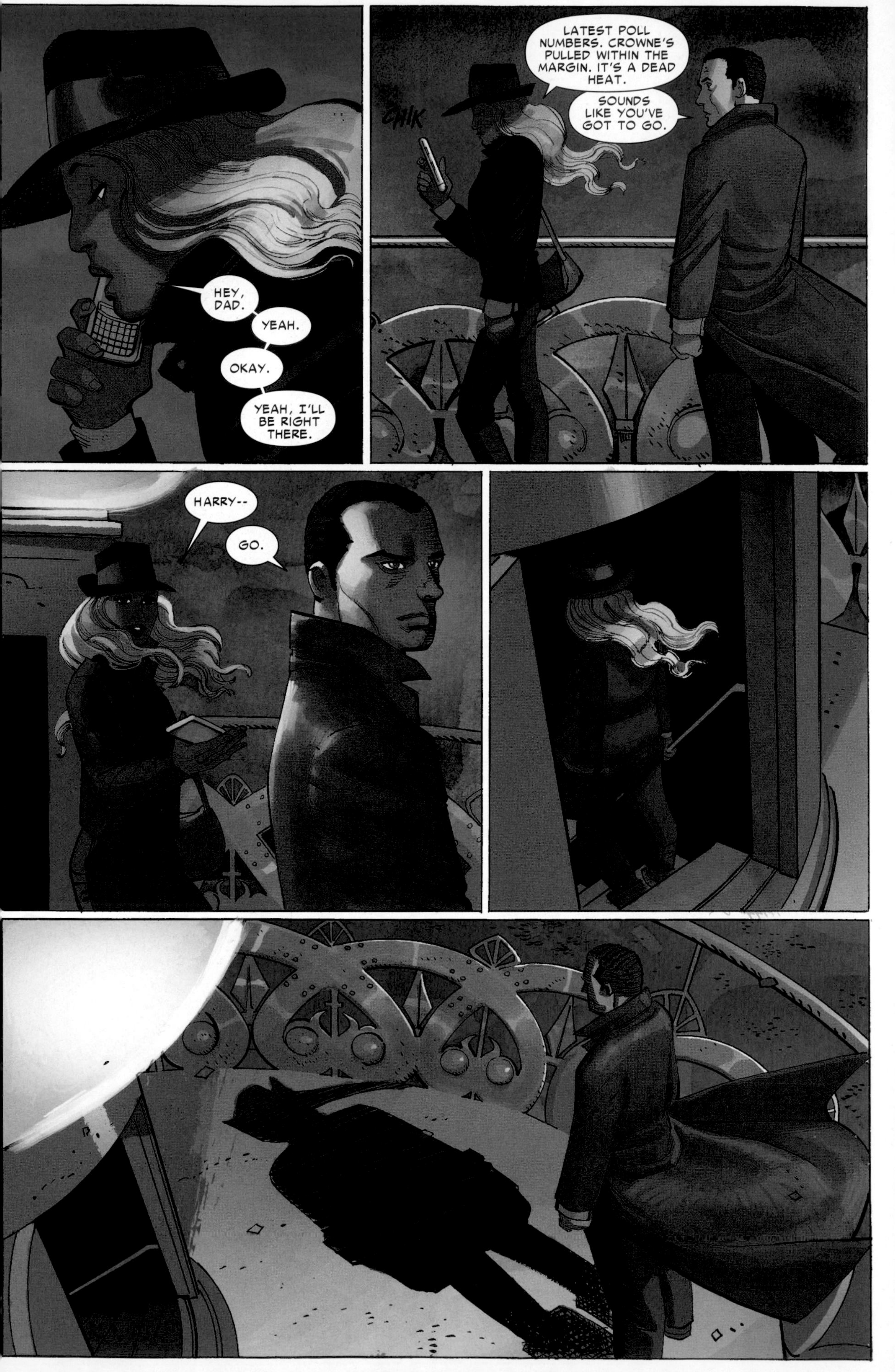
HEY, DAD.
YEAH.
OKAY.
YEAH, I'LL BE RIGHT THERE.
CHIK
LATEST POLL NUMBERS. CROWNE'S PULLED WITHIN THE MARGIN. IT'S A DEAD HEAT.
SOUNDS LIKE YOU'VE GOT TO GO.
HARRY--
GO.

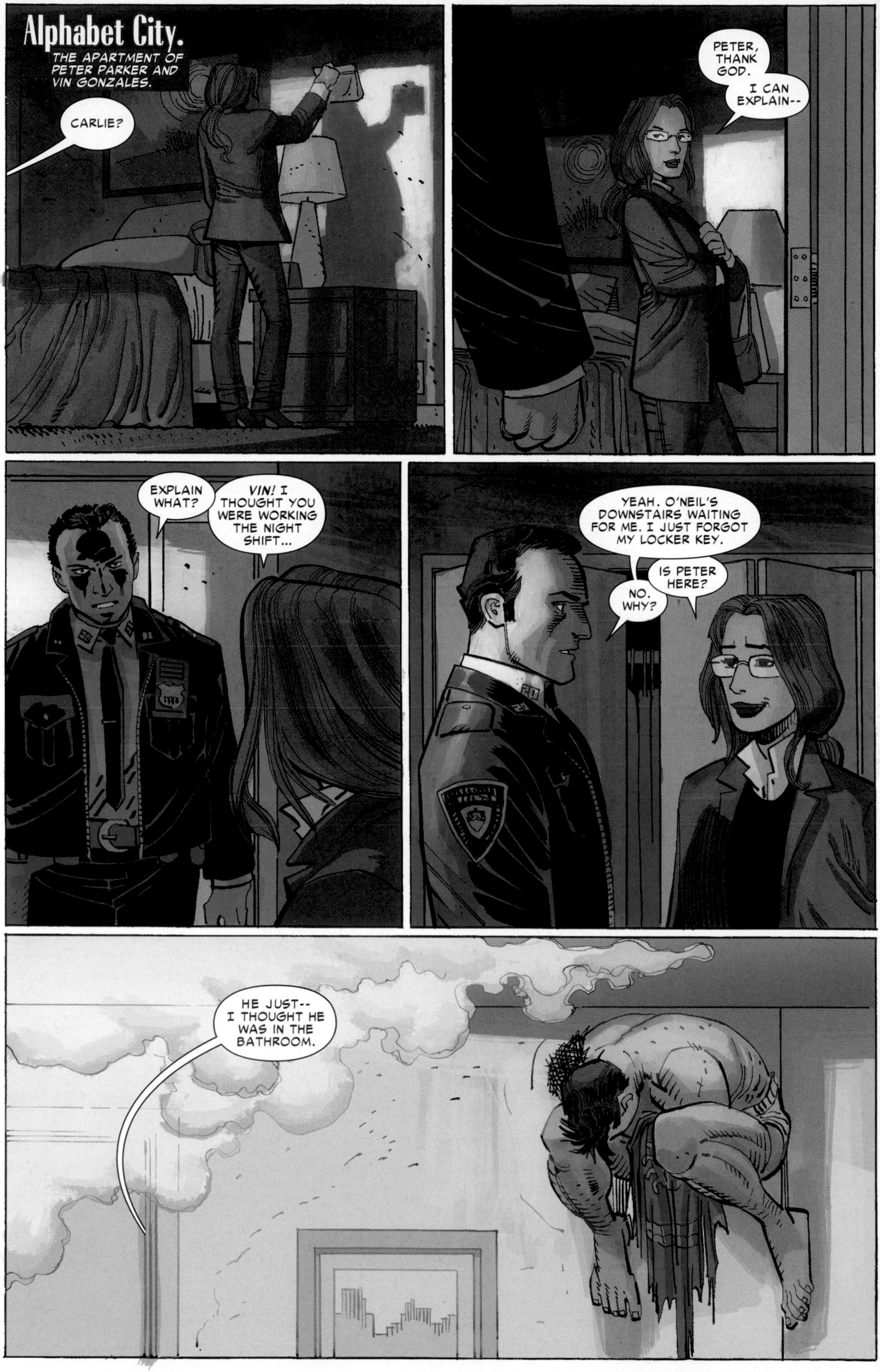
Alphabet City.
THE APARTMENT OF PETER PARKER AND VIN GONZALES.
CARLIE?
PETER, THANK GOD.
I CAN EXPLAIN--
EXPLAIN WHAT?
VIN! I THOUGHT YOU WERE WORKING THE NIGHT SHIFT...
YEAH. O'NEIL'S DOWNSTAIRS WAITING FOR ME. I JUST FORGOT MY LOCKER KEY.
IS PETER HERE?
NO. WHY?
HE JUST-- I THOUGHT HE WAS IN THE BATHROOM.

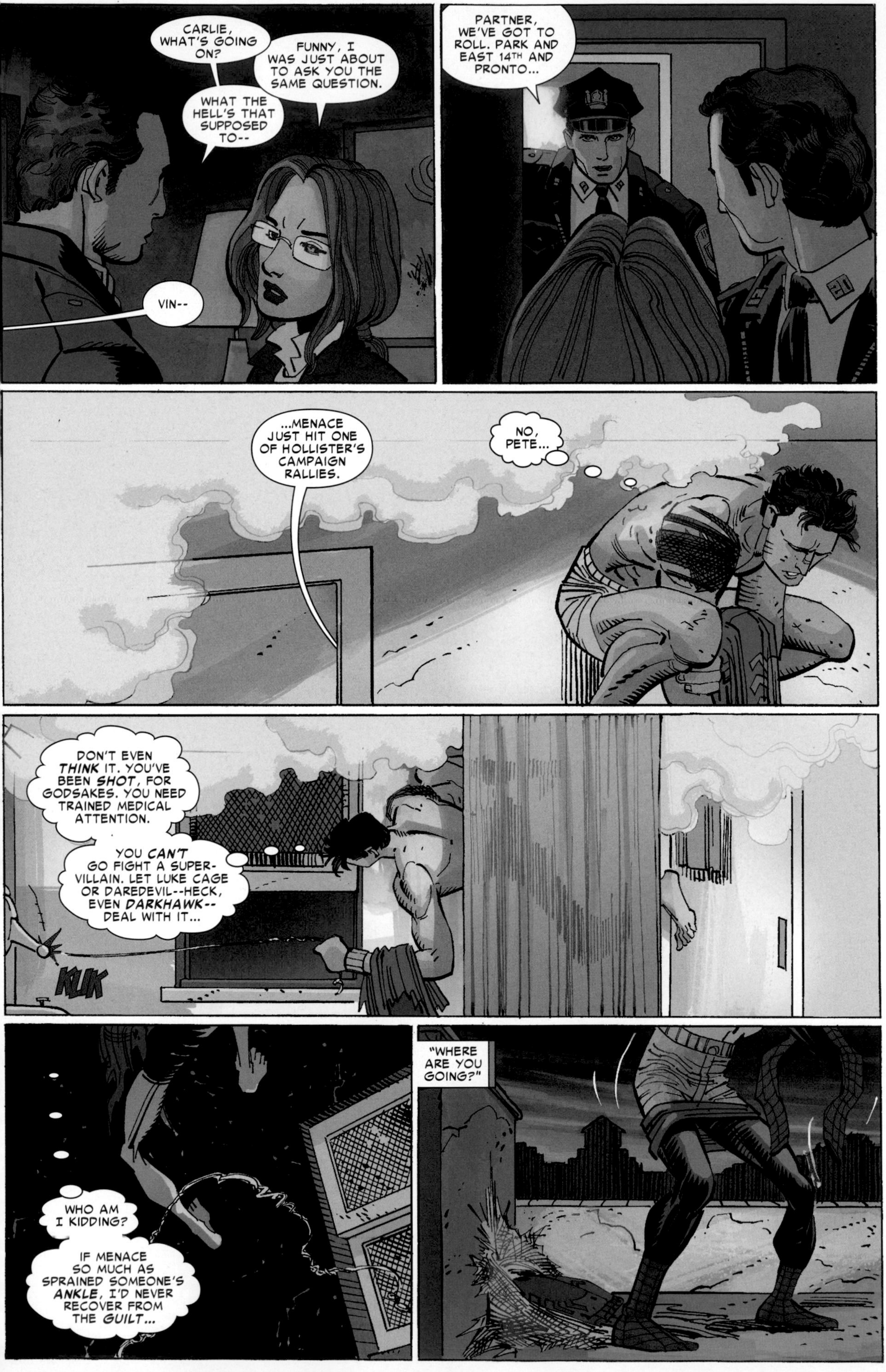
CARLIE, WHAT'S GOING ON?
FUNNY, I WAS JUST ABOUT TO ASK YOU THE SAME QUESTION.
WHAT THE HELL'S THAT SUPPOSED TO--
VIN--
PARTNER, WE'VE GOT TO ROLL. PARK AND EAST 14TH AND PRONTO...
...MENACE JUST HIT ONE OF HOLLISTER'S CAMPAIGN RALLIES.
NO, PETE...
DON'T EVEN THINK IT. YOU'VE BEEN SHOT, FOR GODSAKES. YOU NEED TRAINED MEDICAL ATTENTION.
YOU CAN'T GO FIGHT A SUPER-VILLAIN. LET LUKE CAGE OR DAREDEVIL--HECK, EVEN DARKHAWK--DEAL WITH IT...
KLIK
WHO AM I KIDDING?
IF MENACE SO MUCH AS SPRAINED SOMEONE'S ANKLE, I'D NEVER RECOVER FROM THE GUILT...
"WHERE ARE YOU GOING?"

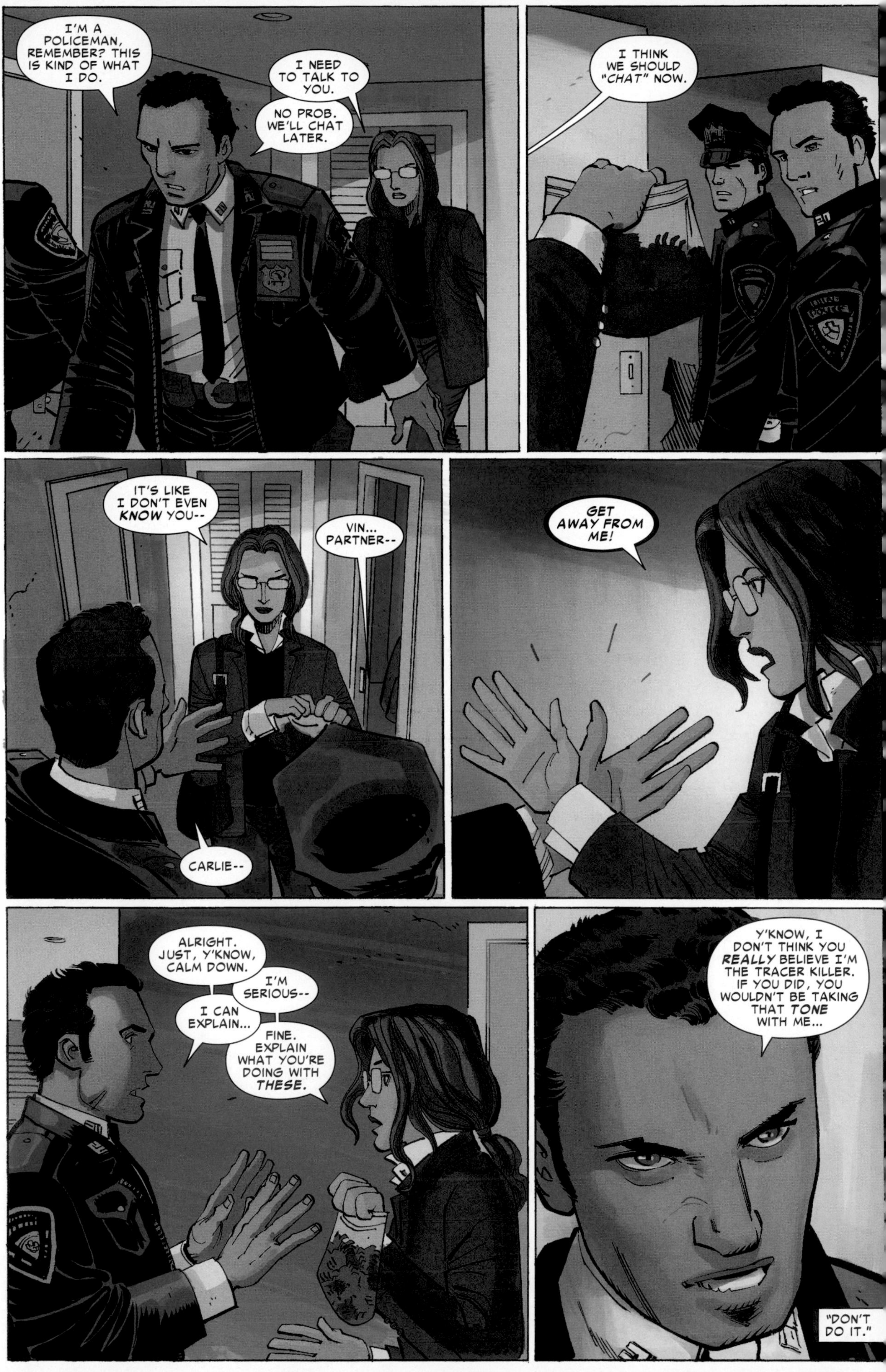
I'M A POLICEMAN, REMEMBER? THIS IS KIND OF WHAT I DO.
I NEED TO TALK TO YOU.
NO PROB. WE'LL CHAT LATER.
I THINK WE SHOULD "CHAT" NOW.
IT'S LIKE I DON'T EVEN KNOW YOU--
VIN... PARTNER--
CARLIE--
GET AWAY FROM ME!
ALRIGHT. JUST, Y'KNOW, CALM DOWN.
I'M SERIOUS--
I CAN EXPLAIN...
FINE. EXPLAIN WHAT YOU'RE DOING WITH THESE.
Y'KNOW, I DON'T THINK YOU REALLY BELIEVE I'M THE TRACER KILLER. IF YOU DID, YOU WOULDN'T BE TAKING THAT TONE WITH ME...
"DON'T DO IT."

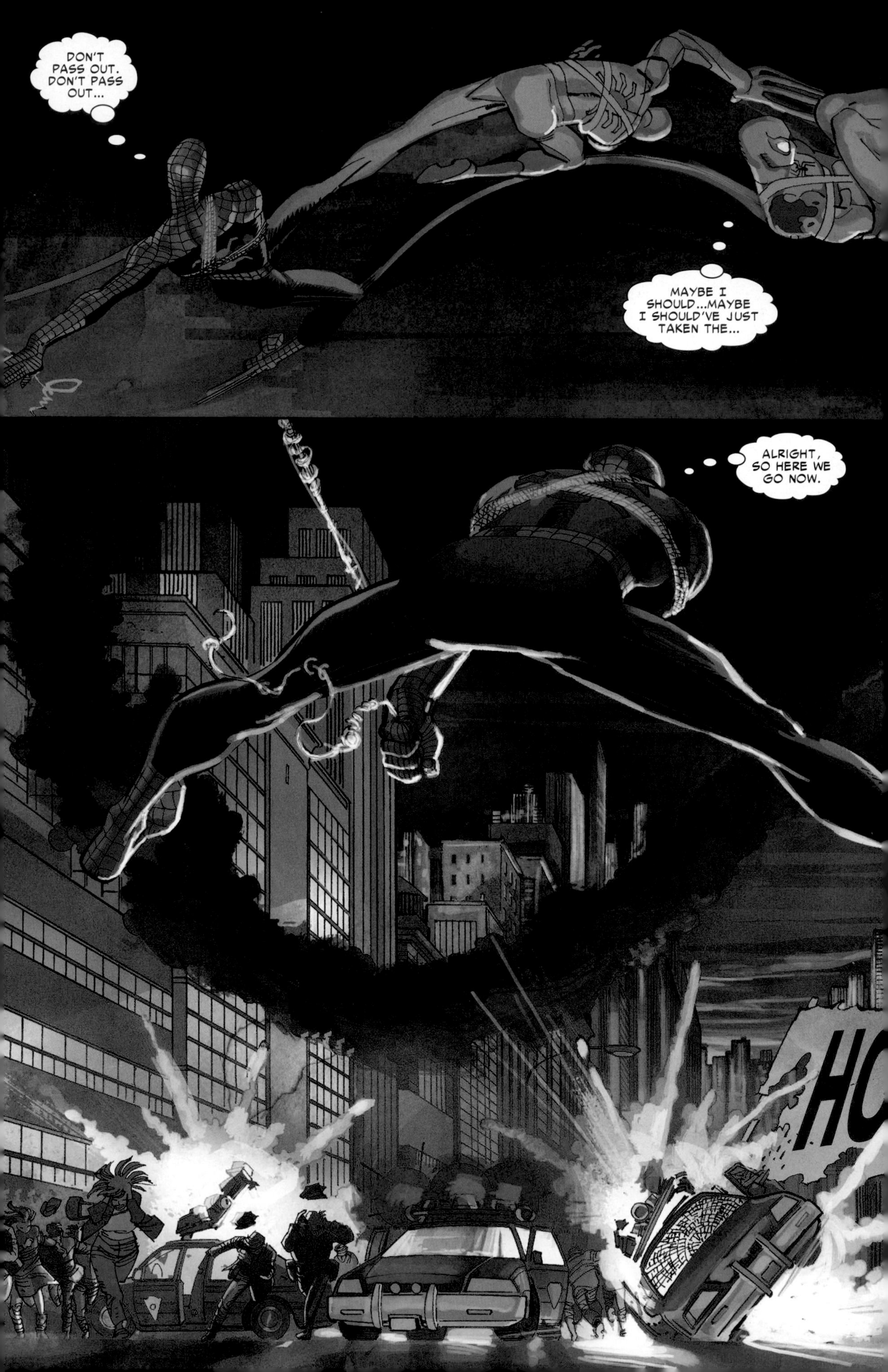
DON'T PASS OUT. DON'T PASS OUT...
MAYBE I SHOULD...MAYBE I SHOULD'VE JUST TAKEN THE...
ALRIGHT, SO HERE WE GO NOW.

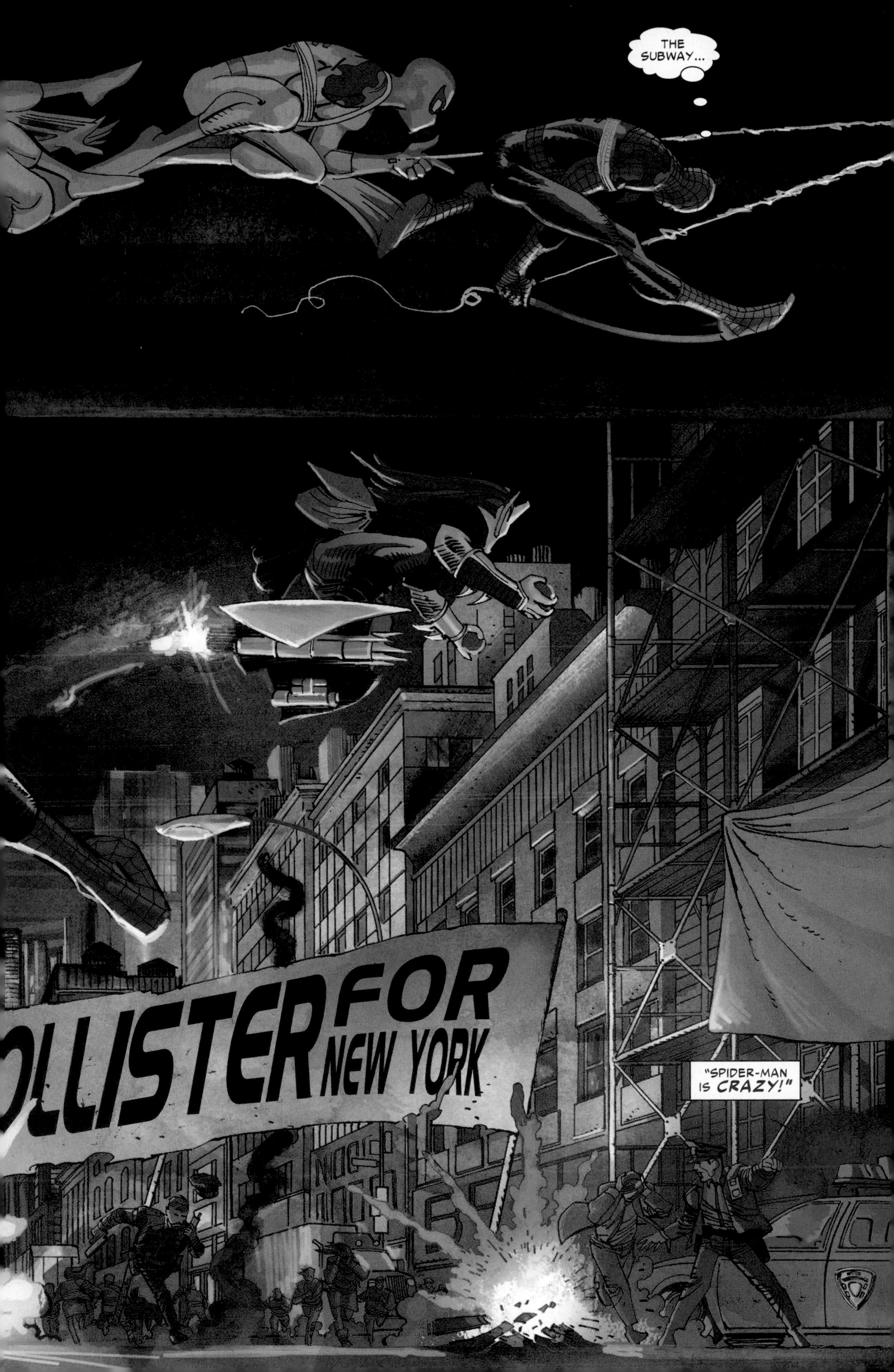
THE SUBWAY...
OLLISTER FOR NEW YORK
"SPIDER-MAN IS CRAZY!"

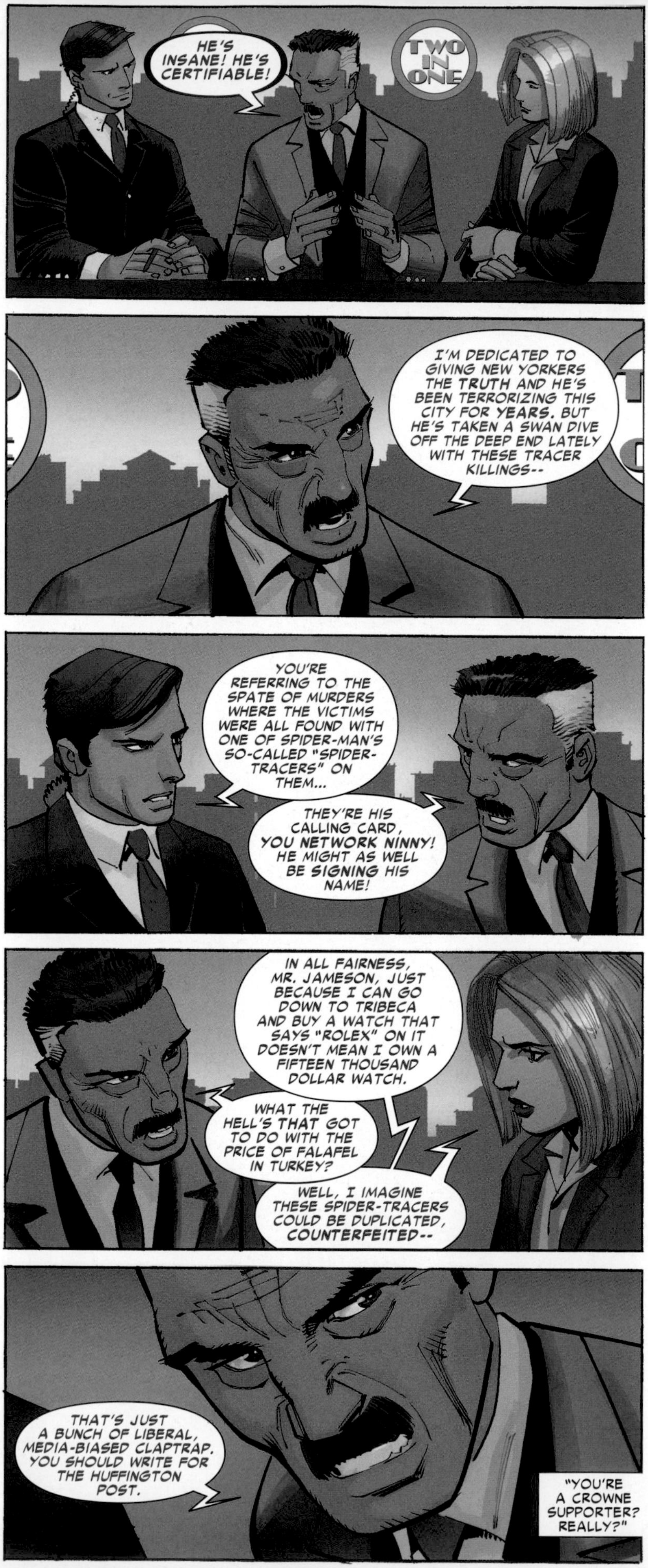
HE'S INSANE! HE'S CERTIFIABLE!
TWO IN ONE
I'M DEDICATED TO GIVING NEW YORKERS THE TRUTH AND HE'S BEEN TERRORIZING THIS CITY FOR YEARS. BUT HE'S TAKEN A SWAN DIVE OFF THE DEEP END LATELY WITH THESE TRACER KILLINGS--
YOU'RE REFERRING TO THE SPATE OF MURDERS WHERE THE VICTIMS WERE ALL FOUND WITH ONE OF SPIDER-MAN'S SO-CALLED "SPIDER-TRACERS" ON THEM...
THEY'RE HIS CALLING CARD, YOU NETWORK NINNY! HE MIGHT AS WELL BE SIGNING HIS NAME!
IN ALL FAIRNESS, MR. JAMESON, JUST BECAUSE I CAN GO DOWN TO TRIBECA AND BUY A WATCH THAT SAYS "ROLEX" ON IT DOESN'T MEAN I OWN A FIFTEEN THOUSAND DOLLAR WATCH.
WHAT THE HELL'S THAT GOT TO DO WITH THE PRICE OF FALAFEL IN TURKEY?
WELL, I IMAGINE THESE SPIDER-TRACERS COULD BE DUPLICATED, COUNTERFEITED--
THAT'S JUST A BUNCH OF LIBERAL, MEDIA-BIASED CLAPTRAP. YOU SHOULD WRITE FOR THE HUFFINGTON POST.
"YOU'RE A CROWNE SUPPORTER? REALLY?"

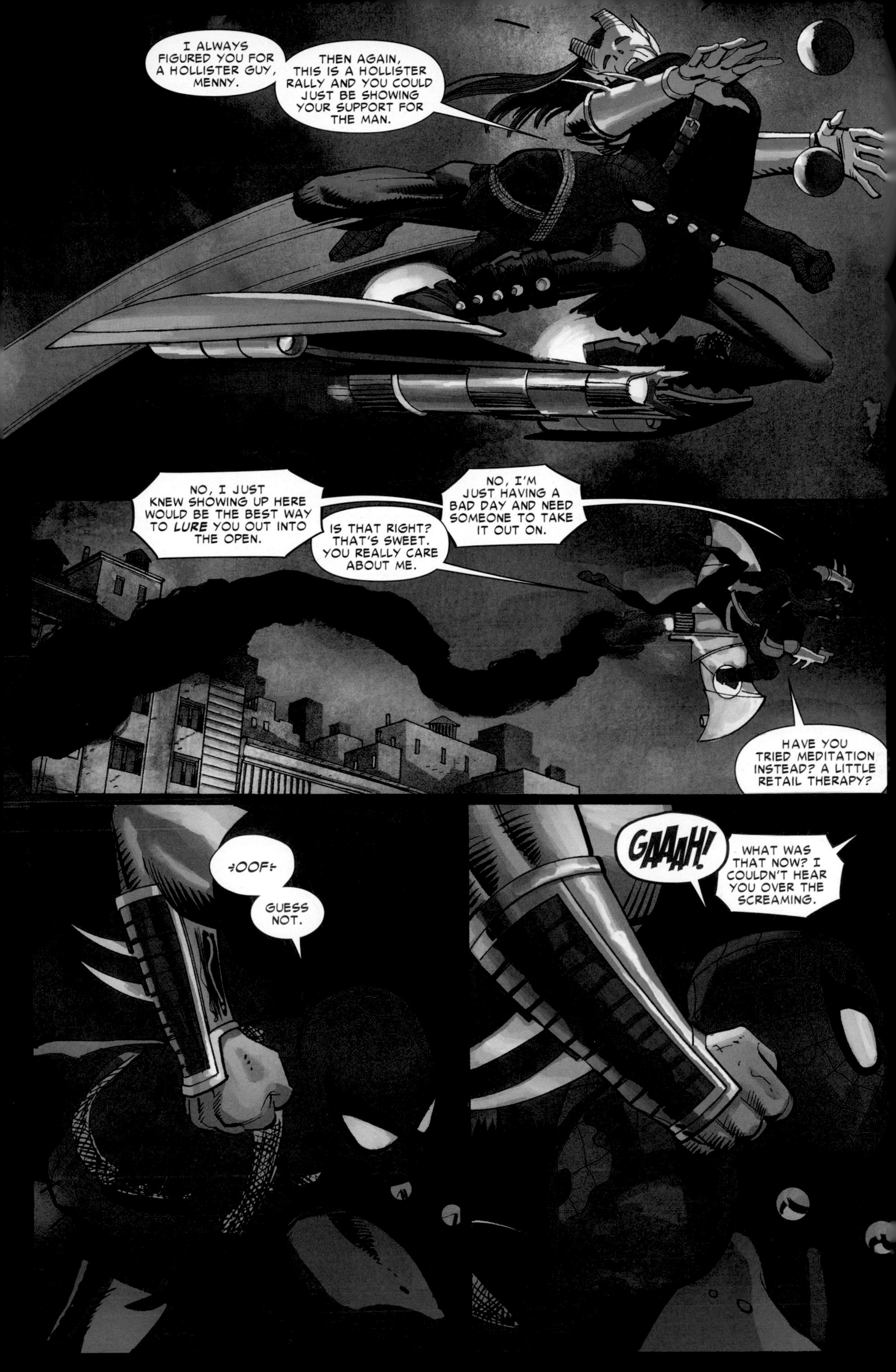
I ALWAYS FIGURED YOU FOR A HOLLISTER GUY, MENNY.
THEN AGAIN, THIS IS A HOLLISTER RALLY AND YOU COULD JUST BE SHOWING YOUR SUPPORT FOR THE MAN.
NO, I JUST KNEW SHOWING UP HERE WOULD BE THE BEST WAY TO LURE YOU OUT INTO THE OPEN.
IS THAT RIGHT? THAT'S SWEET. YOU REALLY CARE ABOUT ME.
NO, I'M JUST HAVING A BAD DAY AND NEED SOMEONE TO TAKE IT OUT ON.
HAVE YOU TRIED MEDITATION INSTEAD? A LITTLE RETAIL THERAPY?
OOF
GUESS NOT.
GAAAH!
WHAT WAS THAT NOW? I COULDN'T HEAR YOU OVER THE SCREAMING.

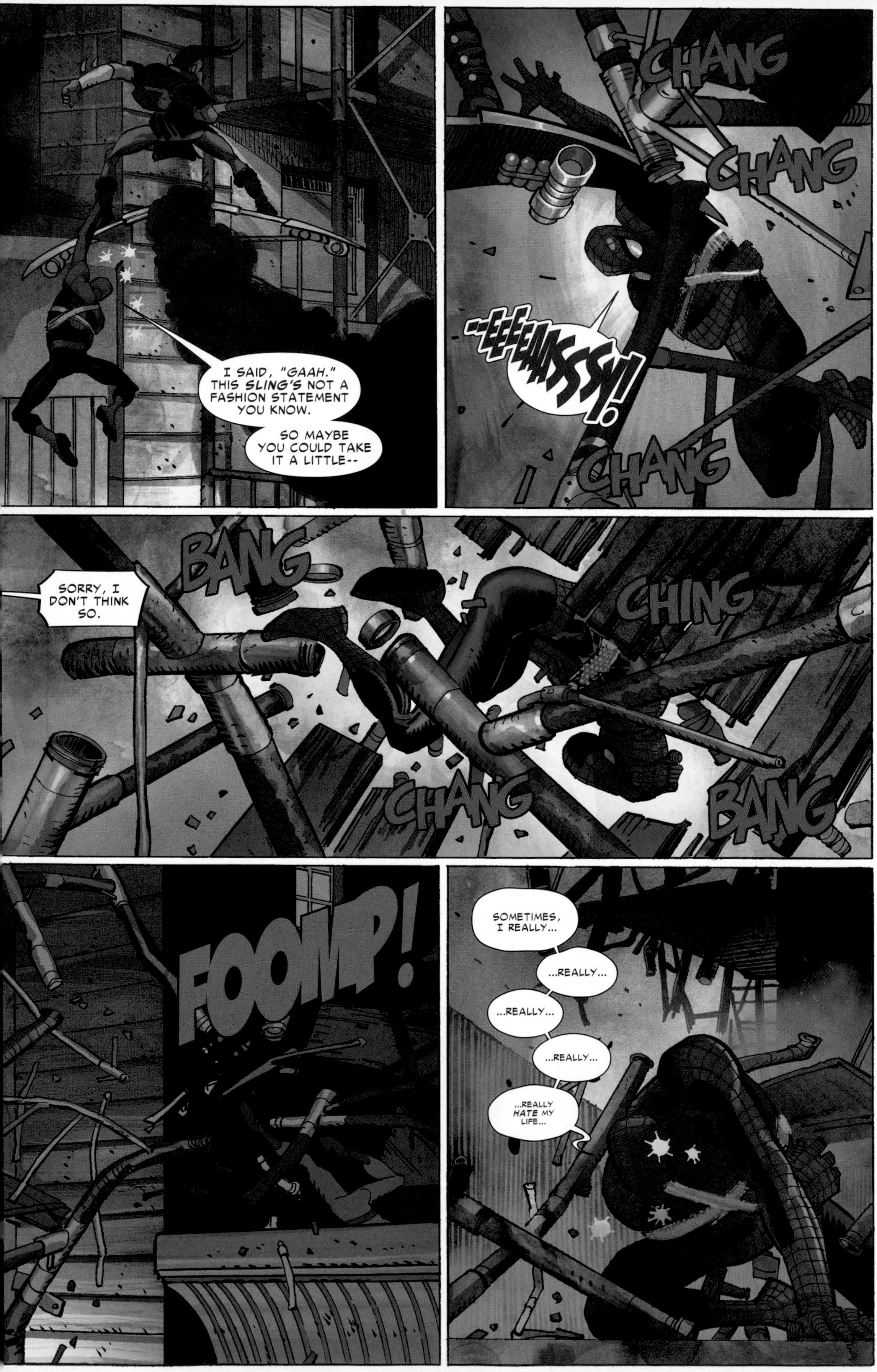
I SAID, "GAAH." THIS SLING'S NOT A FASHION STATEMENT YOU KNOW.
SO MAYBE YOU COULD TAKE IT A LITTLE--
CHANG
CHANG
--EEEEAASSSY!
CHANG
BANG
SORRY, I DON'T THINK SO.
CHING
CHANG
BANG
FOOMP!
SOMETIMES, I REALLY...
...REALLY...
...REALLY...
...REALLY...
...REALLY HATE MY LIFE...

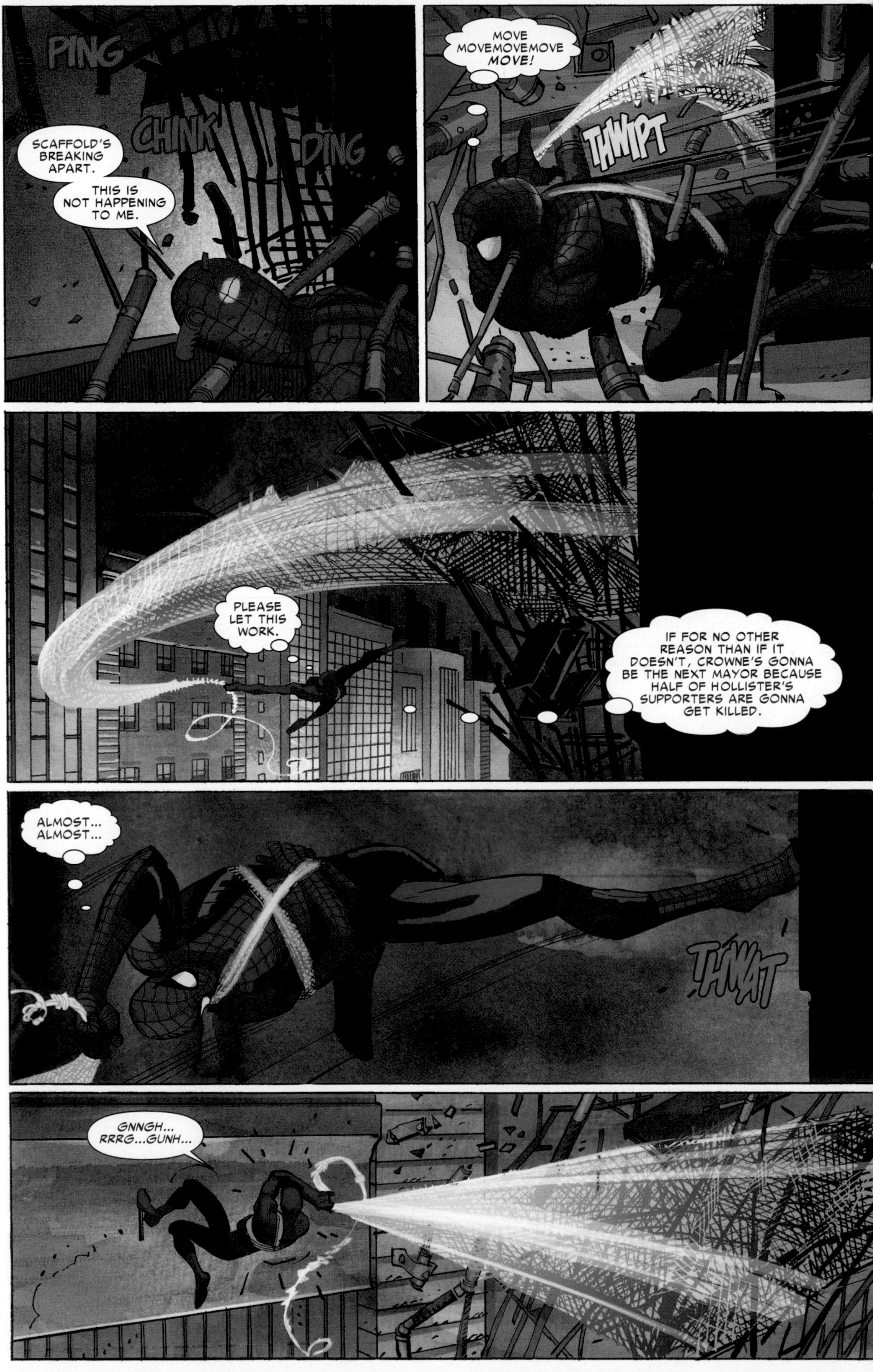
PING
CHINK
DING
SCAFFOLD'S BREAKING APART.
THIS IS NOT HAPPENING TO ME.
MOVE MOVEMOVEMOVE *MOVE!*
THWIPT
PLEASE LET THIS WORK.
IF FOR NO OTHER REASON THAN IF IT DOESN'T, CROWNE'S GONNA BE THE NEXT MAYOR BECAUSE HALF OF HOLLISTER'S SUPPORTERS ARE GONNA GET KILLED.
ALMOST... ALMOST...
THWAT
GNNGH... RRRG...GUNH...

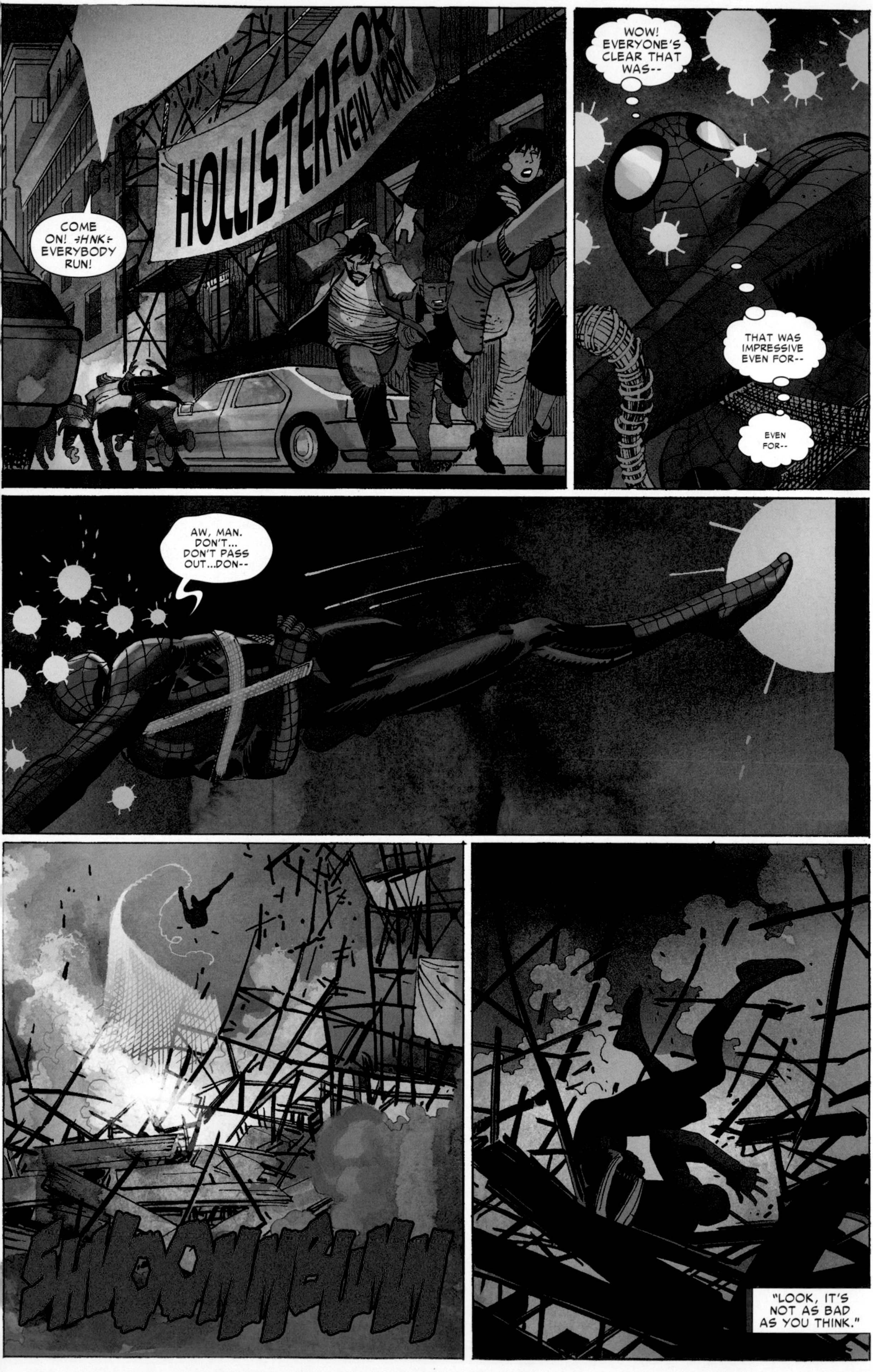
HOLLISTER FOR NEW YORK
COME ON! =HNK= EVERYBODY RUN!
WOW! EVERYONE'S CLEAR THAT WAS--
THAT WAS IMPRESSIVE EVEN FOR--
EVEN FOR--
AW, MAN. DON'T... DON'T PASS OUT...DON--
SHHOOMMPUMM
"LOOK, IT'S NOT AS BAD AS YOU THINK."

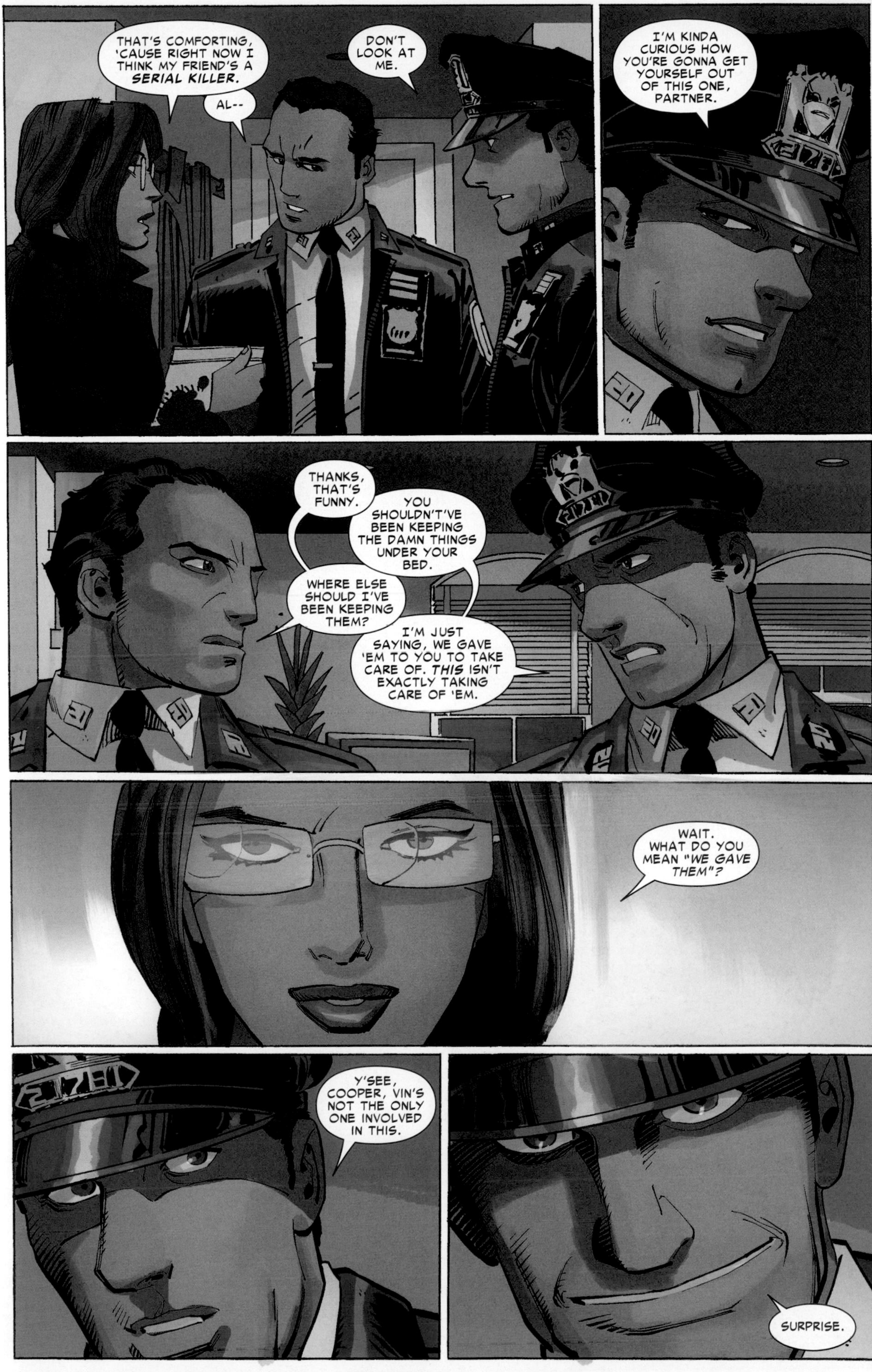
THAT'S COMFORTING, 'CAUSE RIGHT NOW I THINK MY FRIEND'S A *SERIAL KILLER.*
AL--
DON'T LOOK AT ME.
I'M KINDA CURIOUS HOW YOU'RE GONNA GET YOURSELF OUT OF THIS ONE, PARTNER.
THANKS, THAT'S FUNNY.
YOU SHOULDN'T'VE BEEN KEEPING THE DAMN THINGS UNDER YOUR BED.
WHERE ELSE SHOULD I'VE BEEN KEEPING THEM?
I'M JUST SAYING, WE GAVE 'EM TO YOU TO TAKE CARE OF. *THIS* ISN'T EXACTLY TAKING CARE OF 'EM.
WAIT. WHAT DO YOU MEAN "*WE GAVE THEM*"?
Y'SEE, COOPER, VIN'S NOT THE ONLY ONE INVOLVED IN THIS.
SURPRISE.

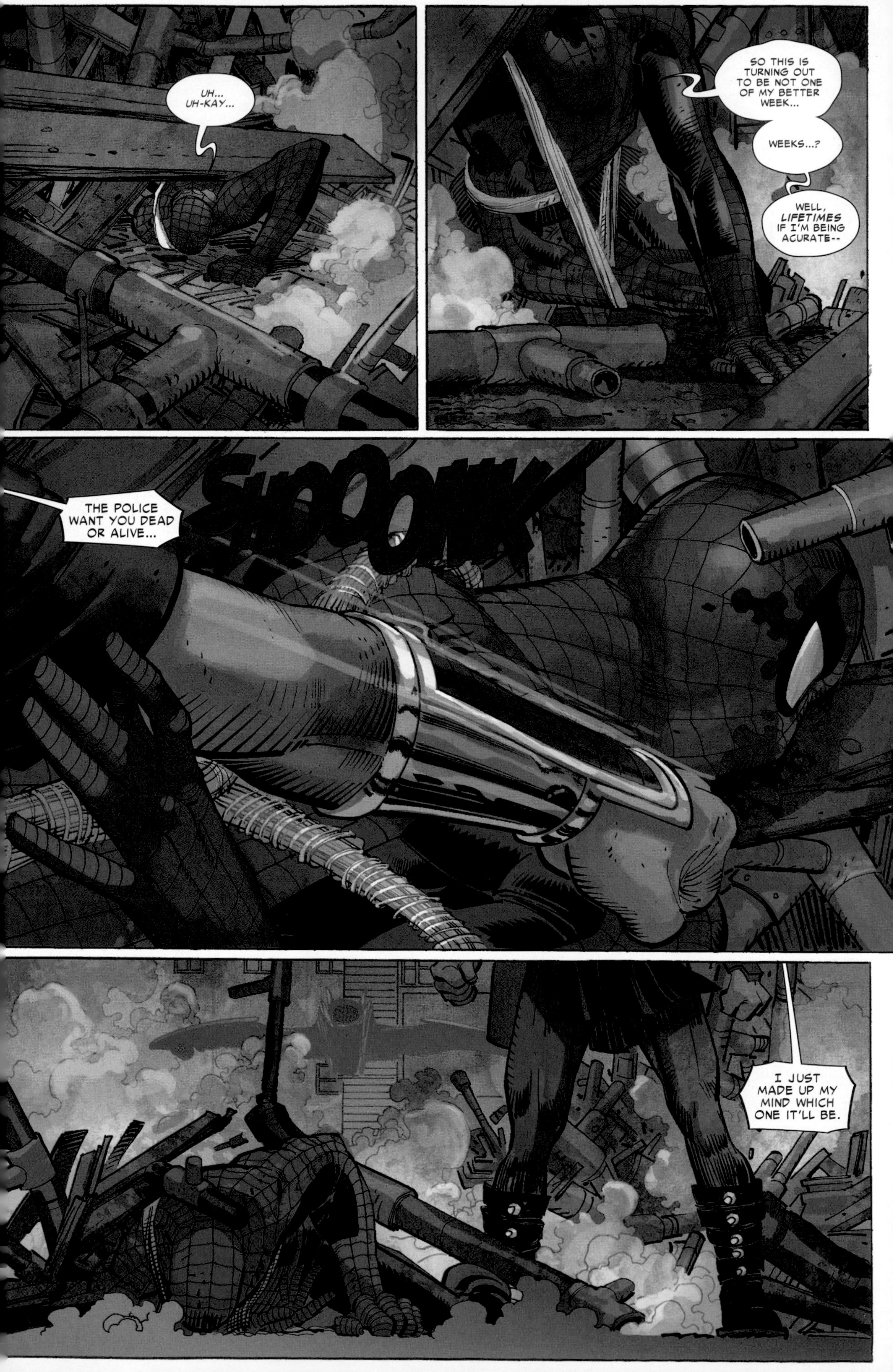
UH... UH-KAY...
SO THIS IS TURNING OUT TO BE NOT ONE OF MY BETTER WEEK...
WEEKS...?
WELL, *LIFETIMES* IF I'M BEING ACURATE--
SHOOOMK
THE POLICE WANT YOU DEAD OR ALIVE...
I JUST MADE UP MY MIND WHICH ONE IT'LL BE.

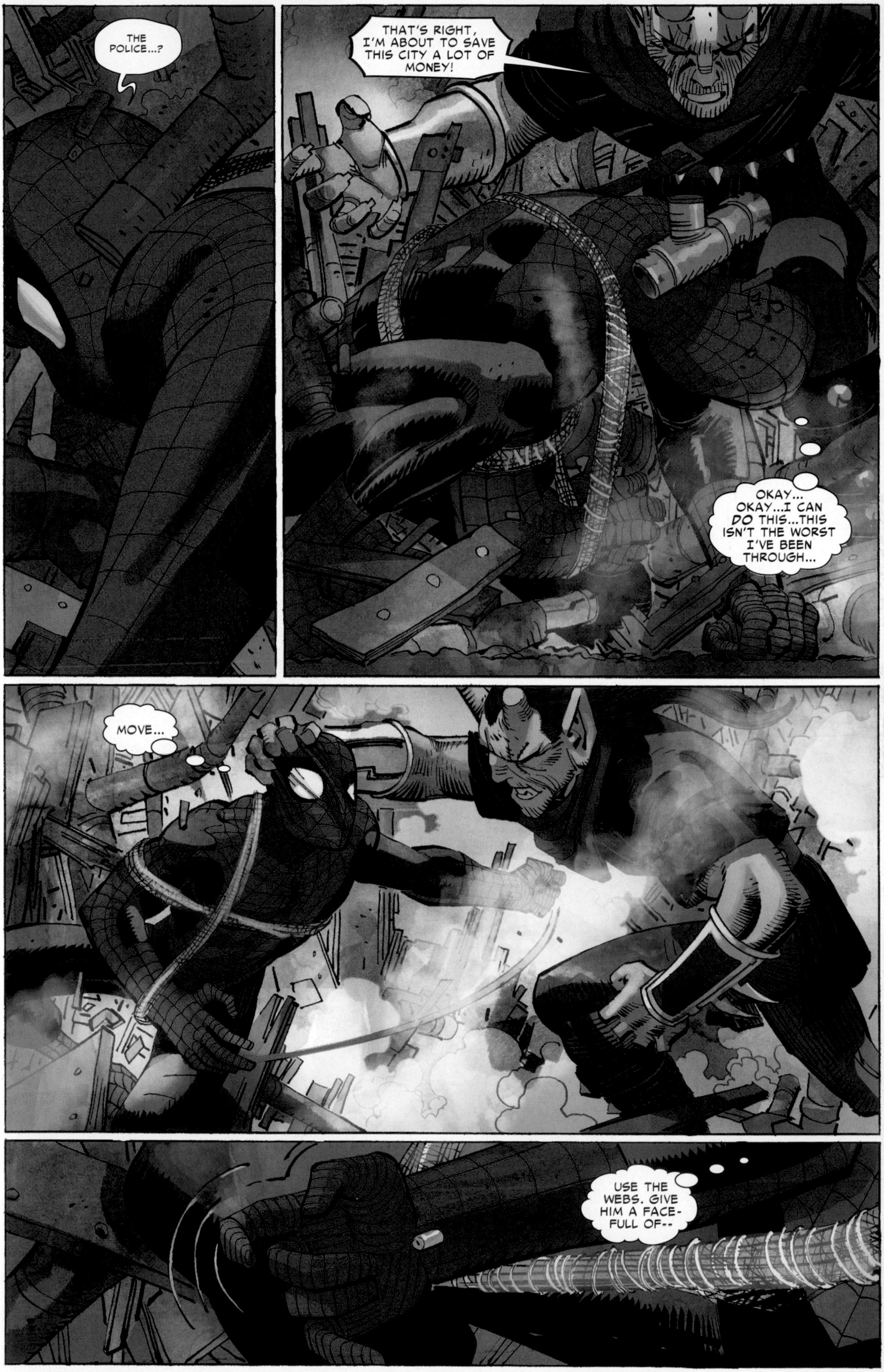
THE POLICE...?
THAT'S RIGHT, I'M ABOUT TO SAVE THIS CITY A LOT OF MONEY!
OKAY... OKAY...I CAN DO THIS...THIS ISN'T THE WORST I'VE BEEN THROUGH...
MOVE...
USE THE WEBS. GIVE HIM A FACE-FULL OF--

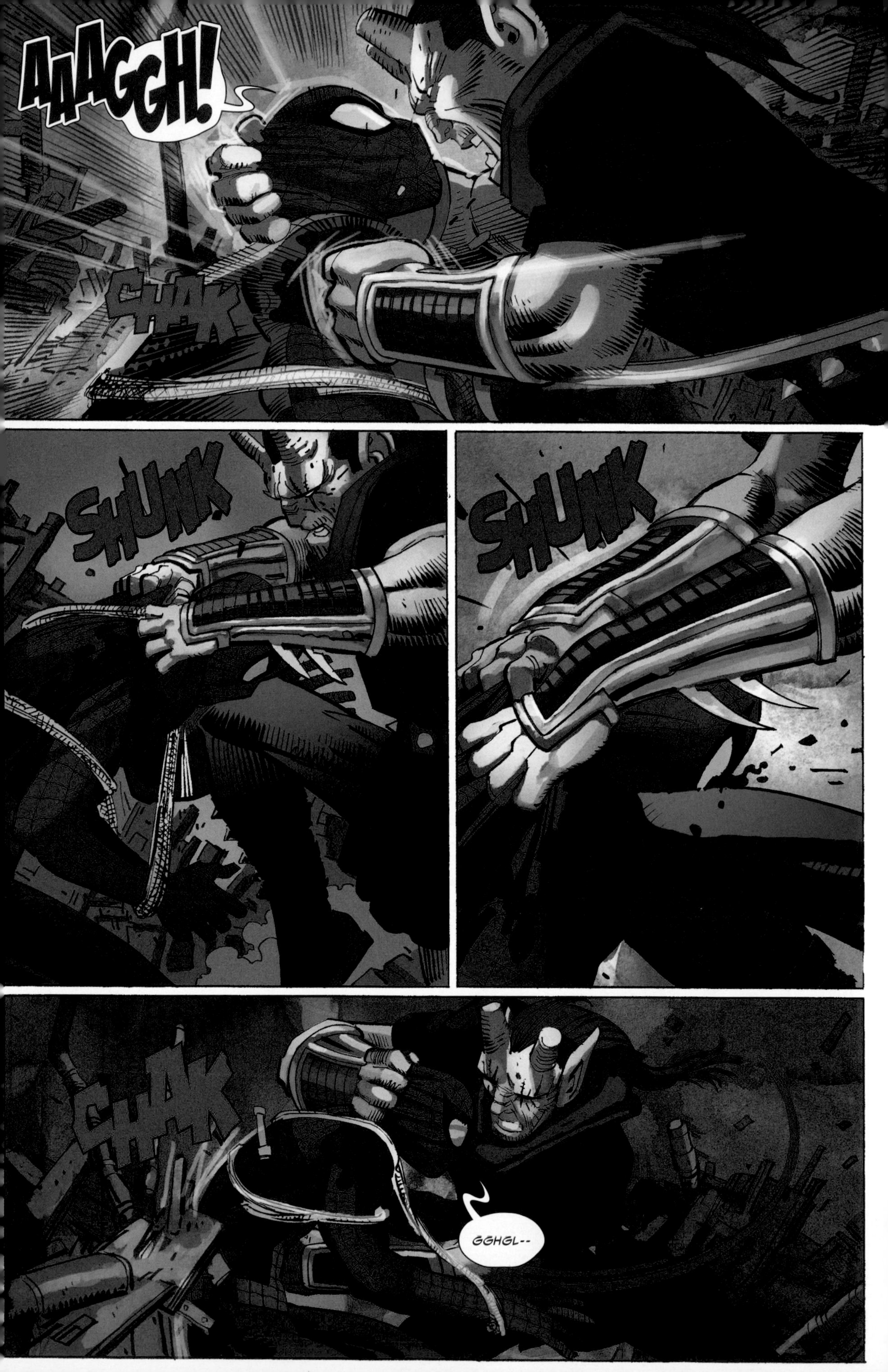
AAAGGH!
CHAK
SHUNK
SHUNK
CHAK
GGHGL--

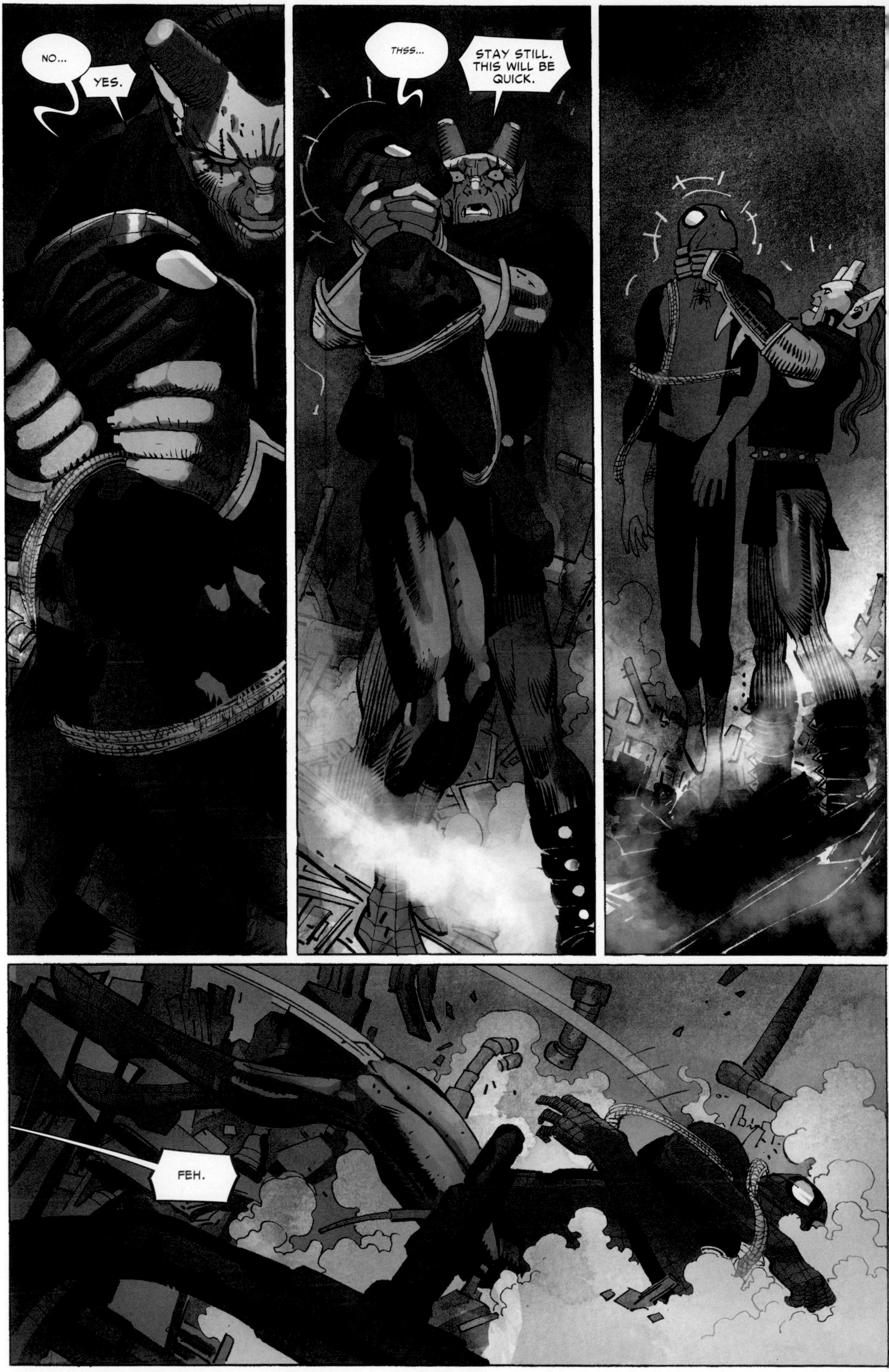
NO...
YES.
THSS...
STAY STILL. THIS WILL BE QUICK.
FEH.

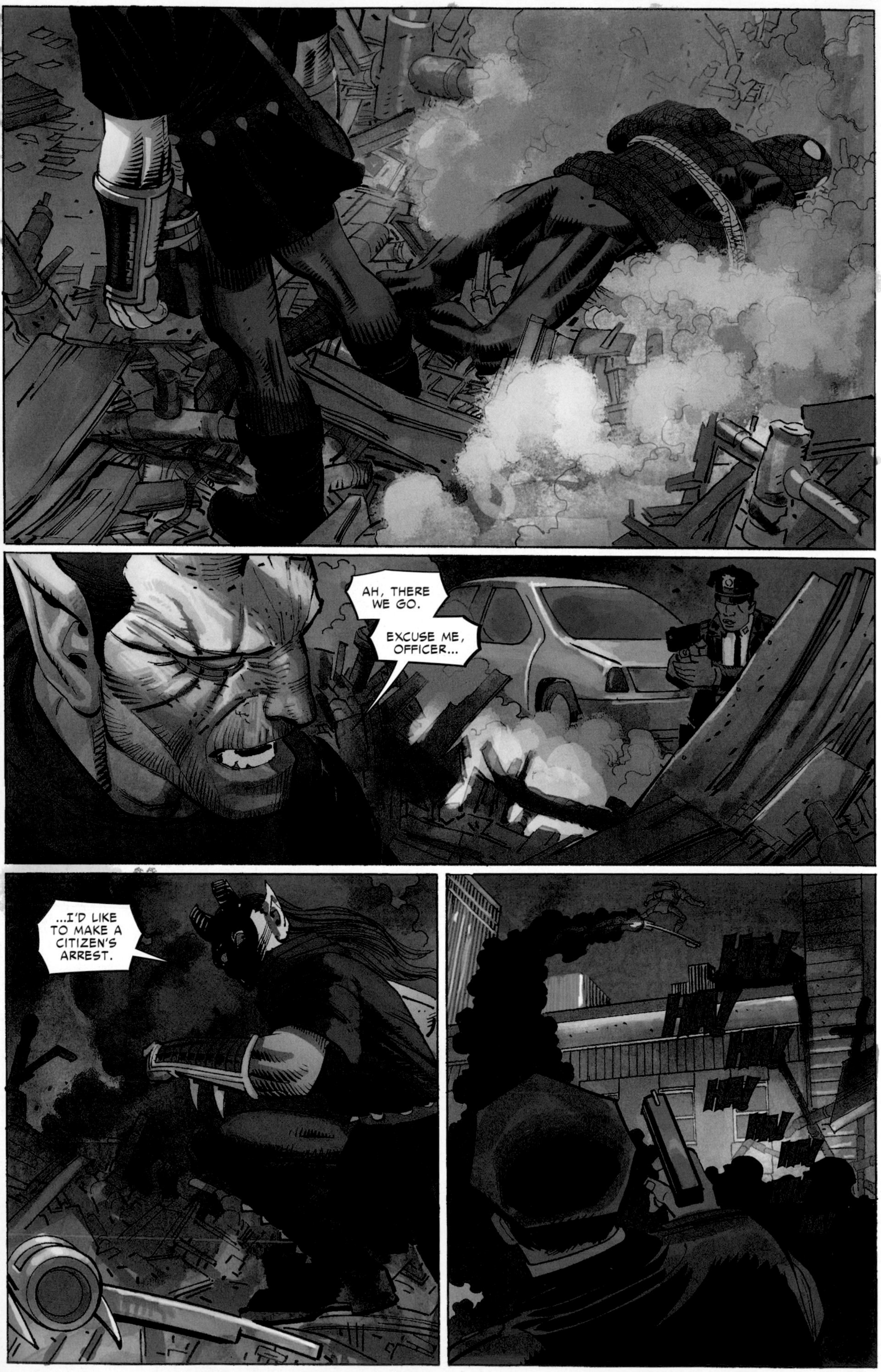
AH, THERE WE GO.
EXCUSE ME, OFFICER...
...I'D LIKE TO MAKE A CITIZEN'S ARREST.

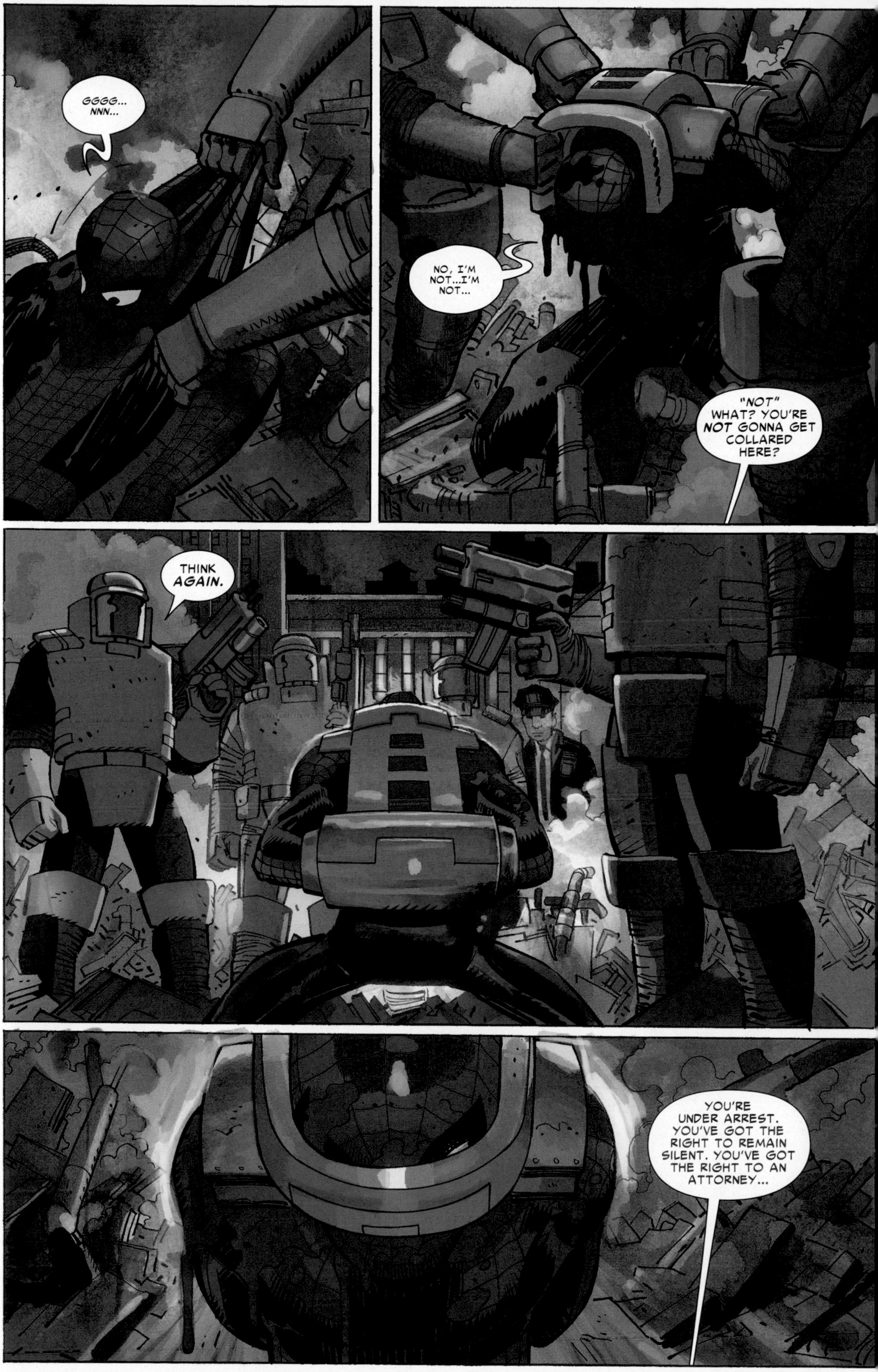
GGGG... NNN...
NO, I'M NOT...I'M NOT...
"NOT" WHAT? YOU'RE NOT GONNA GET COLLARED HERE?
THINK AGAIN.
YOU'RE UNDER ARREST. YOU'VE GOT THE RIGHT TO REMAIN SILENT. YOU'VE GOT THE RIGHT TO AN ATTORNEY...

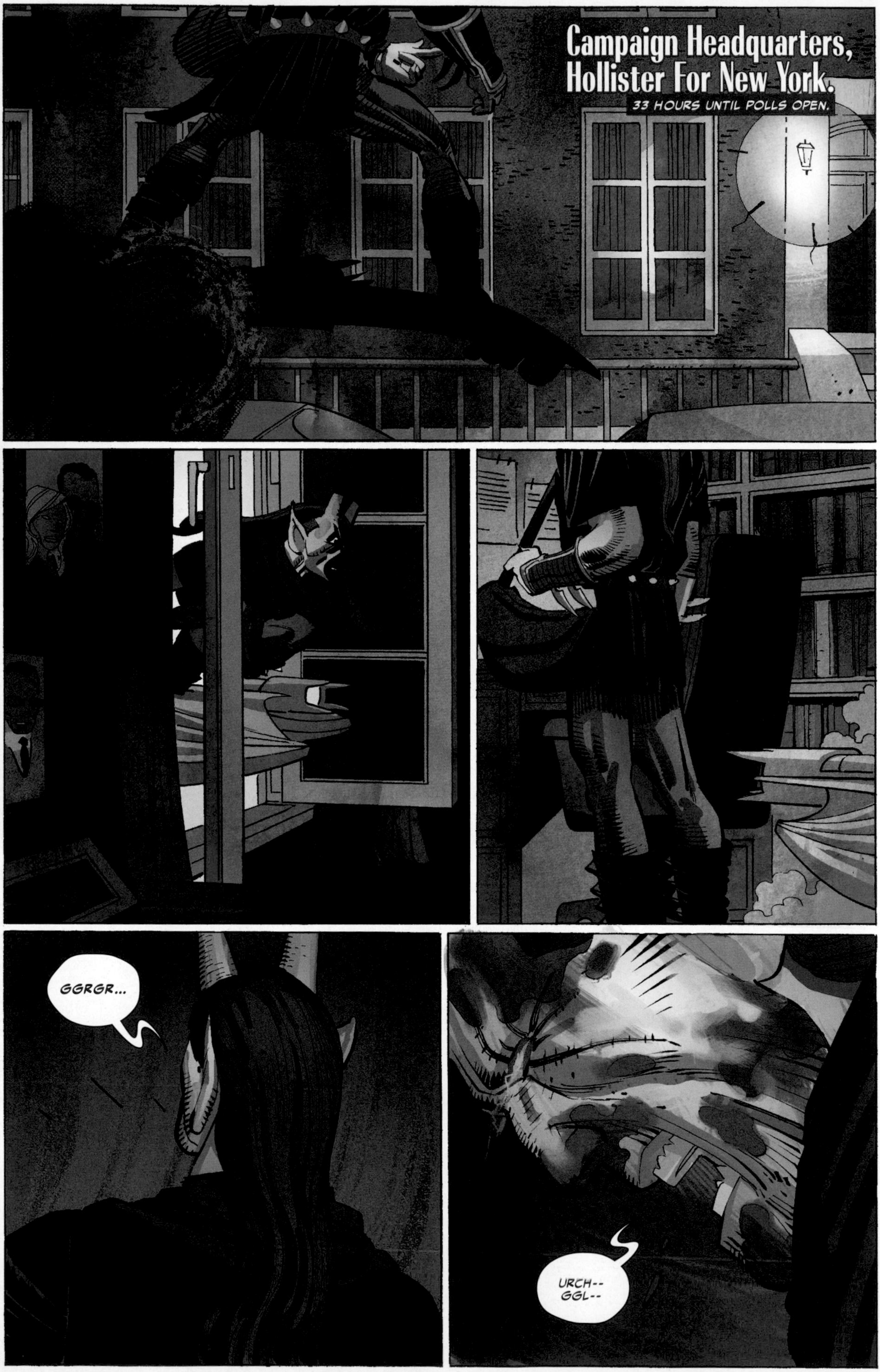
Campaign Headquarters, Hollister For New York.
33 HOURS UNTIL POLLS OPEN.
GGRGR...
URCH-- GGL--

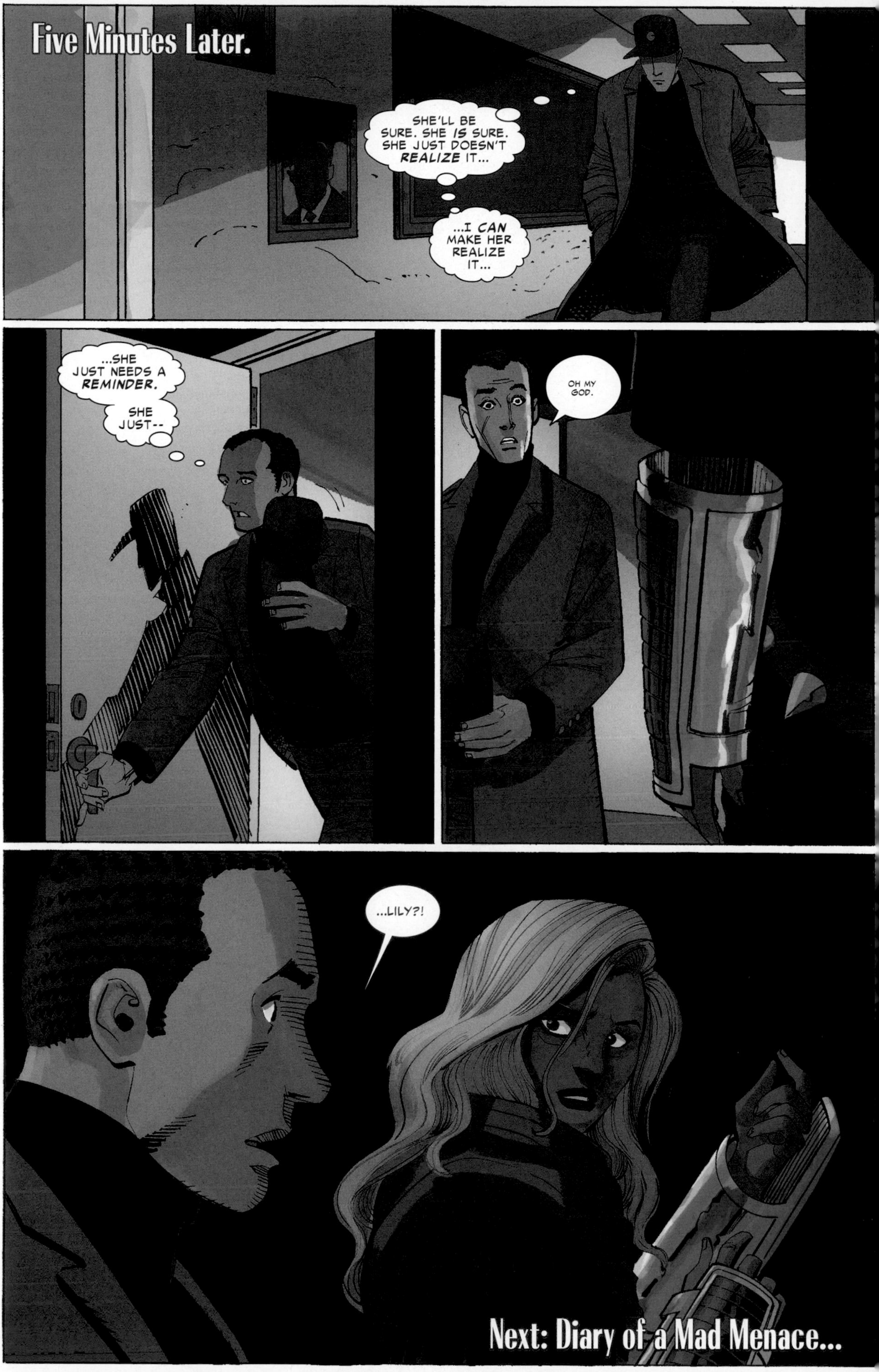
Five Minutes Later.
SHE'LL BE SURE. SHE IS SURE. SHE JUST DOESN'T REALIZE IT...
...I CAN MAKE HER REALIZE IT...
...SHE JUST NEEDS A REMINDER.
SHE JUST--
OH MY GOD.
...LILY?!
Next: Diary of a Mad Menace...

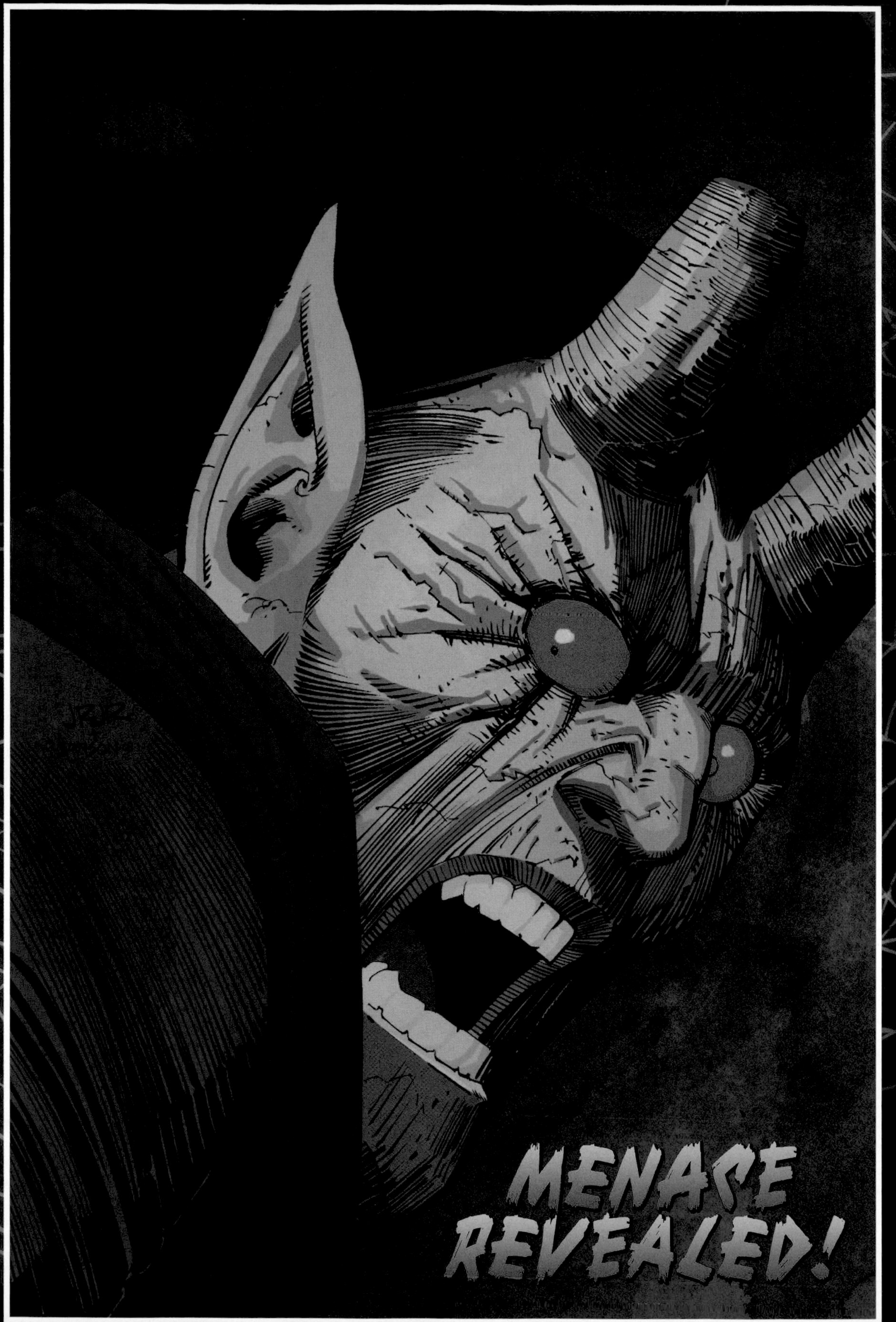
MENACE REVEALED!

AMAZING SPIDER-MAN #586

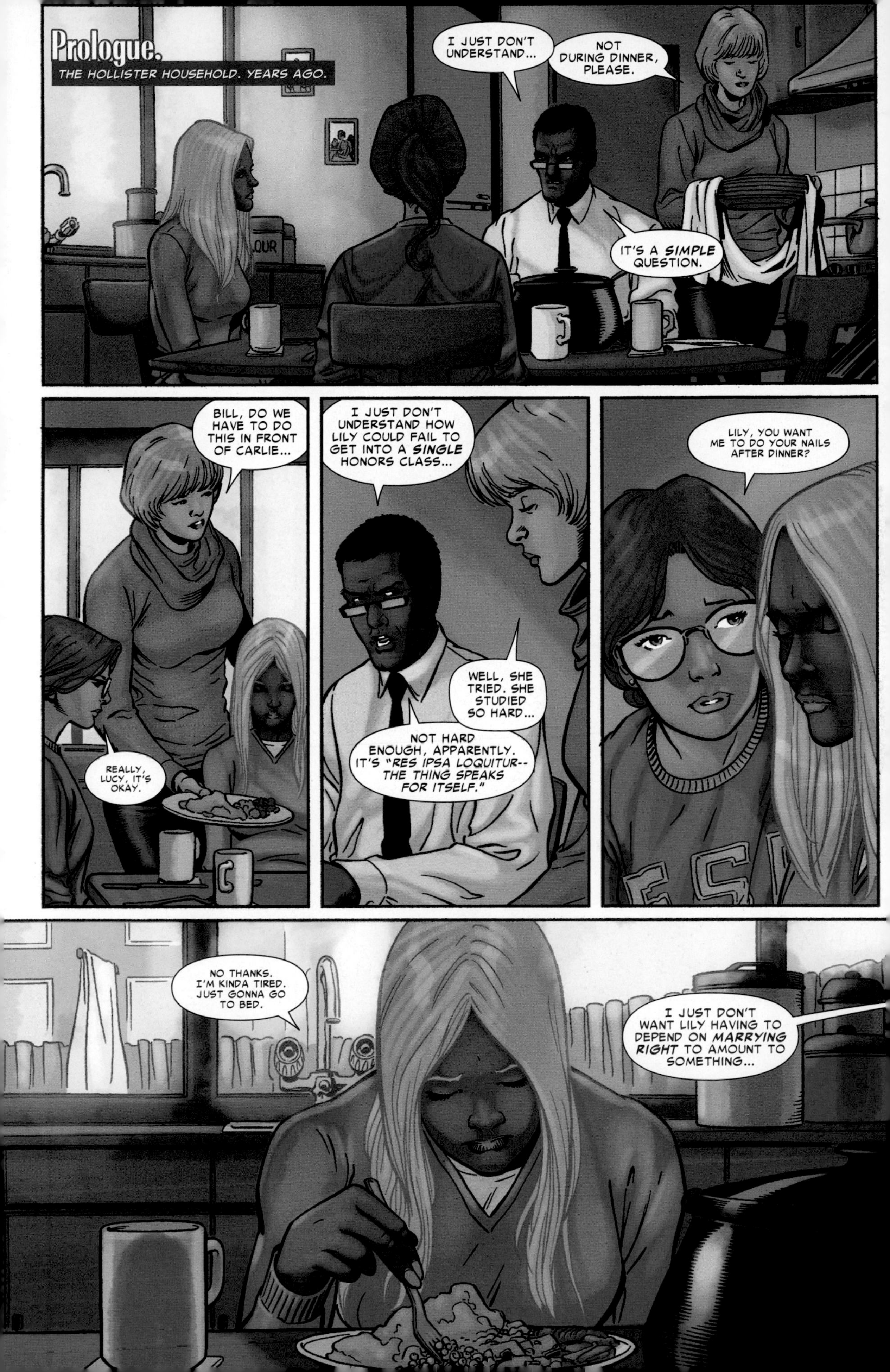
Prologue.
THE HOLLISTER HOUSEHOLD. YEARS AGO.
I JUST DON'T UNDERSTAND...
NOT DURING DINNER, PLEASE.
IT'S A SIMPLE QUESTION.
BILL, DO WE HAVE TO DO THIS IN FRONT OF CARLIE...
REALLY, LUCY, IT'S OKAY.
I JUST DON'T UNDERSTAND HOW LILY COULD FAIL TO GET INTO A SINGLE HONORS CLASS...
WELL, SHE TRIED. SHE STUDIED SO HARD...
NOT HARD ENOUGH, APPARENTLY. IT'S "RES IPSA LOQUITUR-- THE THING SPEAKS FOR ITSELF."
LILY, YOU WANT ME TO DO YOUR NAILS AFTER DINNER?
NO THANKS. I'M KINDA TIRED. JUST GONNA GO TO BED.
I JUST DON'T WANT LILY HAVING TO DEPEND ON MARRYING RIGHT TO AMOUNT TO SOMETHING...

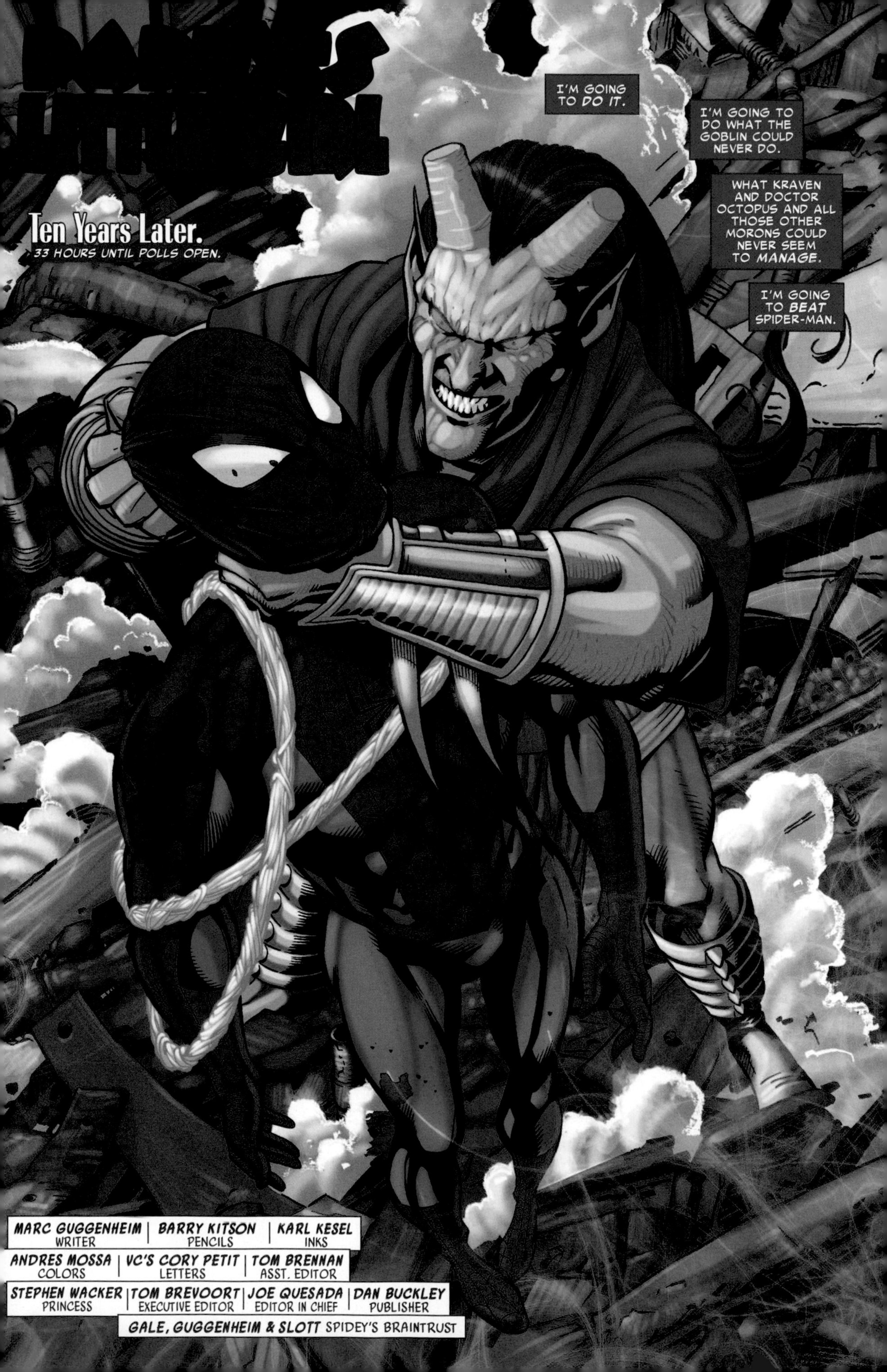
Ten Years Later.
33 HOURS UNTIL POLLS OPEN.
I'M GOING TO DO IT.
I'M GOING TO DO WHAT THE GOBLIN COULD NEVER DO.
WHAT KRAVEN AND DOCTOR OCTOPUS AND ALL THOSE OTHER MORONS COULD NEVER SEEM TO MANAGE.
I'M GOING TO BEAT SPIDER-MAN.
MARC GUGGENHEIM WRITER | BARRY KITSON PENCILS | KARL KESEL INKS
ANDRES MOSSA COLORS | VC'S CORY PETIT LETTERS | TOM BRENNAN ASST. EDITOR
STEPHEN WACKER PRINCESS | TOM BREVOORT EXECUTIVE EDITOR | JOE QUESADA EDITOR IN CHIEF | DAN BUCKLEY PUBLISHER
GALE, GUGGENHEIM & SLOTT SPIDEY'S BRAINTRUST

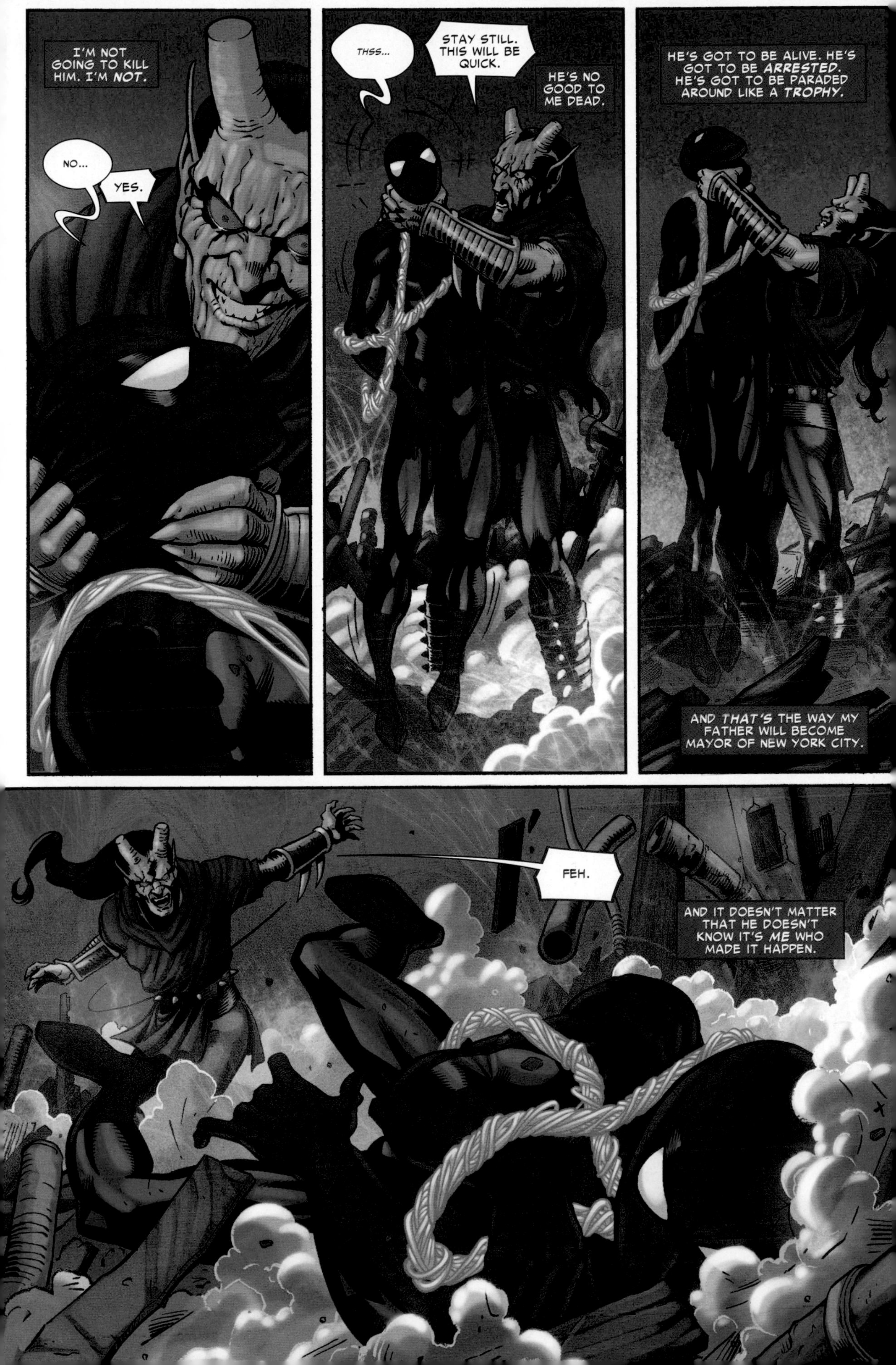

I'M NOT GOING TO KILL HIM. I'M NOT.
NO...
YES.
THSS...
STAY STILL. THIS WILL BE QUICK.
HE'S NO GOOD TO ME DEAD.
HE'S GOT TO BE ALIVE. HE'S GOT TO BE ARRESTED. HE'S GOT TO BE PARADED AROUND LIKE A TROPHY.
AND THAT'S THE WAY MY FATHER WILL BECOME MAYOR OF NEW YORK CITY.
FEH.
AND IT DOESN'T MATTER THAT HE DOESN'T KNOW IT'S ME WHO MADE IT HAPPEN.

I'LL. KNOW.

HA! HA! HA! HA! HA! HA! HA!

HE DOESN'T HAVE TO KNOW.

HE DOESN'T.

THAT'S ALL THAT MATTERS.

HE WOULDN'T UNDERSTAND.

HE NEVER DOES.

HE... NEVER...

GGRGR...

...DOES.

URCH-- GGL--

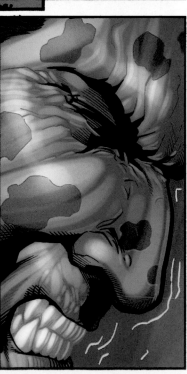

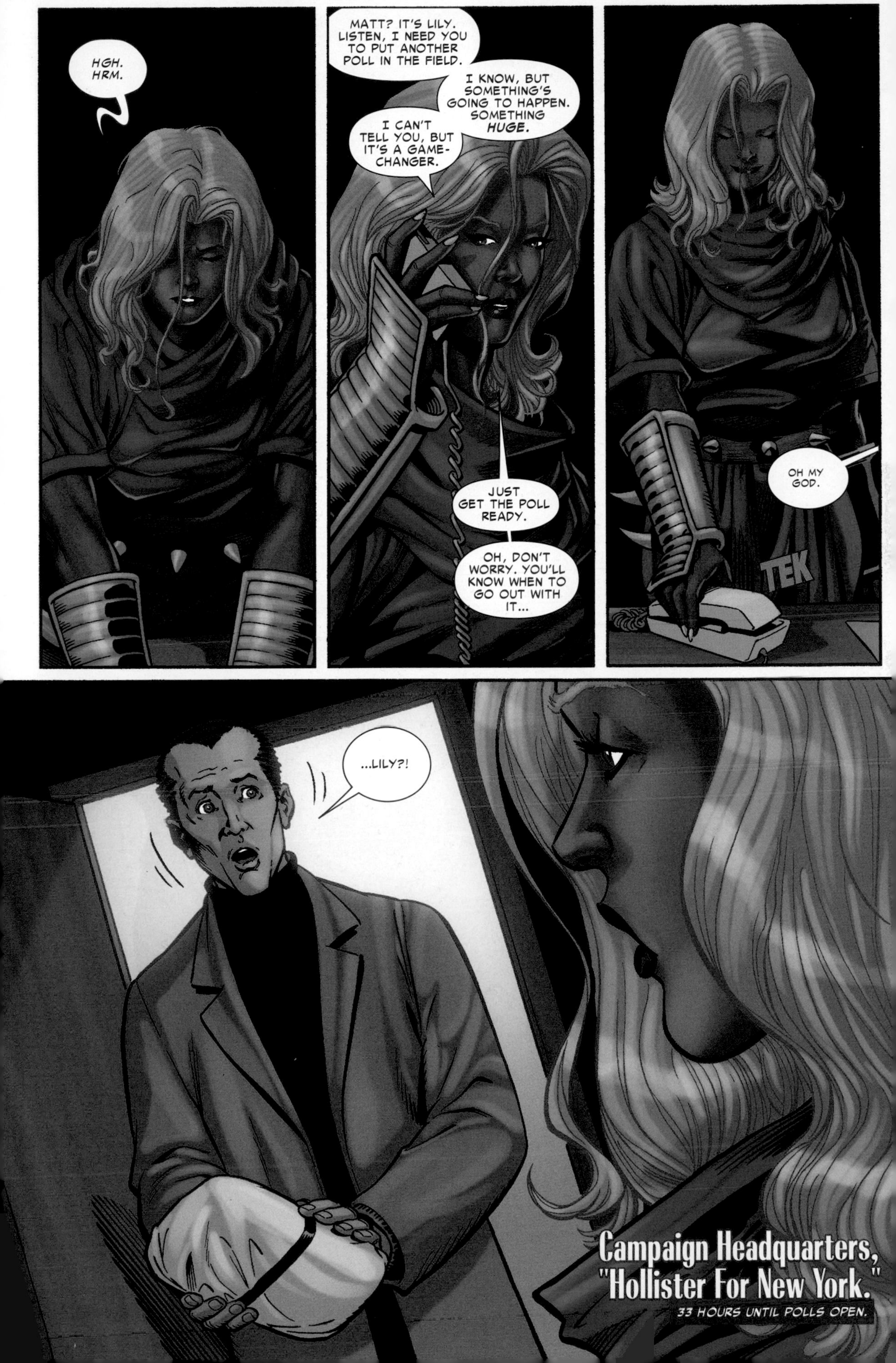
HGH. HRM.
MATT? IT'S LILY. LISTEN, I NEED YOU TO PUT ANOTHER POLL IN THE FIELD.
I KNOW, BUT SOMETHING'S GOING TO HAPPEN. SOMETHING *HUGE.*
I CAN'T TELL YOU, BUT IT'S A GAME-CHANGER.
JUST GET THE POLL READY.
OH, DON'T WORRY. YOU'LL KNOW WHEN TO GO OUT WITH IT...
OH MY GOD.
TEK
...LILY?!
Campaign Headquarters, "Hollister For New York."
33 HOURS UNTIL POLLS OPEN.

WELL? AREN'T YOU GOING TO SAY SOMETHING?

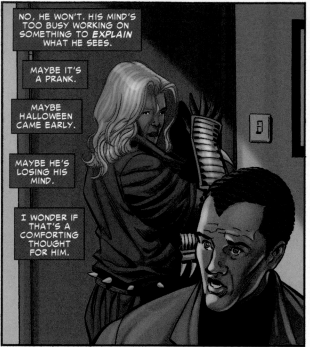

NO, HE WON'T. HIS MIND'S TOO BUSY WORKING ON SOMETHING TO *EXPLAIN* WHAT HE SEES.

MAYBE IT'S A PRANK.

MAYBE HALLOWEEN CAME EARLY.

MAYBE HE'S LOSING HIS MIND.

I WONDER IF THAT'S A COMFORTING THOUGHT FOR HIM.

HARRY, IF YOU'RE GOING TO SAY SOMETHING--

I THINK I'M GOING TO BE SICK.

KNOCK YOURSELF OUT.

LILY--

YOU MIND IF I CHANGE? THE COSTUME GETS UNCOMFORTABLE.

I--

LOOK, THIS DOESN'T HAVE TO BE DIFFICULT.

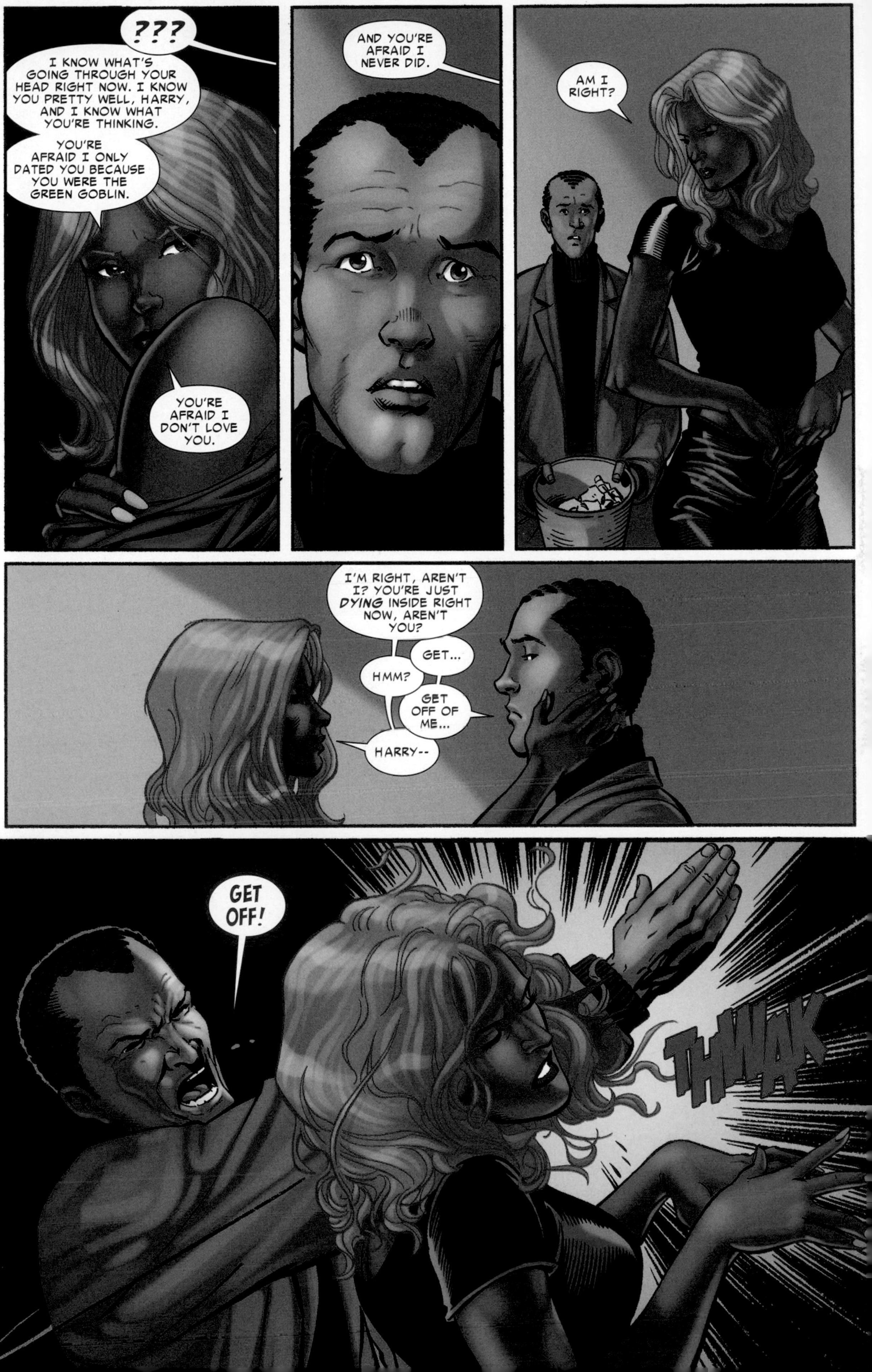
???
I KNOW WHAT'S GOING THROUGH YOUR HEAD RIGHT NOW. I KNOW YOU PRETTY WELL, HARRY, AND I KNOW WHAT YOU'RE THINKING.
YOU'RE AFRAID I ONLY DATED YOU BECAUSE YOU WERE THE GREEN GOBLIN.
YOU'RE AFRAID I DON'T LOVE YOU.
AND YOU'RE AFRAID I NEVER DID.
AM I RIGHT?
I'M RIGHT, AREN'T I? YOU'RE JUST *DYING* INSIDE RIGHT NOW, AREN'T YOU?
GET...
HMM?
GET OFF OF ME...
HARRY--
GET OFF!
THWAK

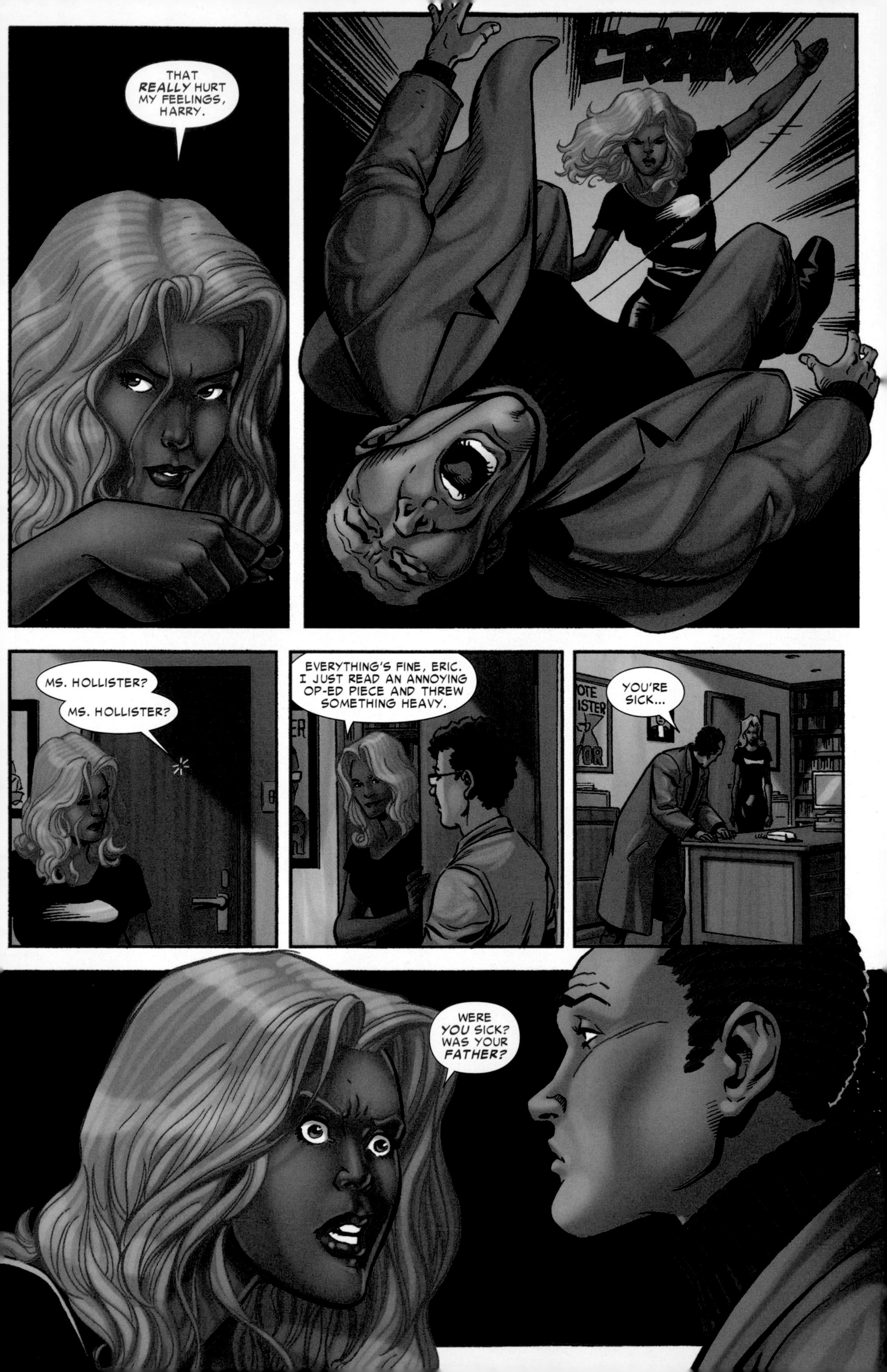
THAT REALLY HURT MY FEELINGS, HARRY.
CRAK
MS. HOLLISTER?
MS. HOLLISTER?
EVERYTHING'S FINE, ERIC. I JUST READ AN ANNOYING OP-ED PIECE AND THREW SOMETHING HEAVY.
YOU'RE SICK...
WERE YOU SICK? WAS YOUR FATHER?

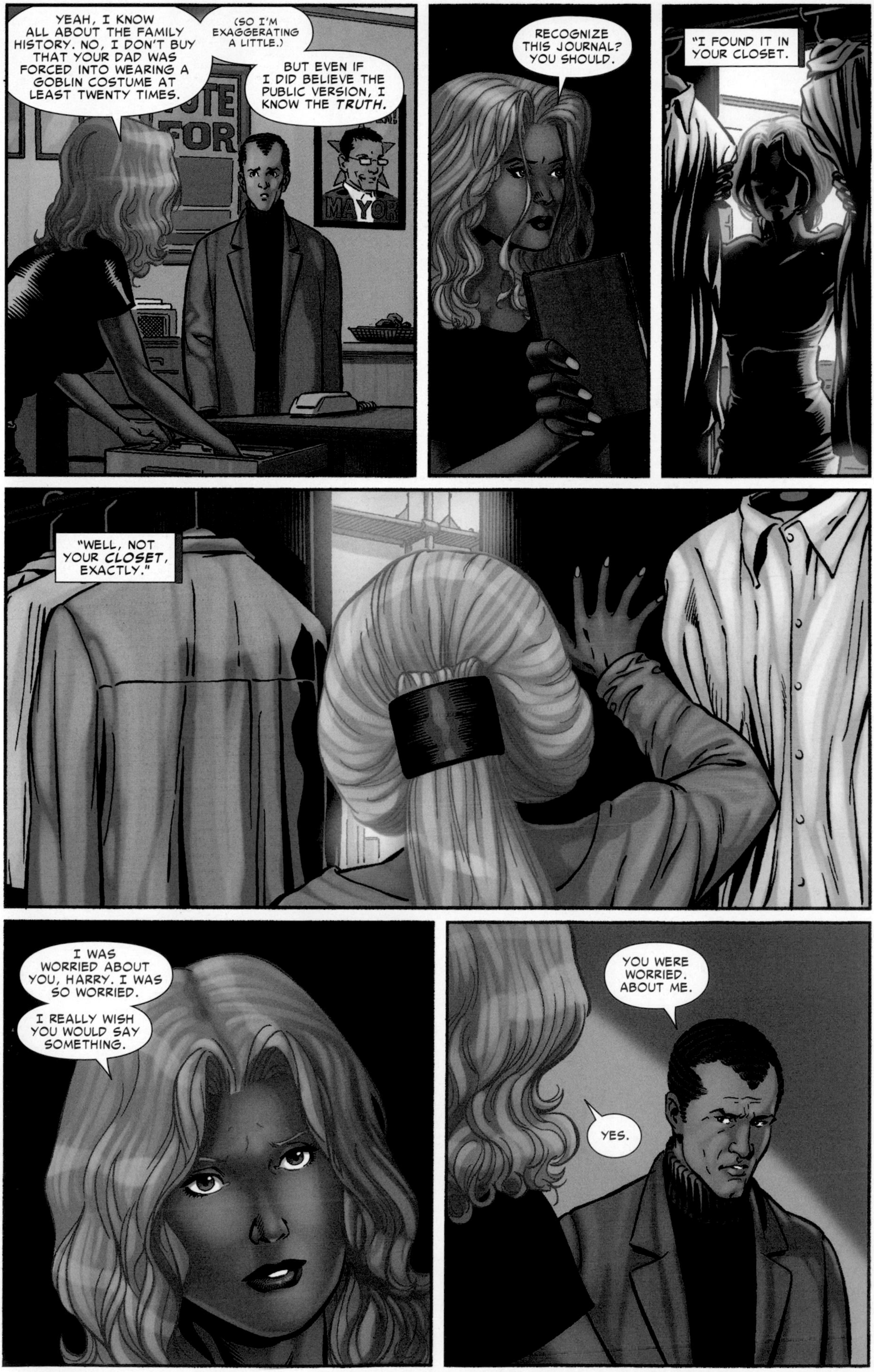
YEAH, I KNOW ALL ABOUT THE FAMILY HISTORY. NO, I DON'T BUY THAT YOUR DAD WAS FORCED INTO WEARING A GOBLIN COSTUME AT LEAST TWENTY TIMES.
(SO I'M EXAGGERATING A LITTLE.)
BUT EVEN IF I DID BELIEVE THE PUBLIC VERSION, I KNOW THE TRUTH.
VOTE FOR
MAYOR
RECOGNIZE THIS JOURNAL? YOU SHOULD.
"I FOUND IT IN YOUR CLOSET.
"WELL, NOT YOUR CLOSET, EXACTLY."
I WAS WORRIED ABOUT YOU, HARRY. I WAS SO WORRIED.
I REALLY WISH YOU WOULD SAY SOMETHING.
YOU WERE WORRIED. ABOUT ME.
YES.

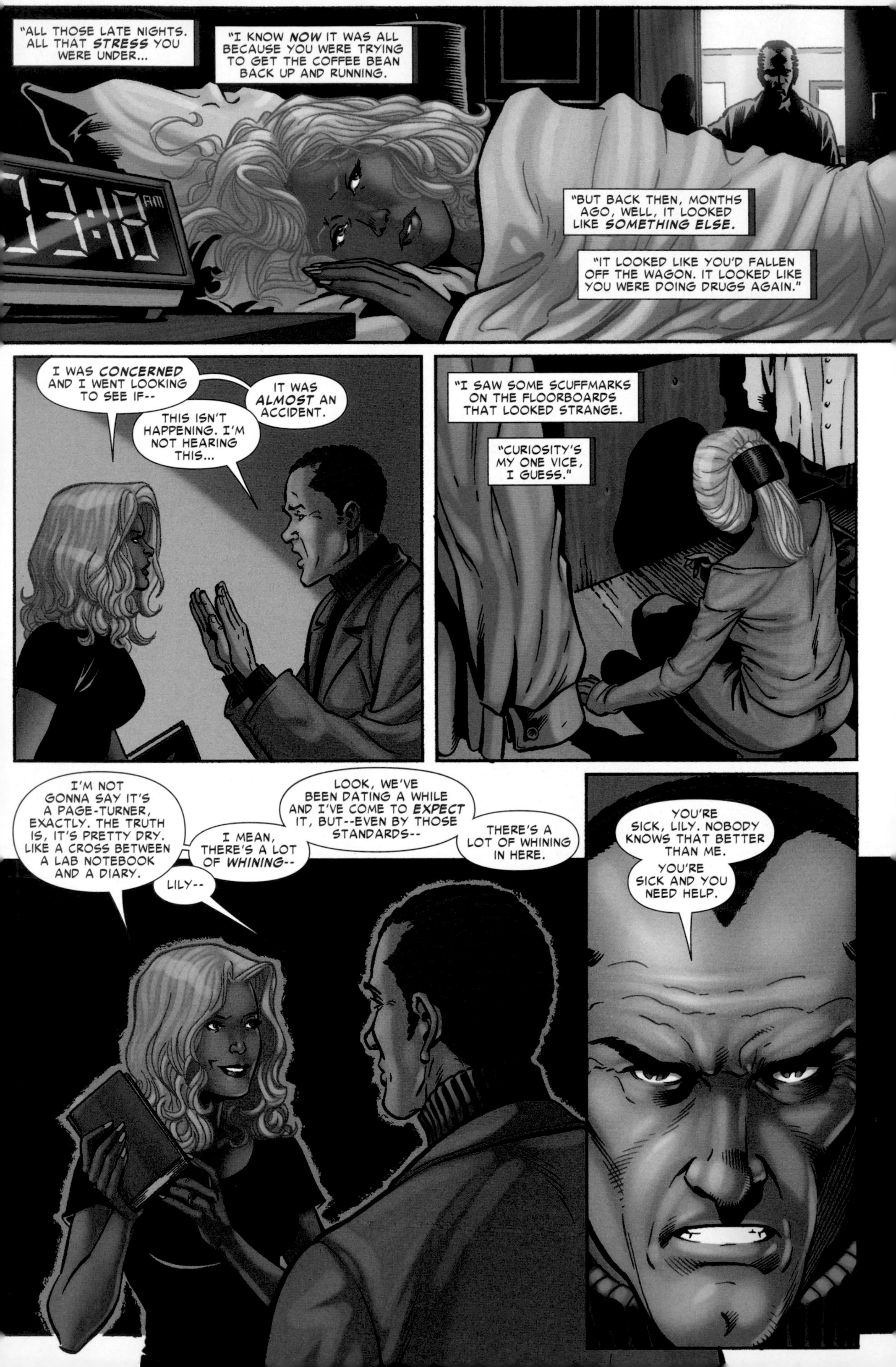

"ALL THOSE LATE NIGHTS. ALL THAT STRESS YOU WERE UNDER...
"I KNOW NOW IT WAS ALL BECAUSE YOU WERE TRYING TO GET THE COFFEE BEAN BACK UP AND RUNNING.
12:18 AM
"BUT BACK THEN, MONTHS AGO, WELL, IT LOOKED LIKE SOMETHING ELSE.
"IT LOOKED LIKE YOU'D FALLEN OFF THE WAGON. IT LOOKED LIKE YOU WERE DOING DRUGS AGAIN."
I WAS CONCERNED AND I WENT LOOKING TO SEE IF--
THIS ISN'T HAPPENING. I'M NOT HEARING THIS...
IT WAS ALMOST AN ACCIDENT.
"I SAW SOME SCUFFMARKS ON THE FLOORBOARDS THAT LOOKED STRANGE.
"CURIOSITY'S MY ONE VICE, I GUESS."
I'M NOT GONNA SAY IT'S A PAGE-TURNER, EXACTLY. THE TRUTH IS, IT'S PRETTY DRY. LIKE A CROSS BETWEEN A LAB NOTEBOOK AND A DIARY.
LILY--
I MEAN, THERE'S A LOT OF WHINING--
LOOK, WE'VE BEEN DATING A WHILE AND I'VE COME TO EXPECT IT, BUT--EVEN BY THOSE STANDARDS--
THERE'S A LOT OF WHINING IN HERE.
YOU'RE SICK, LILY. NOBODY KNOWS THAT BETTER THAN ME.
YOU'RE SICK AND YOU NEED HELP.

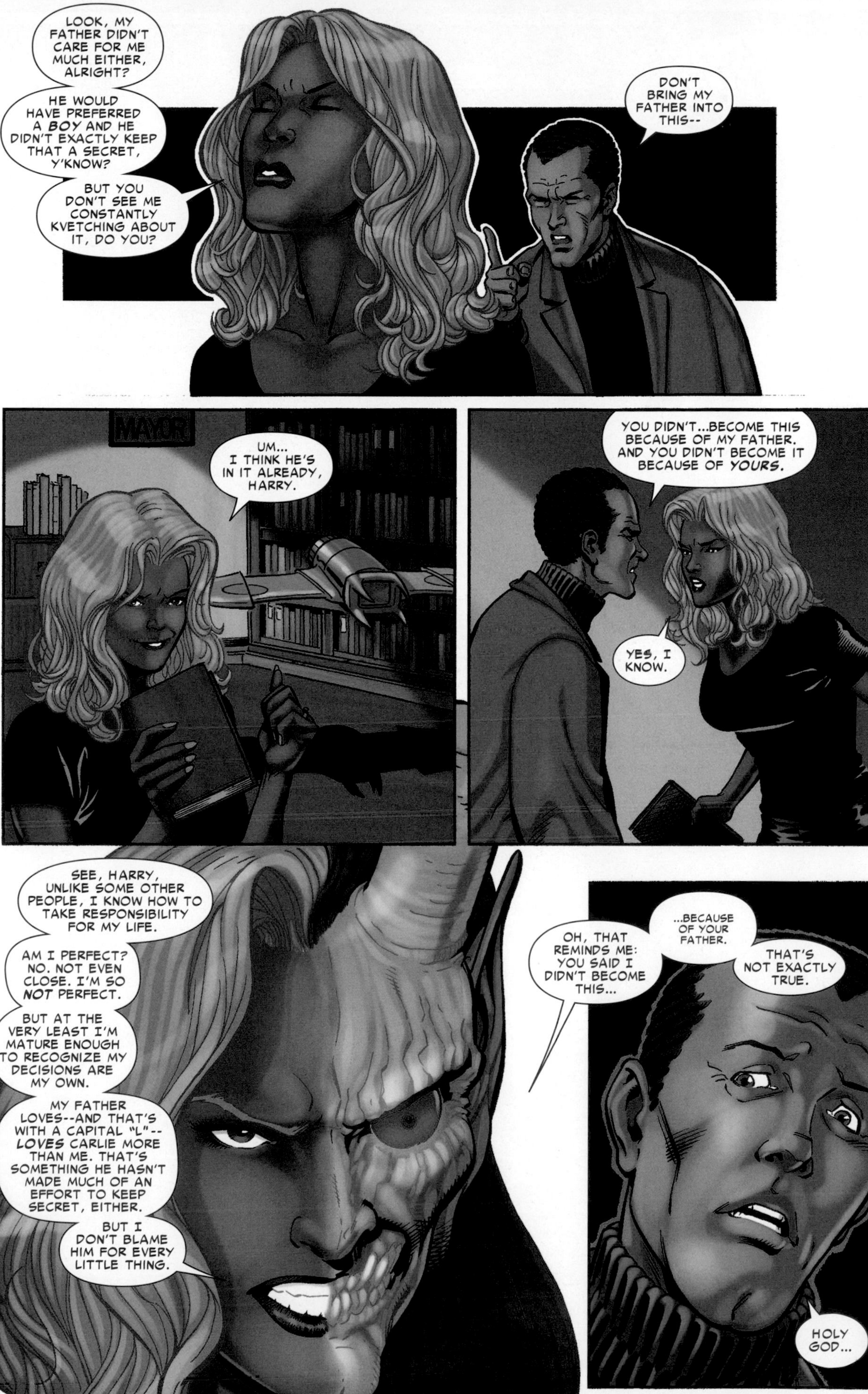
LOOK, MY FATHER DIDN'T CARE FOR ME MUCH EITHER, ALRIGHT?
HE WOULD HAVE PREFERRED A *BOY* AND HE DIDN'T EXACTLY KEEP THAT A SECRET, Y'KNOW?
BUT YOU DON'T SEE ME CONSTANTLY KVETCHING ABOUT IT, DO YOU?
DON'T BRING MY FATHER INTO THIS--
MAYOR
UM... I THINK HE'S IN IT ALREADY, HARRY.
YOU DIDN'T...BECOME THIS BECAUSE OF MY FATHER. AND YOU DIDN'T BECOME IT BECAUSE OF *YOURS.*
YES, I KNOW.
SEE, HARRY, UNLIKE SOME OTHER PEOPLE, I KNOW HOW TO TAKE RESPONSIBILITY FOR MY LIFE.
AM I PERFECT? NO. NOT EVEN CLOSE. I'M SO *NOT* PERFECT.
BUT AT THE VERY LEAST I'M MATURE ENOUGH TO RECOGNIZE MY DECISIONS ARE MY OWN.
MY FATHER LOVES--AND THAT'S WITH A CAPITAL "L"--*LOVES* CARLIE MORE THAN ME. THAT'S SOMETHING HE HASN'T MADE MUCH OF AN EFFORT TO KEEP SECRET, EITHER.
BUT I DON'T BLAME HIM FOR EVERY LITTLE THING.
OH, THAT REMINDS ME: YOU SAID I DIDN'T BECOME THIS...
...BECAUSE OF YOUR FATHER.
THAT'S NOT EXACTLY TRUE.
HOLY GOD...

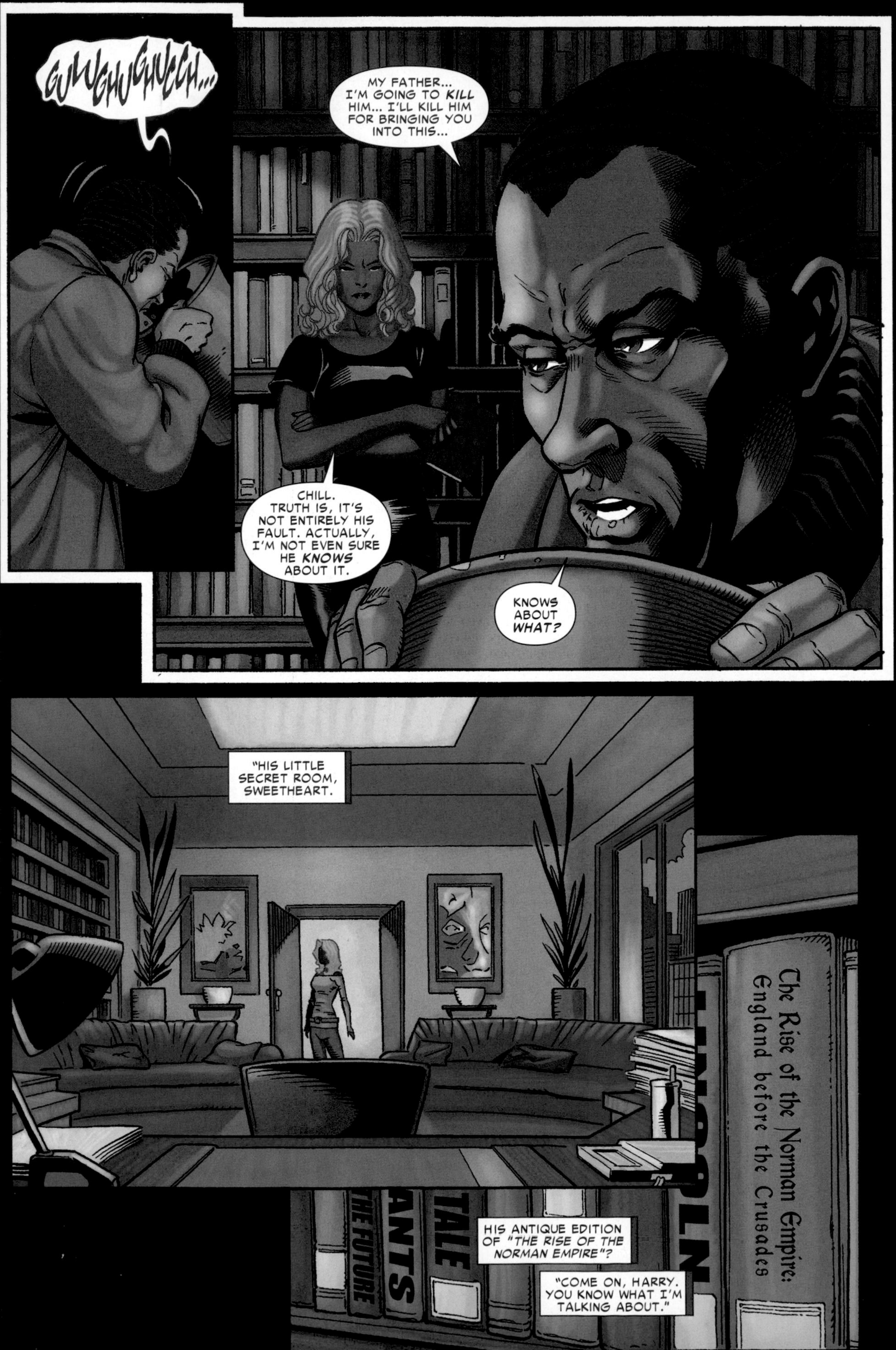
GULUGHUGHUCCH...
MY FATHER... I'M GOING TO KILL HIM... I'LL KILL HIM FOR BRINGING YOU INTO THIS...
CHILL. TRUTH IS, IT'S NOT ENTIRELY HIS FAULT. ACTUALLY, I'M NOT EVEN SURE HE KNOWS ABOUT IT.
KNOWS ABOUT WHAT?
"HIS LITTLE SECRET ROOM, SWEETHEART.
The Rise of the Norman Empire: England before the Crusades
HIS ANTIQUE EDITION OF "THE RISE OF THE NORMAN EMPIRE"?
"COME ON, HARRY. YOU KNOW WHAT I'M TALKING ABOUT."

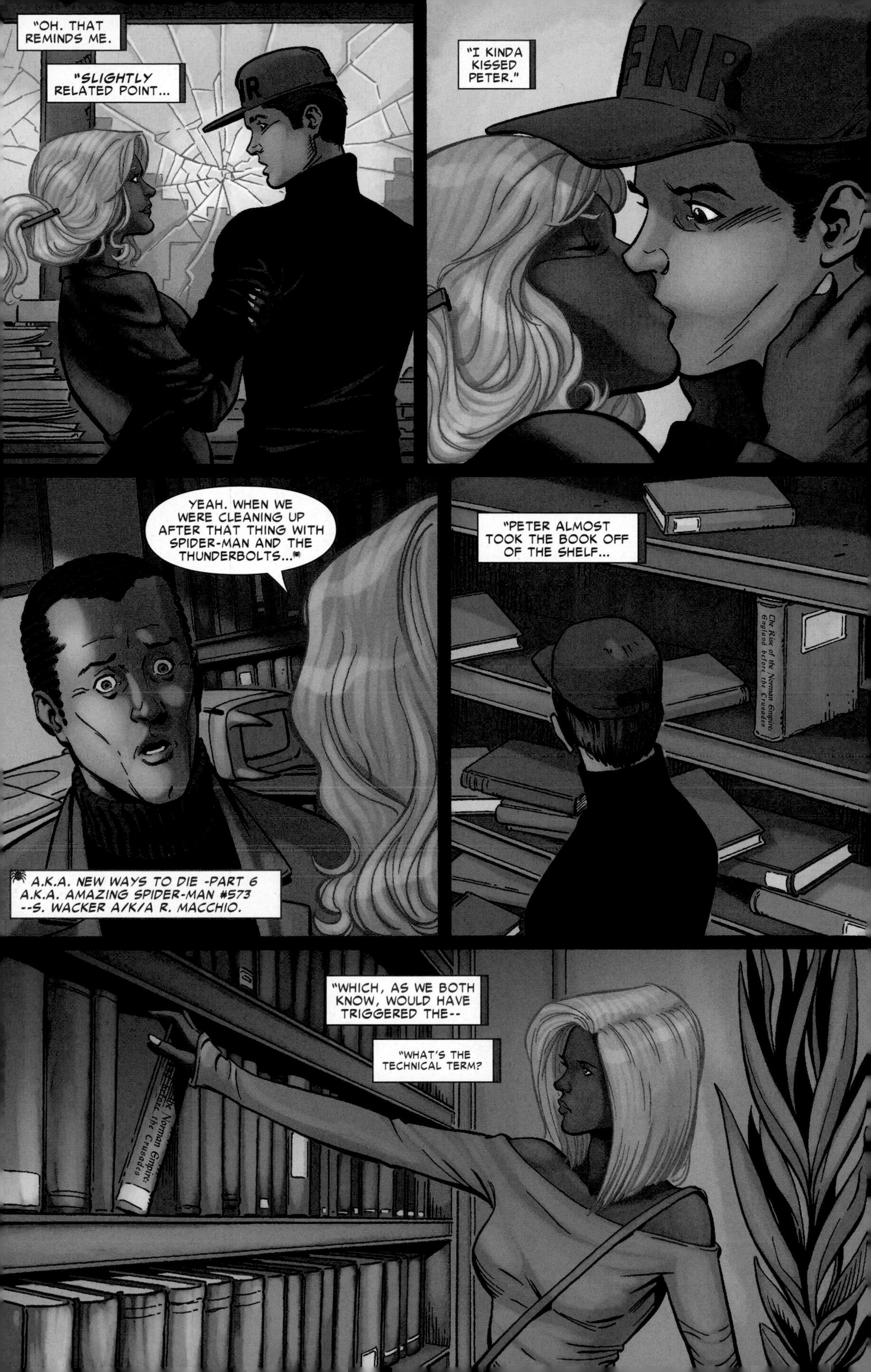
"OH. THAT REMINDS ME.
"SLIGHTLY RELATED POINT...
"I KINDA KISSED PETER."
YEAH. WHEN WE WERE CLEANING UP AFTER THAT THING WITH SPIDER-MAN AND THE THUNDERBOLTS...
A.K.A. NEW WAYS TO DIE -PART 6
A.K.A. AMAZING SPIDER-MAN #573
--S. WACKER A/K/A R. MACCHIO.
"PETER ALMOST TOOK THE BOOK OFF OF THE SHELF...
"WHICH, AS WE BOTH KNOW, WOULD HAVE TRIGGERED THE--
"WHAT'S THE TECHNICAL TERM?

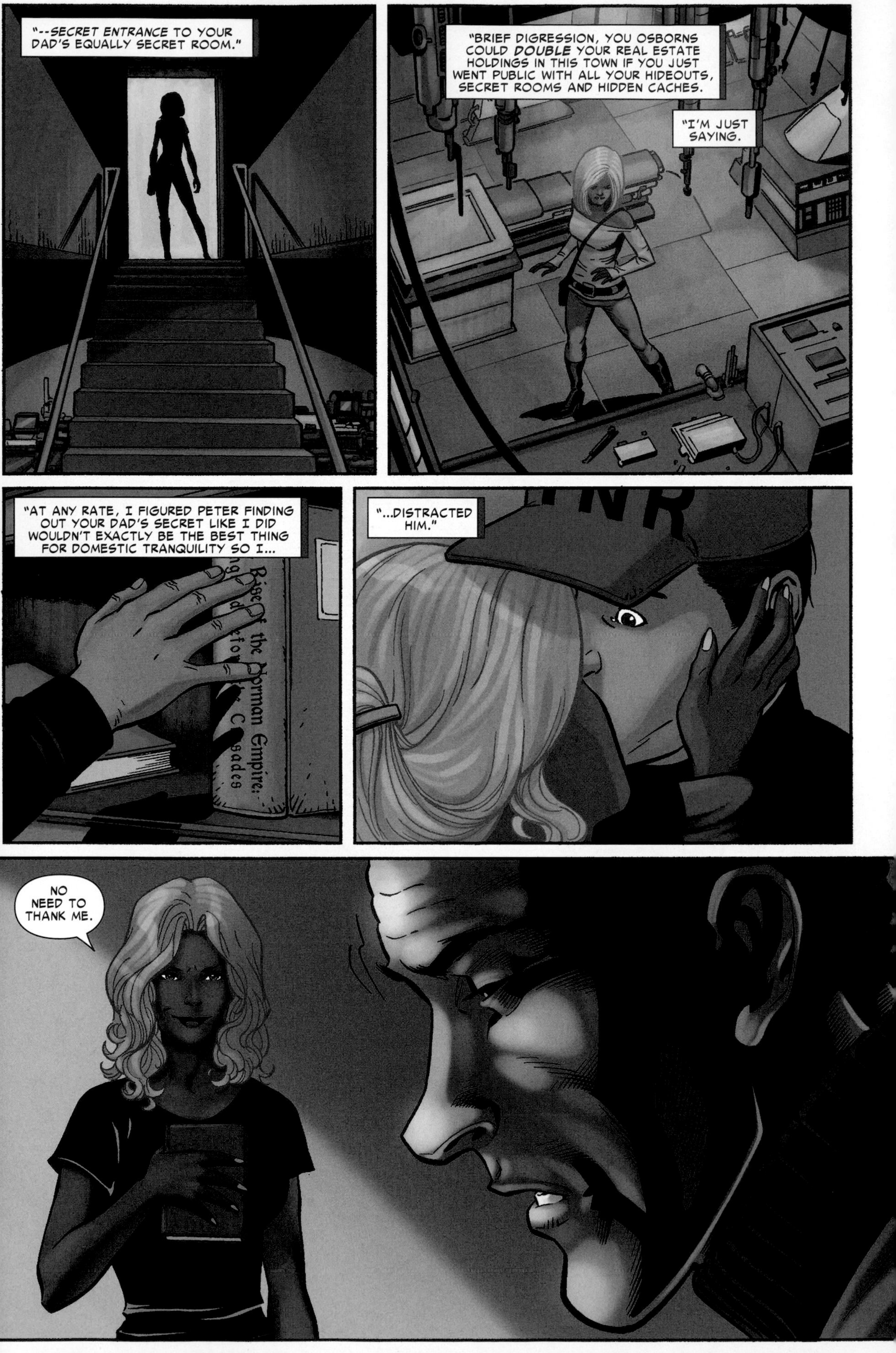
"--SECRET ENTRANCE TO YOUR DAD'S EQUALLY SECRET ROOM."
"BRIEF DIGRESSION, YOU OSBORNS COULD *DOUBLE* YOUR REAL ESTATE HOLDINGS IN THIS TOWN IF YOU JUST WENT PUBLIC WITH ALL YOUR HIDEOUTS, SECRET ROOMS AND HIDDEN CACHES.
"I'M JUST SAYING.
"AT ANY RATE, I FIGURED PETER FINDING OUT YOUR DAD'S SECRET LIKE I DID WOULDN'T EXACTLY BE THE BEST THING FOR DOMESTIC TRANQUILITY SO I...
"...DISTRACTED HIM."
NO NEED TO THANK ME.

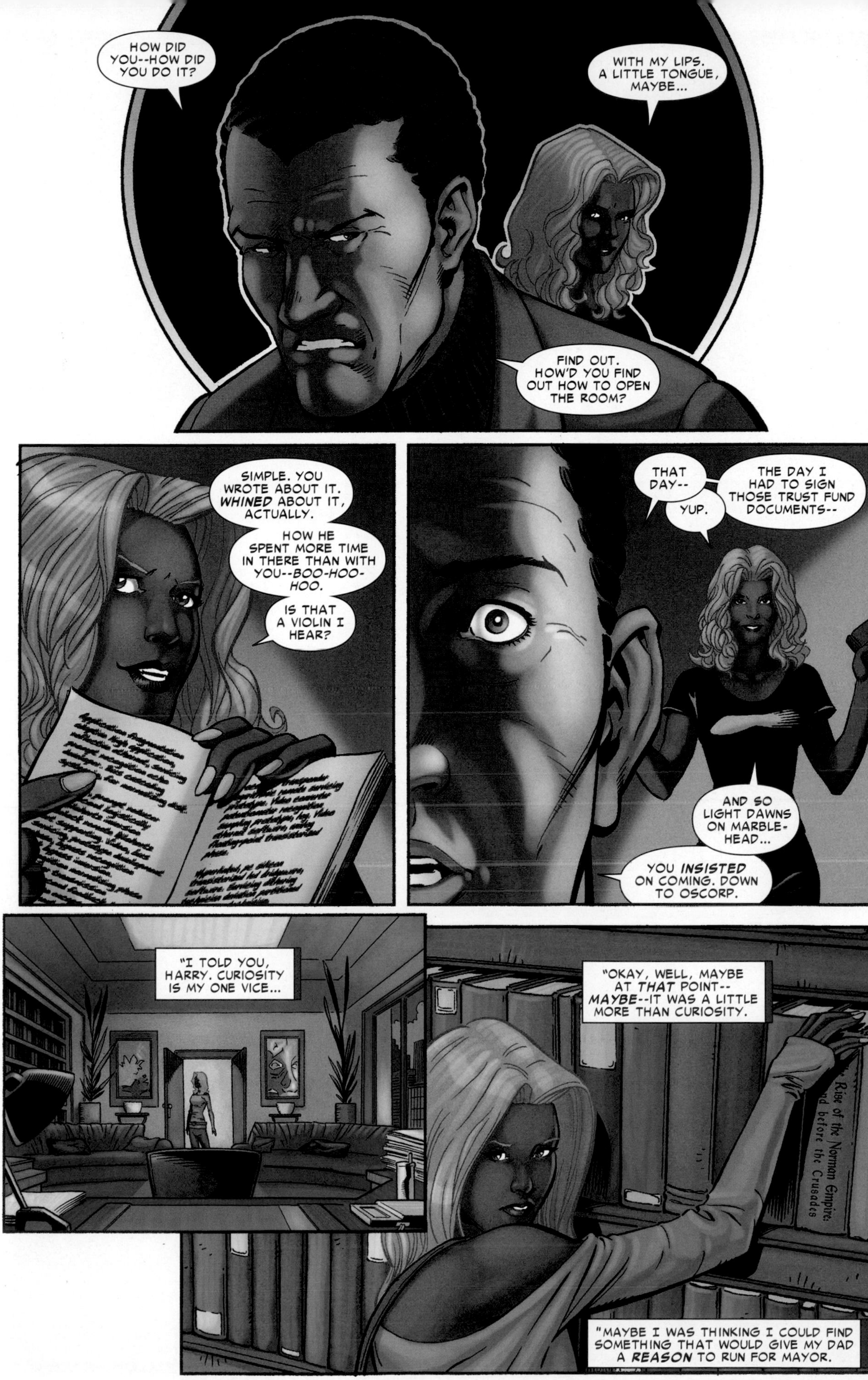
HOW DID YOU--HOW DID YOU DO IT?
WITH MY LIPS. A LITTLE TONGUE, MAYBE...
FIND OUT. HOW'D YOU FIND OUT HOW TO OPEN THE ROOM?
SIMPLE. YOU WROTE ABOUT IT. WHINED ABOUT IT, ACTUALLY.
HOW HE SPENT MORE TIME IN THERE THAN WITH YOU--BOO-HOO-HOO.
IS THAT A VIOLIN I HEAR?
THAT DAY--
THE DAY I HAD TO SIGN THOSE TRUST FUND DOCUMENTS--
YUP.
AND SO LIGHT DAWNS ON MARBLE-HEAD...
YOU INSISTED ON COMING. DOWN TO OSCORP.
"I TOLD YOU, HARRY. CURIOSITY IS MY ONE VICE...
"OKAY, WELL, MAYBE AT THAT POINT--MAYBE--IT WAS A LITTLE MORE THAN CURIOSITY.
The Rise of the Norman Empire: and before the Crusades
"MAYBE I WAS THINKING I COULD FIND SOMETHING THAT WOULD GIVE MY DAD A REASON TO RUN FOR MAYOR.

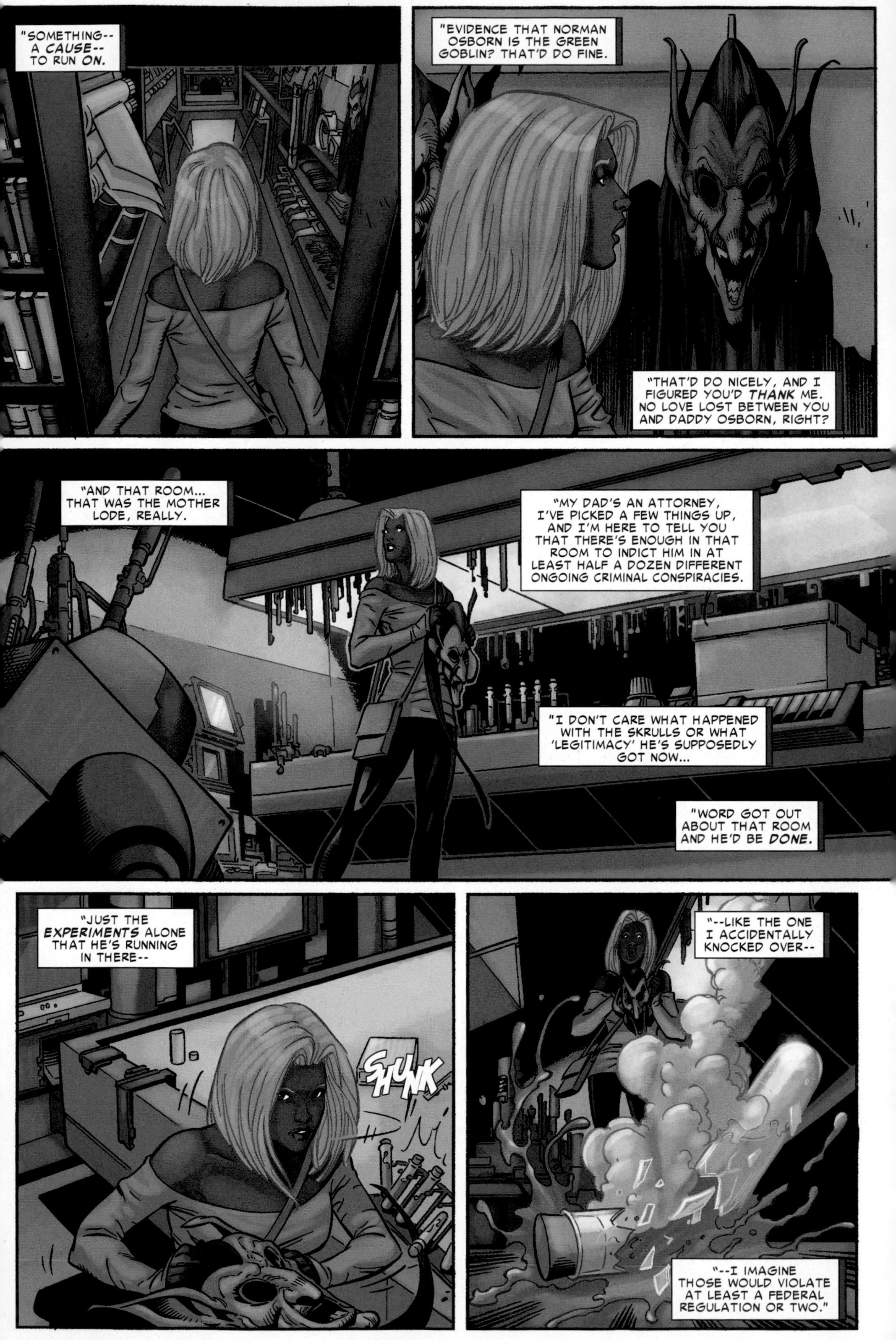
"SOMETHING-- A *CAUSE*-- TO RUN *ON*.
"EVIDENCE THAT NORMAN OSBORN IS THE GREEN GOBLIN? THAT'D DO FINE.
"THAT'D DO NICELY, AND I FIGURED YOU'D *THANK* ME. NO LOVE LOST BETWEEN YOU AND DADDY OSBORN, RIGHT?
"AND THAT ROOM... THAT WAS THE MOTHER LODE, REALLY.
"MY DAD'S AN ATTORNEY, I'VE PICKED A FEW THINGS UP, AND I'M HERE TO TELL YOU THAT THERE'S ENOUGH IN THAT ROOM TO INDICT HIM IN AT LEAST HALF A DOZEN DIFFERENT ONGOING CRIMINAL CONSPIRACIES.
"I DON'T CARE WHAT HAPPENED WITH THE SKRULLS OR WHAT 'LEGITIMACY' HE'S SUPPOSEDLY GOT NOW...
"WORD GOT OUT ABOUT THAT ROOM AND HE'D BE *DONE*.
"JUST THE *EXPERIMENTS* ALONE THAT HE'S RUNNING IN THERE--
SHUNK
"--LIKE THE ONE I ACCIDENTALLY KNOCKED OVER--
"--I IMAGINE THOSE WOULD VIOLATE AT LEAST A FEDERAL REGULATION OR TWO."

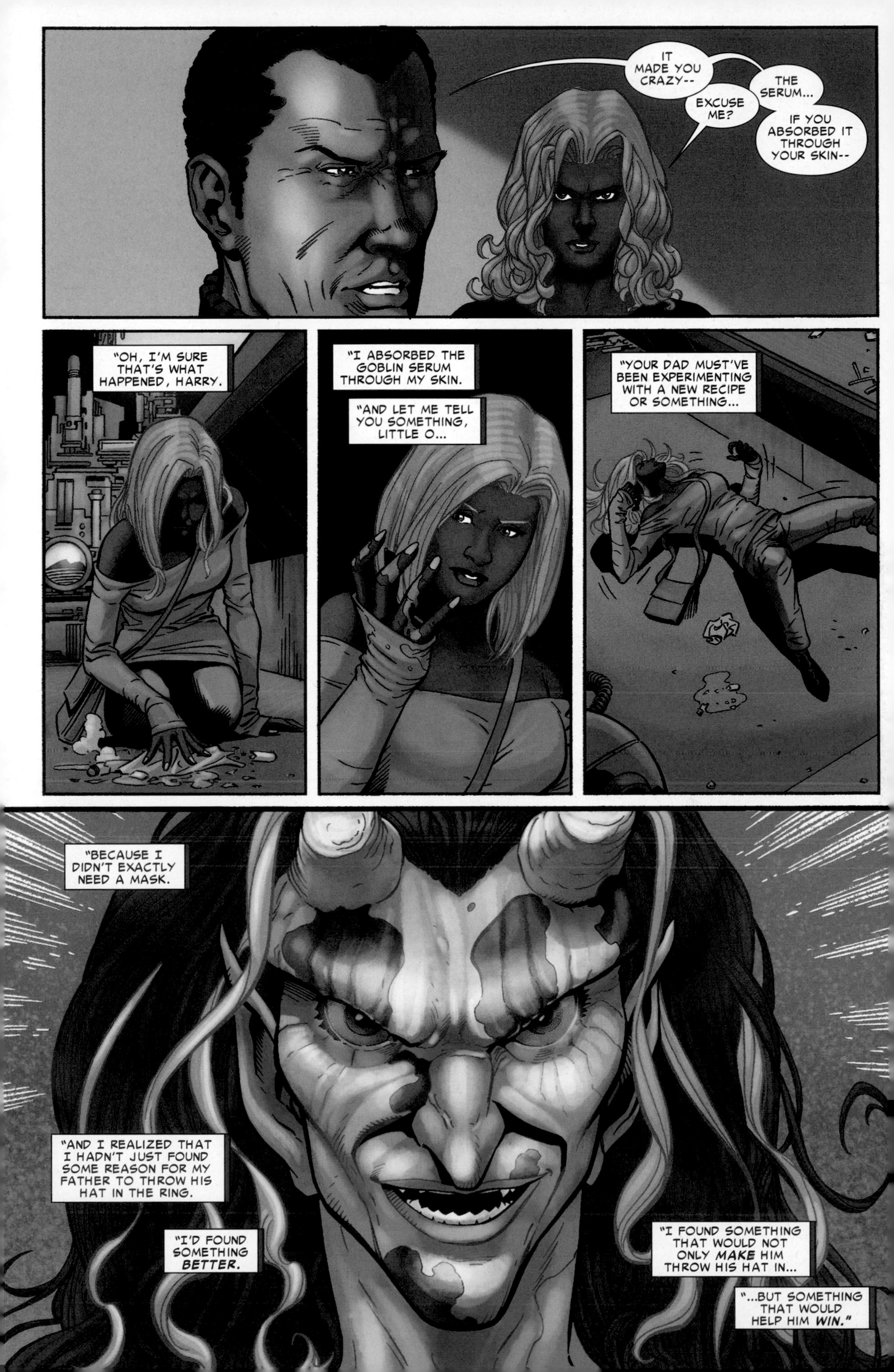
IT MADE YOU CRAZY--
EXCUSE ME?
THE SERUM...
IF YOU ABSORBED IT THROUGH YOUR SKIN--
"OH, I'M SURE THAT'S WHAT HAPPENED, HARRY.
"I ABSORBED THE GOBLIN SERUM THROUGH MY SKIN.
"AND LET ME TELL YOU SOMETHING, LITTLE O...
"YOUR DAD MUST'VE BEEN EXPERIMENTING WITH A NEW RECIPE OR SOMETHING...
"BECAUSE I DIDN'T EXACTLY NEED A MASK.
"AND I REALIZED THAT I HADN'T JUST FOUND SOME REASON FOR MY FATHER TO THROW HIS HAT IN THE RING.
"I'D FOUND SOMETHING BETTER.
"I FOUND SOMETHING THAT WOULD NOT ONLY MAKE HIM THROW HIS HAT IN...
"...BUT SOMETHING THAT WOULD HELP HIM WIN."

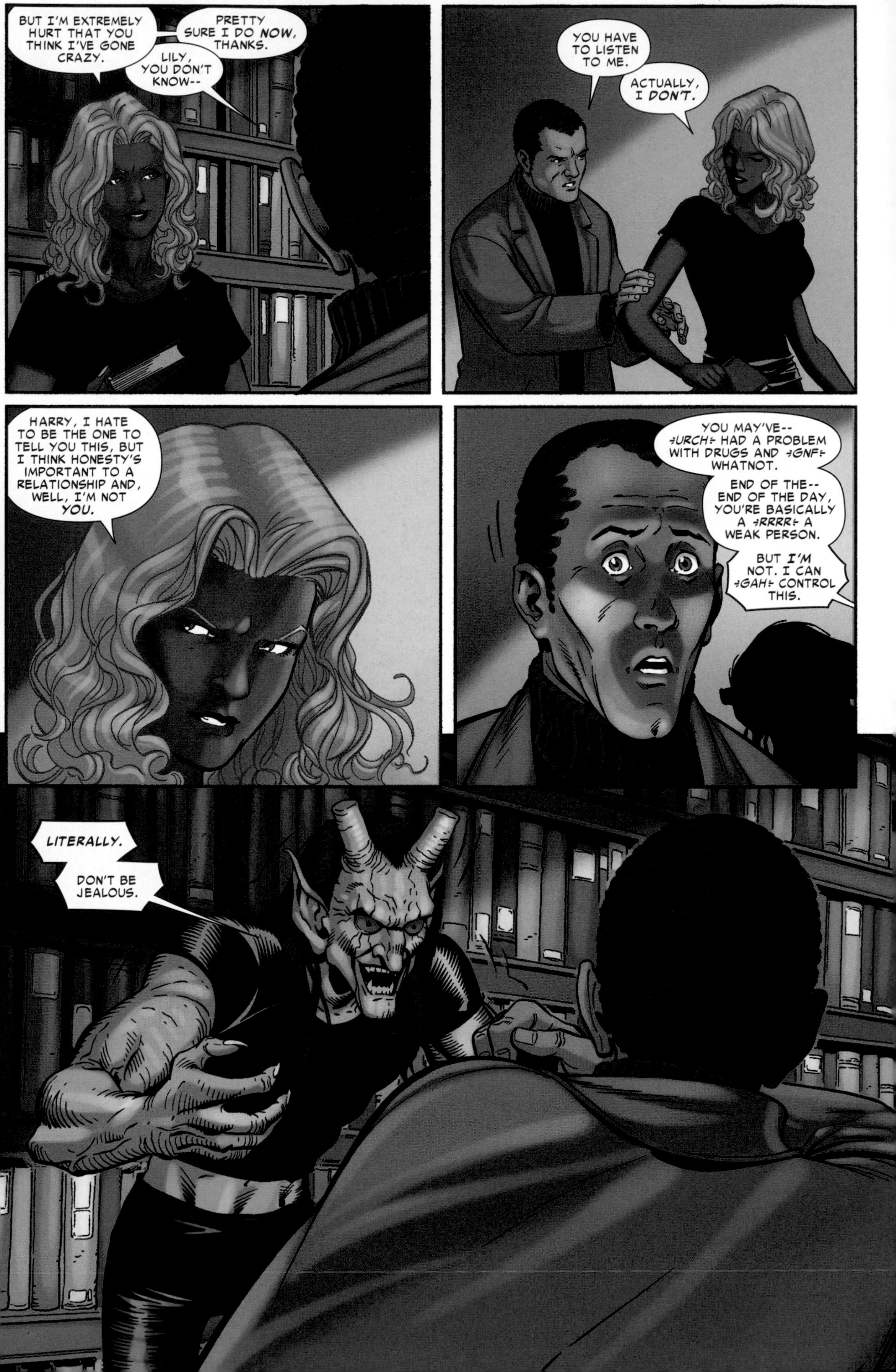
BUT I'M EXTREMELY HURT THAT YOU THINK I'VE GONE CRAZY.
PRETTY SURE I DO NOW, THANKS.
LILY, YOU DON'T KNOW--
YOU HAVE TO LISTEN TO ME.
ACTUALLY, I DON'T.
HARRY, I HATE TO BE THE ONE TO TELL YOU THIS, BUT I THINK HONESTY'S IMPORTANT TO A RELATIONSHIP AND, WELL, I'M NOT YOU.
YOU MAY'VE-- =URCH= HAD A PROBLEM WITH DRUGS AND =GNF= WHATNOT.
END OF THE-- END OF THE DAY, YOU'RE BASICALLY A =RRRR= A WEAK PERSON.
BUT I'M NOT. I CAN =GAH= CONTROL THIS.
LITERALLY.
DON'T BE JEALOUS.

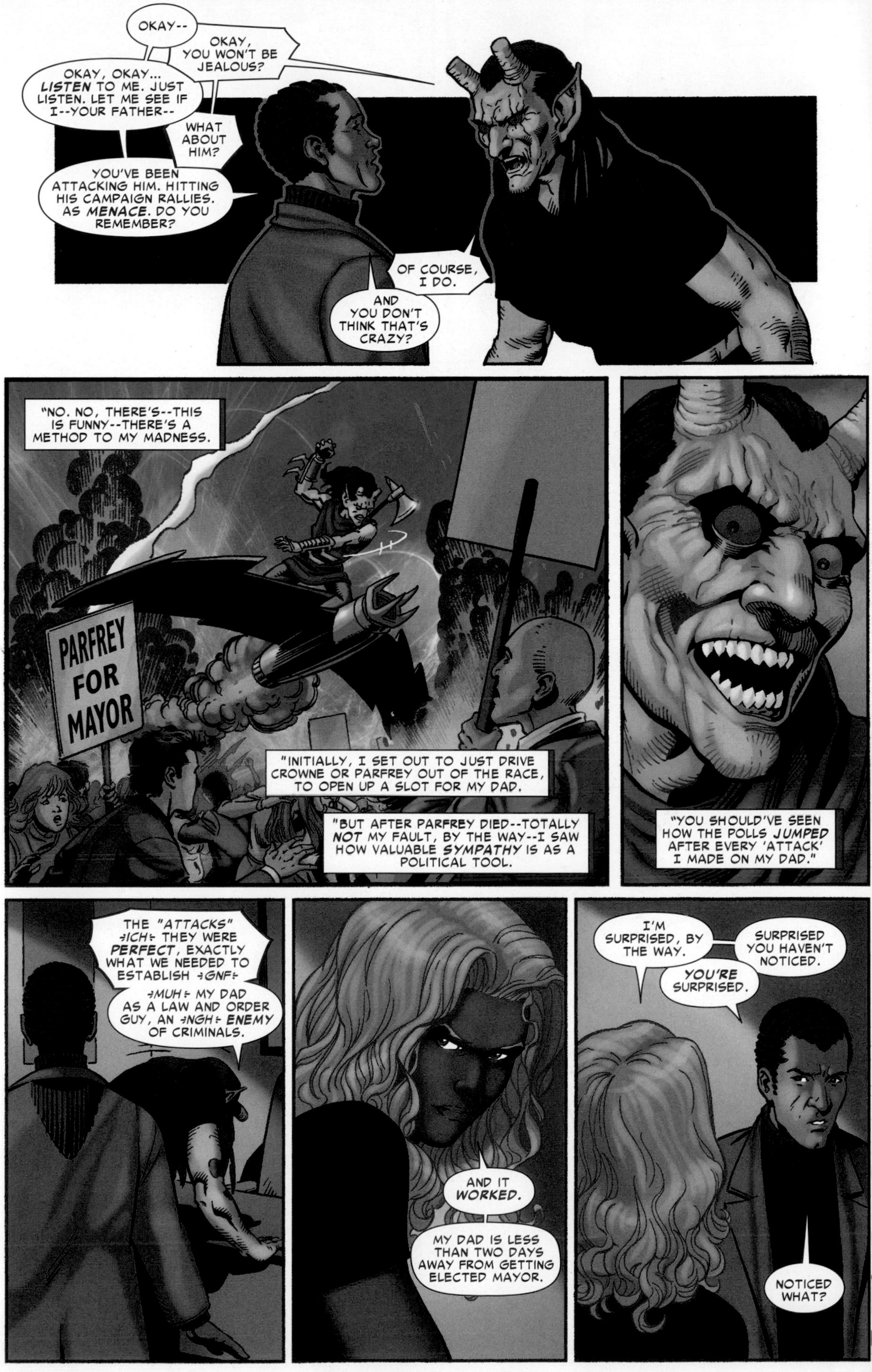
OKAY--
OKAY, YOU WON'T BE JEALOUS?
OKAY, OKAY... LISTEN TO ME. JUST LISTEN. LET ME SEE IF I--YOUR FATHER--
WHAT ABOUT HIM?
YOU'VE BEEN ATTACKING HIM. HITTING HIS CAMPAIGN RALLIES. AS MENACE. DO YOU REMEMBER?
OF COURSE, I DO.
AND YOU DON'T THINK THAT'S CRAZY?
"NO. NO, THERE'S--THIS IS FUNNY--THERE'S A METHOD TO MY MADNESS.
PARFREY FOR MAYOR
"INITIALLY, I SET OUT TO JUST DRIVE CROWNE OR PARFREY OUT OF THE RACE, TO OPEN UP A SLOT FOR MY DAD.
"BUT AFTER PARFREY DIED--TOTALLY NOT MY FAULT, BY THE WAY--I SAW HOW VALUABLE SYMPATHY IS AS A POLITICAL TOOL.
"YOU SHOULD'VE SEEN HOW THE POLLS JUMPED AFTER EVERY 'ATTACK' I MADE ON MY DAD."
THE "ATTACKS" ≠ICH≠ THEY WERE PERFECT, EXACTLY WHAT WE NEEDED TO ESTABLISH ≠GNF≠
≠MUH≠ MY DAD AS A LAW AND ORDER GUY, AN ≠NGH≠ ENEMY OF CRIMINALS.
AND IT WORKED.
MY DAD IS LESS THAN TWO DAYS AWAY FROM GETTING ELECTED MAYOR.
I'M SURPRISED, BY THE WAY.
SURPRISED YOU HAVEN'T NOTICED.
YOU'RE SURPRISED.
NOTICED WHAT?

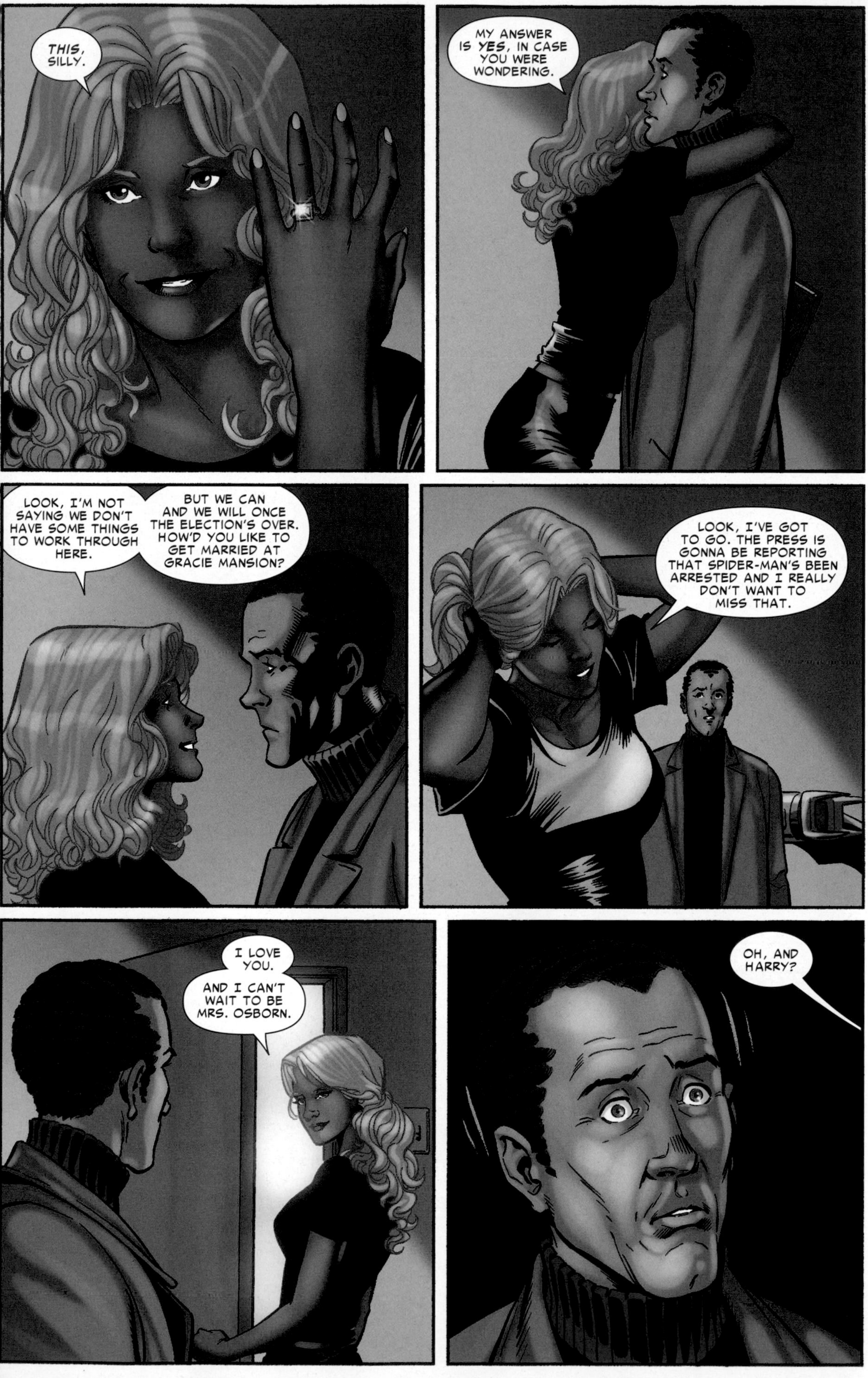
THIS, SILLY.
MY ANSWER IS YES, IN CASE YOU WERE WONDERING.
LOOK, I'M NOT SAYING WE DON'T HAVE SOME THINGS TO WORK THROUGH HERE.
BUT WE CAN AND WE WILL ONCE THE ELECTION'S OVER. HOW'D YOU LIKE TO GET MARRIED AT GRACIE MANSION?
LOOK, I'VE GOT TO GO. THE PRESS IS GONNA BE REPORTING THAT SPIDER-MAN'S BEEN ARRESTED AND I REALLY DON'T WANT TO MISS THAT.
I LOVE YOU.
AND I CAN'T WAIT TO BE MRS. OSBORN.
OH, AND HARRY?

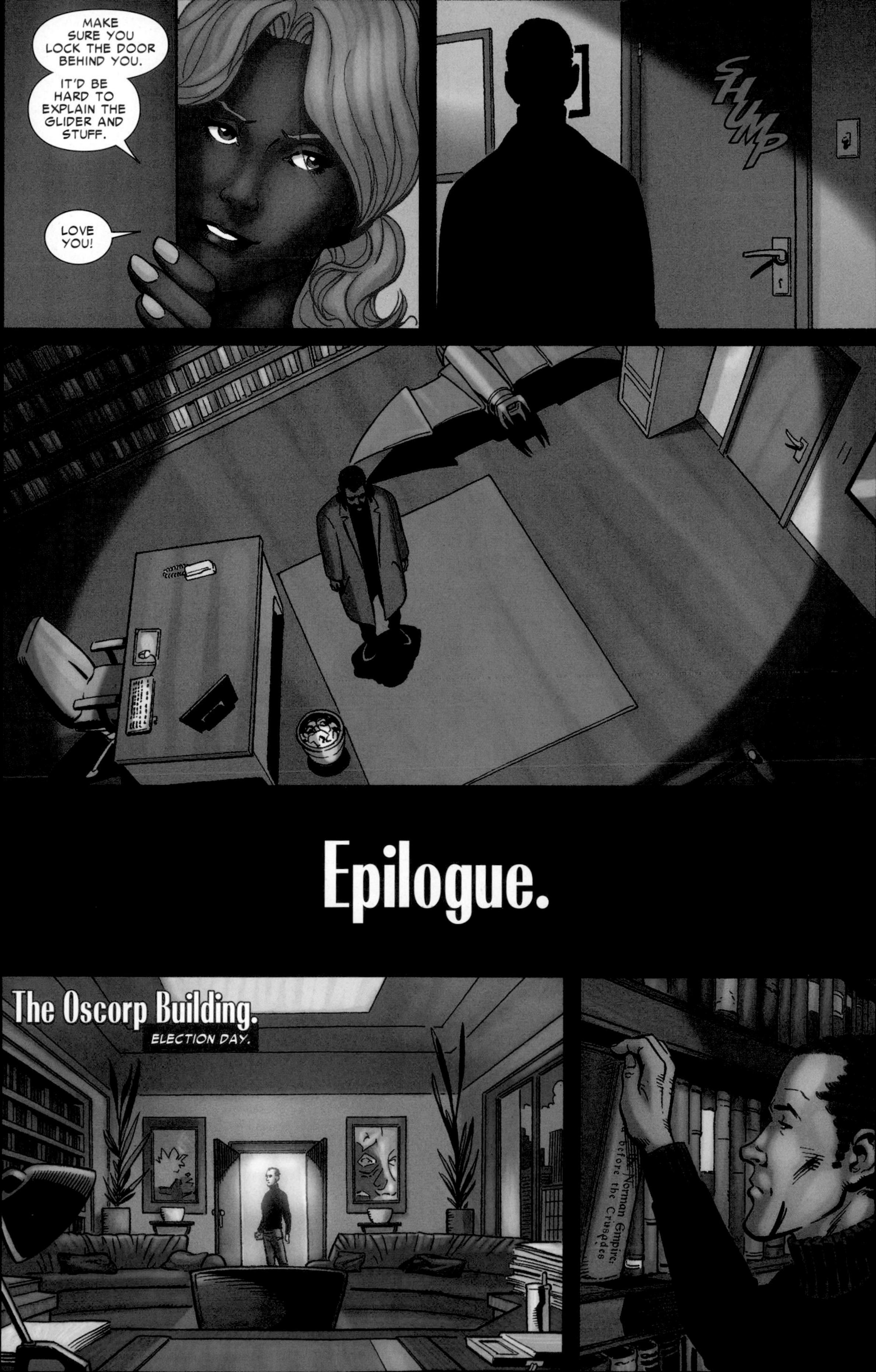
MAKE SURE YOU LOCK THE DOOR BEHIND YOU.
IT'D BE HARD TO EXPLAIN THE GLIDER AND STUFF.
LOVE YOU!
SHUMP
Epilogue.
The Oscorp Building.
ELECTION DAY.
Norman Empire, before the Crusades

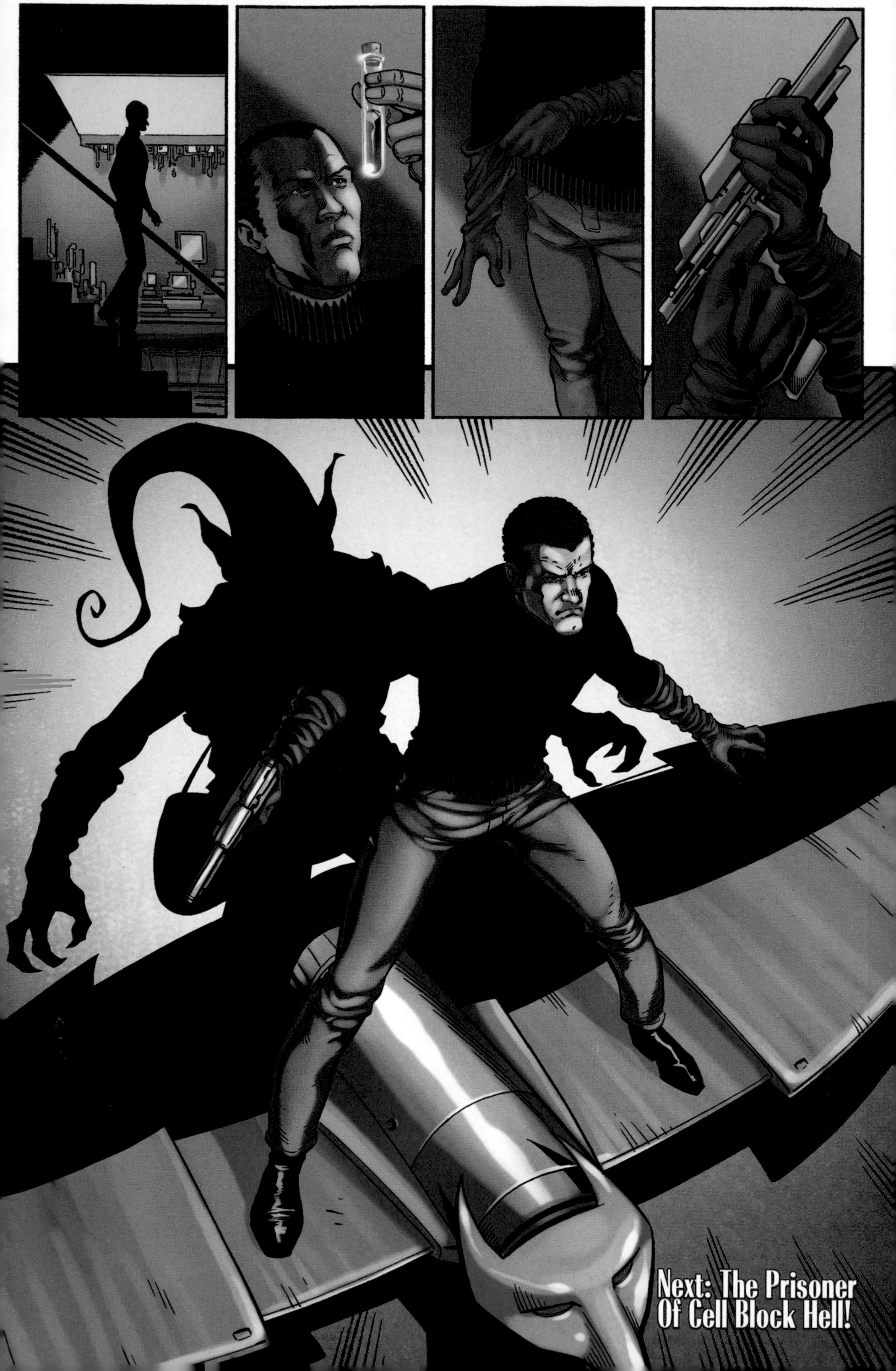
Next: The Prisoner Of Cell Block Hell!

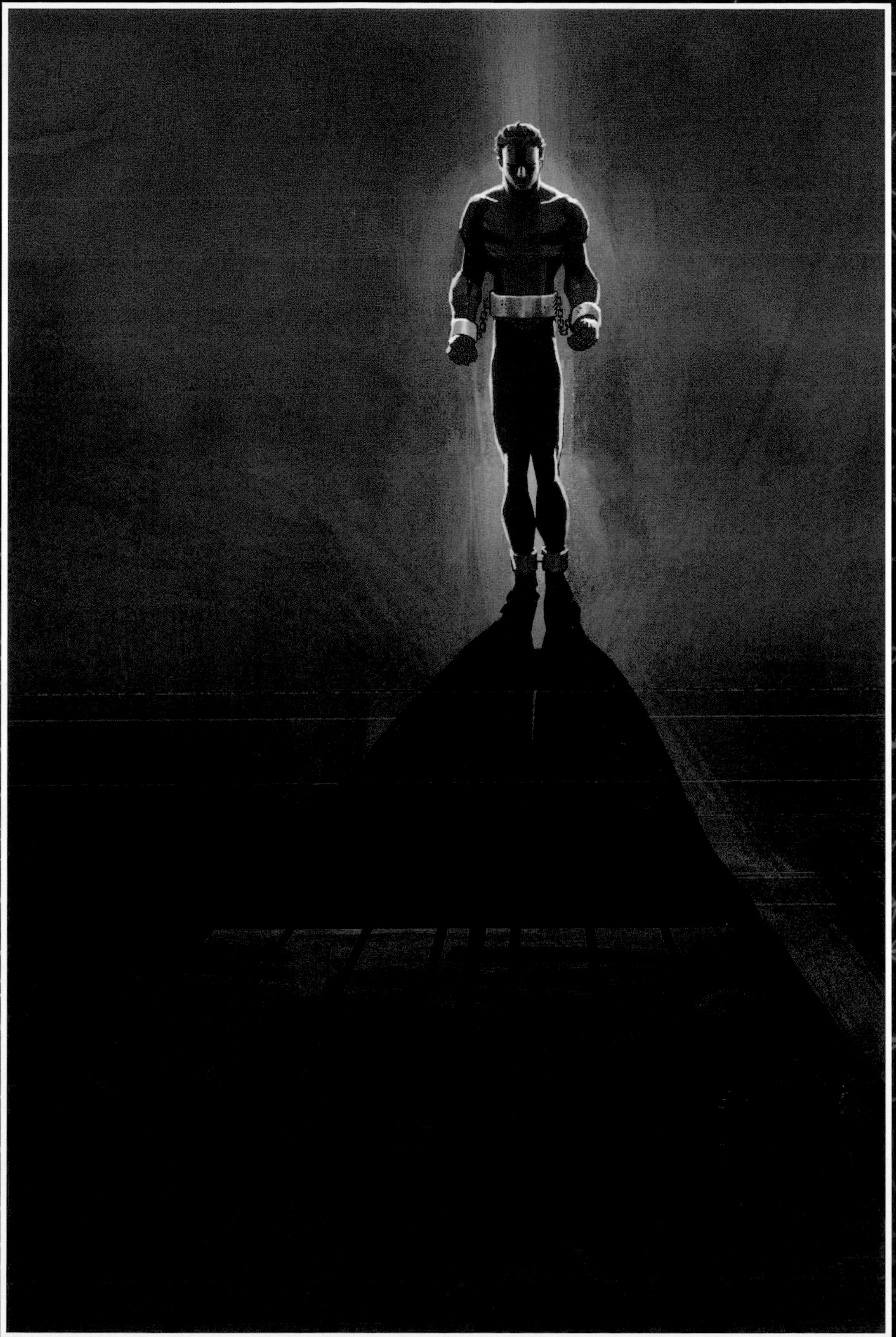

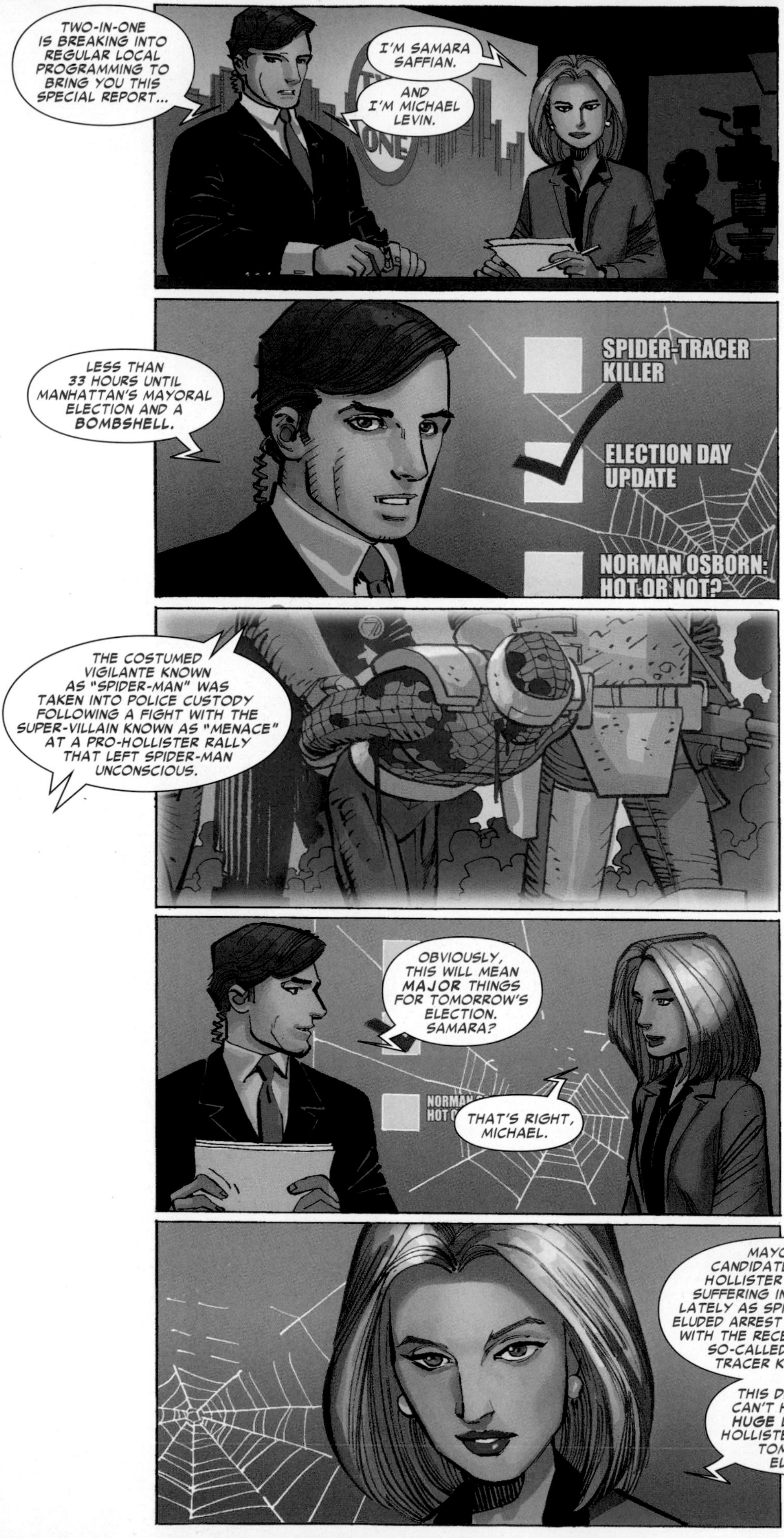
TWO-IN-ONE IS BREAKING INTO REGULAR LOCAL PROGRAMMING TO BRING YOU THIS SPECIAL REPORT...
I'M SAMARA SAFFIAN.
AND I'M MICHAEL LEVIN.
LESS THAN 33 HOURS UNTIL MANHATTAN'S MAYORAL ELECTION AND A BOMBSHELL.
SPIDER-TRACER KILLER
ELECTION DAY UPDATE
NORMAN OSBORN: HOT OR NOT?
THE COSTUMED VIGILANTE KNOWN AS "SPIDER-MAN" WAS TAKEN INTO POLICE CUSTODY FOLLOWING A FIGHT WITH THE SUPER-VILLAIN KNOWN AS "MENACE" AT A PRO-HOLLISTER RALLY THAT LEFT SPIDER-MAN UNCONSCIOUS.
OBVIOUSLY, THIS WILL MEAN MAJOR THINGS FOR TOMORROW'S ELECTION. SAMARA?
THAT'S RIGHT, MICHAEL.
MAYORAL CANDIDATE WILLIAM HOLLISTER HAS BEEN SUFFERING IN THE POLLS LATELY AS SPIDER-MAN HAS ELUDED ARREST IN CONNECTION WITH THE RECENT SPATE OF SO-CALLED "SPIDER-TRACER KILLINGS."
THIS DEVELOPMENT CAN'T HELP BUT PAY HUGE DIVIDENDS TO HOLLISTER GOING INTO TOMORROW'S ELECTION.

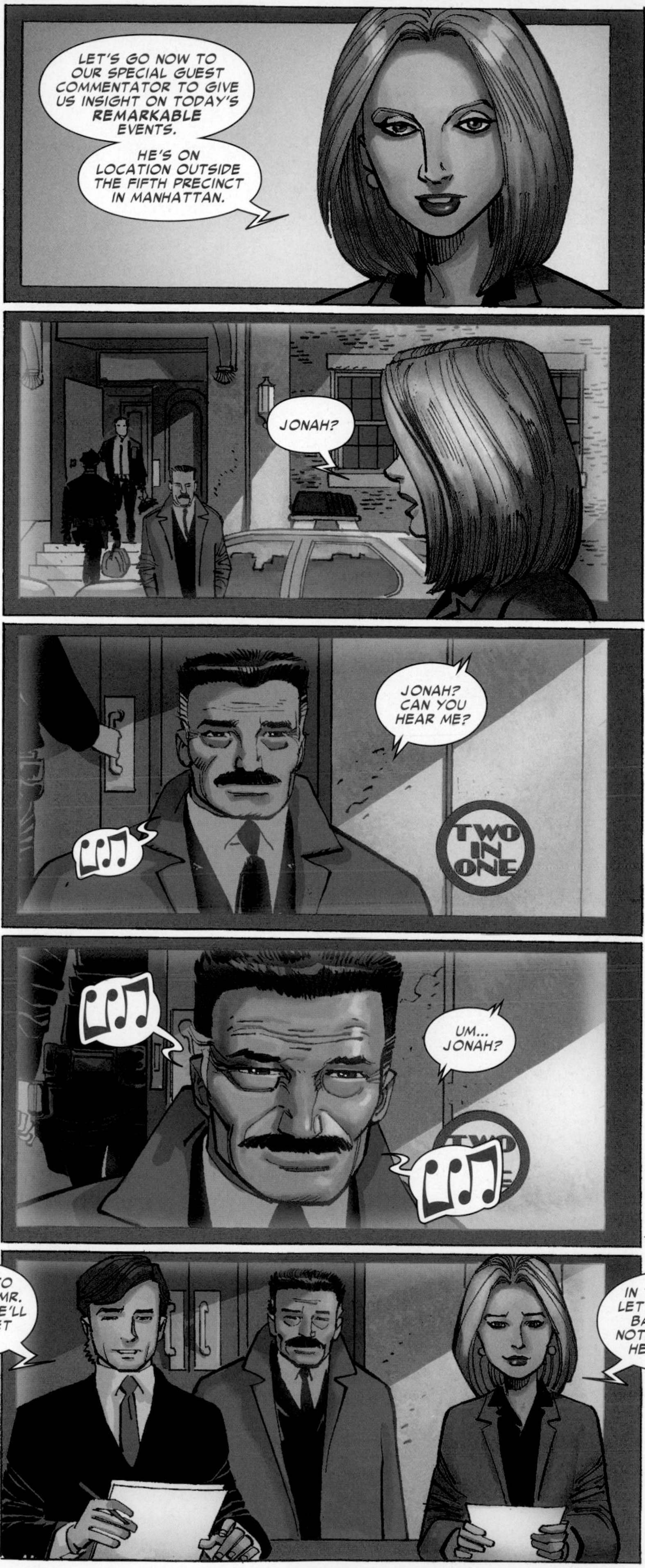
LET'S GO NOW TO OUR SPECIAL GUEST COMMENTATOR TO GIVE US INSIGHT ON TODAY'S REMARKABLE EVENTS.
HE'S ON LOCATION OUTSIDE THE FIFTH PRECINCT IN MANHATTAN.
JONAH?
JONAH? CAN YOU HEAR ME?
TWO IN ONE
UM... JONAH?
WE SEEM TO HAVE LOST MR. JAMESON. WE'LL TRY TO GET HIM BACK.
IN THE MEANTIME, LET'S TAKE A LOOK BACK ON OTHER NOTEWORTHY SUPER HERO ARRESTS...

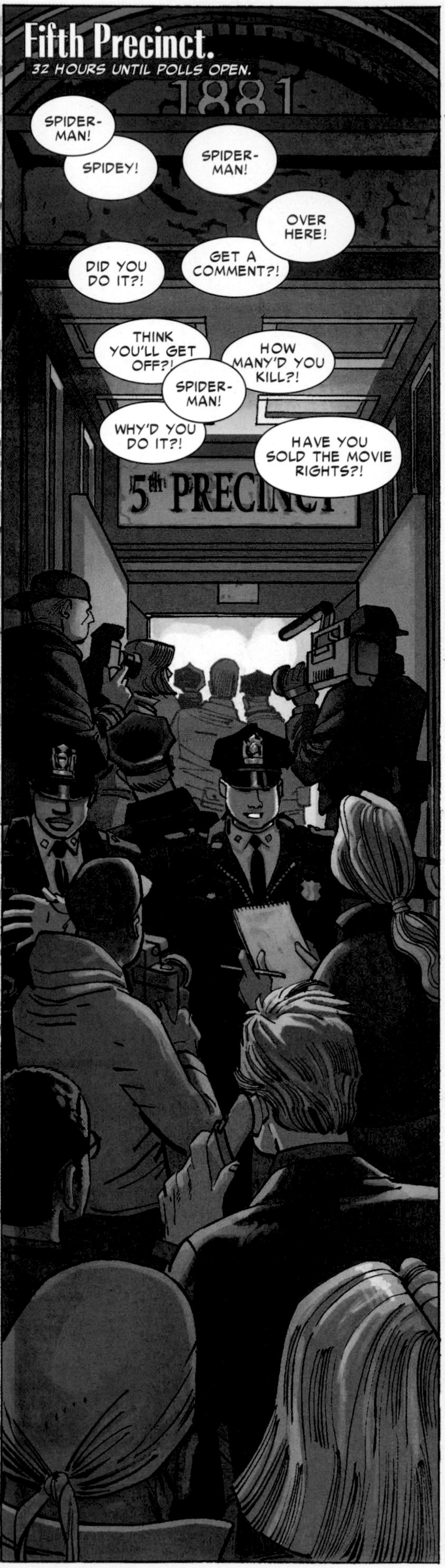
Fifth Precinct.
32 HOURS UNTIL POLLS OPEN.
1881
SPIDER-MAN!
SPIDEY!
SPIDER-MAN!
OVER HERE!
DID YOU DO IT?!
GET A COMMENT?!
THINK YOU'LL GET OFF?!
HOW MANY'D YOU KILL?!
SPIDER-MAN!
WHY'D YOU DO IT?!
HAVE YOU SOLD THE MOVIE RIGHTS?!
5th PRECINCT

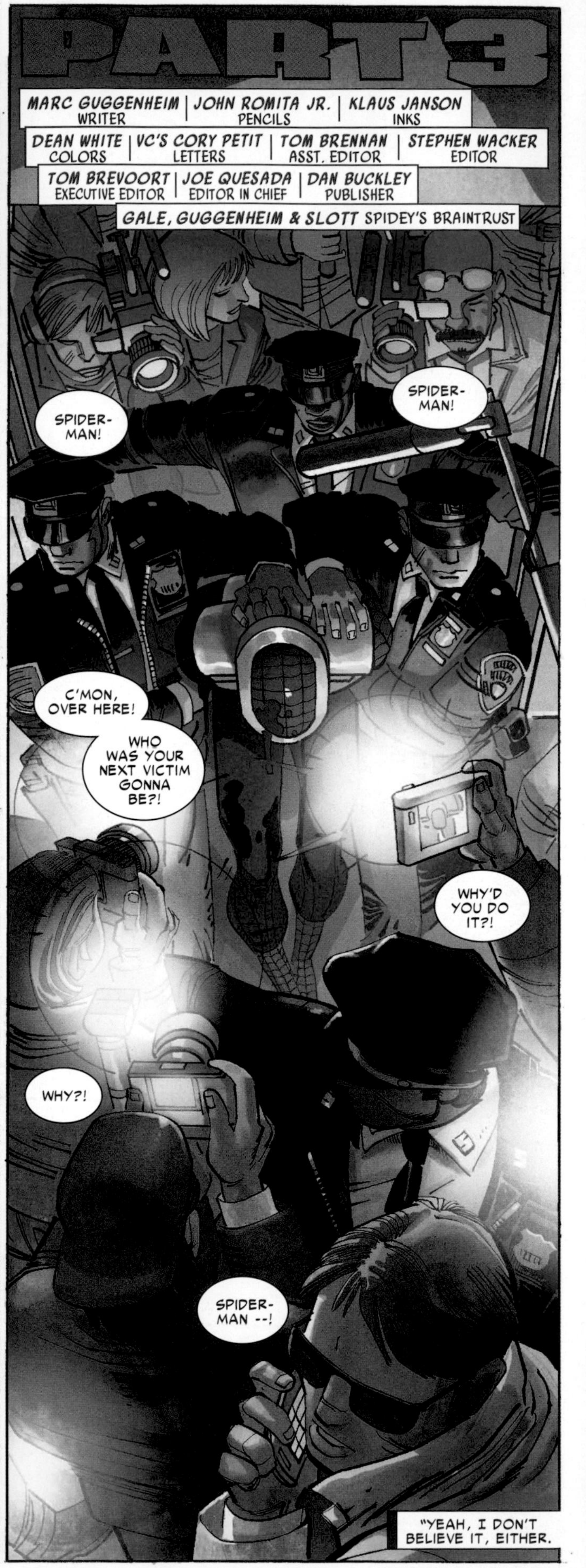
PART 3
MARC GUGGENHEIM WRITER | JOHN ROMITA JR. PENCILS | KLAUS JANSON INKS
DEAN WHITE COLORS | VC'S CORY PETIT LETTERS | TOM BRENNAN ASST. EDITOR | STEPHEN WACKER EDITOR
TOM BREVOORT EXECUTIVE EDITOR | JOE QUESADA EDITOR IN CHIEF | DAN BUCKLEY PUBLISHER
GALE, GUGGENHEIM & SLOTT SPIDEY'S BRAINTRUST
SPIDER-MAN!
SPIDER-MAN!
C'MON, OVER HERE!
WHO WAS YOUR NEXT VICTIM GONNA BE?!
WHY'D YOU DO IT?!
WHY?!
SPIDER-MAN --!
"YEAH, I DON'T BELIEVE IT, EITHER.

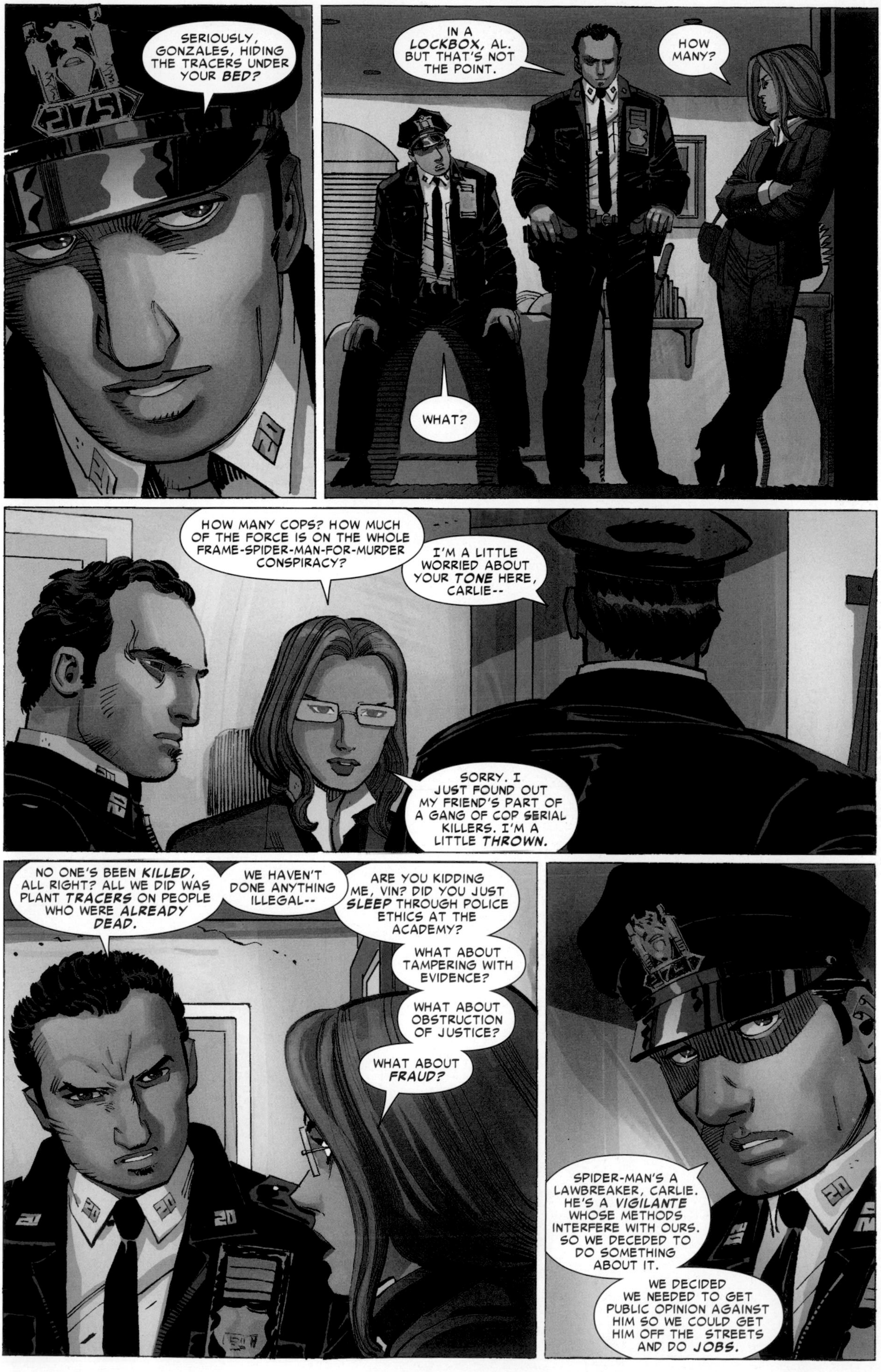
SERIOUSLY, GONZALES, HIDING THE TRACERS UNDER YOUR BED?
IN A LOCKBOX, AL. BUT THAT'S NOT THE POINT.
HOW MANY?
WHAT?
HOW MANY COPS? HOW MUCH OF THE FORCE IS ON THE WHOLE FRAME-SPIDER-MAN-FOR-MURDER CONSPIRACY?
I'M A LITTLE WORRIED ABOUT YOUR TONE HERE, CARLIE--
SORRY. I JUST FOUND OUT MY FRIEND'S PART OF A GANG OF COP SERIAL KILLERS. I'M A LITTLE THROWN.
NO ONE'S BEEN KILLED, ALL RIGHT? ALL WE DID WAS PLANT TRACERS ON PEOPLE WHO WERE ALREADY DEAD.
WE HAVEN'T DONE ANYTHING ILLEGAL--
ARE YOU KIDDING ME, VIN? DID YOU JUST SLEEP THROUGH POLICE ETHICS AT THE ACADEMY?
WHAT ABOUT TAMPERING WITH EVIDENCE?
WHAT ABOUT OBSTRUCTION OF JUSTICE?
WHAT ABOUT FRAUD?
SPIDER-MAN'S A LAWBREAKER, CARLIE. HE'S A VIGILANTE WHOSE METHODS INTERFERE WITH OURS. SO WE DECEDED TO DO SOMETHING ABOUT IT.
WE DECIDED WE NEEDED TO GET PUBLIC OPINION AGAINST HIM SO WE COULD GET HIM OFF THE STREETS AND DO JOBS.

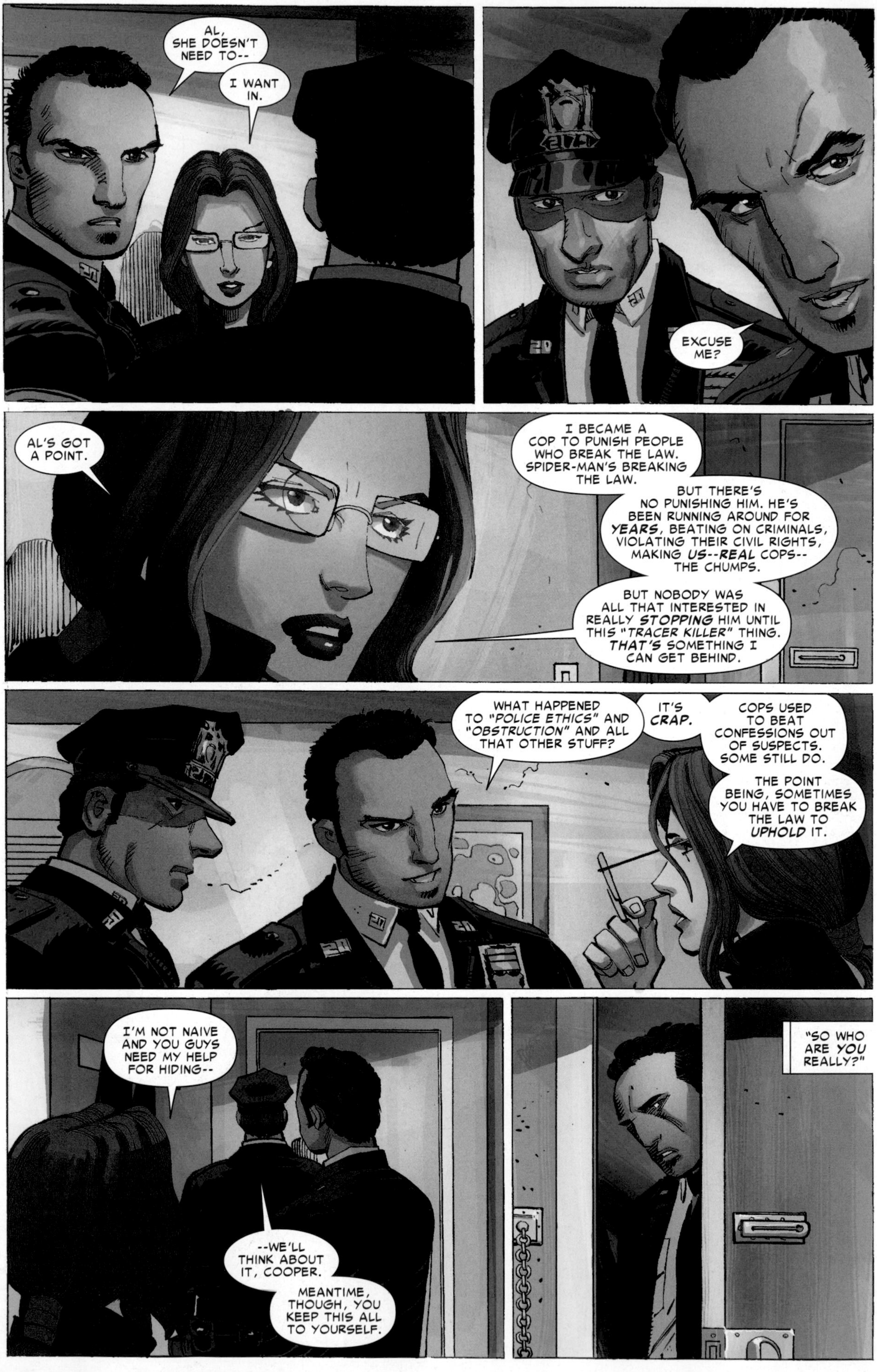
AL, SHE DOESN'T NEED TO--
I WANT IN.
EXCUSE ME?
AL'S GOT A POINT.
I BECAME A COP TO PUNISH PEOPLE WHO BREAK THE LAW. SPIDER-MAN'S BREAKING THE LAW.
BUT THERE'S NO PUNISHING HIM. HE'S BEEN RUNNING AROUND FOR YEARS, BEATING ON CRIMINALS, VIOLATING THEIR CIVIL RIGHTS, MAKING US--REAL COPS--THE CHUMPS.
BUT NOBODY WAS ALL THAT INTERESTED IN REALLY STOPPING HIM UNTIL THIS "TRACER KILLER" THING. THAT'S SOMETHING I CAN GET BEHIND.
WHAT HAPPENED TO "POLICE ETHICS" AND "OBSTRUCTION" AND ALL THAT OTHER STUFF?
IT'S CRAP.
COPS USED TO BEAT CONFESSIONS OUT OF SUSPECTS. SOME STILL DO.
THE POINT BEING, SOMETIMES YOU HAVE TO BREAK THE LAW TO UPHOLD IT.
I'M NOT NAIVE AND YOU GUYS NEED MY HELP FOR HIDING--
--WE'LL THINK ABOUT IT, COOPER.
MEANTIME, THOUGH, YOU KEEP THIS ALL TO YOURSELF.
"SO WHO ARE YOU REALLY?"

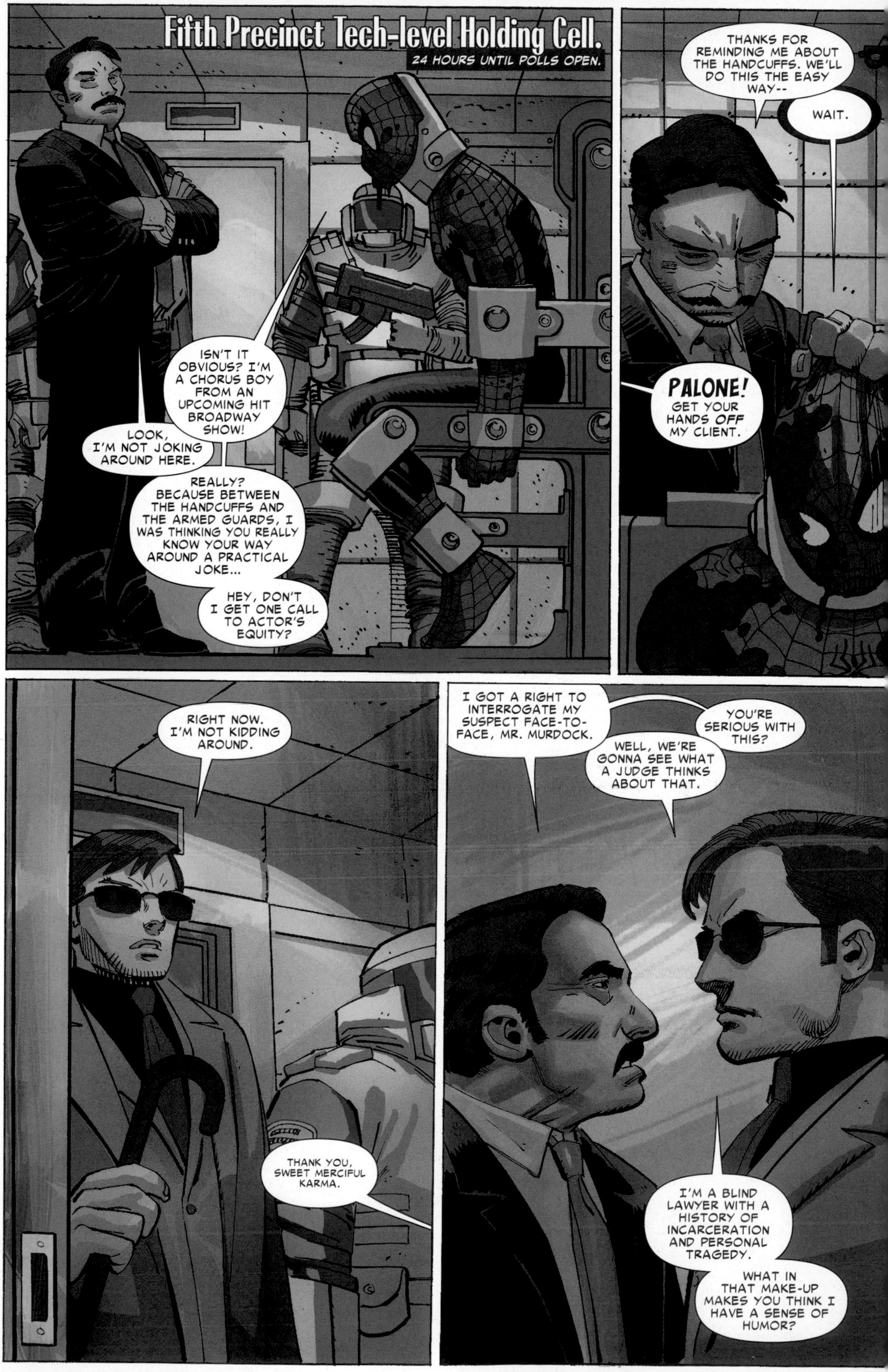
Fifth Precinct Tech-level Holding Cell.
24 HOURS UNTIL POLLS OPEN.
LOOK, I'M NOT JOKING AROUND HERE.
ISN'T IT OBVIOUS? I'M A CHORUS BOY FROM AN UPCOMING HIT BROADWAY SHOW!
REALLY? BECAUSE BETWEEN THE HANDCUFFS AND THE ARMED GUARDS, I WAS THINKING YOU REALLY KNOW YOUR WAY AROUND A PRACTICAL JOKE...
HEY, DON'T I GET ONE CALL TO ACTOR'S EQUITY?
THANKS FOR REMINDING ME ABOUT THE HANDCUFFS. WE'LL DO THIS THE EASY WAY--
WAIT.
PALONE! GET YOUR HANDS OFF MY CLIENT.
RIGHT NOW. I'M NOT KIDDING AROUND.
THANK YOU, SWEET MERCIFUL KARMA.
I GOT A RIGHT TO INTERROGATE MY SUSPECT FACE-TO-FACE, MR. MURDOCK.
YOU'RE SERIOUS WITH THIS?
WELL, WE'RE GONNA SEE WHAT A JUDGE THINKS ABOUT THAT.
I'M A BLIND LAWYER WITH A HISTORY OF INCARCERATION AND PERSONAL TRAGEDY.
WHAT IN THAT MAKE-UP MAKES YOU THINK I HAVE A SENSE OF HUMOR?

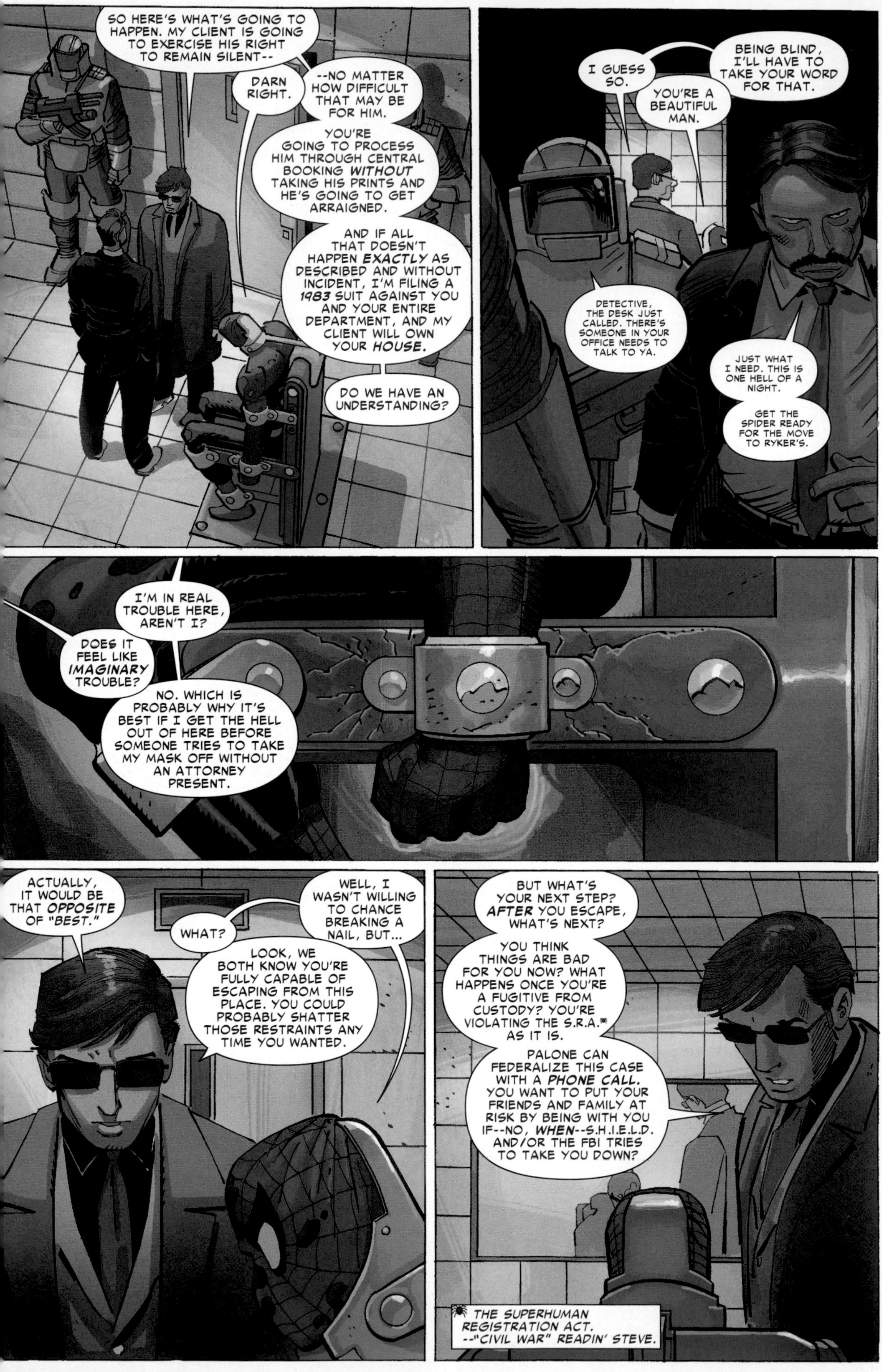
SO HERE'S WHAT'S GOING TO HAPPEN. MY CLIENT IS GOING TO EXERCISE HIS RIGHT TO REMAIN SILENT--
DARN RIGHT.
--NO MATTER HOW DIFFICULT THAT MAY BE FOR HIM.
YOU'RE GOING TO PROCESS HIM THROUGH CENTRAL BOOKING WITHOUT TAKING HIS PRINTS AND HE'S GOING TO GET ARRAIGNED.
AND IF ALL THAT DOESN'T HAPPEN EXACTLY AS DESCRIBED AND WITHOUT INCIDENT, I'M FILING A 1983 SUIT AGAINST YOU AND YOUR ENTIRE DEPARTMENT, AND MY CLIENT WILL OWN YOUR HOUSE.
DO WE HAVE AN UNDERSTANDING?
I GUESS SO.
BEING BLIND, I'LL HAVE TO TAKE YOUR WORD FOR THAT.
YOU'RE A BEAUTIFUL MAN.
DETECTIVE, THE DESK JUST CALLED. THERE'S SOMEONE IN YOUR OFFICE NEEDS TO TALK TO YA.
JUST WHAT I NEED. THIS IS ONE HELL OF A NIGHT.
GET THE SPIDER READY FOR THE MOVE TO RYKER'S.
I'M IN REAL TROUBLE HERE, AREN'T I?
DOES IT FEEL LIKE IMAGINARY TROUBLE?
NO. WHICH IS PROBABLY WHY IT'S BEST IF I GET THE HELL OUT OF HERE BEFORE SOMEONE TRIES TO TAKE MY MASK OFF WITHOUT AN ATTORNEY PRESENT.
ACTUALLY, IT WOULD BE THAT OPPOSITE OF "BEST."
WHAT?
WELL, I WASN'T WILLING TO CHANCE BREAKING A NAIL, BUT...
LOOK, WE BOTH KNOW YOU'RE FULLY CAPABLE OF ESCAPING FROM THIS PLACE. YOU COULD PROBABLY SHATTER THOSE RESTRAINTS ANY TIME YOU WANTED.
BUT WHAT'S YOUR NEXT STEP? AFTER YOU ESCAPE, WHAT'S NEXT?
YOU THINK THINGS ARE BAD FOR YOU NOW? WHAT HAPPENS ONCE YOU'RE A FUGITIVE FROM CUSTODY? YOU'RE VIOLATING THE S.R.A.* AS IT IS.
PALONE CAN FEDERALIZE THIS CASE WITH A PHONE CALL. YOU WANT TO PUT YOUR FRIENDS AND FAMILY AT RISK BY BEING WITH YOU IF--NO, WHEN--S.H.I.E.L.D. AND/OR THE FBI TRIES TO TAKE YOU DOWN?
*THE SUPERHUMAN REGISTRATION ACT. --"CIVIL WAR" READIN' STEVE.

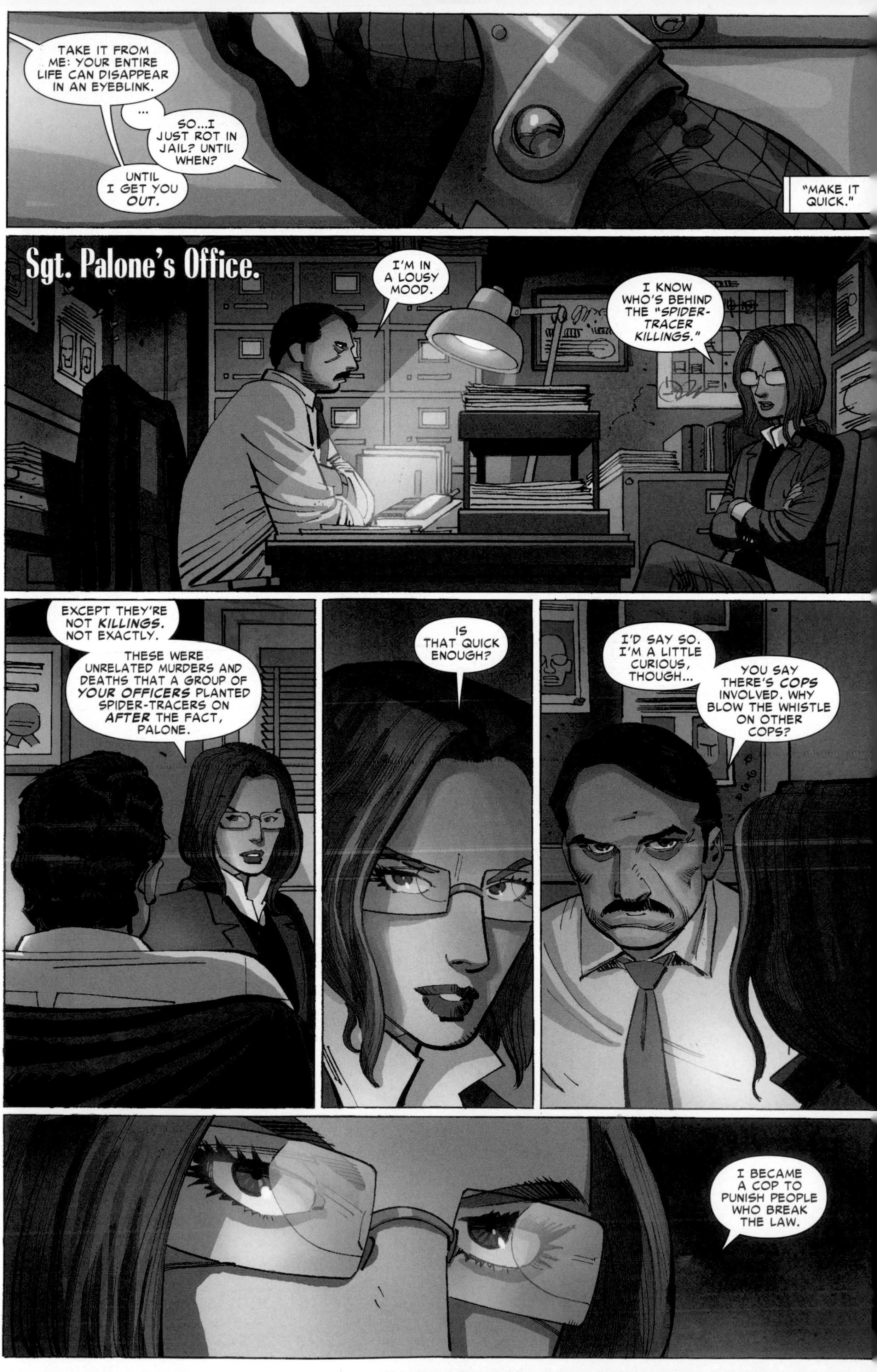

TAKE IT FROM ME: YOUR ENTIRE LIFE CAN DISAPPEAR IN AN EYEBLINK.
...
SO...I JUST ROT IN JAIL? UNTIL WHEN?
UNTIL I GET YOU OUT.
"MAKE IT QUICK."
Sgt. Palone's Office.
I'M IN A LOUSY MOOD.
I KNOW WHO'S BEHIND THE "SPIDER-TRACER KILLINGS."
EXCEPT THEY'RE NOT KILLINGS. NOT EXACTLY.
THESE WERE UNRELATED MURDERS AND DEATHS THAT A GROUP OF YOUR OFFICERS PLANTED SPIDER-TRACERS ON AFTER THE FACT, PALONE.
IS THAT QUICK ENOUGH?
I'D SAY SO. I'M A LITTLE CURIOUS, THOUGH...
YOU SAY THERE'S COPS INVOLVED. WHY BLOW THE WHISTLE ON OTHER COPS?
I BECAME A COP TO PUNISH PEOPLE WHO BREAK THE LAW.

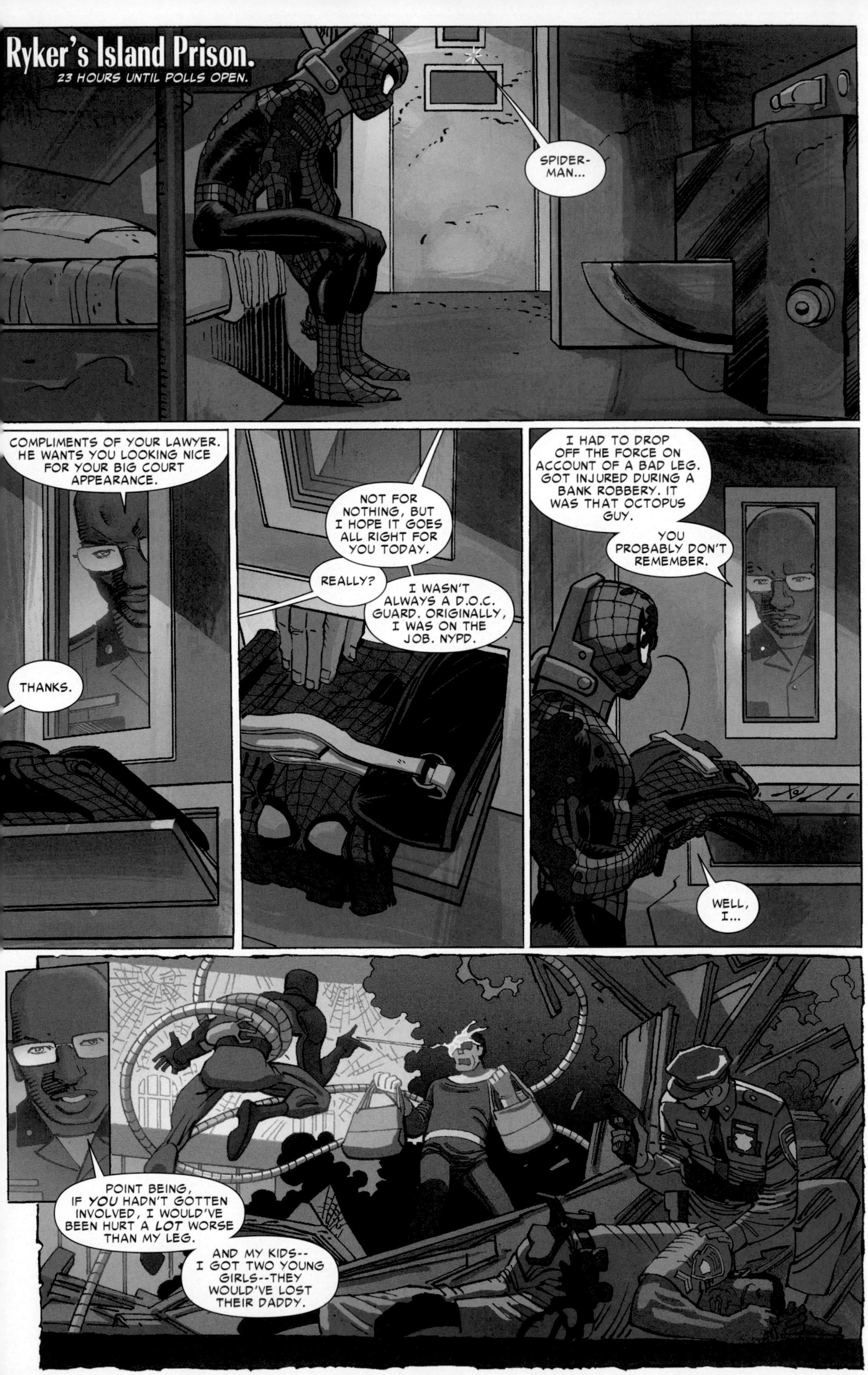
Ryker's Island Prison.
23 HOURS UNTIL POLLS OPEN.
SPIDER-MAN...
COMPLIMENTS OF YOUR LAWYER. HE WANTS YOU LOOKING NICE FOR YOUR BIG COURT APPEARANCE.
THANKS.
NOT FOR NOTHING, BUT I HOPE IT GOES ALL RIGHT FOR YOU TODAY.
REALLY?
I WASN'T ALWAYS A D.O.C. GUARD. ORIGINALLY, I WAS ON THE JOB. NYPD.
I HAD TO DROP OFF THE FORCE ON ACCOUNT OF A BAD LEG. GOT INJURED DURING A BANK ROBBERY. IT WAS THAT OCTOPUS GUY.
YOU PROBABLY DON'T REMEMBER.
WELL, I...
POINT BEING, IF *YOU* HADN'T GOTTEN INVOLVED, I WOULD'VE BEEN HURT A *LOT* WORSE THAN MY LEG.
AND MY KIDS-- I GOT TWO YOUNG GIRLS--THEY WOULD'VE LOST THEIR DADDY.

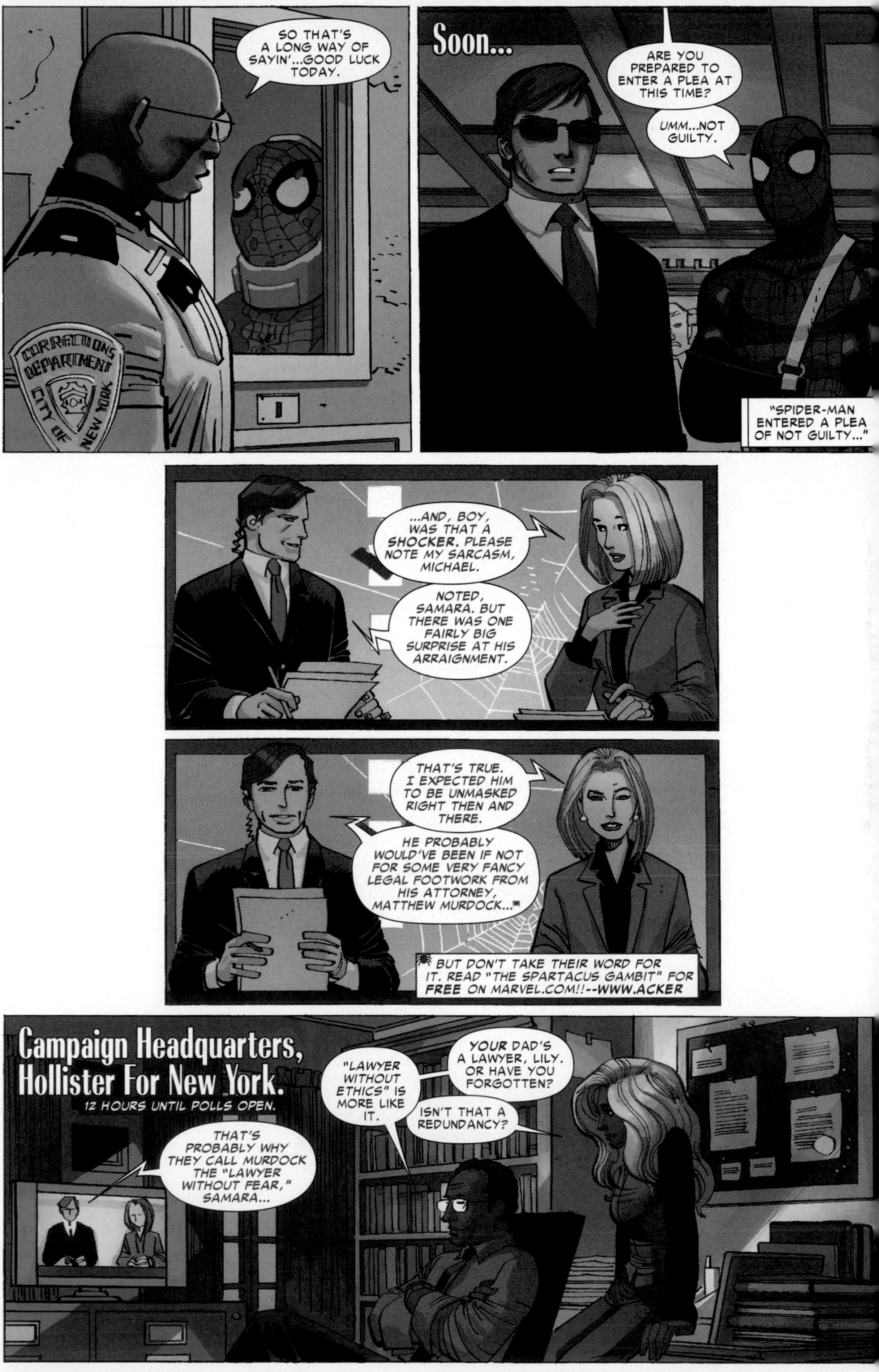
SO THAT'S A LONG WAY OF SAYIN'...GOOD LUCK TODAY.
CORRECTIONS DEPARTMENT CITY OF NEW YORK
Soon...
ARE YOU PREPARED TO ENTER A PLEA AT THIS TIME?
UMM...NOT GUILTY.
"SPIDER-MAN ENTERED A PLEA OF NOT GUILTY..."
...AND, BOY, WAS THAT A SHOCKER. PLEASE NOTE MY SARCASM, MICHAEL.
NOTED, SAMARA. BUT THERE WAS ONE FAIRLY BIG SURPRISE AT HIS ARRAIGNMENT.
THAT'S TRUE. I EXPECTED HIM TO BE UNMASKED RIGHT THEN AND THERE.
HE PROBABLY WOULD'VE BEEN IF NOT FOR SOME VERY FANCY LEGAL FOOTWORK FROM HIS ATTORNEY, MATTHEW MURDOCK...*
* BUT DON'T TAKE THEIR WORD FOR IT. READ "THE SPARTACUS GAMBIT" FOR FREE ON MARVEL.COM!!--WWW.ACKER
Campaign Headquarters, Hollister For New York.
12 HOURS UNTIL POLLS OPEN.
THAT'S PROBABLY WHY THEY CALL MURDOCK THE "LAWYER WITHOUT FEAR," SAMARA...
"LAWYER WITHOUT ETHICS" IS MORE LIKE IT.
YOUR DAD'S A LAWYER, LILY. OR HAVE YOU FORGOTTEN?
ISN'T THAT A REDUNDANCY?

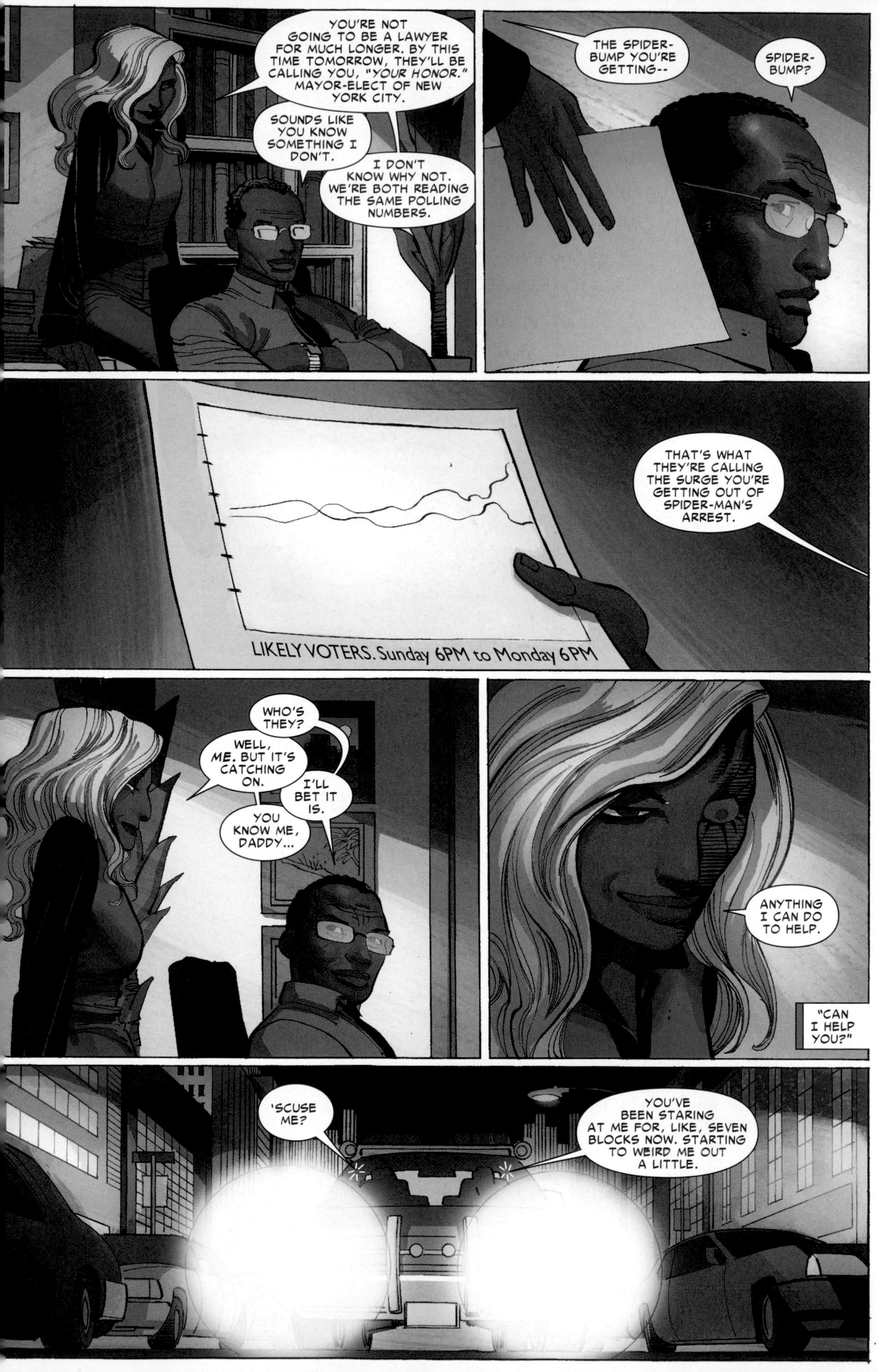
YOU'RE NOT GOING TO BE A LAWYER FOR MUCH LONGER. BY THIS TIME TOMORROW, THEY'LL BE CALLING YOU, "YOUR HONOR." MAYOR-ELECT OF NEW YORK CITY.
SOUNDS LIKE YOU KNOW SOMETHING I DON'T.
I DON'T KNOW WHY NOT. WE'RE BOTH READING THE SAME POLLING NUMBERS.
THE SPIDER-BUMP YOU'RE GETTING--
SPIDER-BUMP?
THAT'S WHAT THEY'RE CALLING THE SURGE YOU'RE GETTING OUT OF SPIDER-MAN'S ARREST.
LIKELY VOTERS. Sunday 6PM to Monday 6PM
WHO'S THEY?
WELL, ME. BUT IT'S CATCHING ON.
I'LL BET IT IS.
YOU KNOW ME, DADDY...
ANYTHING I CAN DO TO HELP.
"CAN I HELP YOU?"
'SCUSE ME?
YOU'VE BEEN STARING AT ME FOR, LIKE, SEVEN BLOCKS NOW. STARTING TO WEIRD ME OUT A LITTLE.

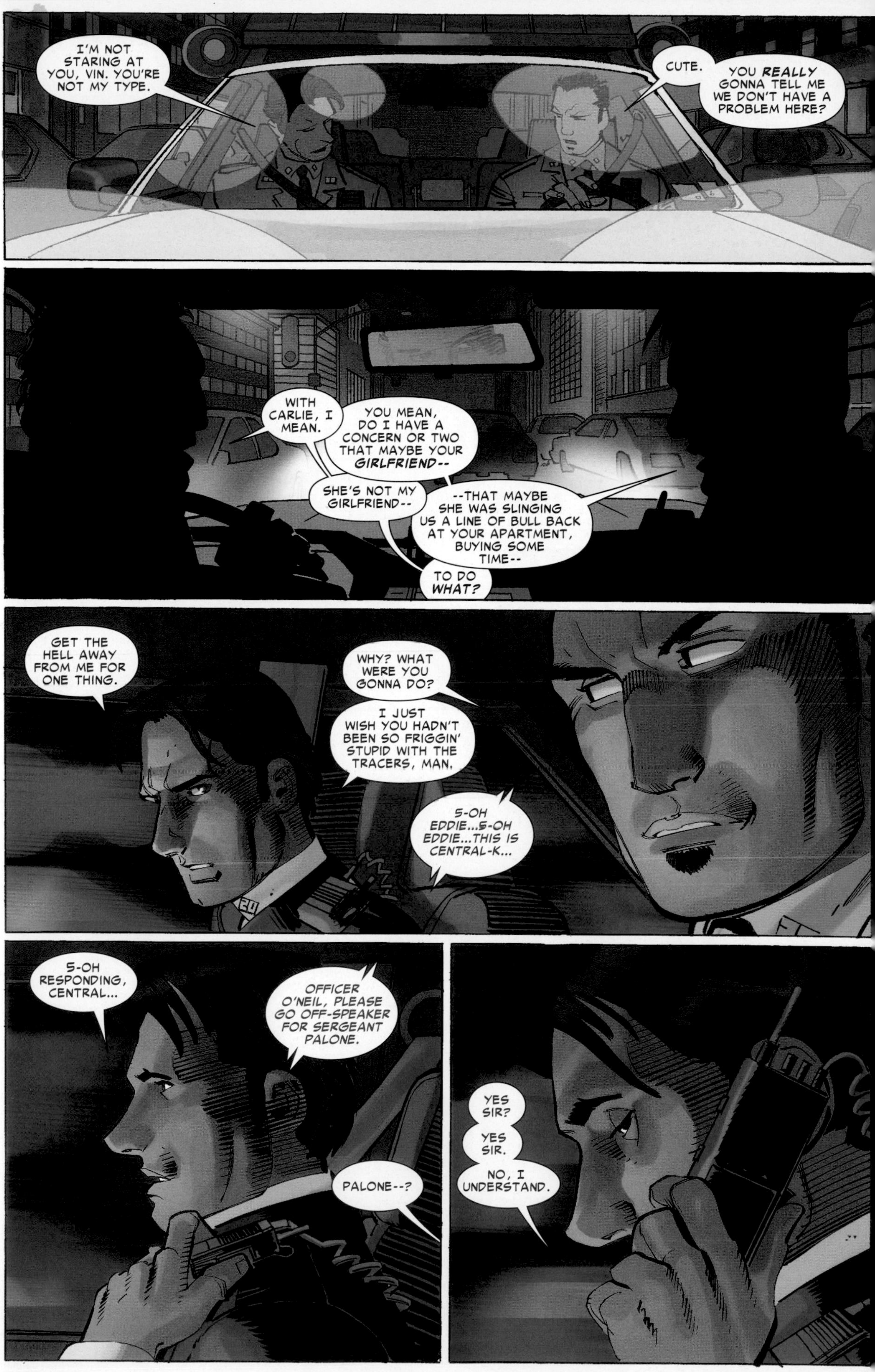
I'M NOT STARING AT YOU, VIN. YOU'RE NOT MY TYPE.
CUTE.
YOU REALLY GONNA TELL ME WE DON'T HAVE A PROBLEM HERE?
WITH CARLIE, I MEAN.
YOU MEAN, DO I HAVE A CONCERN OR TWO THAT MAYBE YOUR GIRLFRIEND--
SHE'S NOT MY GIRLFRIEND--
--THAT MAYBE SHE WAS SLINGING US A LINE OF BULL BACK AT YOUR APARTMENT, BUYING SOME TIME--
TO DO WHAT?
GET THE HELL AWAY FROM ME FOR ONE THING.
WHY? WHAT WERE YOU GONNA DO?
I JUST WISH YOU HADN'T BEEN SO FRIGGIN' STUPID WITH THE TRACERS, MAN.
5-OH EDDIE...5-OH EDDIE...THIS IS CENTRAL-K...
5-OH RESPONDING, CENTRAL...
OFFICER O'NEIL, PLEASE GO OFF-SPEAKER FOR SERGEANT PALONE.
PALONE--?
YES SIR?
YES SIR.
NO, I UNDERSTAND.

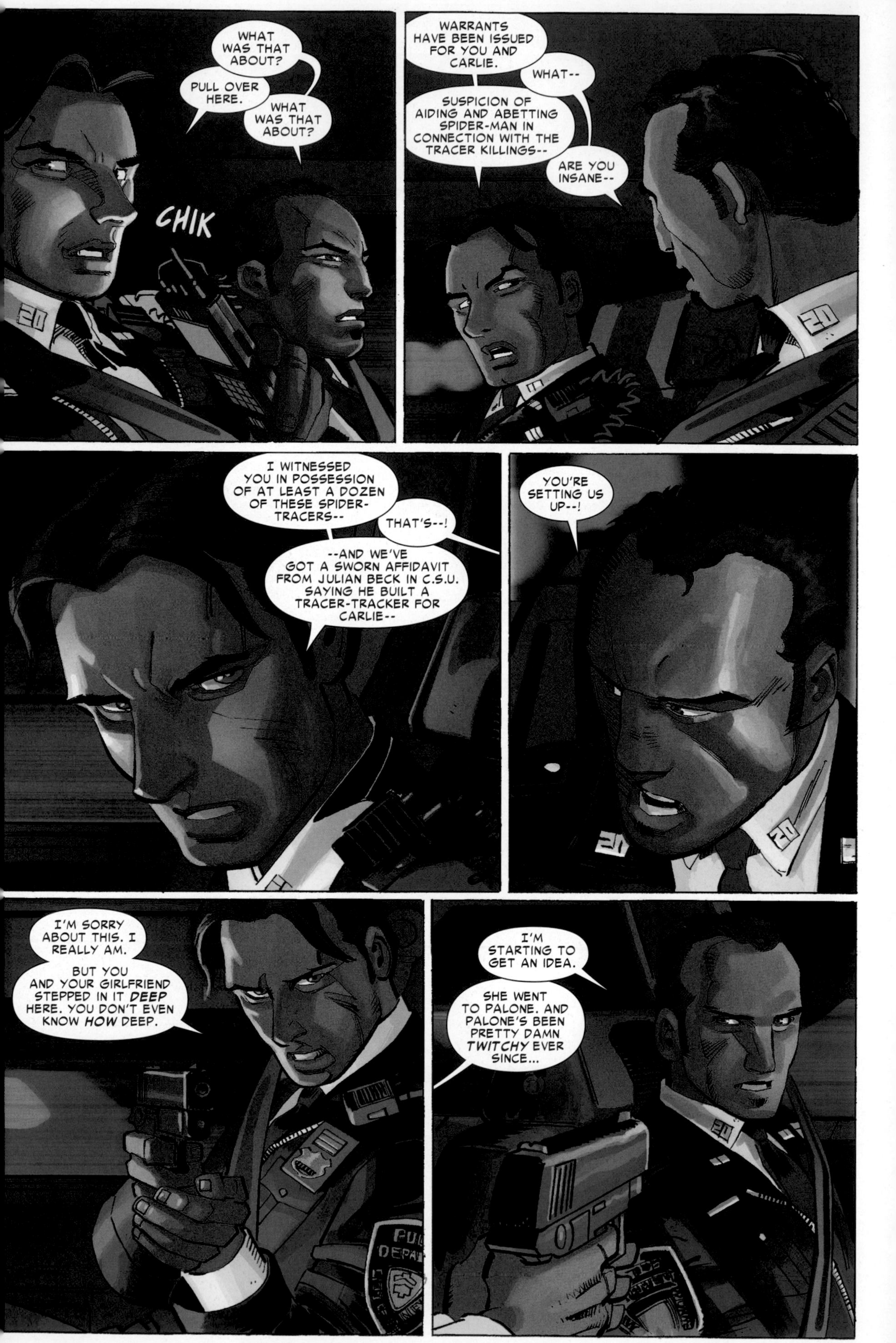
WHAT WAS THAT ABOUT?
PULL OVER HERE.
WHAT WAS THAT ABOUT?
CHIK
WARRANTS HAVE BEEN ISSUED FOR YOU AND CARLIE.
WHAT--
SUSPICION OF AIDING AND ABETTING SPIDER-MAN IN CONNECTION WITH THE TRACER KILLINGS--
ARE YOU INSANE--
I WITNESSED YOU IN POSSESSION OF AT LEAST A DOZEN OF THESE SPIDER-TRACERS--
THAT'S--!
--AND WE'VE GOT A SWORN AFFIDAVIT FROM JULIAN BECK IN C.S.U. SAYING HE BUILT A TRACER-TRACKER FOR CARLIE--
YOU'RE SETTING US UP--!
I'M SORRY ABOUT THIS. I REALLY AM.
BUT YOU AND YOUR GIRLFRIEND STEPPED IN IT *DEEP* HERE. YOU DON'T EVEN KNOW *HOW* DEEP.
I'M STARTING TO GET AN IDEA.
SHE WENT TO PALONE. AND PALONE'S BEEN PRETTY DAMN *TWITCHY* EVER SINCE...

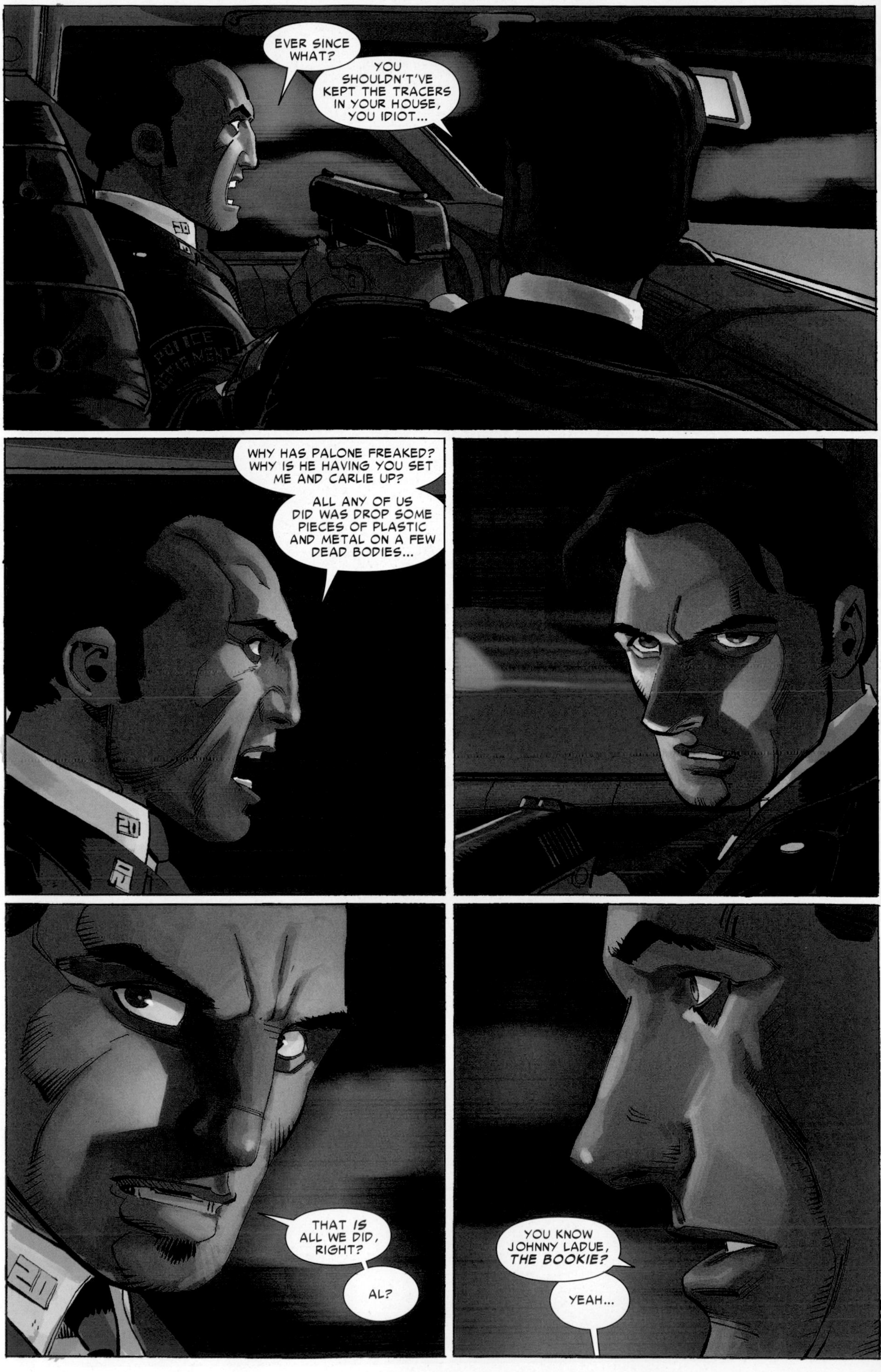
EVER SINCE WHAT?
YOU SHOULDN'T'VE KEPT THE TRACERS IN YOUR HOUSE, YOU IDIOT...
POLICE DEPARTMENT
WHY HAS PALONE FREAKED? WHY IS HE HAVING YOU SET ME AND CARLIE UP?
ALL ANY OF US DID WAS DROP SOME PIECES OF PLASTIC AND METAL ON A FEW DEAD BODIES...
THAT IS ALL WE DID, RIGHT?
AL?
YOU KNOW JOHNNY LADUE, THE BOOKIE?
YEAH...

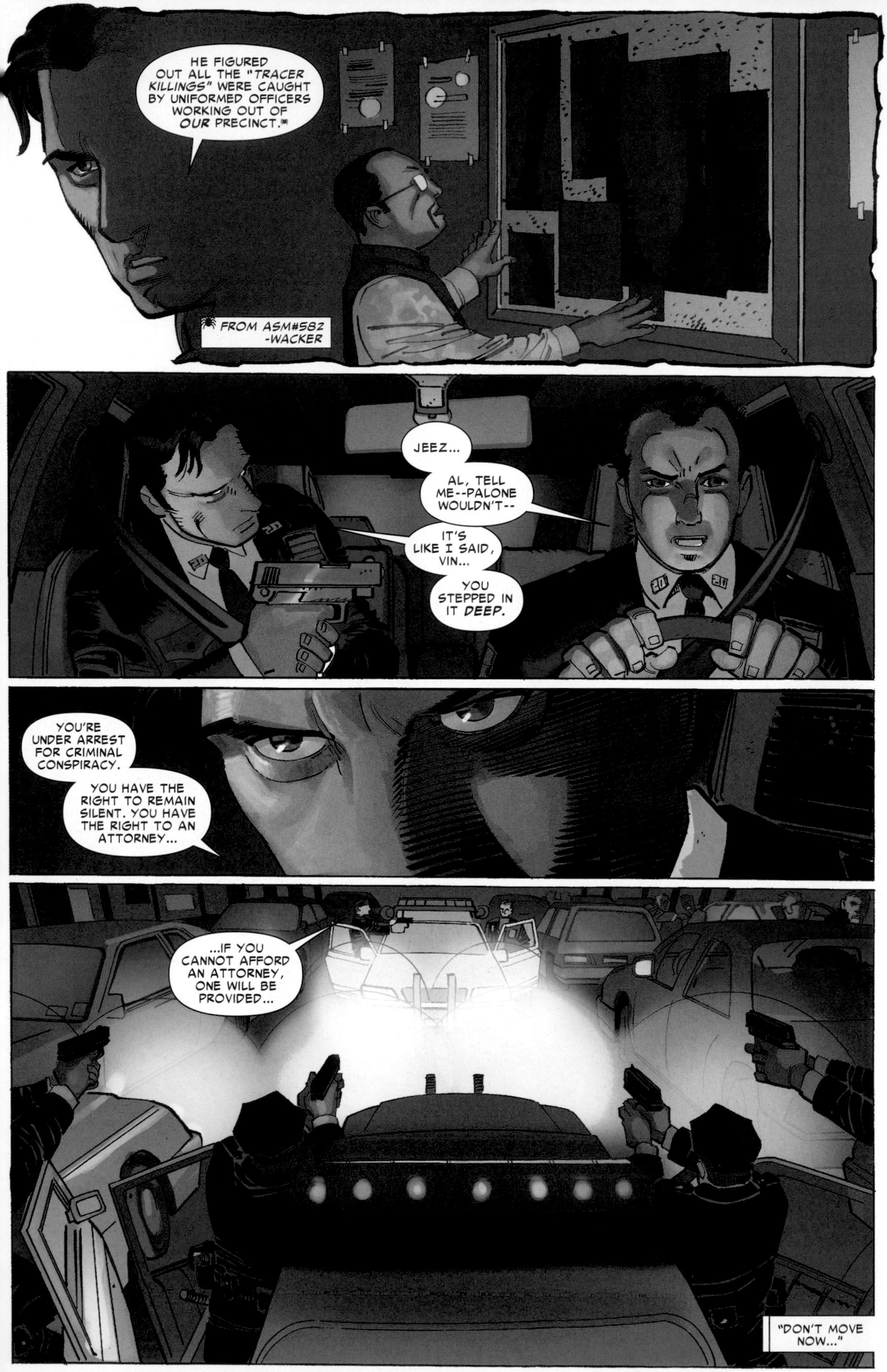

HE FIGURED OUT ALL THE "TRACER KILLINGS" WERE CAUGHT BY UNIFORMED OFFICERS WORKING OUT OF OUR PRECINCT.*
*FROM ASM#582 -WACKER
JEEZ...
AL, TELL ME--PALONE WOULDN'T--
IT'S LIKE I SAID, VIN...
YOU STEPPED IN IT DEEP.
YOU'RE UNDER ARREST FOR CRIMINAL CONSPIRACY.
YOU HAVE THE RIGHT TO REMAIN SILENT. YOU HAVE THE RIGHT TO AN ATTORNEY...
...IF YOU CANNOT AFFORD AN ATTORNEY, ONE WILL BE PROVIDED...
"DON'T MOVE NOW..."

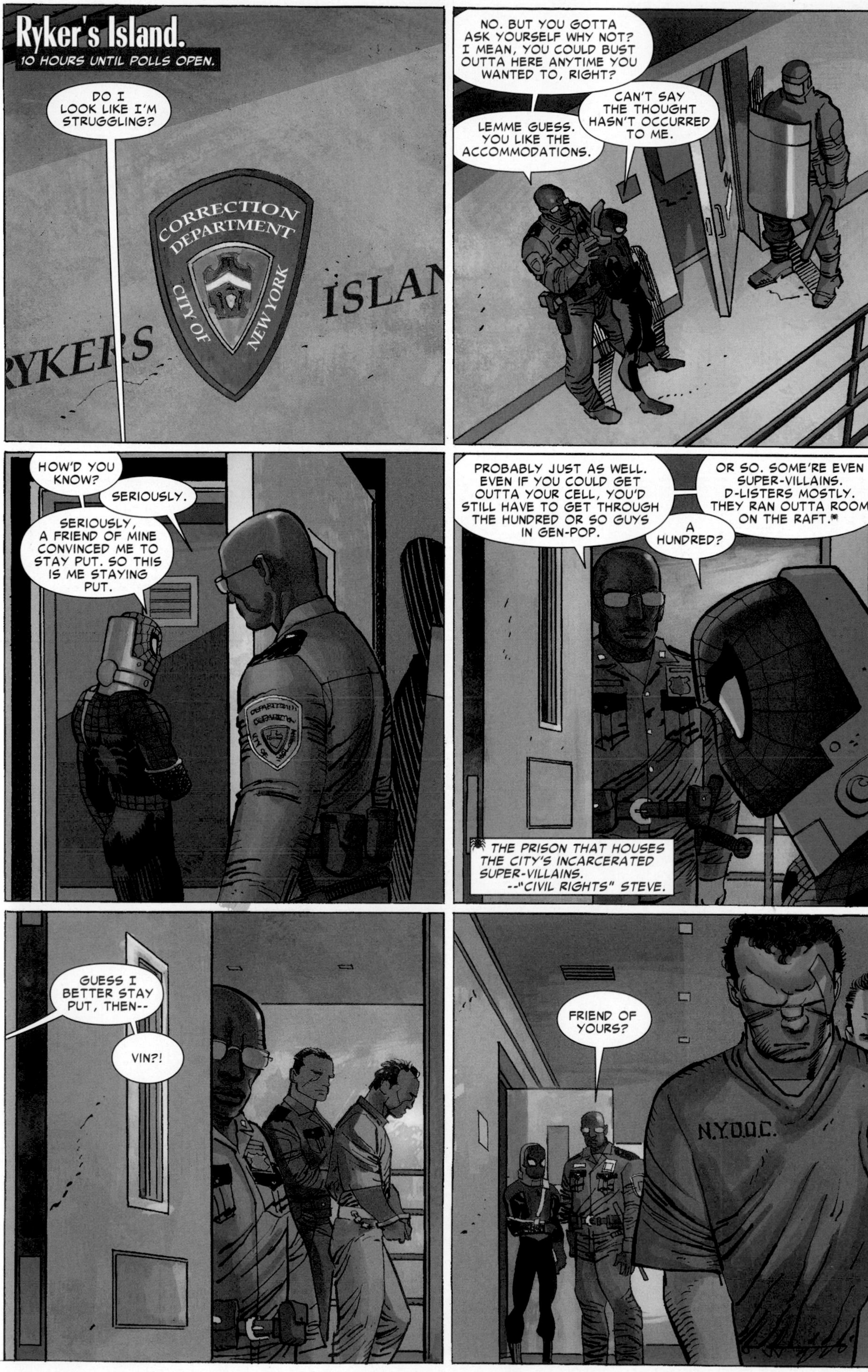
Ryker's Island.
10 HOURS UNTIL POLLS OPEN.
DO I LOOK LIKE I'M STRUGGLING?
CORRECTION DEPARTMENT
CITY OF NEW YORK
RYKERS ISLAN
NO. BUT YOU GOTTA ASK YOURSELF WHY NOT? I MEAN, YOU COULD BUST OUTTA HERE ANYTIME YOU WANTED TO, RIGHT?
LEMME GUESS. YOU LIKE THE ACCOMMODATIONS.
CAN'T SAY THE THOUGHT HASN'T OCCURRED TO ME.
HOW'D YOU KNOW?
SERIOUSLY.
SERIOUSLY, A FRIEND OF MINE CONVINCED ME TO STAY PUT. SO THIS IS ME STAYING PUT.
PROBABLY JUST AS WELL. EVEN IF YOU COULD GET OUTTA YOUR CELL, YOU'D STILL HAVE TO GET THROUGH THE HUNDRED OR SO GUYS IN GEN-POP.
A HUNDRED?
OR SO. SOME'RE EVEN SUPER-VILLAINS. D-LISTERS MOSTLY. THEY RAN OUTTA ROOM ON THE RAFT.*
*THE PRISON THAT HOUSES THE CITY'S INCARCERATED SUPER-VILLAINS. --"CIVIL RIGHTS" STEVE.
GUESS I BETTER STAY PUT, THEN--
VIN?!
FRIEND OF YOURS?
N.Y.D.O.C.

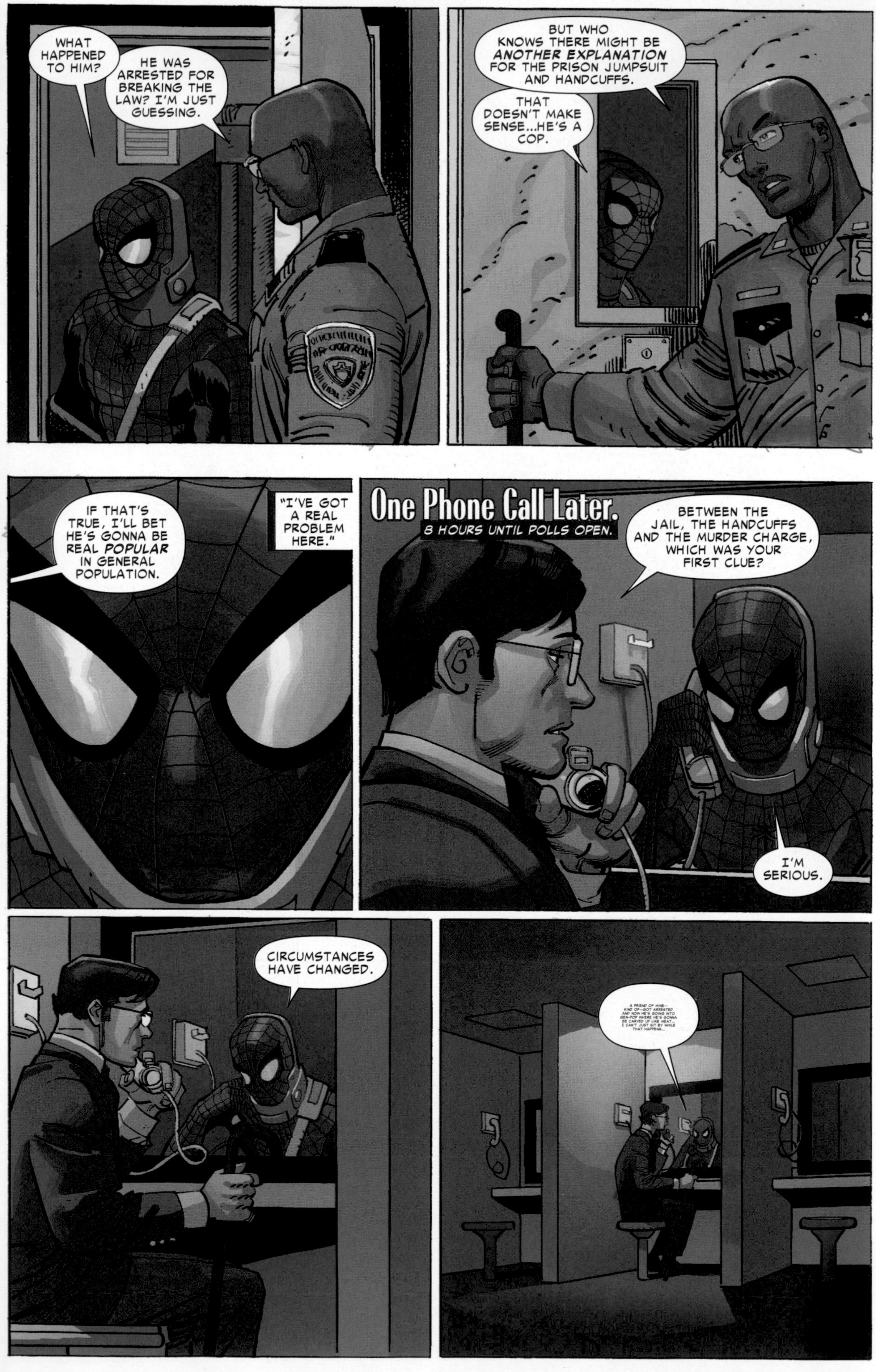
WHAT HAPPENED TO HIM?
HE WAS ARRESTED FOR BREAKING THE LAW? I'M JUST GUESSING.
BUT WHO KNOWS THERE MIGHT BE *ANOTHER EXPLANATION* FOR THE PRISON JUMPSUIT AND HANDCUFFS.
THAT DOESN'T MAKE SENSE...HE'S A COP.
IF THAT'S TRUE, I'LL BET HE'S GONNA BE REAL *POPULAR* IN GENERAL POPULATION.
"I'VE GOT A REAL PROBLEM HERE."
One Phone Call Later.
8 HOURS UNTIL POLLS OPEN.
BETWEEN THE JAIL, THE HANDCUFFS AND THE MURDER CHARGE, WHICH WAS YOUR FIRST CLUE?
I'M SERIOUS.
CIRCUMSTANCES HAVE CHANGED.
A FRIEND OF MINE-- KIND OF--GOT ARRESTED AND NOW HE'S GOING INTO GEN-POP WHERE HE'S GONNA BE CARVED UP LIKE MEAT... I CAN'T JUST SIT BY WHILE THAT HAPPENS...

Election Day.

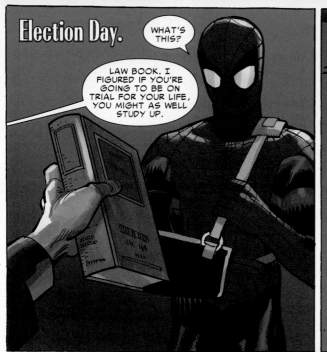

WHAT'S THIS?

LAW BOOK. I FIGURED IF YOU'RE GOING TO BE ON TRIAL FOR YOUR LIFE, YOU MIGHT AS WELL STUDY UP.

I THOUGHT YOU WERE GOING TO GET ME OUT OF THIS.

I'M TRYING TO KEEP YOUR MASK ON AND GET YOU OUT OF THAT CIVIL SUIT.※

※ SPIDEY WAS SLAPPED WITH A LAWSUIT BY A GUY HE RESCUED WAAAAAY BACK IN ISSUE #550. --"SUMMARY JUDGMENT" STEVE.

IT'S GOING TO TAKE A LITTLE MORE THAN WHAT I'VE GOT PLANNED TO GET THE *CRIMINAL* CHARGES AGAINST YOU DROPPED.

WHAT DO YOU HAVE PLANNED?

IF I TOLD YOU, IT WOULDN'T BE A SURPRISE.

YOU CAN SPOIL IT FOR ME. SOMETHING TELLS ME I'M GOING TO PAY ATTENTION ANYWAY.

"WELL, YOU'LL NEVER BELIEVE WHAT HAPPENED NEXT."

I KNOW *I* DON'T BELIEVE IT, MICHAEL.

THE JUDGE RULED THAT SPIDER-MAN'S MASK STAYS ON.

BUT THAT WASN'T THE SURPRISING PART.

THOUGH I CERTAINLY DIDN'T SEE THAT COMING.

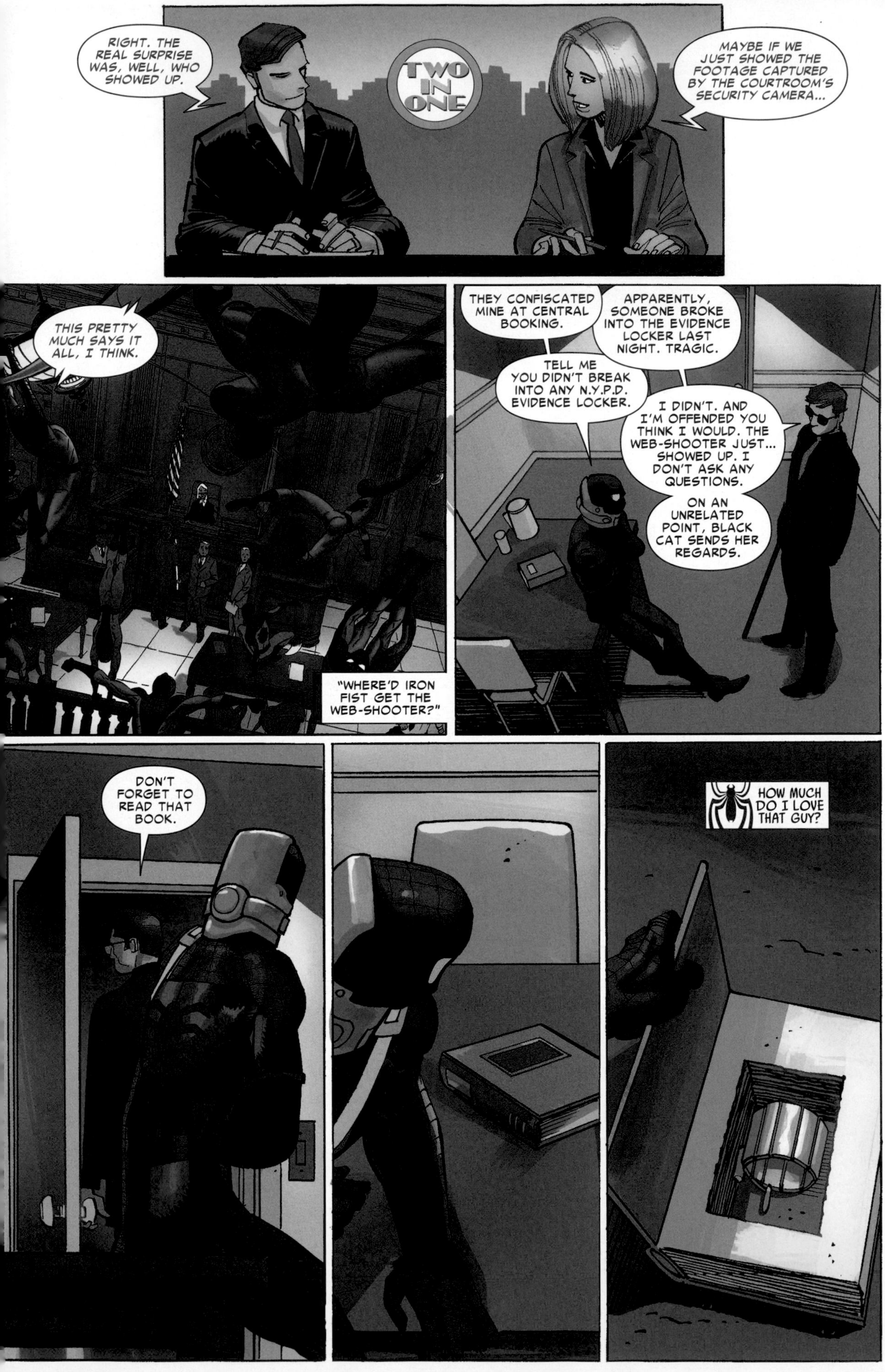
RIGHT. THE REAL SURPRISE WAS, WELL, WHO SHOWED UP.
TWO IN ONE
MAYBE IF WE JUST SHOWED THE FOOTAGE CAPTURED BY THE COURTROOM'S SECURITY CAMERA...
THIS PRETTY MUCH SAYS IT ALL, I THINK.
"WHERE'D IRON FIST GET THE WEB-SHOOTER?"
THEY CONFISCATED MINE AT CENTRAL BOOKING.
APPARENTLY, SOMEONE BROKE INTO THE EVIDENCE LOCKER LAST NIGHT. TRAGIC.
TELL ME YOU DIDN'T BREAK INTO ANY N.Y.P.D. EVIDENCE LOCKER.
I DIDN'T. AND I'M OFFENDED YOU THINK I WOULD. THE WEB-SHOOTER JUST... SHOWED UP. I DON'T ASK ANY QUESTIONS.
ON AN UNRELATED POINT, BLACK CAT SENDS HER REGARDS.
DON'T FORGET TO READ THAT BOOK.
HOW MUCH DO I LOVE THAT GUY?

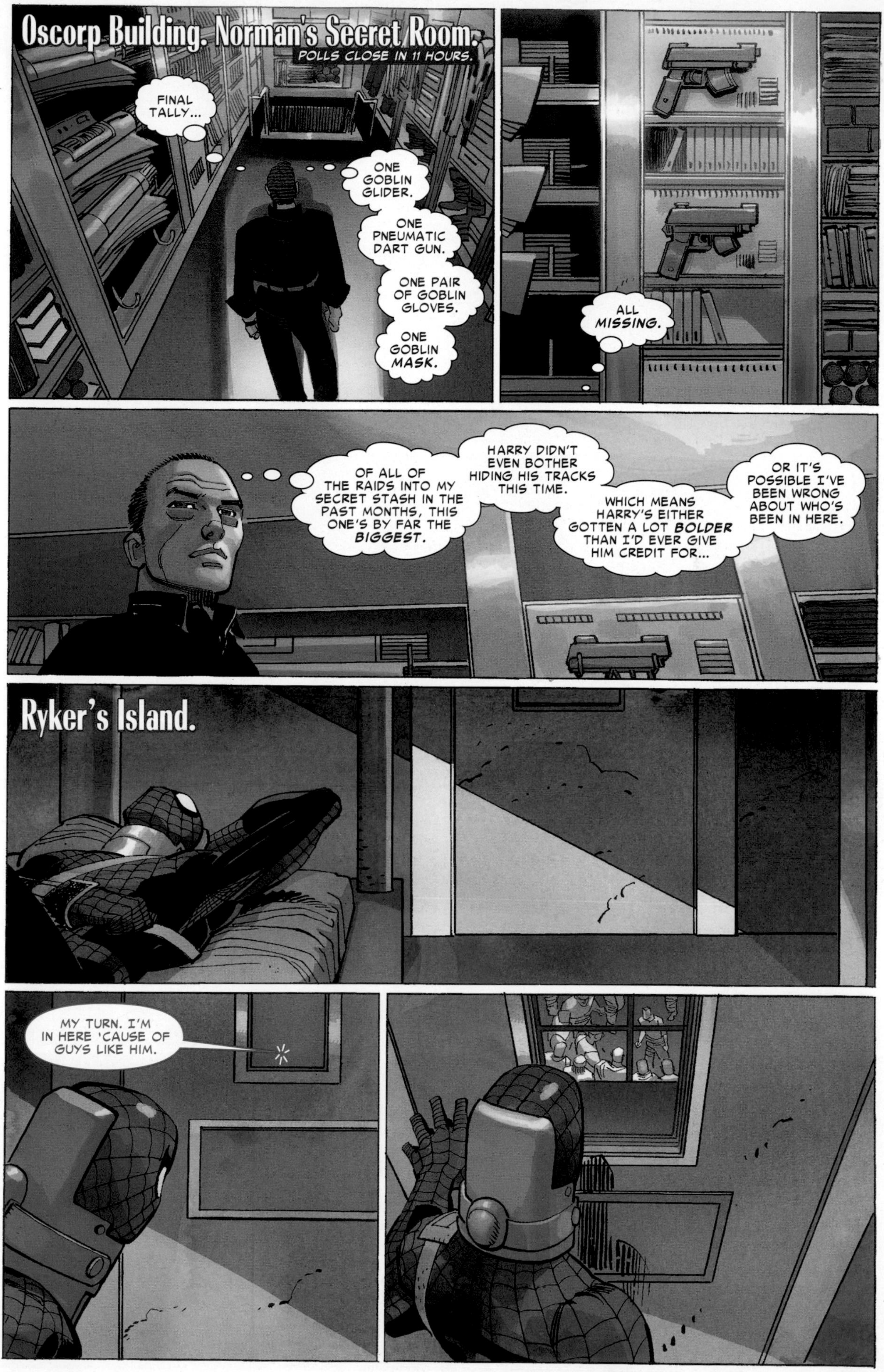
Oscorp Building. Norman's Secret Room.
POLLS CLOSE IN 11 HOURS.
FINAL TALLY...
ONE GOBLIN GLIDER.
ONE PNEUMATIC DART GUN.
ONE PAIR OF GOBLIN GLOVES.
ONE GOBLIN MASK.
ALL MISSING.
OF ALL OF THE RAIDS INTO MY SECRET STASH IN THE PAST MONTHS, THIS ONE'S BY FAR THE BIGGEST.
HARRY DIDN'T EVEN BOTHER HIDING HIS TRACKS THIS TIME.
WHICH MEANS HARRY'S EITHER GOTTEN A LOT BOLDER THAN I'D EVER GIVE HIM CREDIT FOR...
OR IT'S POSSIBLE I'VE BEEN WRONG ABOUT WHO'S BEEN IN HERE.
Ryker's Island.
MY TURN. I'M IN HERE 'CAUSE OF GUYS LIKE HIM.

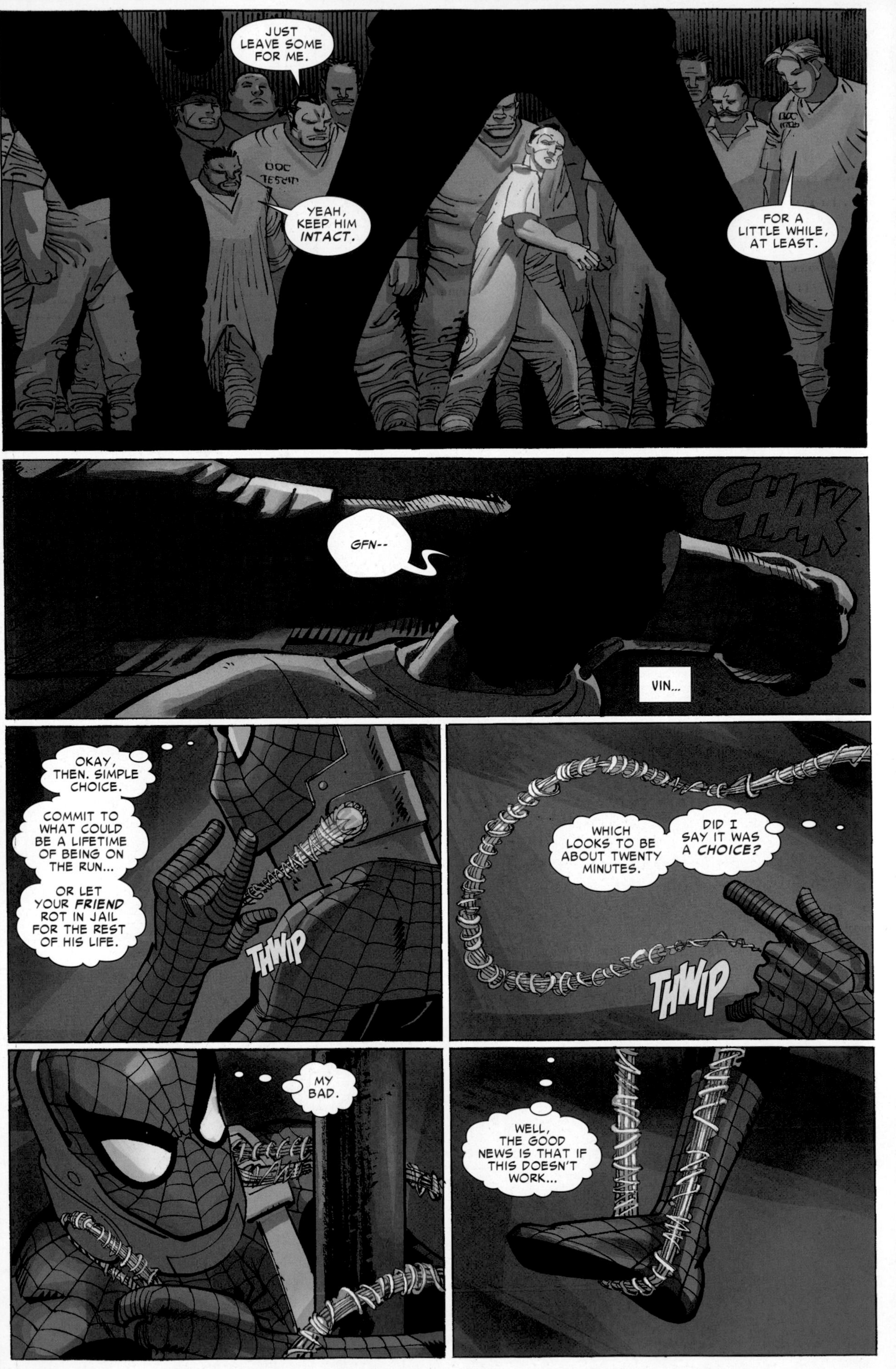
JUST LEAVE SOME FOR ME.
YEAH, KEEP HIM INTACT.
FOR A LITTLE WHILE, AT LEAST.
CHAK
GFN--
VIN...
OKAY, THEN. SIMPLE CHOICE.
COMMIT TO WHAT COULD BE A LIFETIME OF BEING ON THE RUN...
OR LET YOUR FRIEND ROT IN JAIL FOR THE REST OF HIS LIFE.
THWIP
DID I SAY IT WAS A CHOICE?
WHICH LOOKS TO BE ABOUT TWENTY MINUTES.
THWIP
MY BAD.
WELL, THE GOOD NEWS IS THAT IF THIS DOESN'T WORK...

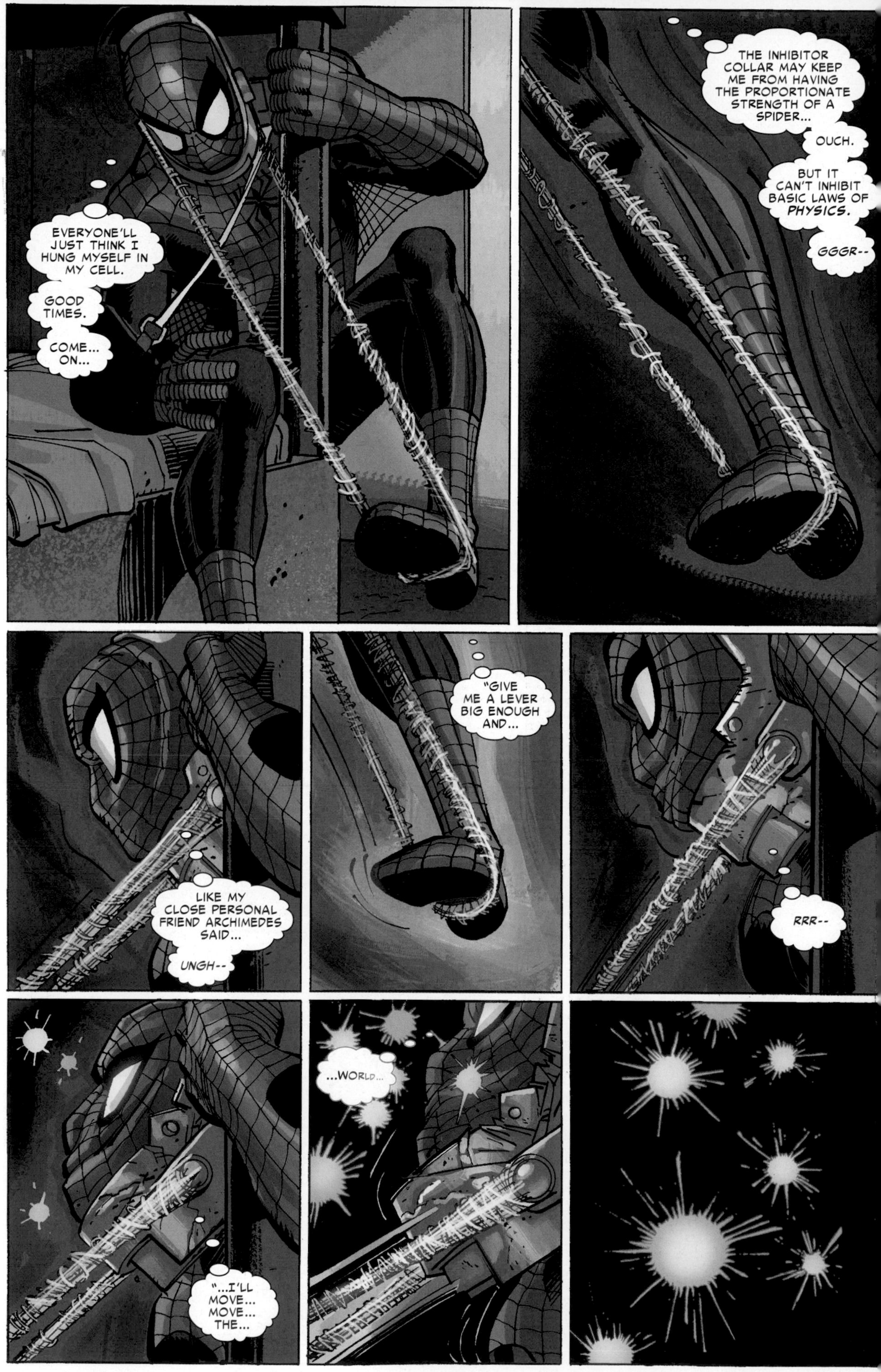
EVERYONE'LL JUST THINK I HUNG MYSELF IN MY CELL.
GOOD TIMES.
COME... ON...
THE INHIBITOR COLLAR MAY KEEP ME FROM HAVING THE PROPORTIONATE STRENGTH OF A SPIDER...
OUCH.
BUT IT CAN'T INHIBIT BASIC LAWS OF PHYSICS.
GGGR--
LIKE MY CLOSE PERSONAL FRIEND ARCHIMEDES SAID...
UNGH--
"GIVE ME A LEVER BIG ENOUGH AND...
RRR--
"...I'LL MOVE... MOVE... THE...
...WORLD...

YEAH, BABY. GONNA ROAST US SOME PORK TODAY...

NGH... GH...

CHAK

UGNF--

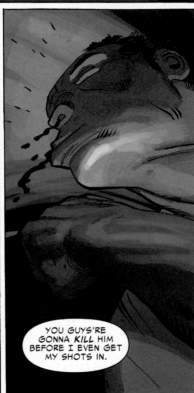

YOU GUYS'RE GONNA *KILL* HIM BEFORE I EVEN GET MY SHOTS IN.

WHAT ABOUT *MY* SHOTS?

WHAT ABOUT 'EM?

HEY, SAILORS...

I THINK I'VE GOT A SOLUTION THAT MIGHT WORK FOR *EVERYBODY*...

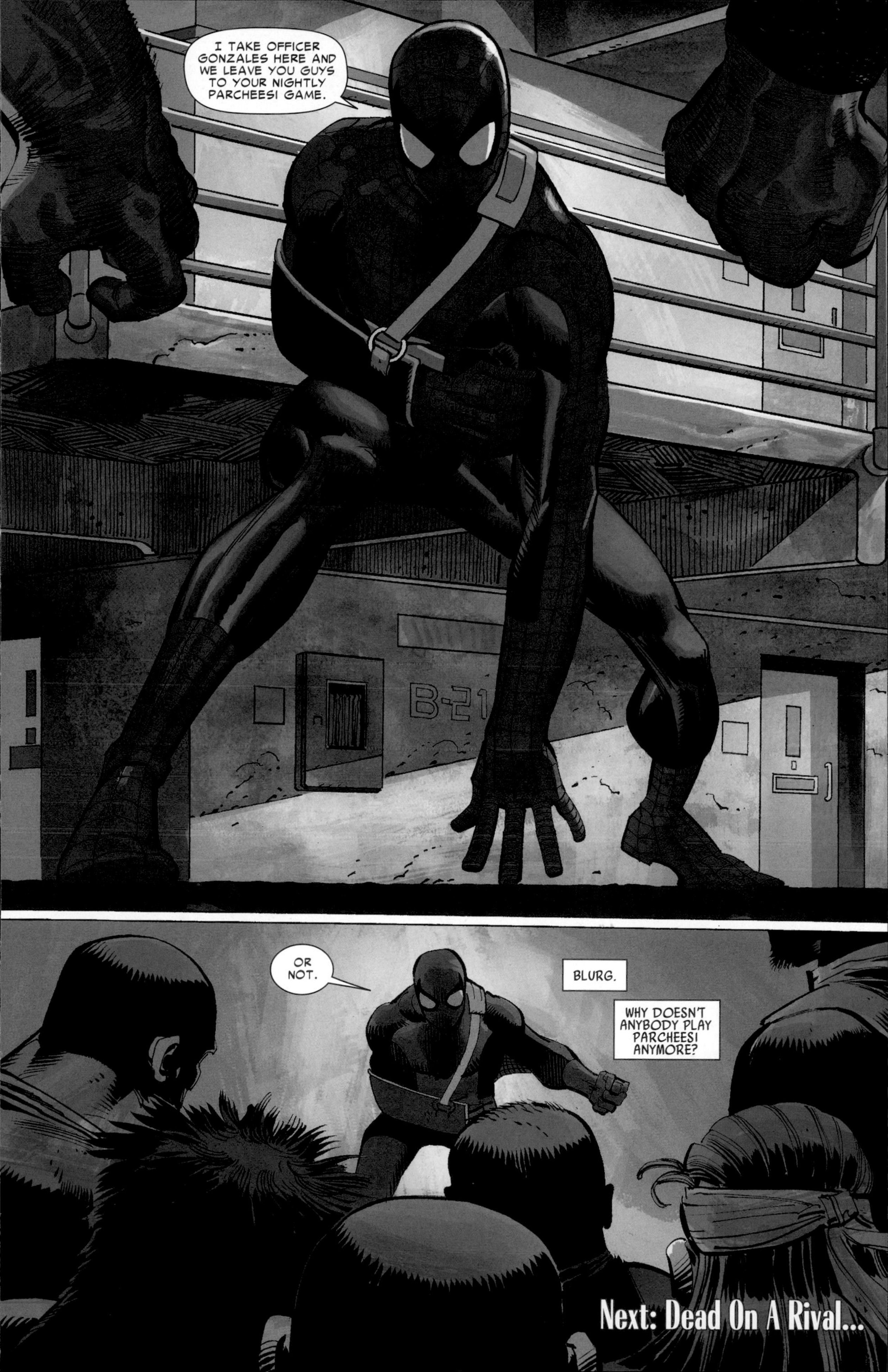
I TAKE OFFICER GONZALES HERE AND WE LEAVE YOU GUYS TO YOUR NIGHTLY PARCHEESI GAME.
B-21
OR NOT.
BLURG.
WHY DOESN'T ANYBODY PLAY PARCHEESI ANYMORE?
Next: Dead On A Rival...

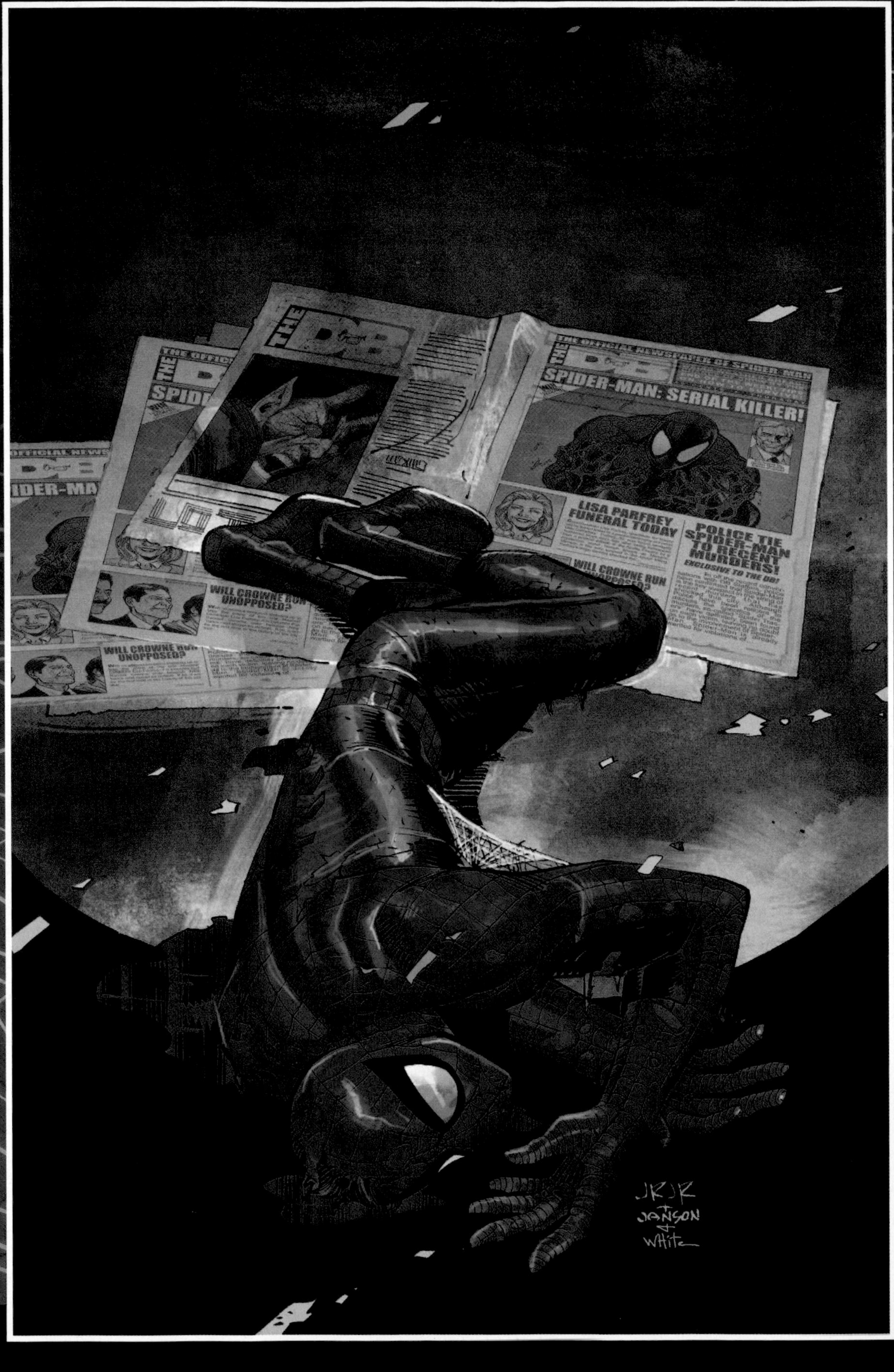
THE DB
SPIDER-MAN: SERIAL KILLER!
LISA PARFREY FUNERAL TODAY
POLICE TIE SPIDER-MAN TO RECENT MURDERS!
EXCLUSIVE TO THE DB!
WILL CROWNE RUN UNOPPOSED?
JRJR + JANSON + White

AMAZING SPIDER-MAN #588

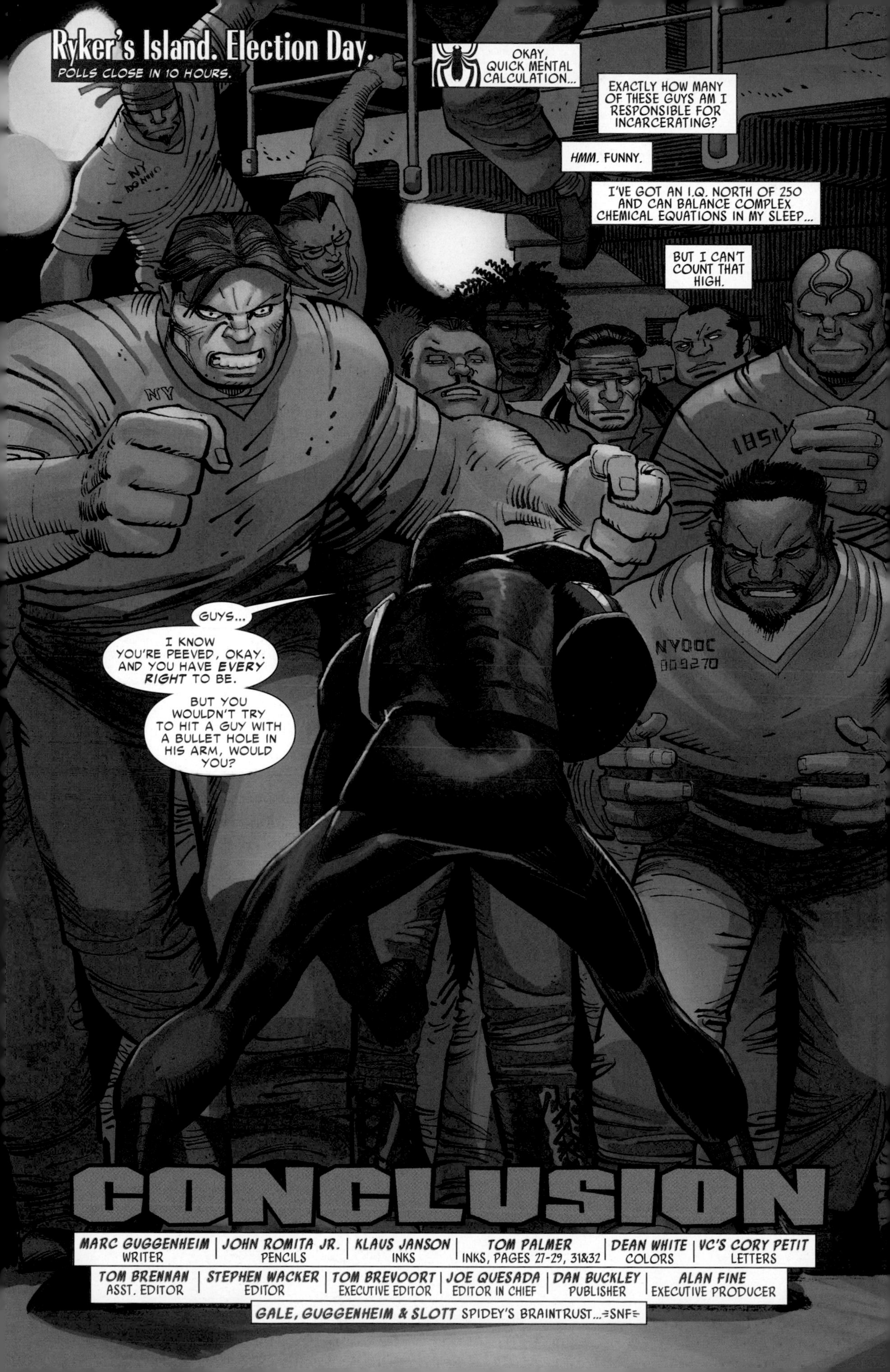
Ryker's Island. Election Day.
POLLS CLOSE IN 10 HOURS.
OKAY, QUICK MENTAL CALCULATION...
EXACTLY HOW MANY OF THESE GUYS AM I RESPONSIBLE FOR INCARCERATING?
HMM. FUNNY.
I'VE GOT AN I.Q. NORTH OF 250 AND CAN BALANCE COMPLEX CHEMICAL EQUATIONS IN MY SLEEP...
BUT I CAN'T COUNT THAT HIGH.
GUYS...
I KNOW YOU'RE PEEVED, OKAY. AND YOU HAVE EVERY RIGHT TO BE.
BUT YOU WOULDN'T TRY TO HIT A GUY WITH A BULLET HOLE IN HIS ARM, WOULD YOU?
NY
1851
NYDOC 009270
CONCLUSION
MARC GUGGENHEIM WRITER | JOHN ROMITA JR. PENCILS | KLAUS JANSON INKS | TOM PALMER INKS, PAGES 27-29, 31&32 | DEAN WHITE COLORS | VC'S CORY PETIT LETTERS
TOM BRENNAN ASST. EDITOR | STEPHEN WACKER EDITOR | TOM BREVOORT EXECUTIVE EDITOR | JOE QUESADA EDITOR IN CHIEF | DAN BUCKLEY PUBLISHER | ALAN FINE EXECUTIVE PRODUCER
GALE, GUGGENHEIM & SLOTT SPIDEY'S BRAINTRUST... =SNF=

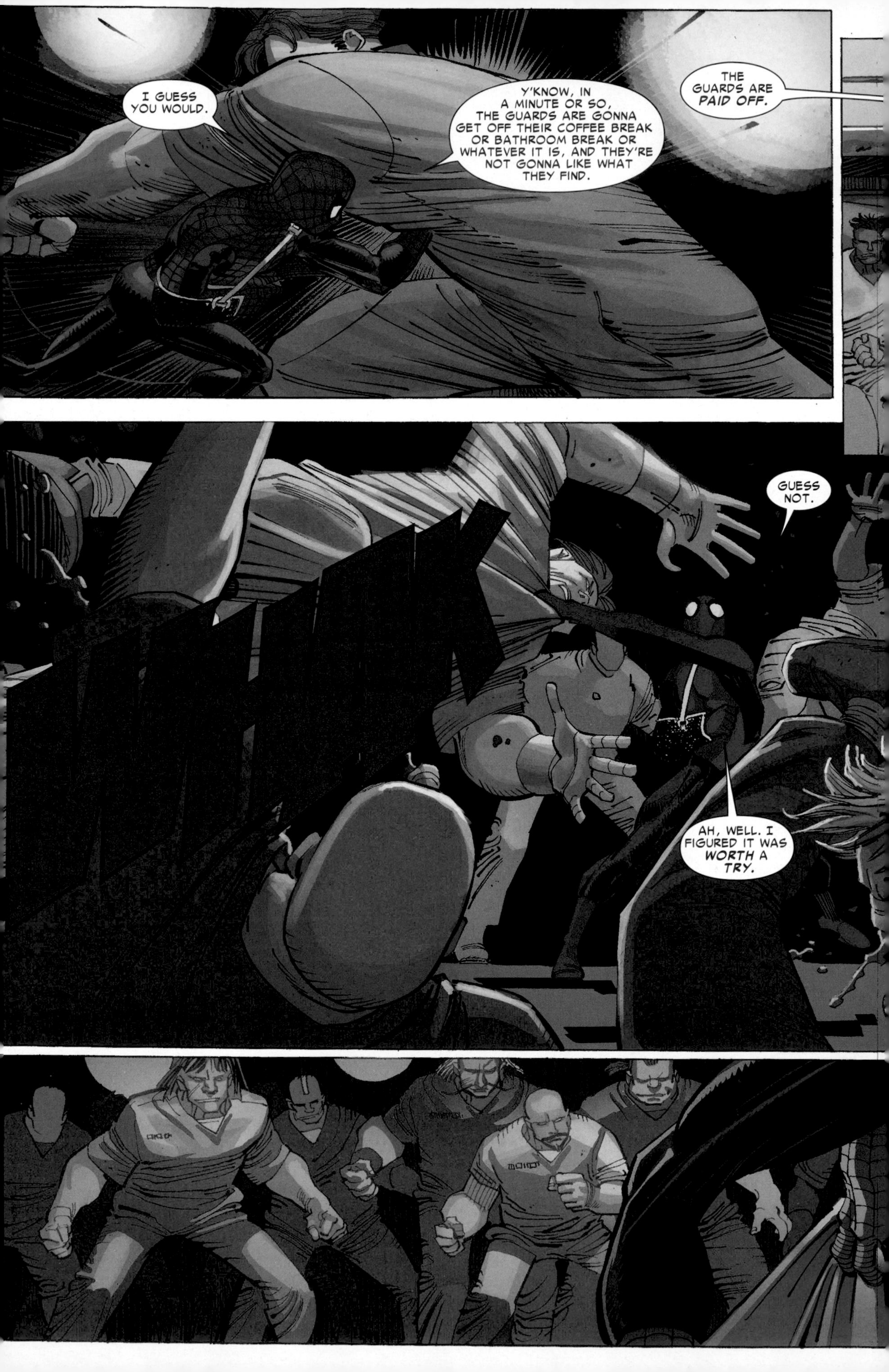
I GUESS YOU WOULD.
Y'KNOW, IN A MINUTE OR SO, THE GUARDS ARE GONNA GET OFF THEIR COFFEE BREAK OR BATHROOM BREAK OR WHATEVER IT IS, AND THEY'RE NOT GONNA LIKE WHAT THEY FIND.
THE GUARDS ARE *PAID OFF.*
GUESS NOT.
AH, WELL. I FIGURED IT WAS *WORTH* A *TRY.*

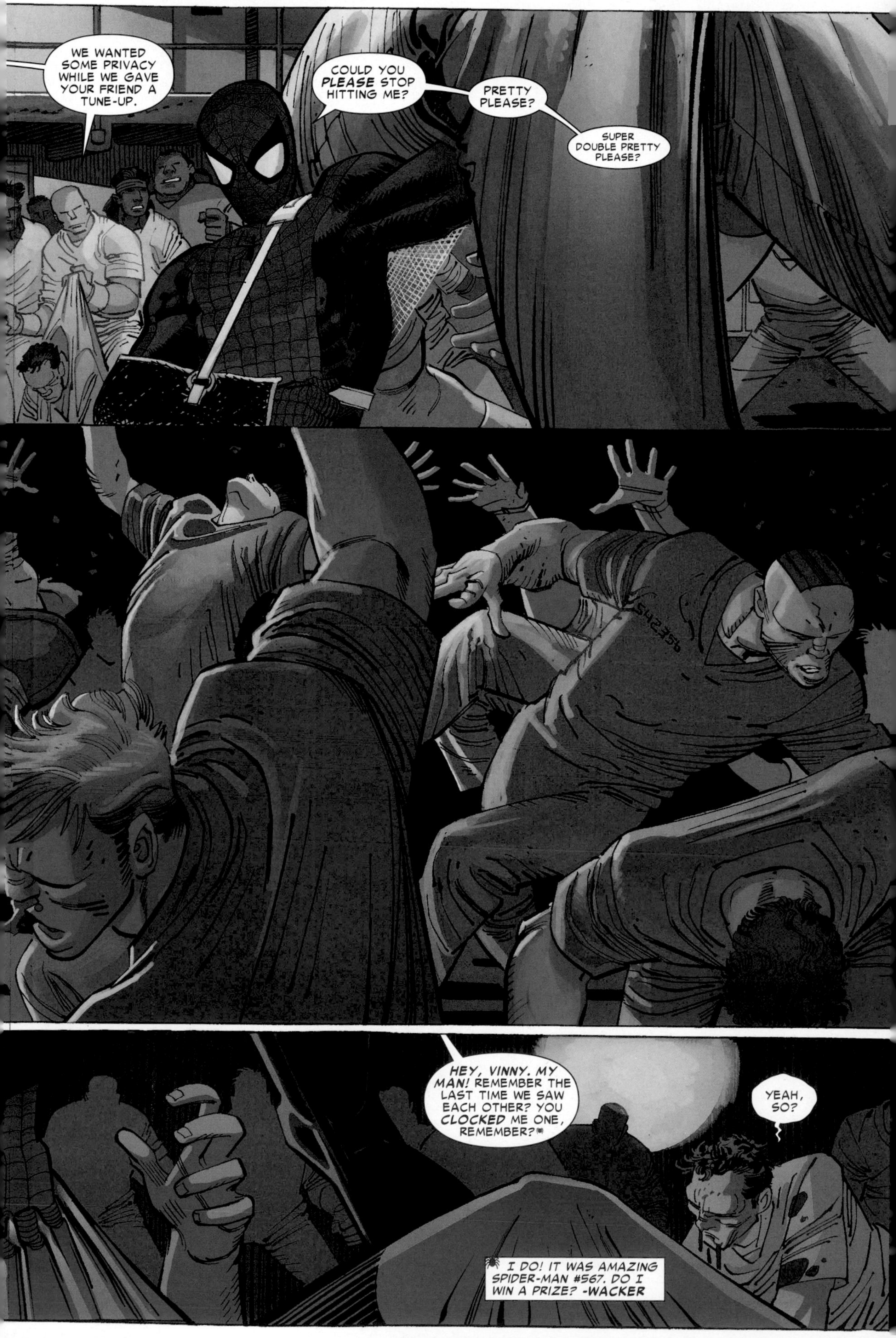
WE WANTED SOME PRIVACY WHILE WE GAVE YOUR FRIEND A TUNE-UP.
COULD YOU *PLEASE* STOP HITTING ME?
PRETTY PLEASE?
SUPER DOUBLE PRETTY PLEASE?
542356
HEY, VINNY. MY MAN! REMEMBER THE LAST TIME WE SAW EACH OTHER? YOU *CLOCKED* ME ONE, REMEMBER?
YEAH, SO?
I DO! IT WAS AMAZING SPIDER-MAN #567. DO I WIN A PRIZE? -WACKER

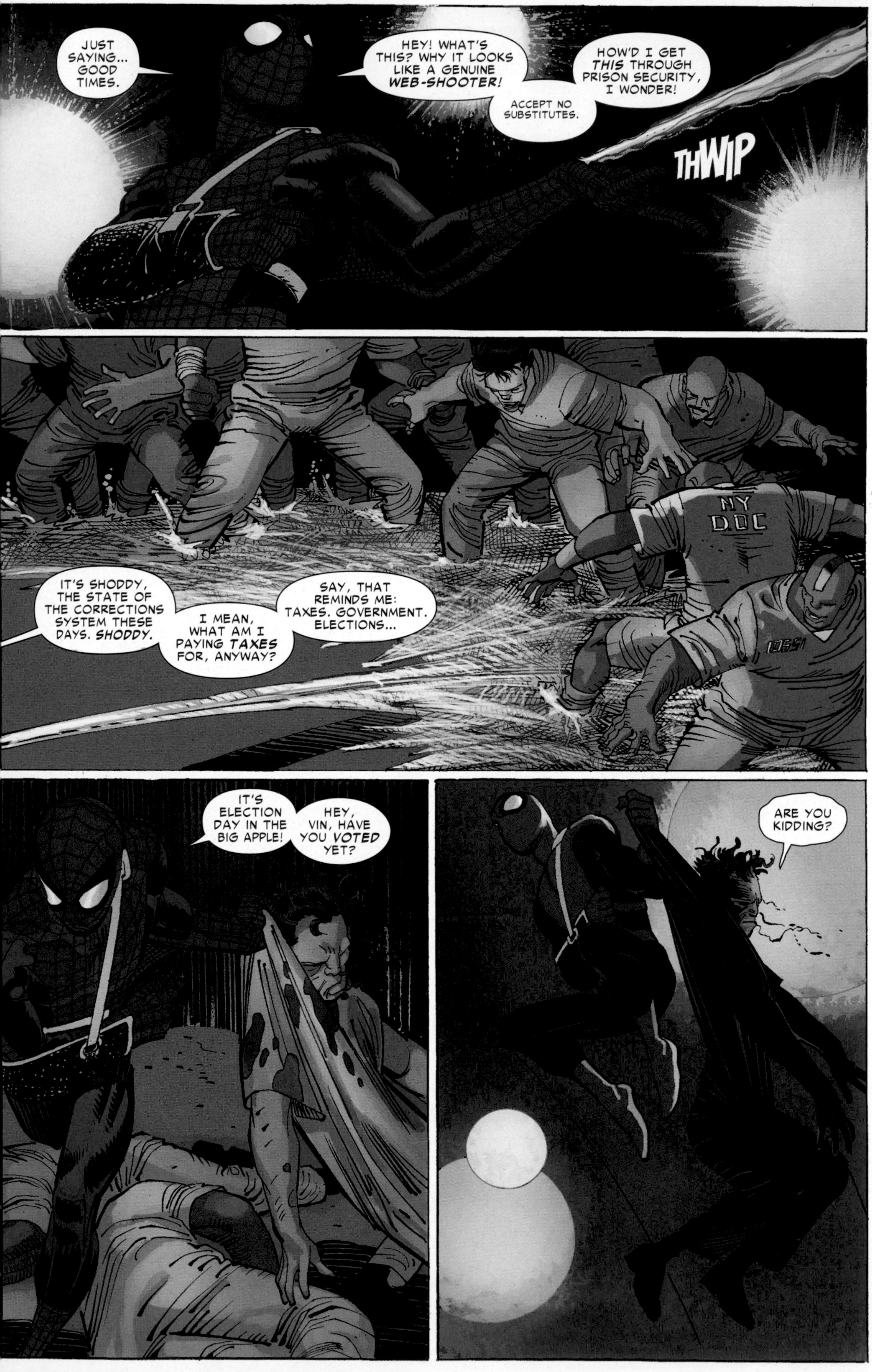

JUST SAYING... GOOD TIMES.
HEY! WHAT'S THIS? WHY IT LOOKS LIKE A GENUINE *WEB-SHOOTER*!
ACCEPT NO SUBSTITUTES.
HOW'D I GET *THIS* THROUGH PRISON SECURITY, I WONDER!
THWIP
NY D.O.C
IT'S SHODDY, THE STATE OF THE CORRECTIONS SYSTEM THESE DAYS. *SHODDY.*
I MEAN, WHAT AM I PAYING *TAXES* FOR, ANYWAY?
SAY, THAT REMINDS ME: TAXES. GOVERNMENT. ELECTIONS...
IT'S ELECTION DAY IN THE BIG APPLE!
HEY, VIN, HAVE YOU *VOTED* YET?
ARE YOU KIDDING?

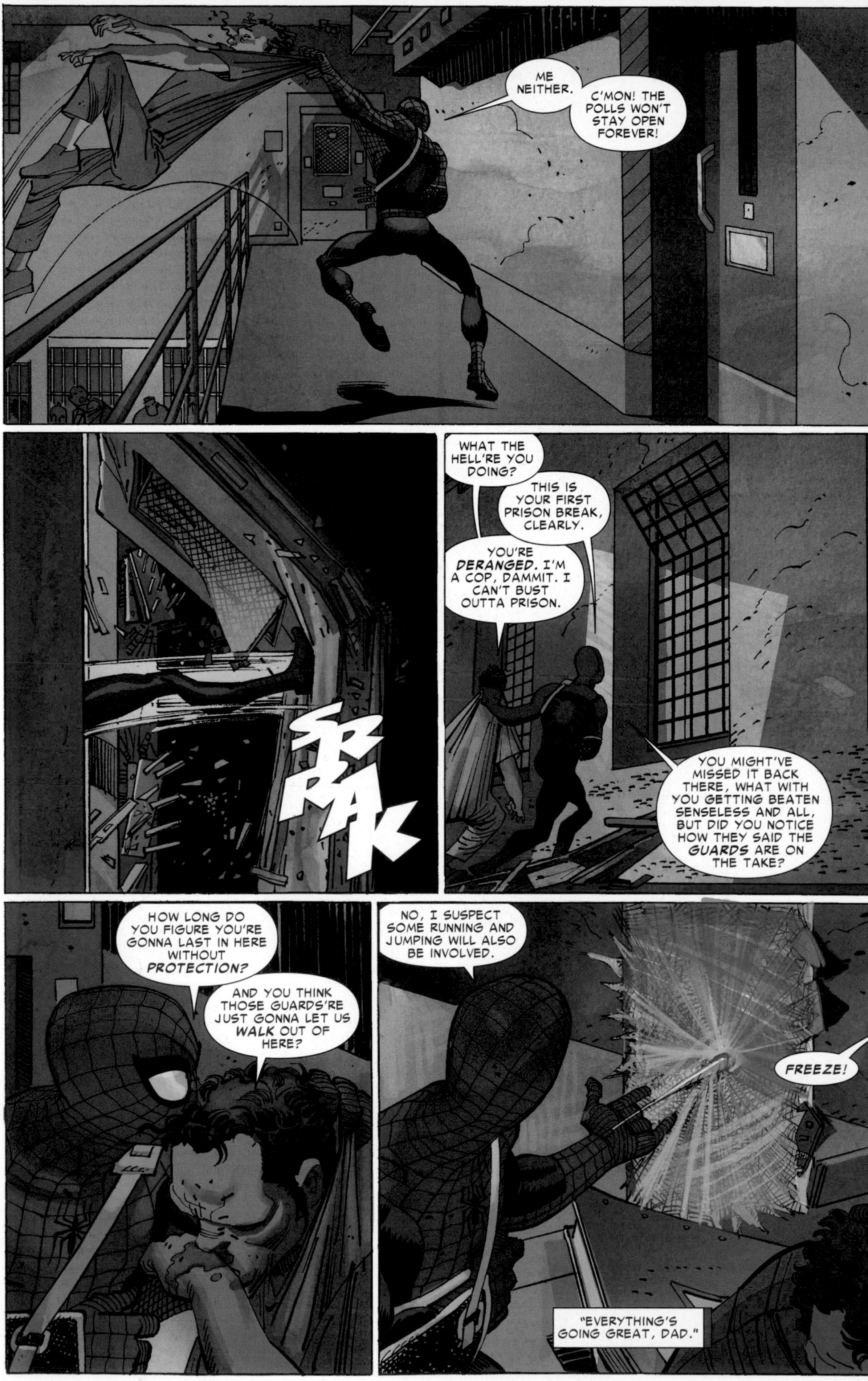
ME NEITHER.
C'MON! THE POLLS WON'T STAY OPEN FOREVER!
SRAK
WHAT THE HELL'RE YOU DOING?
THIS IS YOUR FIRST PRISON BREAK, CLEARLY.
YOU'RE DERANGED. I'M A COP, DAMMIT. I CAN'T BUST OUTTA PRISON.
YOU MIGHT'VE MISSED IT BACK THERE, WHAT WITH YOU GETTING BEATEN SENSELESS AND ALL, BUT DID YOU NOTICE HOW THEY SAID THE GUARDS ARE ON THE TAKE?
HOW LONG DO YOU FIGURE YOU'RE GONNA LAST IN HERE WITHOUT PROTECTION?
AND YOU THINK THOSE GUARDS'RE JUST GONNA LET US WALK OUT OF HERE?
NO, I SUSPECT SOME RUNNING AND JUMPING WILL ALSO BE INVOLVED.
FREEZE!
"EVERYTHING'S GOING GREAT, DAD."

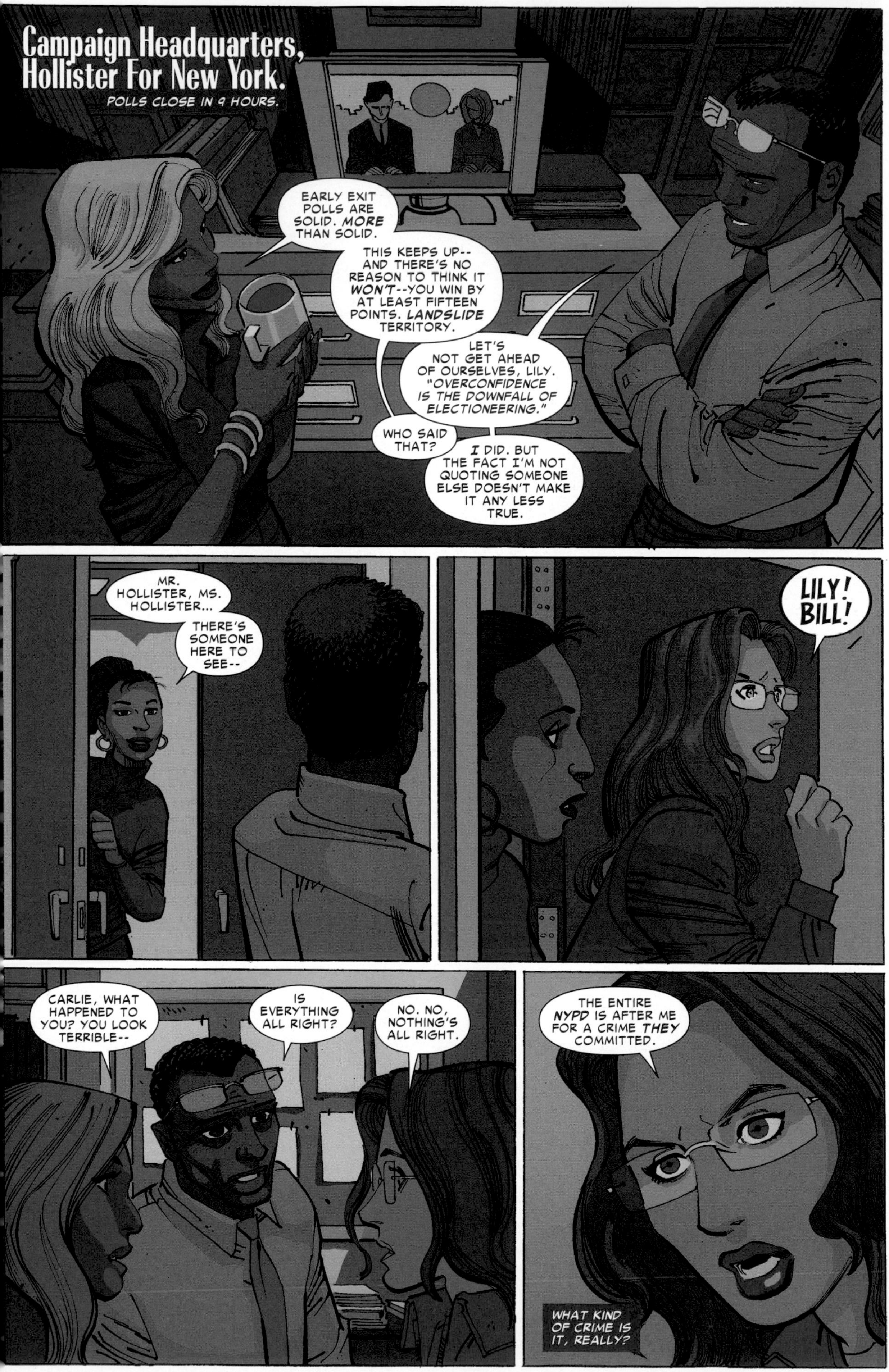
Campaign Headquarters, Hollister For New York.
POLLS CLOSE IN 9 HOURS.
EARLY EXIT POLLS ARE SOLID. MORE THAN SOLID.
THIS KEEPS UP-- AND THERE'S NO REASON TO THINK IT WON'T--YOU WIN BY AT LEAST FIFTEEN POINTS. LANDSLIDE TERRITORY.
LET'S NOT GET AHEAD OF OURSELVES, LILY. "OVERCONFIDENCE IS THE DOWNFALL OF ELECTIONEERING."
WHO SAID THAT?
I DID. BUT THE FACT I'M NOT QUOTING SOMEONE ELSE DOESN'T MAKE IT ANY LESS TRUE.
MR. HOLLISTER, MS. HOLLISTER...
THERE'S SOMEONE HERE TO SEE--
LILY! BILL!
CARLIE, WHAT HAPPENED TO YOU? YOU LOOK TERRIBLE--
IS EVERYTHING ALL RIGHT?
NO. NO, NOTHING'S ALL RIGHT.
THE ENTIRE NYPD IS AFTER ME FOR A CRIME THEY COMMITTED.
WHAT KIND OF CRIME IS IT, REALLY?

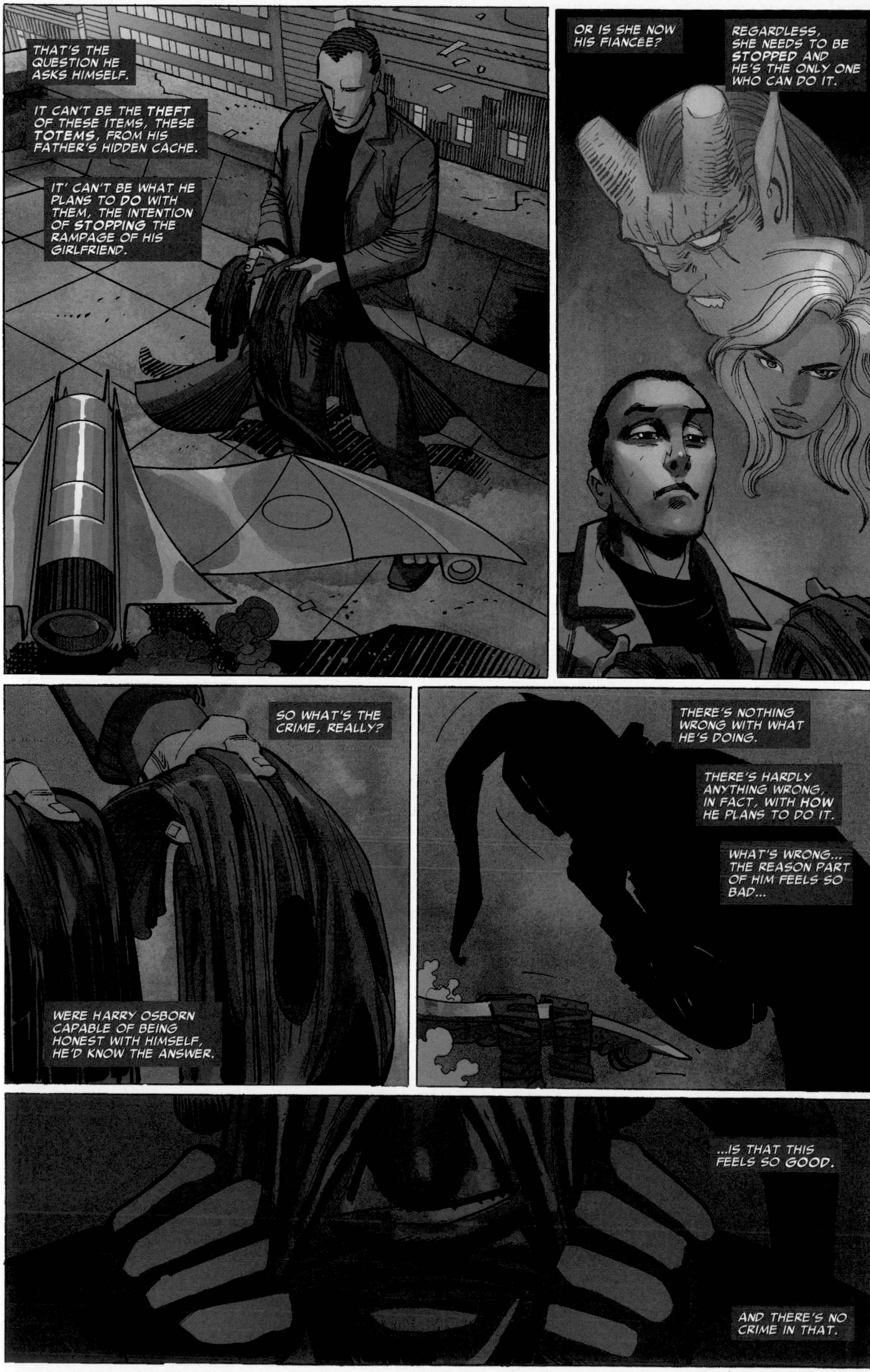
THAT'S THE QUESTION HE ASKS HIMSELF.
IT CAN'T BE THE THEFT OF THESE ITEMS, THESE TOTEMS, FROM HIS FATHER'S HIDDEN CACHE.
IT' CAN'T BE WHAT HE PLANS TO DO WITH THEM, THE INTENTION OF STOPPING THE RAMPAGE OF HIS GIRLFRIEND.
OR IS SHE NOW HIS FIANCEE?
REGARDLESS, SHE NEEDS TO BE STOPPED AND HE'S THE ONLY ONE WHO CAN DO IT.
SO WHAT'S THE CRIME, REALLY?
WERE HARRY OSBORN CAPABLE OF BEING HONEST WITH HIMSELF, HE'D KNOW THE ANSWER.
THERE'S NOTHING WRONG WITH WHAT HE'S DOING.
THERE'S HARDLY ANYTHING WRONG, IN FACT, WITH HOW HE PLANS TO DO IT.
WHAT'S WRONG... THE REASON PART OF HIM FEELS SO BAD...
...IS THAT THIS FEELS SO GOOD.
AND THERE'S NO CRIME IN THAT.

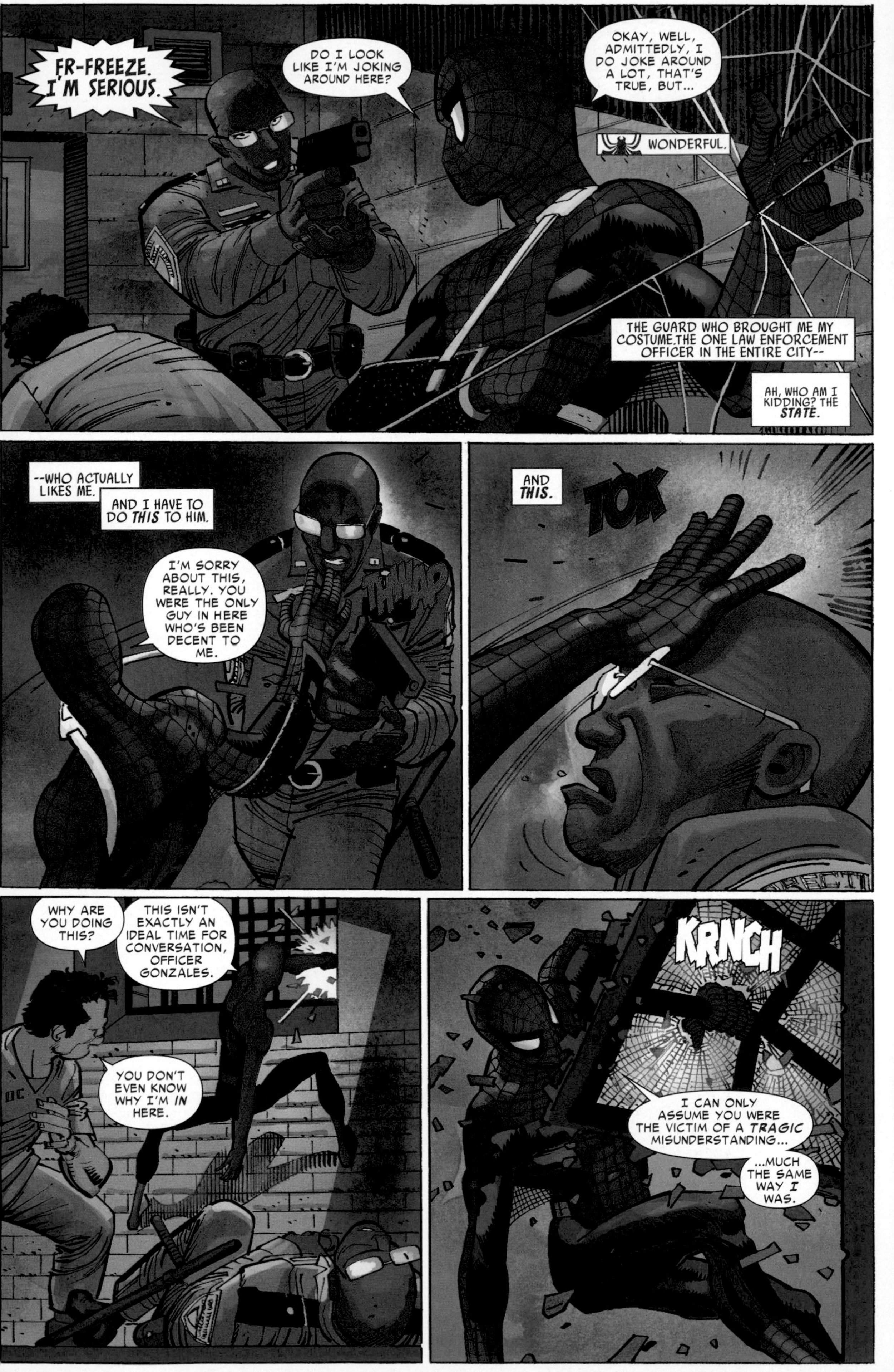
FR-FREEZE. I'M SERIOUS.
DO I LOOK LIKE I'M JOKING AROUND HERE?
OKAY, WELL, ADMITTEDLY, I DO JOKE AROUND A LOT, THAT'S TRUE, BUT...
WONDERFUL.
THE GUARD WHO BROUGHT ME MY COSTUME.THE ONE LAW ENFORCEMENT OFFICER IN THE ENTIRE CITY--
AH, WHO AM I KIDDING? THE STATE.
--WHO ACTUALLY LIKES ME.
AND I HAVE TO DO THIS TO HIM.
I'M SORRY ABOUT THIS, REALLY. YOU WERE THE ONLY GUY IN HERE WHO'S BEEN DECENT TO ME.
THWAP
AND THIS.
TOK
WHY ARE YOU DOING THIS?
THIS ISN'T EXACTLY AN IDEAL TIME FOR CONVERSATION, OFFICER GONZALES.
YOU DON'T EVEN KNOW WHY I'M IN HERE.
KRNCH
I CAN ONLY ASSUME YOU WERE THE VICTIM OF A TRAGIC MISUNDERSTANDING...
...MUCH THE SAME WAY I WAS.

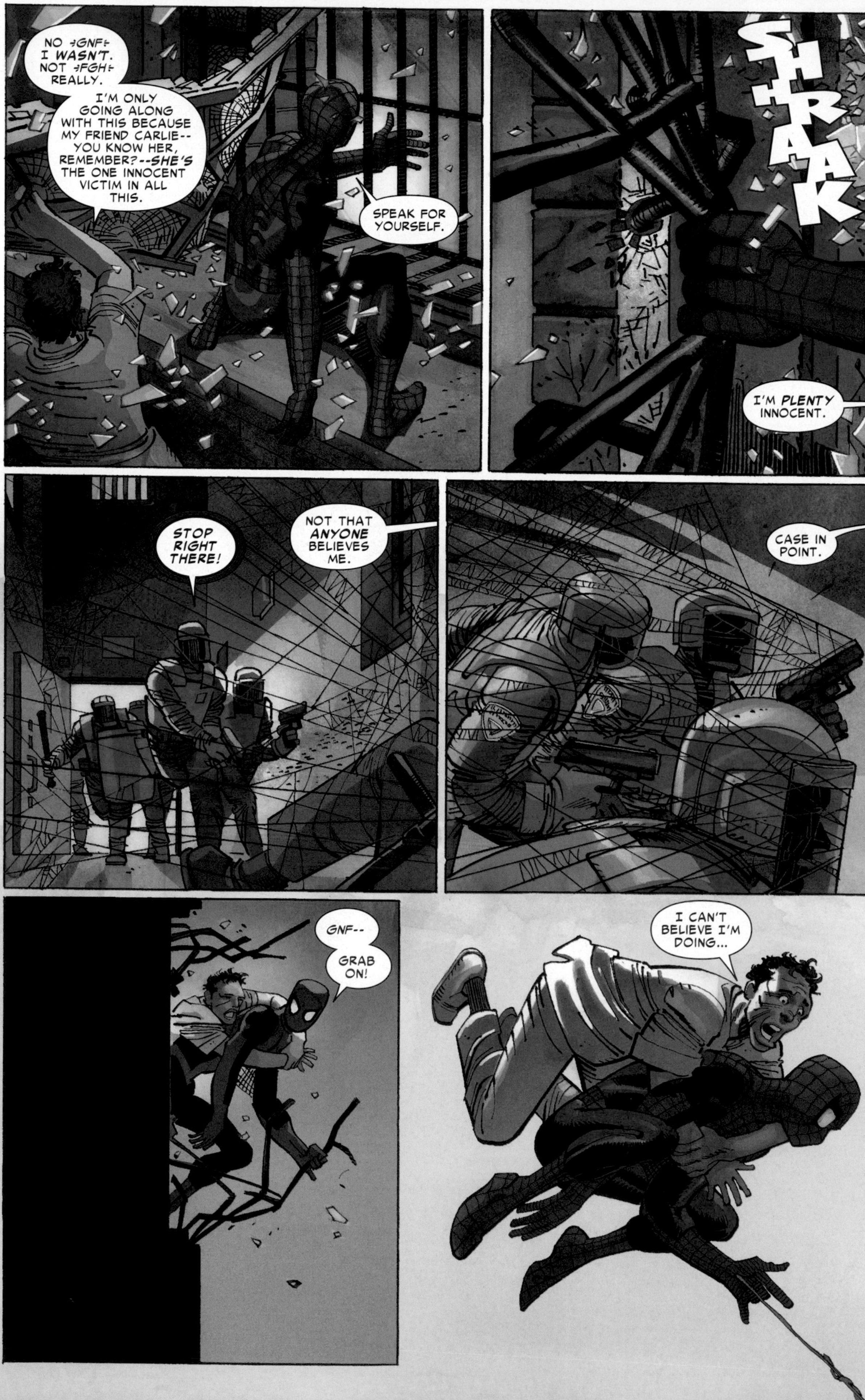
NO ⸗GNF⸗ I WASN'T. NOT ⸗FGH⸗ REALLY.
I'M ONLY GOING ALONG WITH THIS BECAUSE MY FRIEND CARLIE-- YOU KNOW HER, REMEMBER?--SHE'S THE ONE INNOCENT VICTIM IN ALL THIS.
SPEAK FOR YOURSELF.
SHRAK
I'M PLENTY INNOCENT.
STOP RIGHT THERE!
NOT THAT ANYONE BELIEVES ME.
CASE IN POINT.
GNF--
GRAB ON!
I CAN'T BELIEVE I'M DOING...

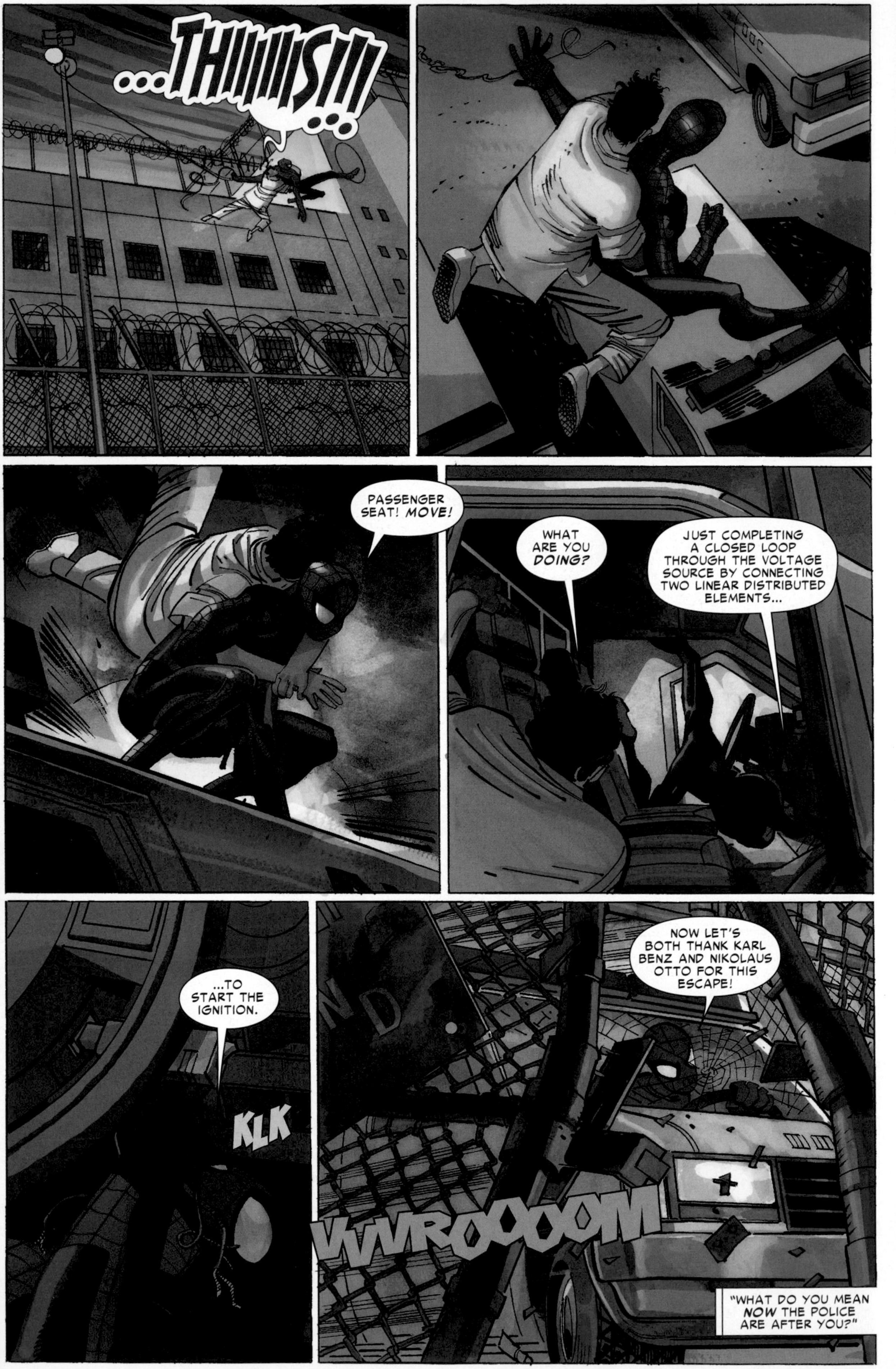
...THWWWSH!!
..!!
PASSENGER SEAT! MOVE!
WHAT ARE YOU DOING?
JUST COMPLETING A CLOSED LOOP THROUGH THE VOLTAGE SOURCE BY CONNECTING TWO LINEAR DISTRIBUTED ELEMENTS...
...TO START THE IGNITION.
KLK
NOW LET'S BOTH THANK KARL BENZ AND NIKOLAUS OTTO FOR THIS ESCAPE!
VVVROOOOOM
"WHAT DO YOU MEAN NOW THE POLICE ARE AFTER YOU?"

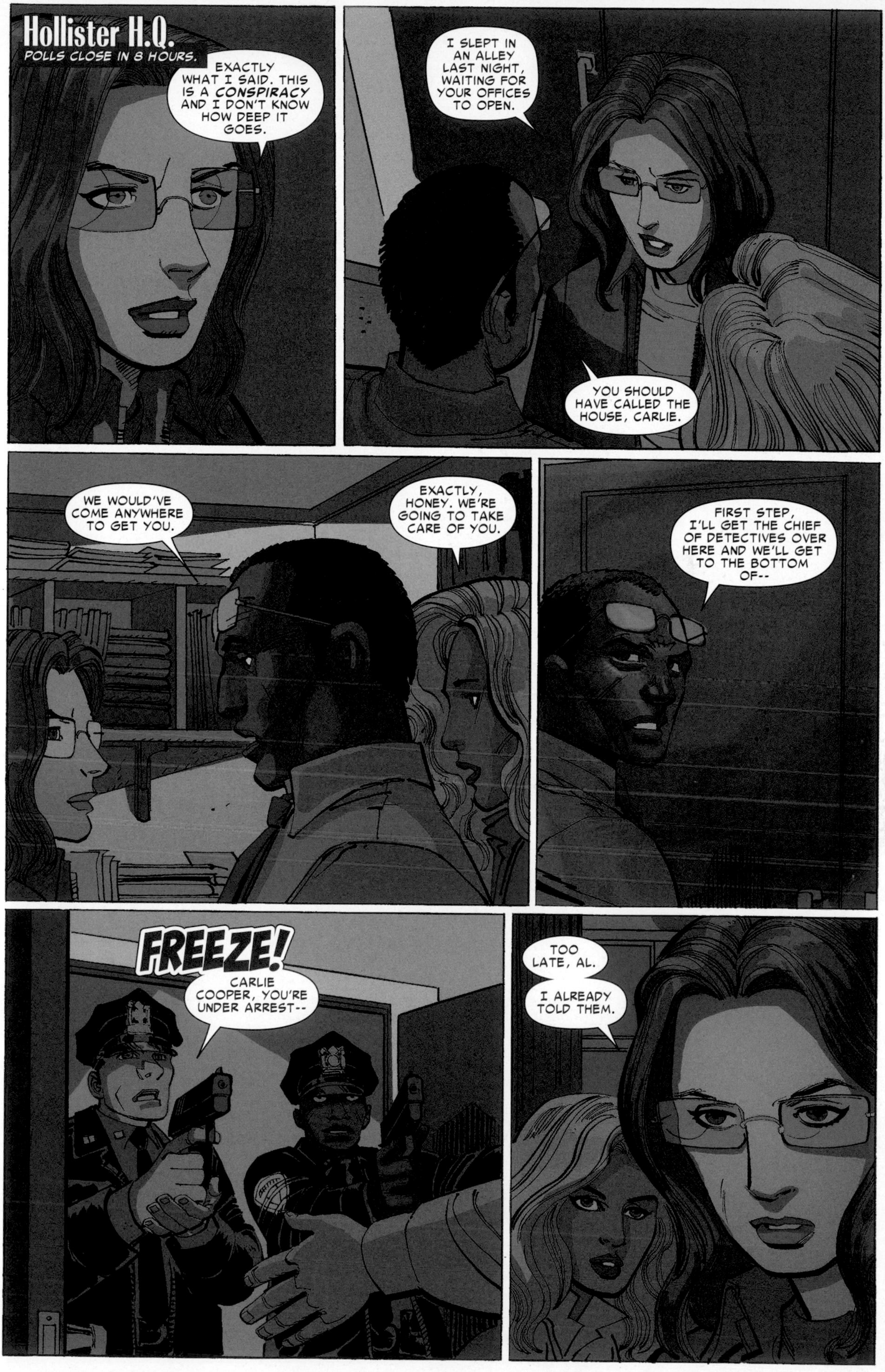
Hollister H.Q.
POLLS CLOSE IN 8 HOURS.
EXACTLY WHAT I SAID. THIS IS A CONSPIRACY AND I DON'T KNOW HOW DEEP IT GOES.
I SLEPT IN AN ALLEY LAST NIGHT, WAITING FOR YOUR OFFICES TO OPEN.
YOU SHOULD HAVE CALLED THE HOUSE, CARLIE.
WE WOULD'VE COME ANYWHERE TO GET YOU.
EXACTLY, HONEY. WE'RE GOING TO TAKE CARE OF YOU.
FIRST STEP, I'LL GET THE CHIEF OF DETECTIVES OVER HERE AND WE'LL GET TO THE BOTTOM OF--
FREEZE!
CARLIE COOPER, YOU'RE UNDER ARREST--
TOO LATE, AL.
I ALREADY TOLD THEM.

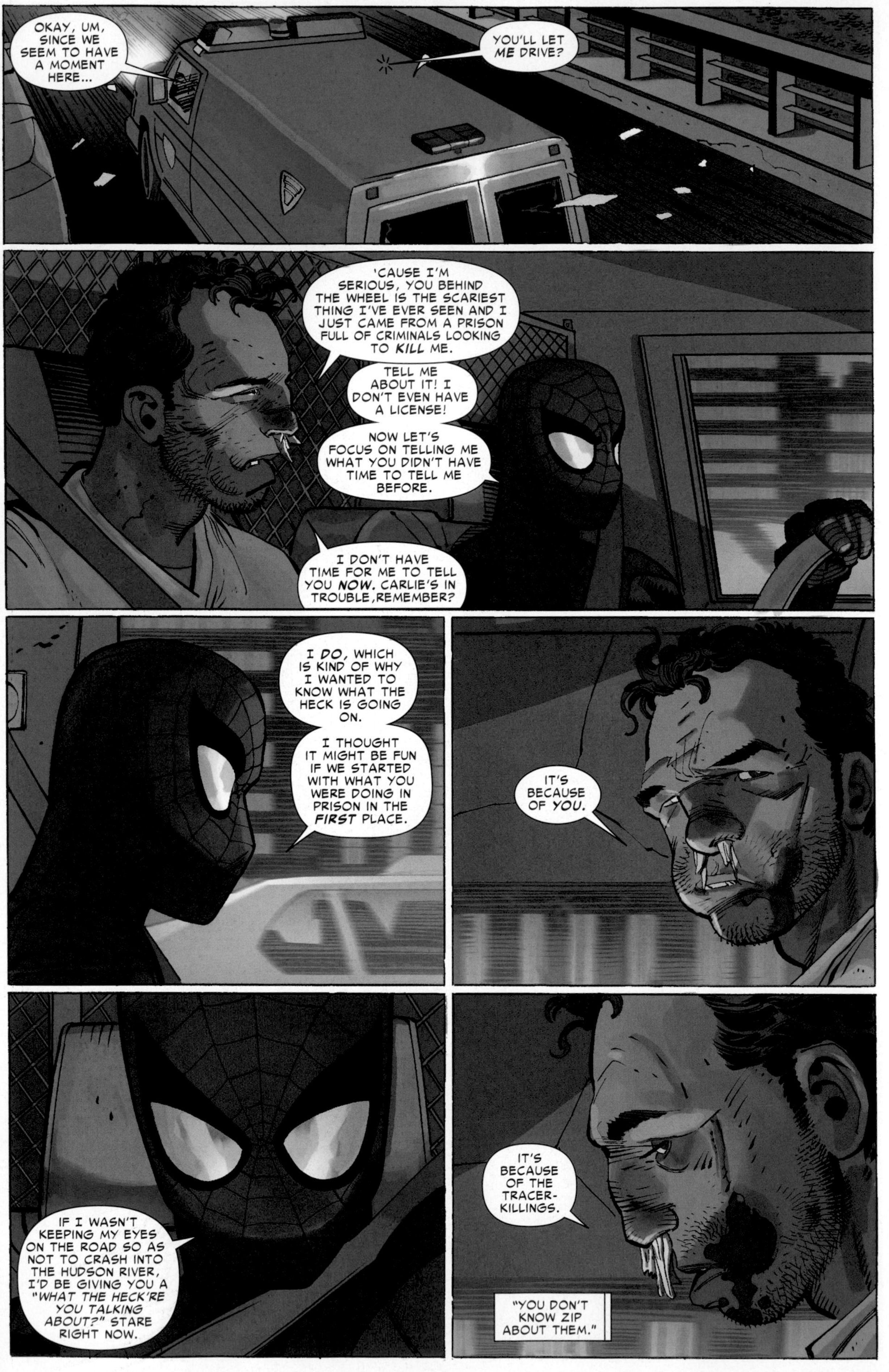
OKAY, UM, SINCE WE SEEM TO HAVE A MOMENT HERE...
YOU'LL LET ME DRIVE?
'CAUSE I'M SERIOUS, YOU BEHIND THE WHEEL IS THE SCARIEST THING I'VE EVER SEEN AND I JUST CAME FROM A PRISON FULL OF CRIMINALS LOOKING TO KILL ME.
TELL ME ABOUT IT! I DON'T EVEN HAVE A LICENSE!
NOW LET'S FOCUS ON TELLING ME WHAT YOU DIDN'T HAVE TIME TO TELL ME BEFORE.
I DON'T HAVE TIME FOR ME TO TELL YOU NOW. CARLIE'S IN TROUBLE, REMEMBER?
I DO, WHICH IS KIND OF WHY I WANTED TO KNOW WHAT THE HECK IS GOING ON.
I THOUGHT IT MIGHT BE FUN IF WE STARTED WITH WHAT YOU WERE DOING IN PRISON IN THE FIRST PLACE.
IT'S BECAUSE OF YOU.
IF I WASN'T KEEPING MY EYES ON THE ROAD SO AS NOT TO CRASH INTO THE HUDSON RIVER, I'D BE GIVING YOU A "WHAT THE HECK'RE YOU TALKING ABOUT?" STARE RIGHT NOW.
IT'S BECAUSE OF THE TRACER-KILLINGS.
"YOU DON'T KNOW ZIP ABOUT THEM."

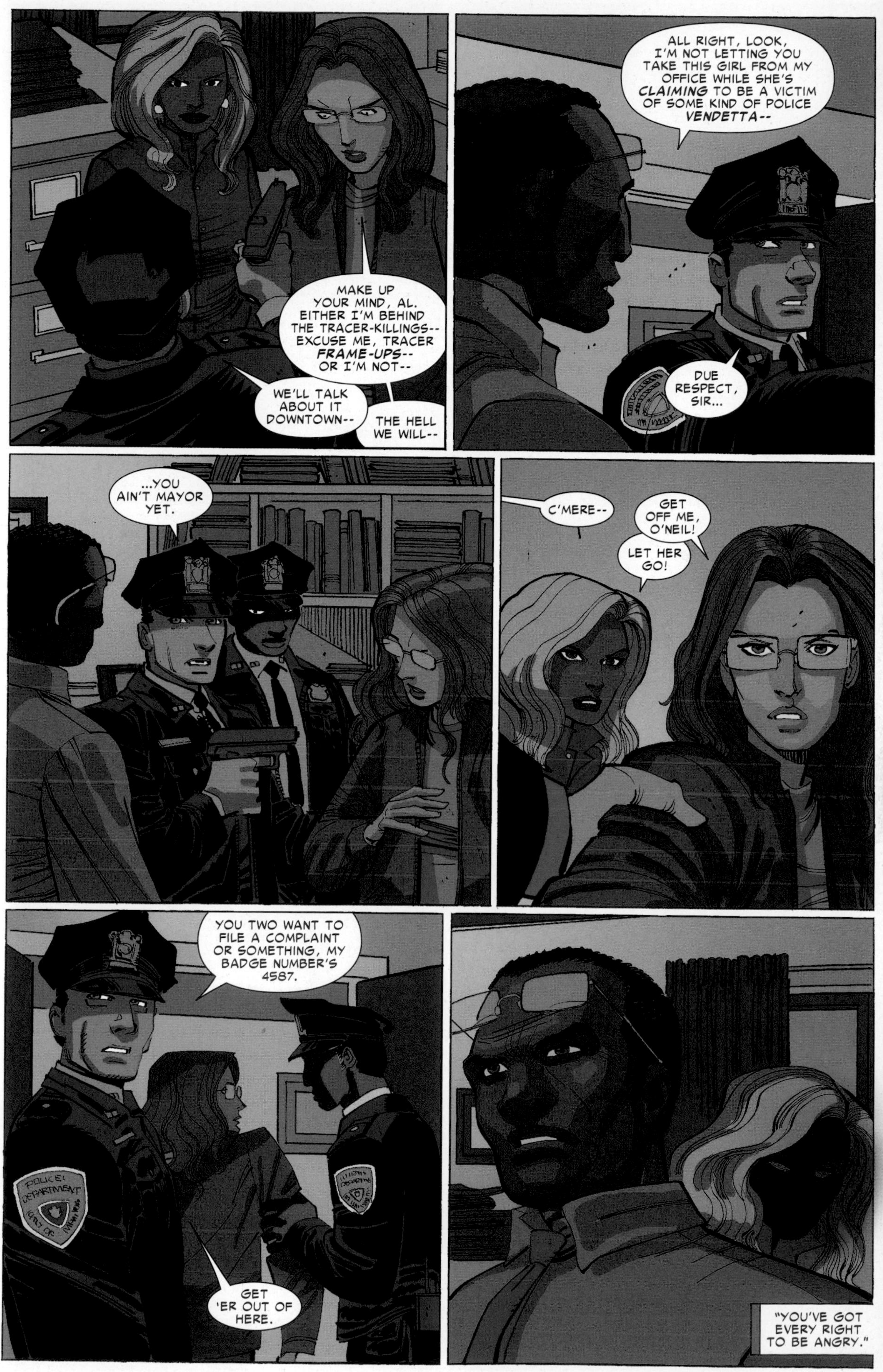
MAKE UP YOUR MIND, AL. EITHER I'M BEHIND THE TRACER-KILLINGS-- EXCUSE ME, TRACER FRAME-UPS-- OR I'M NOT--
WE'LL TALK ABOUT IT DOWNTOWN--
THE HELL WE WILL--
ALL RIGHT, LOOK, I'M NOT LETTING YOU TAKE THIS GIRL FROM MY OFFICE WHILE SHE'S CLAIMING TO BE A VICTIM OF SOME KIND OF POLICE VENDETTA--
DUE RESPECT, SIR...
...YOU AIN'T MAYOR YET.
C'MERE--
GET OFF ME, O'NEIL!
LET HER GO!
YOU TWO WANT TO FILE A COMPLAINT OR SOMETHING, MY BADGE NUMBER'S 4587.
GET 'ER OUT OF HERE.
"YOU'VE GOT EVERY RIGHT TO BE ANGRY."

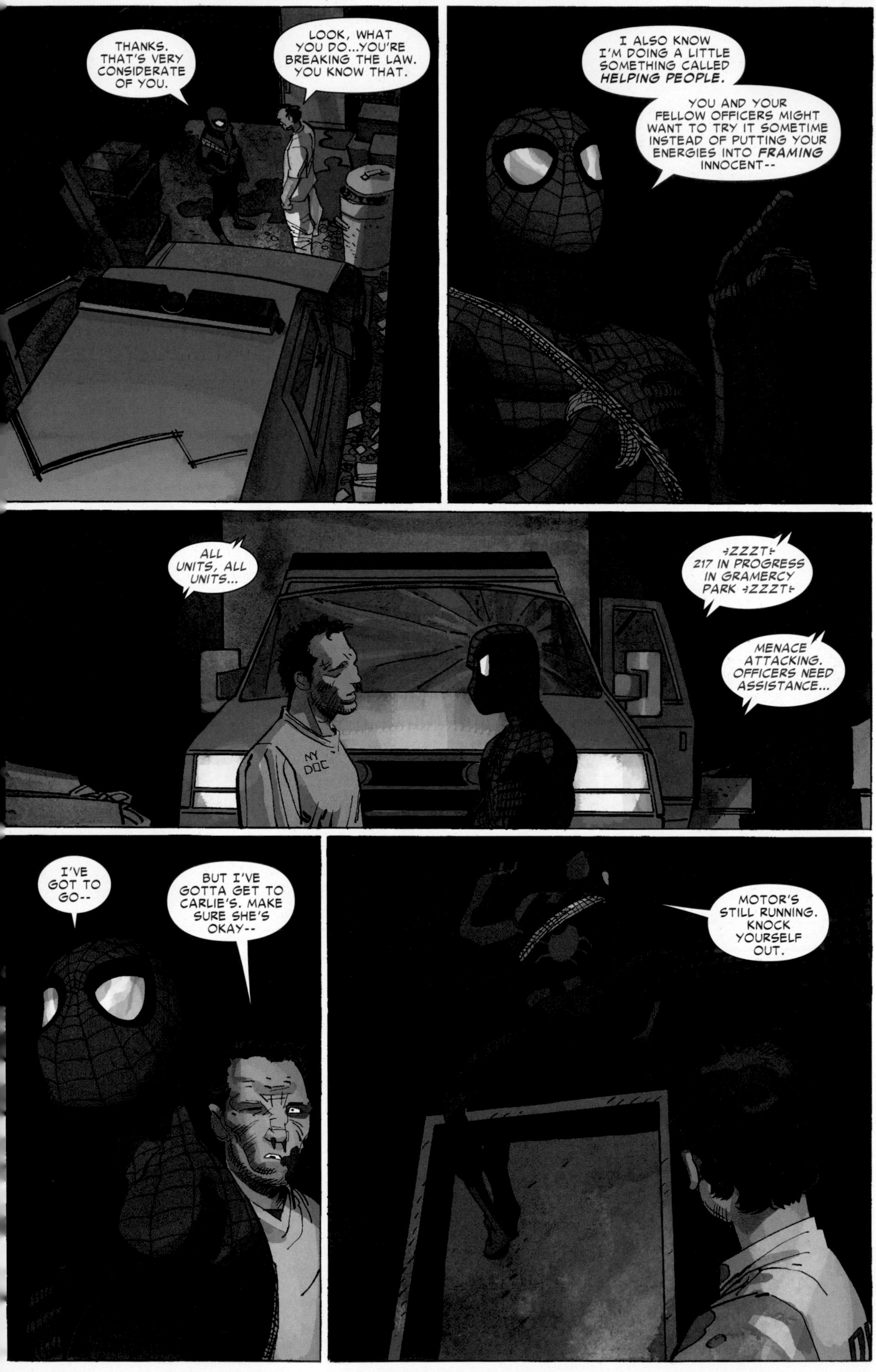
THANKS. THAT'S VERY CONSIDERATE OF YOU.
LOOK, WHAT YOU DO...YOU'RE BREAKING THE LAW. YOU KNOW THAT.
I ALSO KNOW I'M DOING A LITTLE SOMETHING CALLED *HELPING PEOPLE.*
YOU AND YOUR FELLOW OFFICERS MIGHT WANT TO TRY IT SOMETIME INSTEAD OF PUTTING YOUR ENERGIES INTO *FRAMING* INNOCENT--
ALL UNITS, ALL UNITS...
÷ZZZT÷ 217 IN PROGRESS IN GRAMERCY PARK ÷ZZZT÷
MENACE ATTACKING. OFFICERS NEED ASSISTANCE...
NY DOC
I'VE GOT TO GO--
BUT I'VE GOTTA GET TO CARLIE'S. MAKE SURE SHE'S OKAY--
MOTOR'S STILL RUNNING. KNOCK YOURSELF OUT.

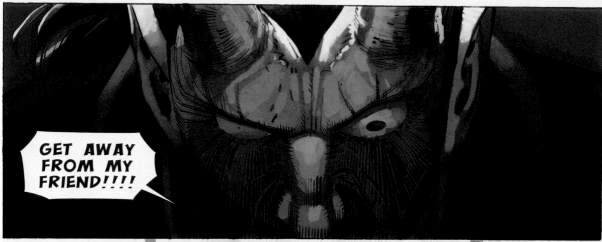

GET AWAY FROM MY FRIEND!!!!

Outside Hollister H.Q.

WHERE THE HELL DID HE COME FROM?!

WHOEVER YOU ARE, MENACE, WE ARE SO *NOT* FRIENDS.

DOESN'T MEAN I'M NOT *GRATEFUL* FOR THE DISTRACTION, THOUGH...

...OR FOR THE CHANCE TO GRAB THOSE KEYS OFF AL'S BELT...

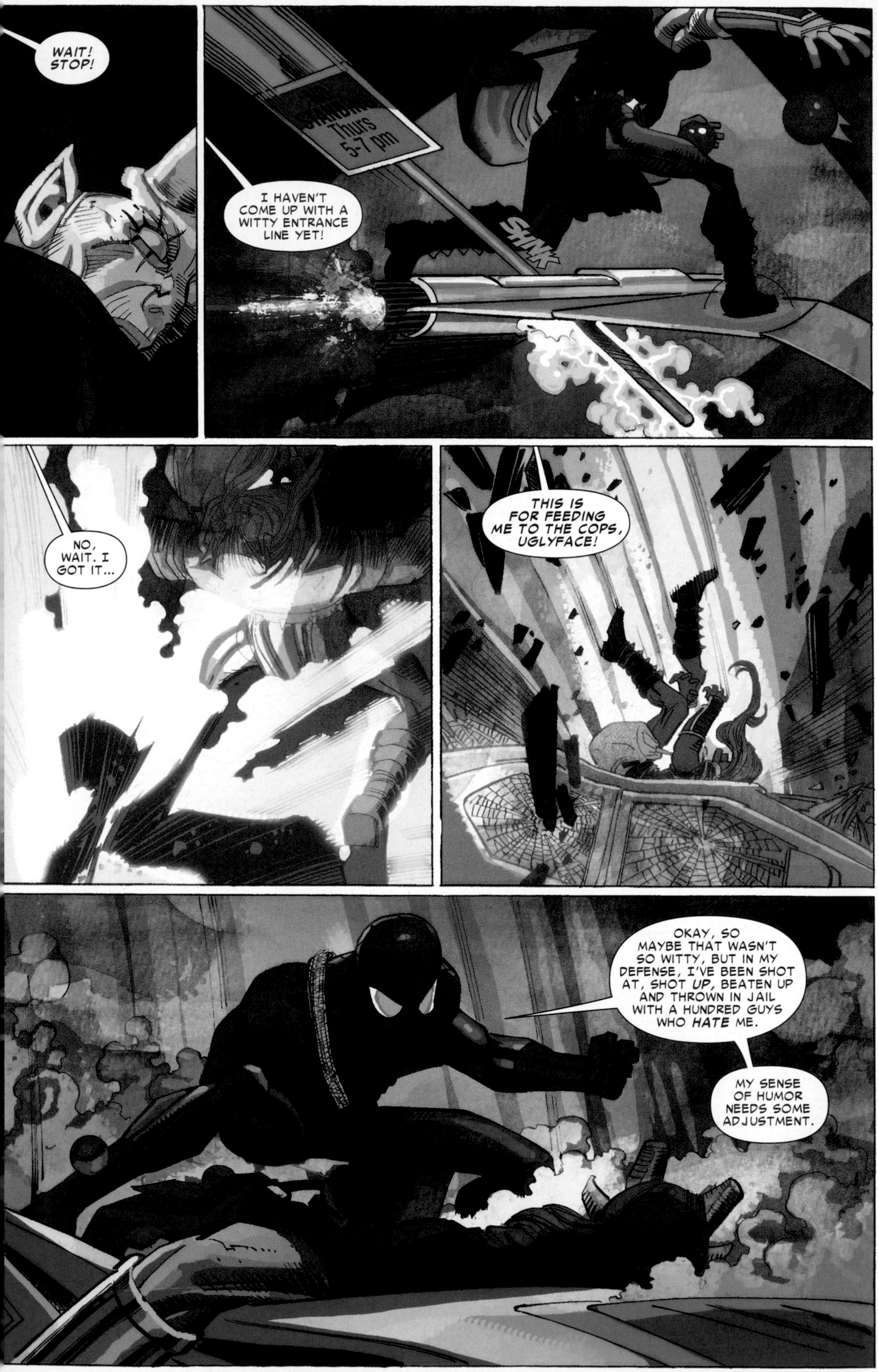

WAIT! STOP!
Thurs 5-7 pm
I HAVEN'T COME UP WITH A WITTY ENTRANCE LINE YET!
SHNK
NO, WAIT. I GOT IT...
THIS IS FOR FEEDING ME TO THE COPS, UGLYFACE!
OKAY, SO MAYBE THAT WASN'T SO WITTY, BUT IN MY DEFENSE, I'VE BEEN SHOT AT, SHOT UP, BEATEN UP AND THROWN IN JAIL WITH A HUNDRED GUYS WHO HATE ME.
MY SENSE OF HUMOR NEEDS SOME ADJUSTMENT.

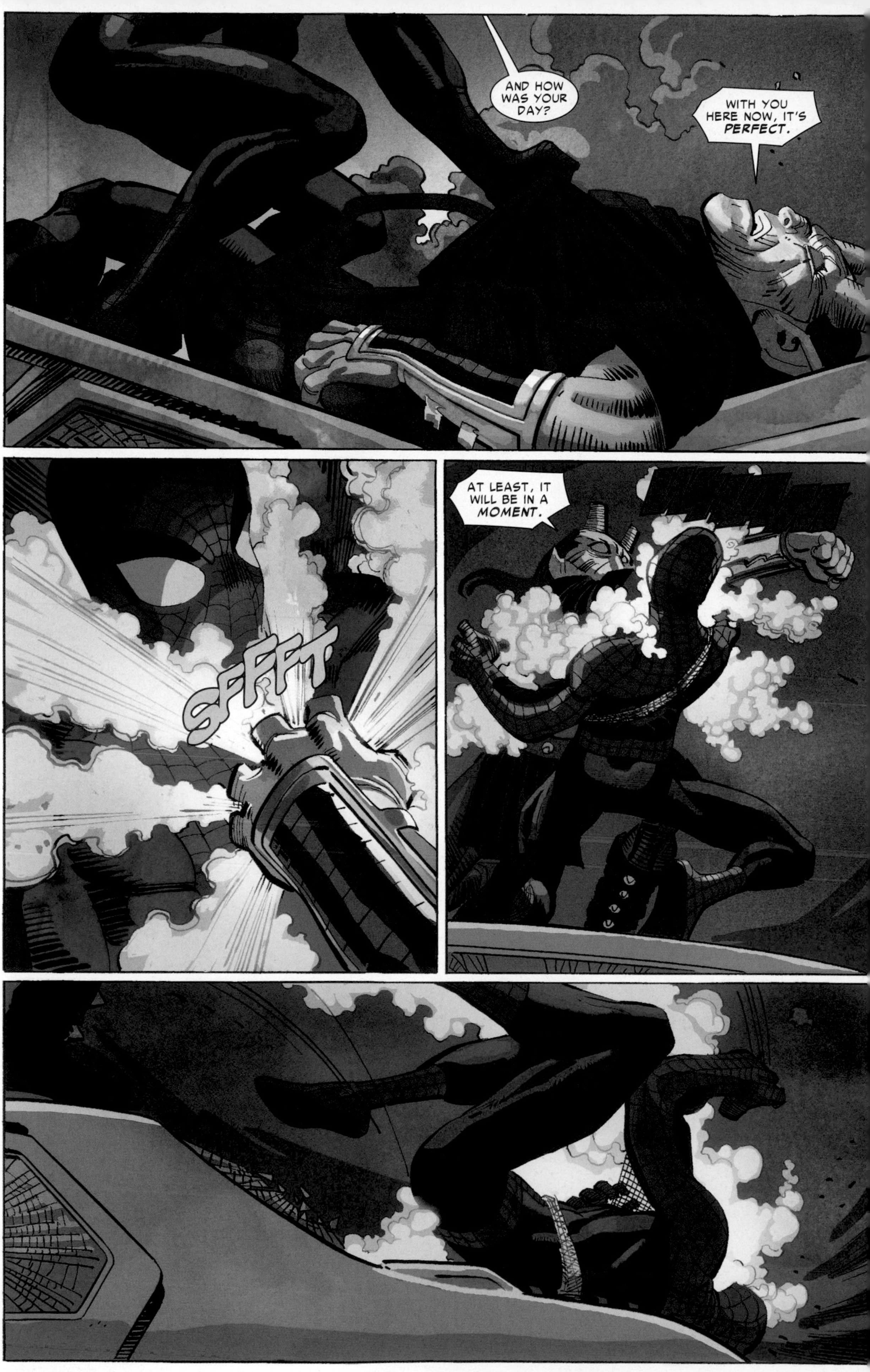
AND HOW WAS YOUR DAY?
WITH YOU HERE NOW, IT'S PERFECT.
SFFFT
AT LEAST, IT WILL BE IN A MOMENT.

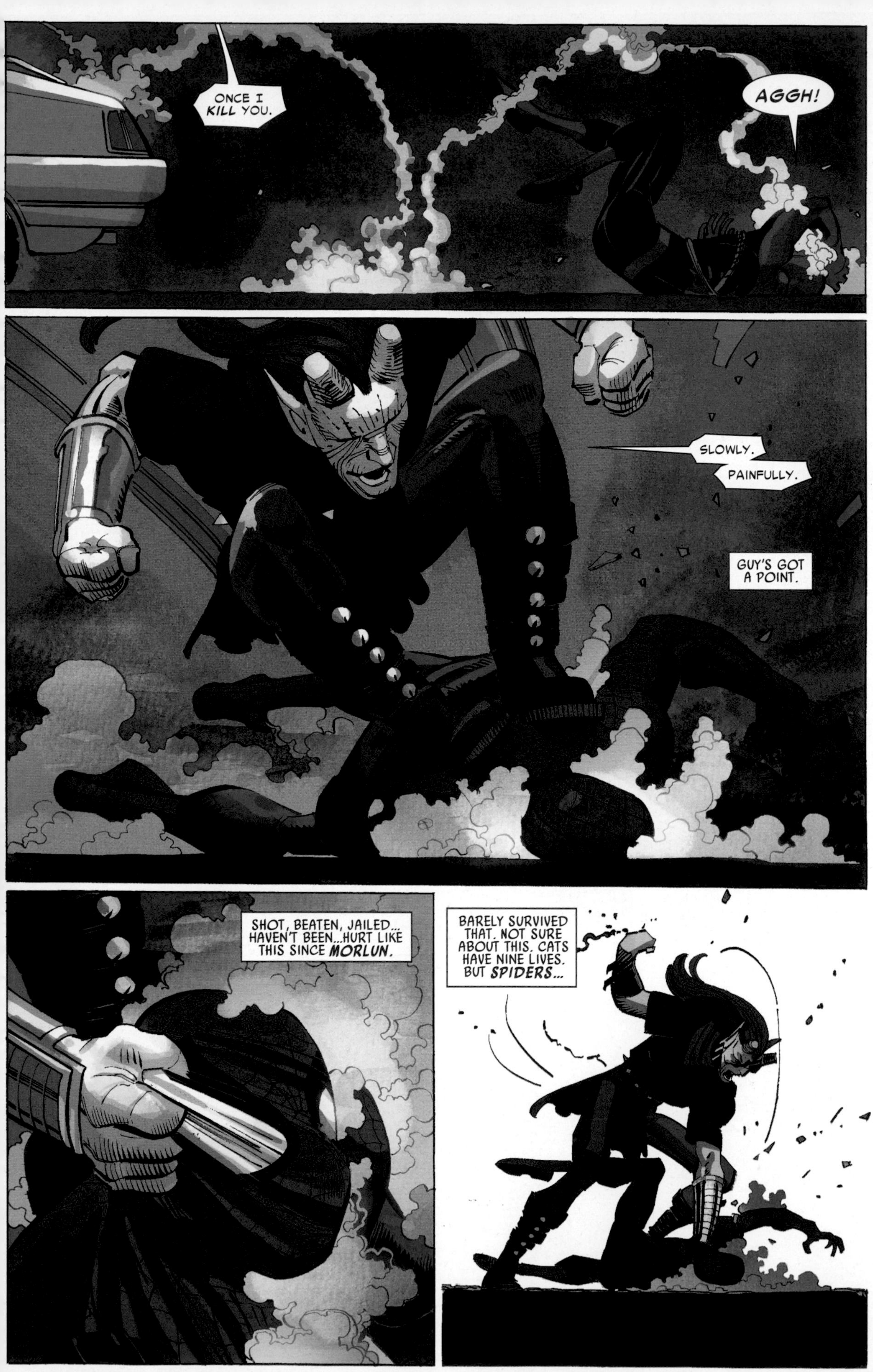
ONCE I KILL YOU.
AGGH!
SLOWLY.
PAINFULLY.
GUY'S GOT A POINT.
SHOT, BEATEN, JAILED... HAVEN'T BEEN...HURT LIKE THIS SINCE MORLUN.
BARELY SURVIVED THAT. NOT SURE ABOUT THIS. CATS HAVE NINE LIVES. BUT SPIDERS...

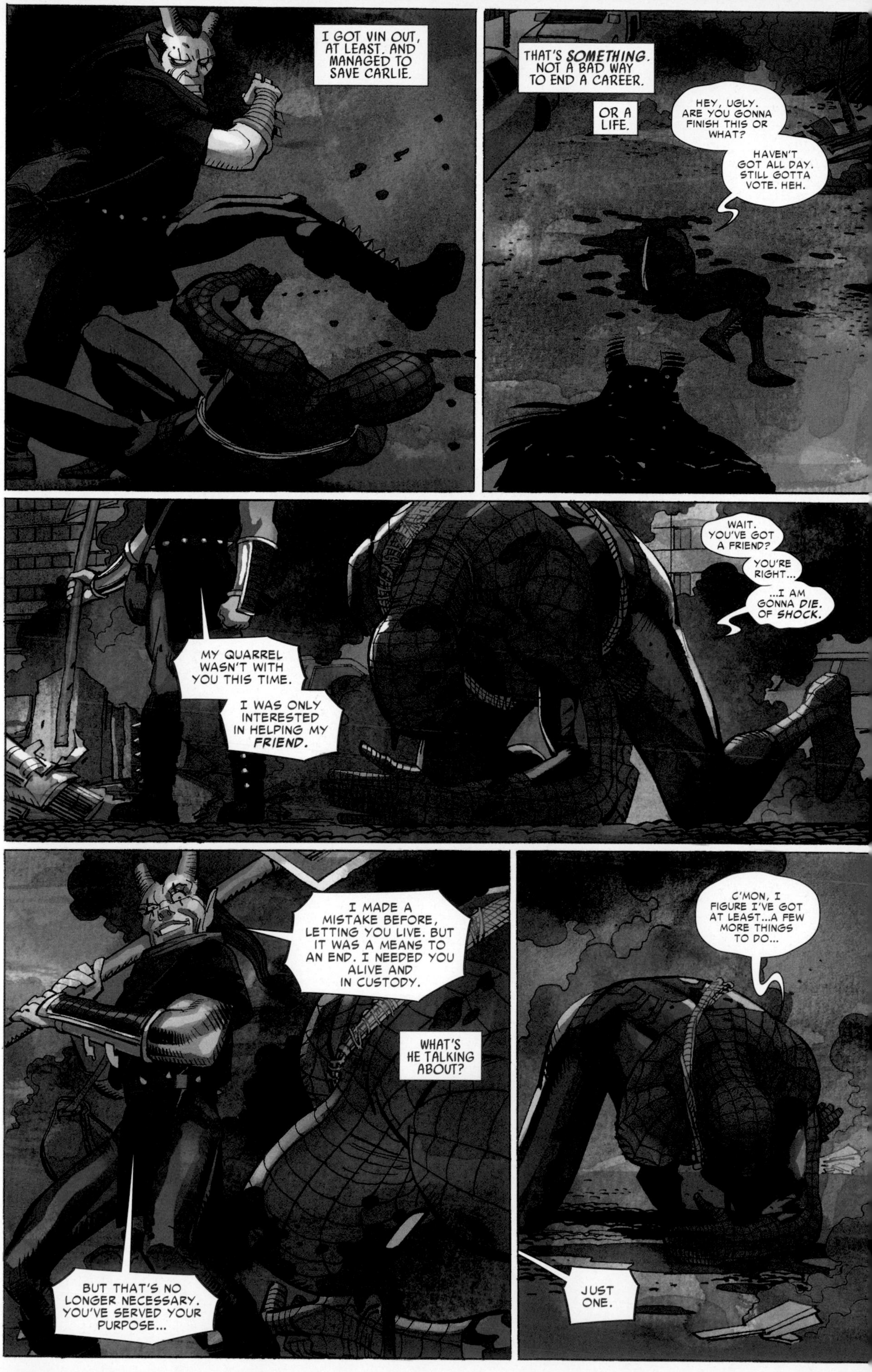
I GOT VIN OUT, AT LEAST. AND MANAGED TO SAVE CARLIE.
THAT'S SOMETHING. NOT A BAD WAY TO END A CAREER.
OR A LIFE.
HEY, UGLY. ARE YOU GONNA FINISH THIS OR WHAT?
HAVEN'T GOT ALL DAY. STILL GOTTA VOTE. HEH.
MY QUARREL WASN'T WITH YOU THIS TIME.
I WAS ONLY INTERESTED IN HELPING MY FRIEND.
WAIT. YOU'VE GOT A FRIEND?
YOU'RE RIGHT...
...I AM GONNA DIE. OF SHOCK.
I MADE A MISTAKE BEFORE, LETTING YOU LIVE. BUT IT WAS A MEANS TO AN END. I NEEDED YOU ALIVE AND IN CUSTODY.
WHAT'S HE TALKING ABOUT?
BUT THAT'S NO LONGER NECESSARY. YOU'VE SERVED YOUR PURPOSE...
C'MON, I FIGURE I'VE GOT AT LEAST...A FEW MORE THINGS TO DO...
JUST ONE.

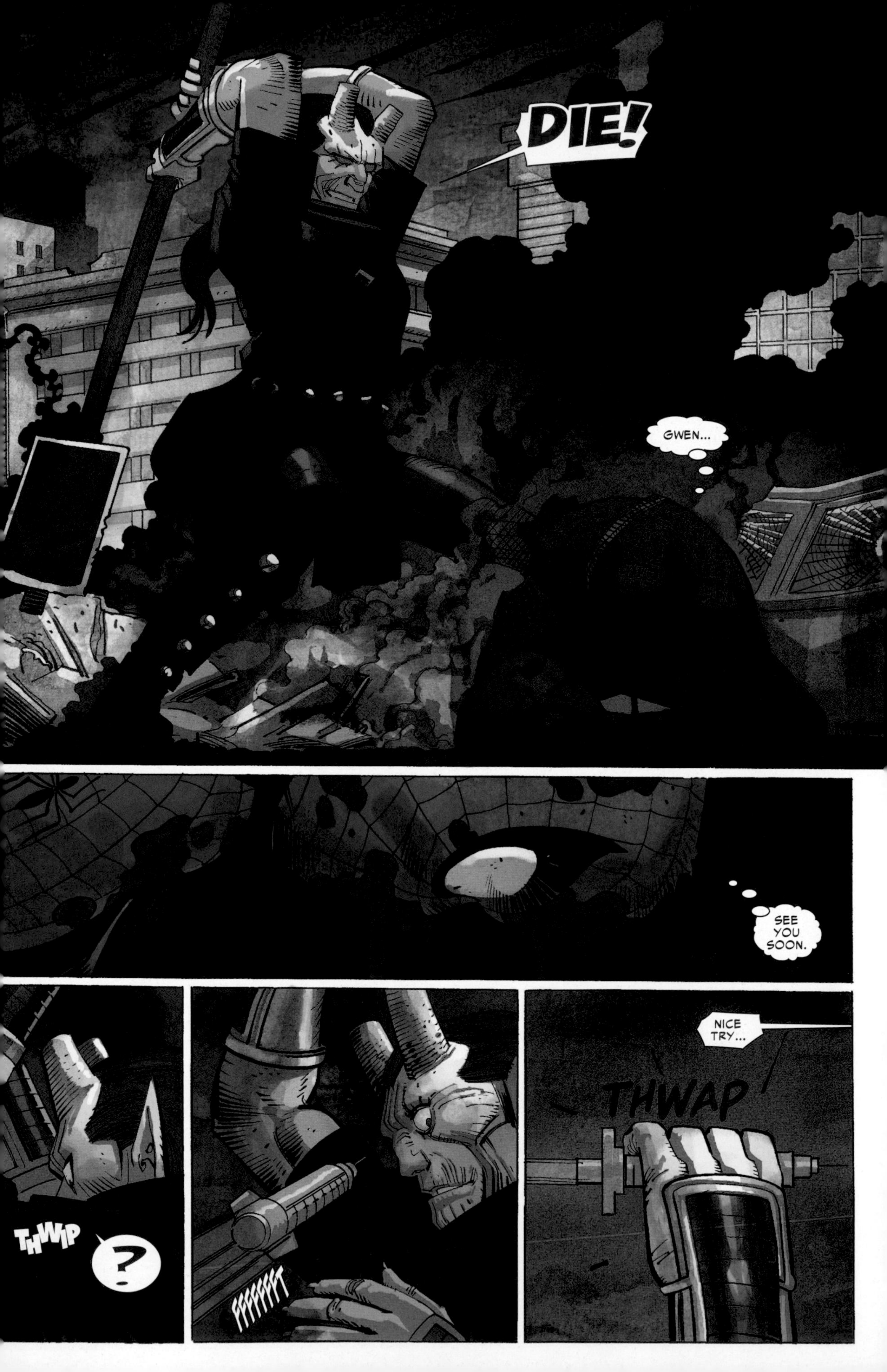
DIE!
GWEN...
SEE YOU SOON.
THWIP
?
FFFFFFFT
NICE TRY...
THWAP

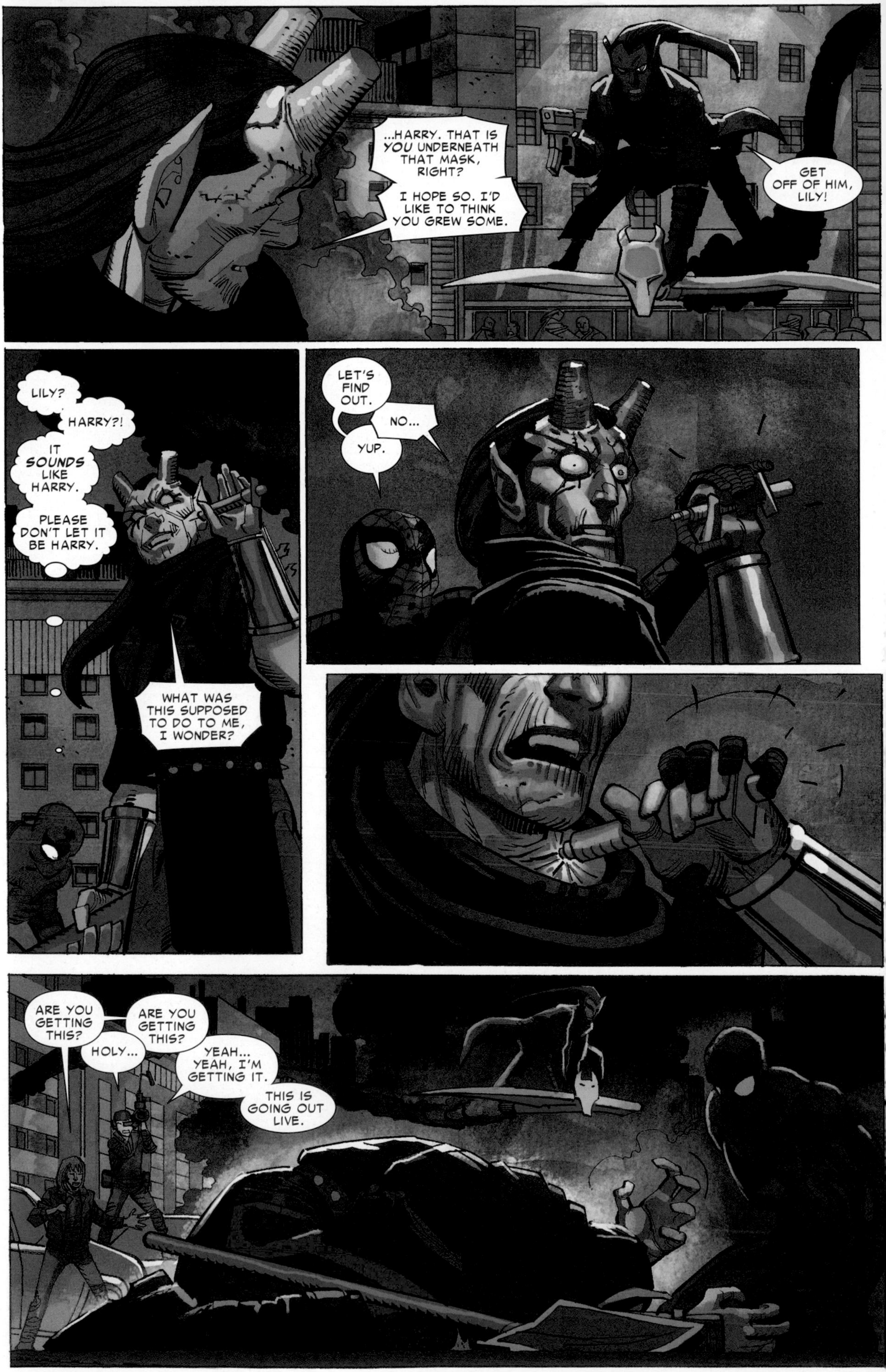

...HARRY. THAT IS YOU UNDERNEATH THAT MASK, RIGHT?
I HOPE SO. I'D LIKE TO THINK YOU GREW SOME.
GET OFF OF HIM, LILY!
LILY?
HARRY?!
IT SOUNDS LIKE HARRY.
PLEASE DON'T LET IT BE HARRY.
WHAT WAS THIS SUPPOSED TO DO TO ME, I WONDER?
LET'S FIND OUT.
NO...
YUP.
ARE YOU GETTING THIS?
ARE YOU GETTING THIS?
HOLY...
YEAH... YEAH, I'M GETTING IT.
THIS IS GOING OUT LIVE.

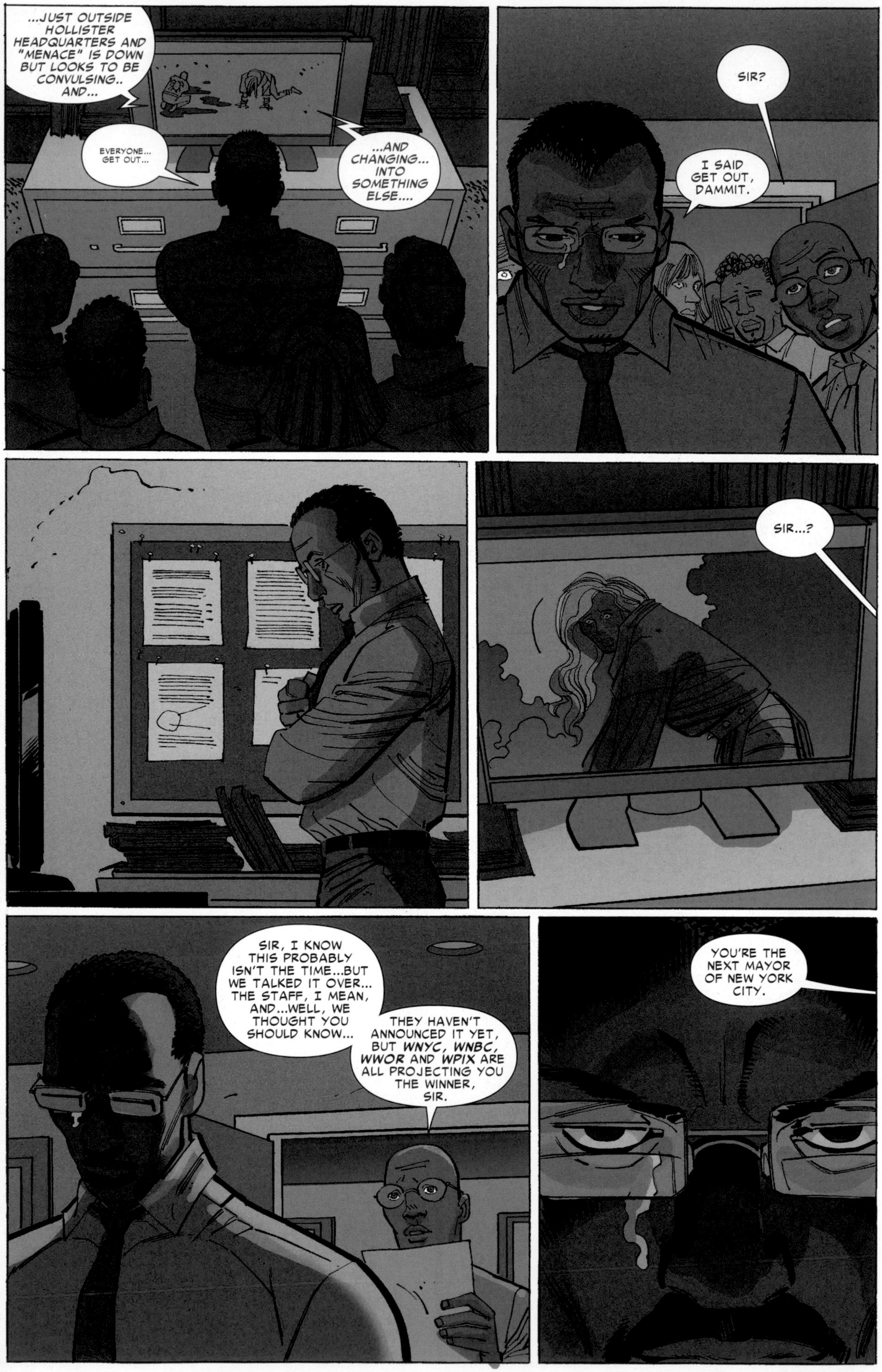
...JUST OUTSIDE HOLLISTER HEADQUARTERS AND "MENACE" IS DOWN BUT LOOKS TO BE CONVULSING.. AND...
EVERYONE... GET OUT...
...AND CHANGING... INTO SOMETHING ELSE....
SIR?
I SAID GET OUT, DAMMIT.
SIR...?
SIR, I KNOW THIS PROBABLY ISN'T THE TIME...BUT WE TALKED IT OVER... THE STAFF, I MEAN, AND...WELL, WE THOUGHT YOU SHOULD KNOW...
THEY HAVEN'T ANNOUNCED IT YET, BUT WNYC, WNBC, WWOR AND WPIX ARE ALL PROJECTING YOU THE WINNER, SIR.
YOU'RE THE NEXT MAYOR OF NEW YORK CITY.

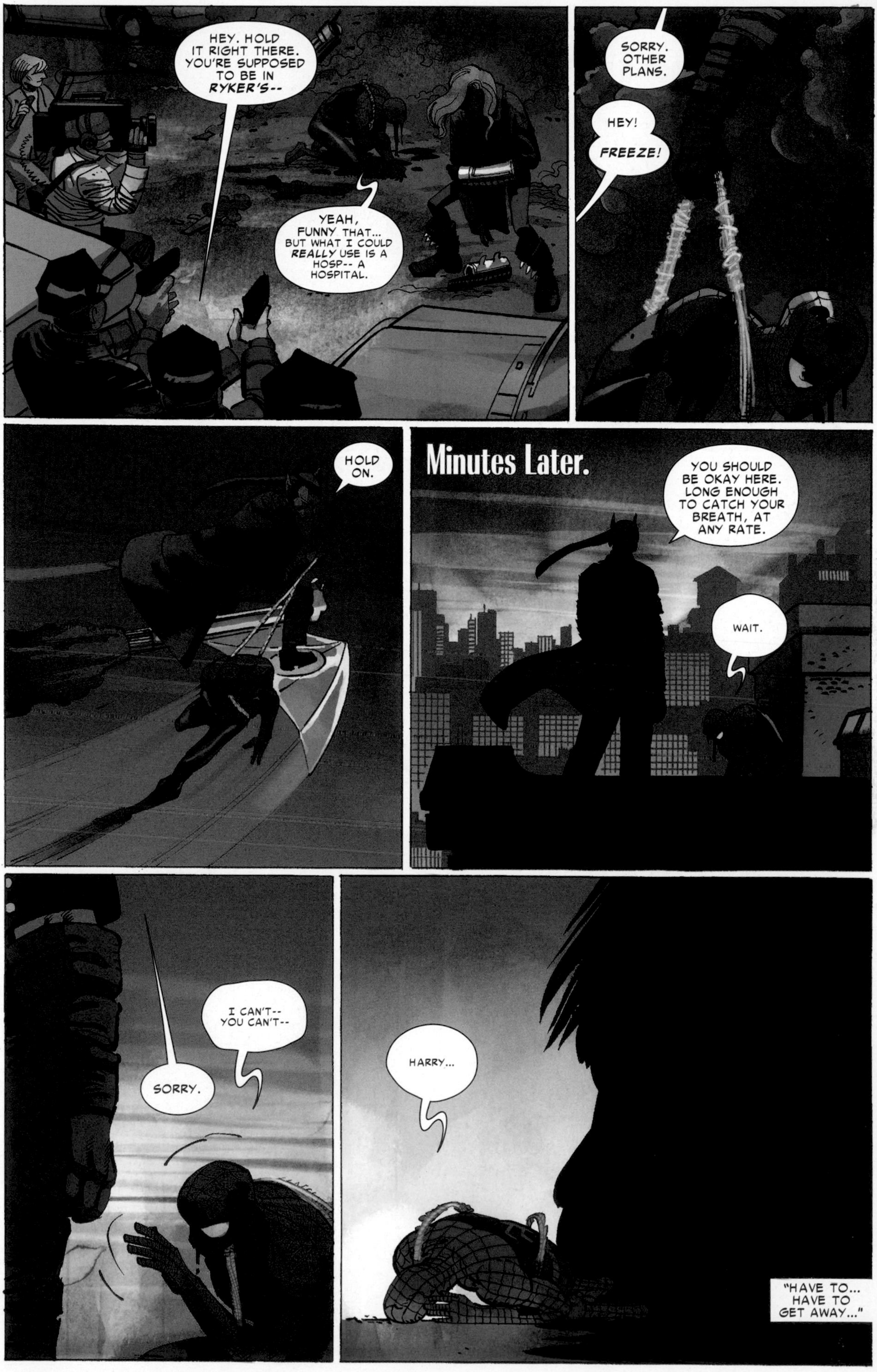
HEY. HOLD IT RIGHT THERE. YOU'RE SUPPOSED TO BE IN RYKER'S--
YEAH, FUNNY THAT... BUT WHAT I COULD REALLY USE IS A HOSP-- A HOSPITAL.
SORRY. OTHER PLANS.
HEY!
FREEZE!
HOLD ON.
Minutes Later.
YOU SHOULD BE OKAY HERE. LONG ENOUGH TO CATCH YOUR BREATH, AT ANY RATE.
WAIT.
I CAN'T-- YOU CAN'T--
SORRY.
HARRY...
"HAVE TO... HAVE TO GET AWAY..."

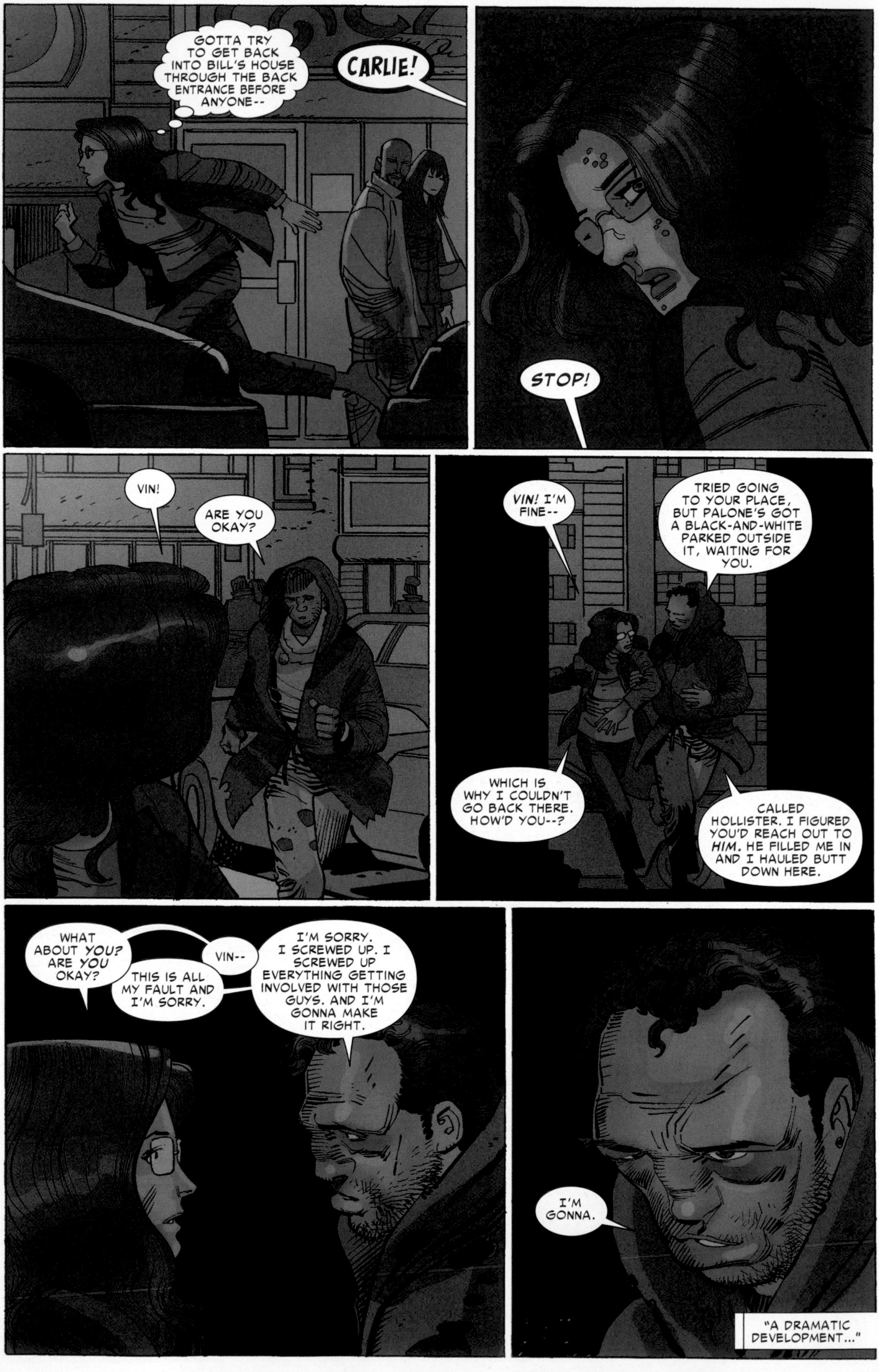
GOTTA TRY TO GET BACK INTO BILL'S HOUSE THROUGH THE BACK ENTRANCE BEFORE ANYONE--
CARLIE!
STOP!
VIN!
ARE YOU OKAY?
VIN! I'M FINE--
TRIED GOING TO YOUR PLACE, BUT PALONE'S GOT A BLACK-AND-WHITE PARKED OUTSIDE IT, WAITING FOR YOU.
WHICH IS WHY I COULDN'T GO BACK THERE. HOW'D YOU--?
CALLED HOLLISTER. I FIGURED YOU'D REACH OUT TO HIM. HE FILLED ME IN AND I HAULED BUTT DOWN HERE.
WHAT ABOUT YOU? ARE YOU OKAY?
VIN--
THIS IS ALL MY FAULT AND I'M SORRY.
I'M SORRY. I SCREWED UP. I SCREWED UP EVERYTHING GETTING INVOLVED WITH THOSE GUYS. AND I'M GONNA MAKE IT RIGHT.
I'M GONNA.
"A DRAMATIC DEVELOPMENT..."

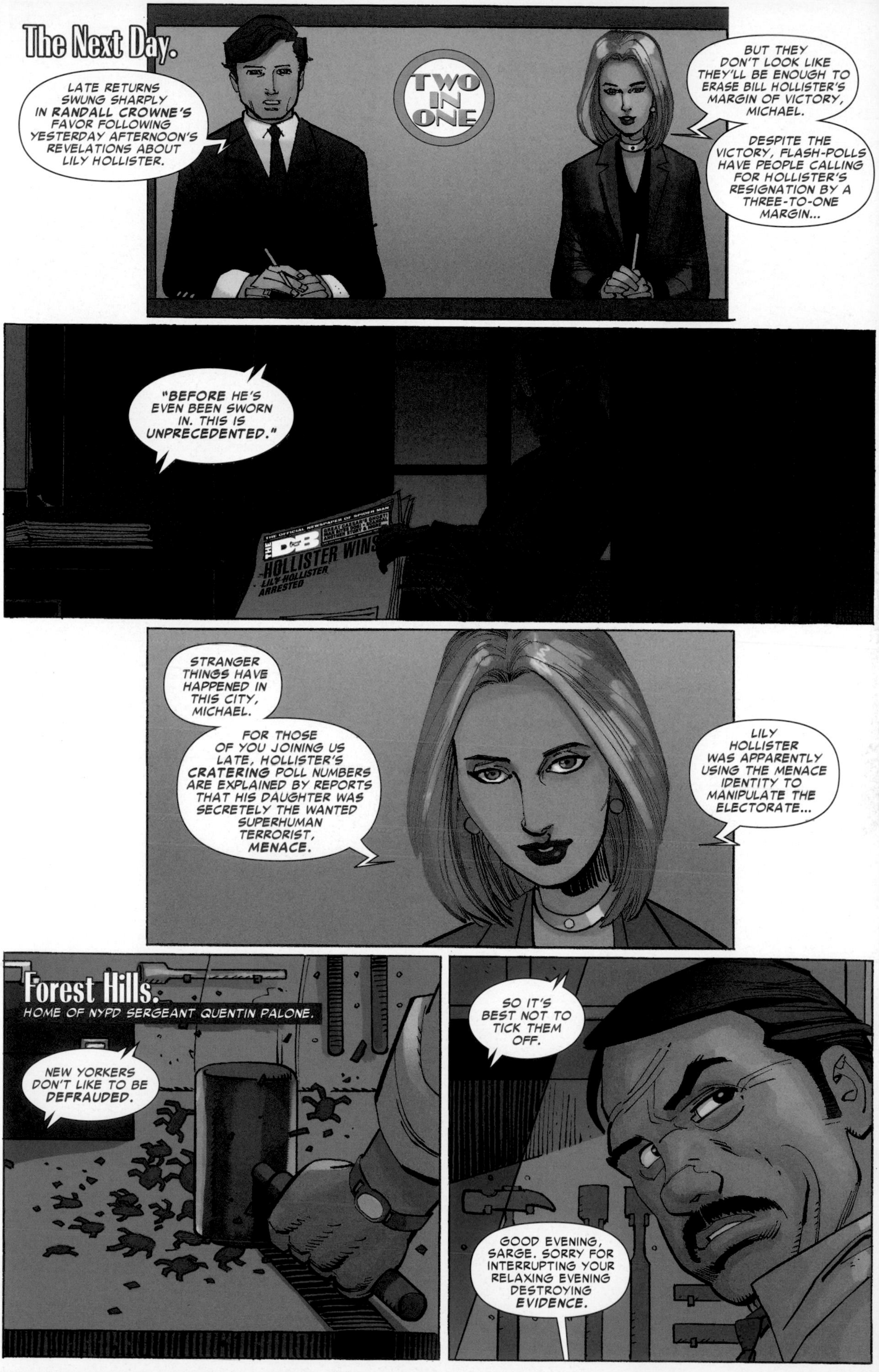
The Next Day.
LATE RETURNS SWUNG SHARPLY IN RANDALL CROWNE'S FAVOR FOLLOWING YESTERDAY AFTERNOON'S REVELATIONS ABOUT LILY HOLLISTER.
TWO IN ONE
BUT THEY DON'T LOOK LIKE THEY'LL BE ENOUGH TO ERASE BILL HOLLISTER'S MARGIN OF VICTORY, MICHAEL.
DESPITE THE VICTORY, FLASH-POLLS HAVE PEOPLE CALLING FOR HOLLISTER'S RESIGNATION BY A THREE-TO-ONE MARGIN...
"BEFORE HE'S EVEN BEEN SWORN IN. THIS IS UNPRECEDENTED."
THE OFFICIAL NEWSPAPER OF SPIDER MAN
THE DB
HOLLISTER WINS
LILY HOLLISTER ARRESTED
STRANGER THINGS HAVE HAPPENED IN THIS CITY, MICHAEL.
FOR THOSE OF YOU JOINING US LATE, HOLLISTER'S CRATERING POLL NUMBERS ARE EXPLAINED BY REPORTS THAT HIS DAUGHTER WAS SECRETELY THE WANTED SUPERHUMAN TERRORIST, MENACE.
LILY HOLLISTER WAS APPARENTLY USING THE MENACE IDENTITY TO MANIPULATE THE ELECTORATE...
Forest Hills.
HOME OF NYPD SERGEANT QUENTIN PALONE.
NEW YORKERS DON'T LIKE TO BE DEFRAUDED.
SO IT'S BEST NOT TO TICK THEM OFF.
GOOD EVENING, SARGE. SORRY FOR INTERRUPTING YOUR RELAXING EVENING DESTROYING EVIDENCE.

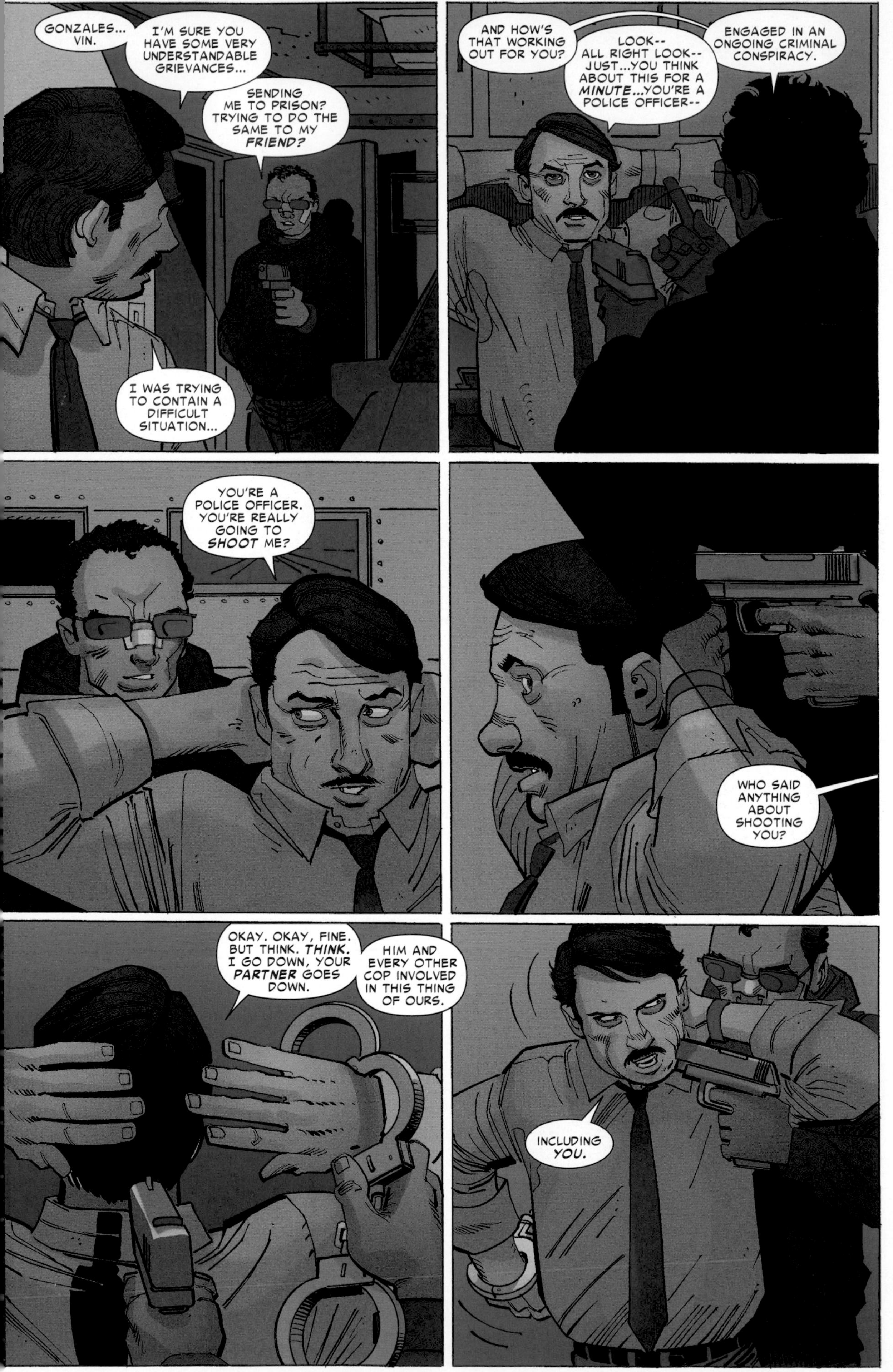
GONZALES... VIN.
I'M SURE YOU HAVE SOME VERY UNDERSTANDABLE GRIEVANCES...
SENDING ME TO PRISON? TRYING TO DO THE SAME TO MY *FRIEND?*
I WAS TRYING TO CONTAIN A DIFFICULT SITUATION...
AND HOW'S THAT WORKING OUT FOR YOU?
ENGAGED IN AN ONGOING CRIMINAL CONSPIRACY.
LOOK-- ALL RIGHT LOOK-- JUST...YOU THINK ABOUT THIS FOR A *MINUTE*...YOU'RE A POLICE OFFICER--
YOU'RE A POLICE OFFICER. YOU'RE REALLY GOING TO *SHOOT* ME?
WHO SAID ANYTHING ABOUT SHOOTING YOU?
OKAY. OKAY, FINE. BUT THINK. *THINK.* I GO DOWN, YOUR *PARTNER* GOES DOWN.
HIM AND EVERY OTHER COP INVOLVED IN THIS THING OF OURS.
INCLUDING *YOU.*

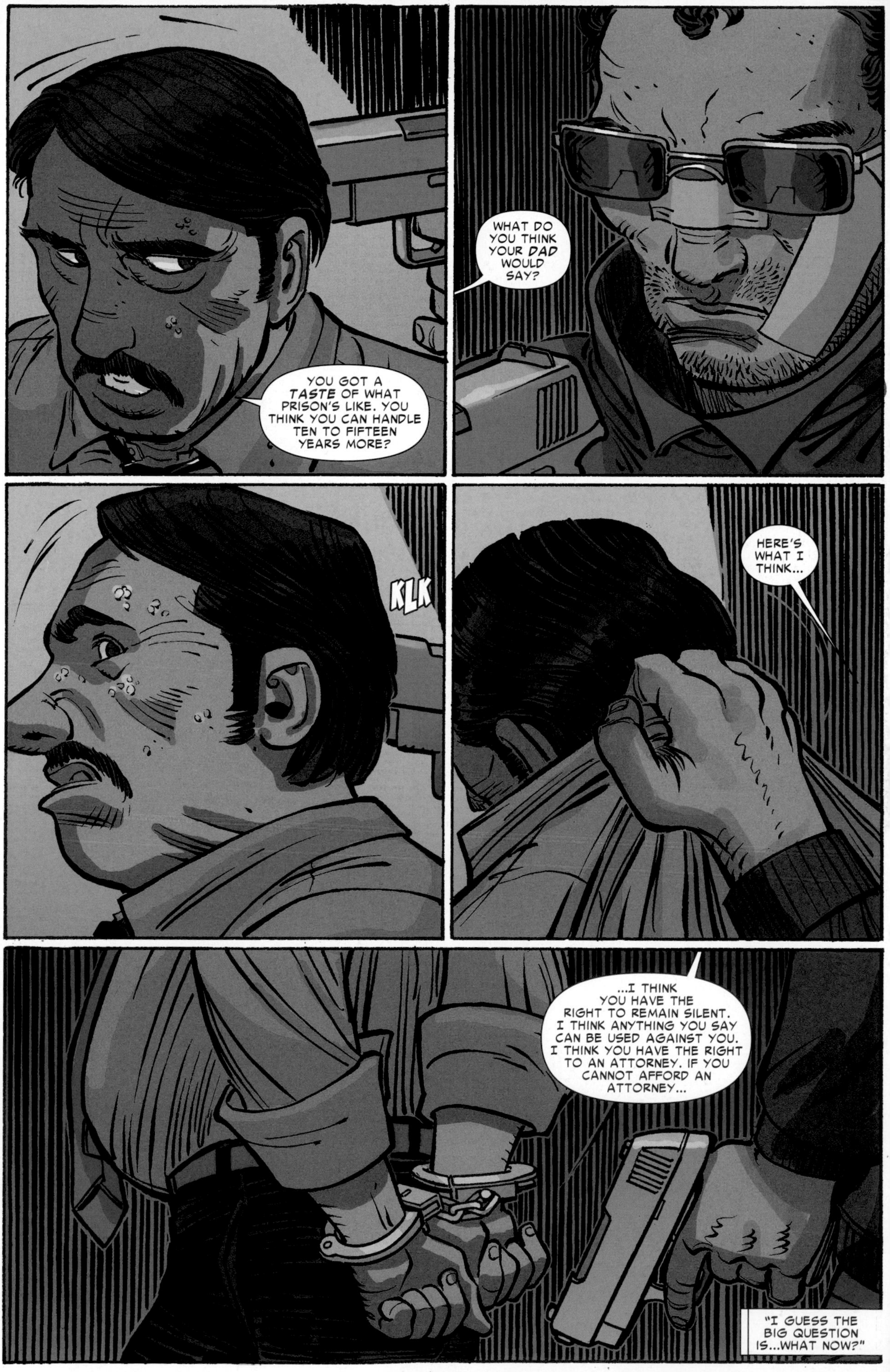
YOU GOT A TASTE OF WHAT PRISON'S LIKE. YOU THINK YOU CAN HANDLE TEN TO FIFTEEN YEARS MORE?
WHAT DO YOU THINK YOUR DAD WOULD SAY?
KLK
HERE'S WHAT I THINK...
...I THINK YOU HAVE THE RIGHT TO REMAIN SILENT. I THINK ANYTHING YOU SAY CAN BE USED AGAINST YOU. I THINK YOU HAVE THE RIGHT TO AN ATTORNEY. IF YOU CANNOT AFFORD AN ATTORNEY...
"I GUESS THE BIG QUESTION IS...WHAT NOW?"

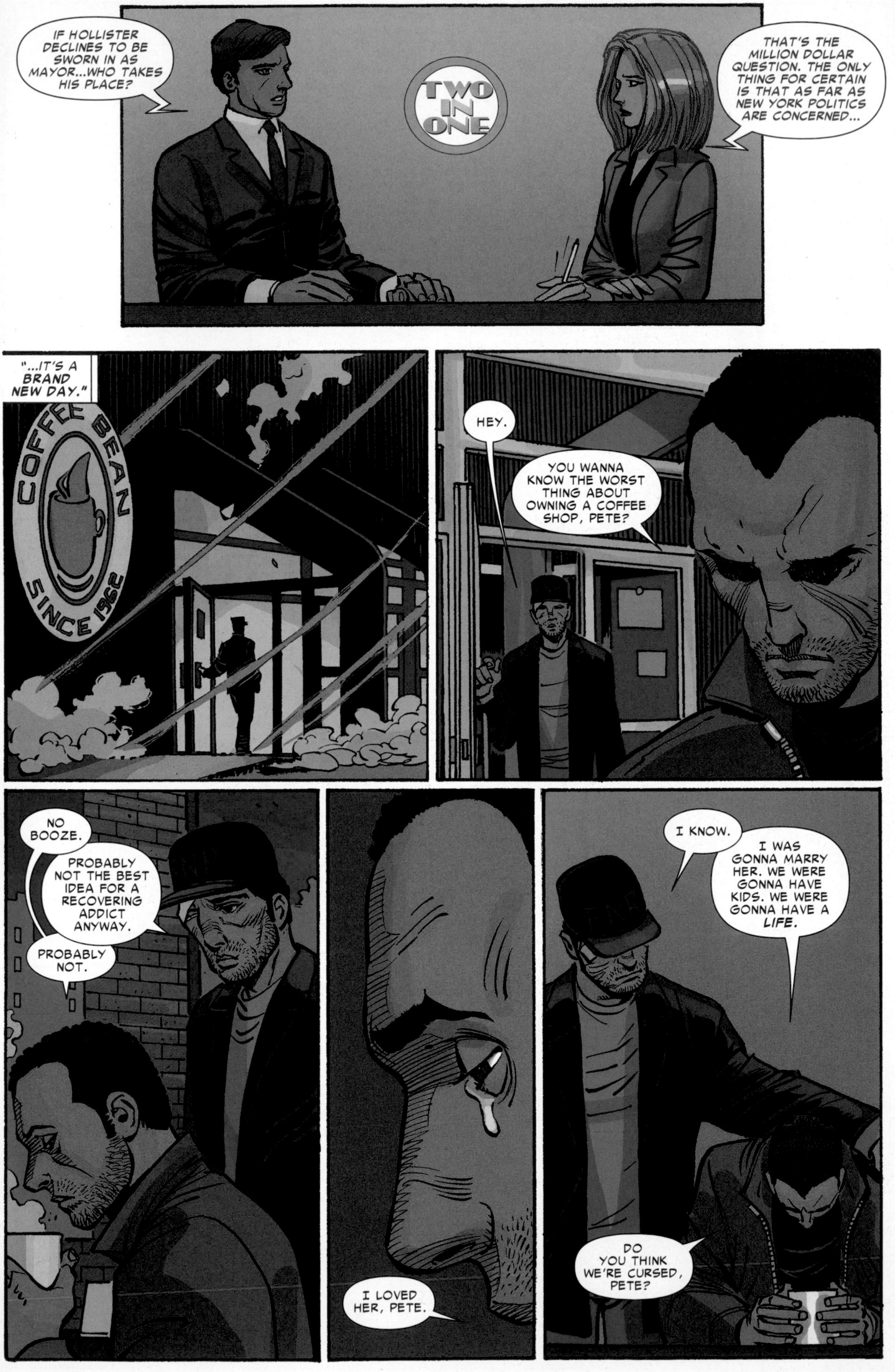
IF HOLLISTER DECLINES TO BE SWORN IN AS MAYOR...WHO TAKES HIS PLACE?
TWO IN ONE
THAT'S THE MILLION DOLLAR QUESTION. THE ONLY THING FOR CERTAIN IS THAT AS FAR AS NEW YORK POLITICS ARE CONCERNED...
"...IT'S A BRAND NEW DAY."
COFFEE BEAN SINCE 1962
HEY.
YOU WANNA KNOW THE WORST THING ABOUT OWNING A COFFEE SHOP, PETE?
NO BOOZE.
PROBABLY NOT THE BEST IDEA FOR A RECOVERING ADDICT ANYWAY.
PROBABLY NOT.
I LOVED HER, PETE.
I KNOW.
I WAS GONNA MARRY HER. WE WERE GONNA HAVE KIDS. WE WERE GONNA HAVE A LIFE.
DO YOU THINK WE'RE CURSED, PETE?

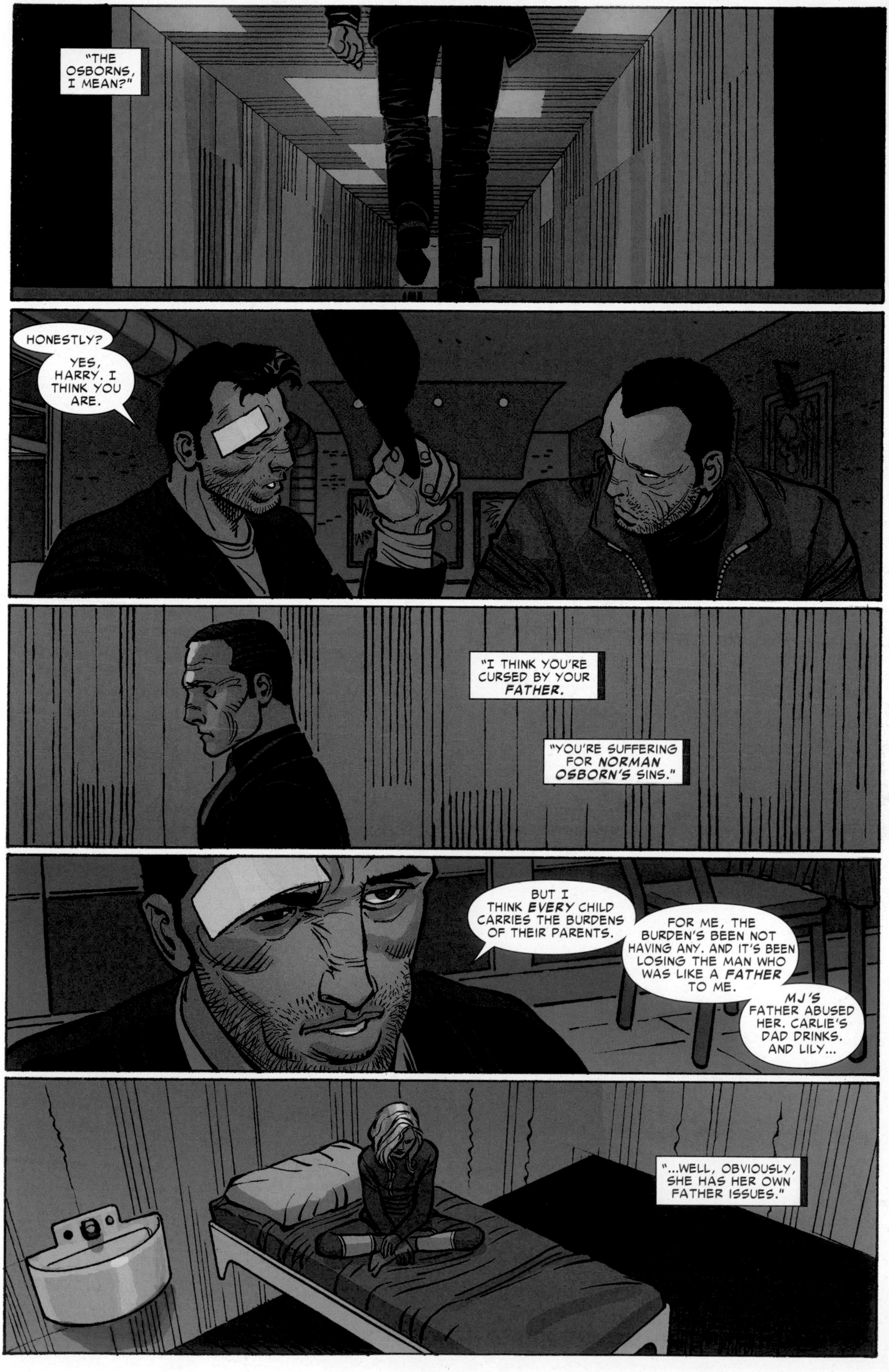
"THE OSBORNS, I MEAN?"
HONESTLY?
YES, HARRY. I THINK YOU ARE.
"I THINK YOU'RE CURSED BY YOUR FATHER.
"YOU'RE SUFFERING FOR NORMAN OSBORN'S SINS."
BUT I THINK EVERY CHILD CARRIES THE BURDENS OF THEIR PARENTS.
FOR ME, THE BURDEN'S BEEN NOT HAVING ANY. AND IT'S BEEN LOSING THE MAN WHO WAS LIKE A FATHER TO ME.
MJ'S FATHER ABUSED HER. CARLIE'S DAD DRINKS. AND LILY...
"...WELL, OBVIOUSLY, SHE HAS HER OWN FATHER ISSUES."

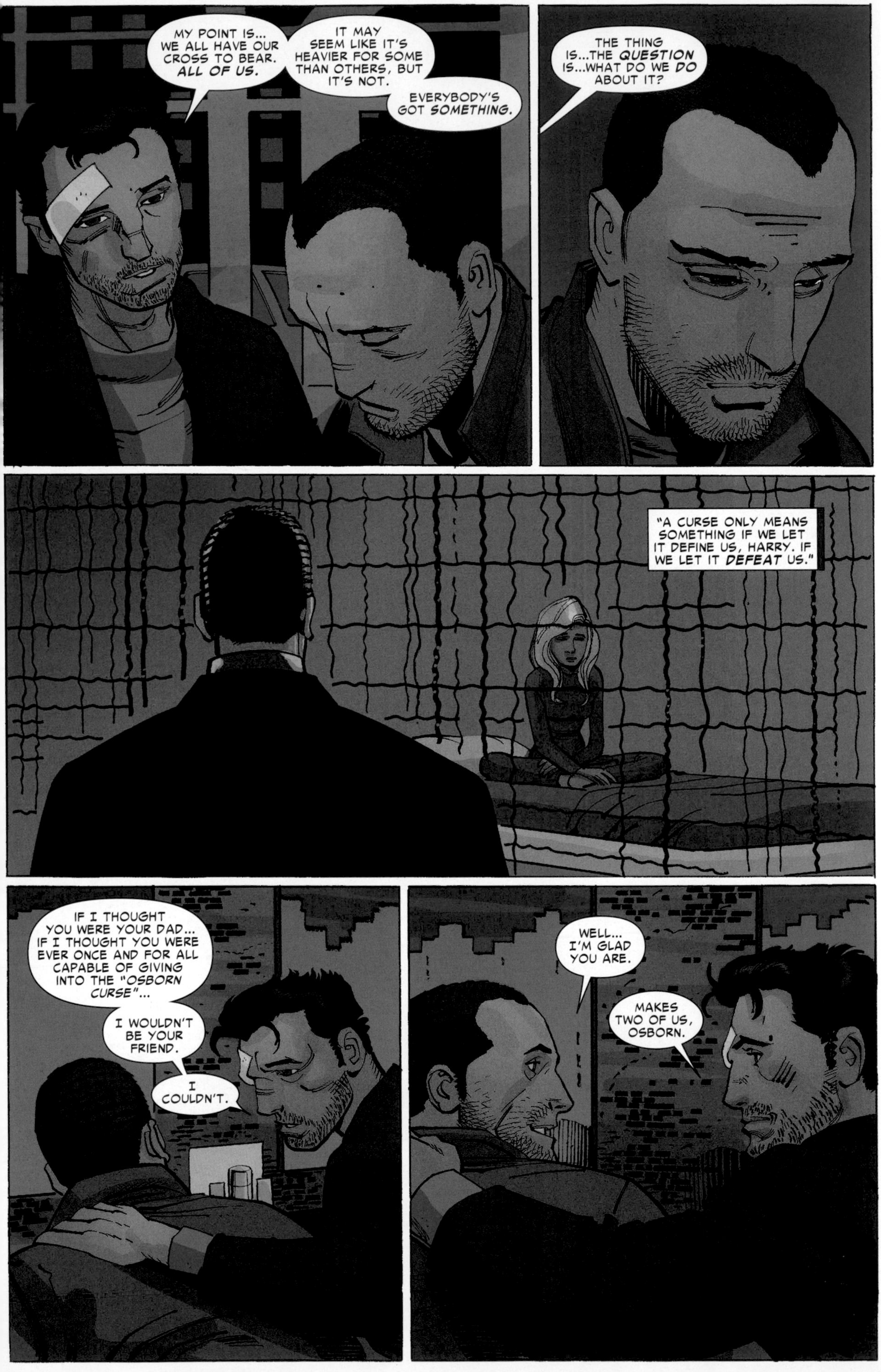
MY POINT IS... WE ALL HAVE OUR CROSS TO BEAR. ALL OF US.
IT MAY SEEM LIKE IT'S HEAVIER FOR SOME THAN OTHERS, BUT IT'S NOT.
EVERYBODY'S GOT SOMETHING.
THE THING IS...THE QUESTION IS...WHAT DO WE DO ABOUT IT?
"A CURSE ONLY MEANS SOMETHING IF WE LET IT DEFINE US, HARRY. IF WE LET IT DEFEAT US."
IF I THOUGHT YOU WERE YOUR DAD... IF I THOUGHT YOU WERE EVER ONCE AND FOR ALL CAPABLE OF GIVING INTO THE "OSBORN CURSE"...
I WOULDN'T BE YOUR FRIEND.
I COULDN'T.
WELL... I'M GLAD YOU ARE.
MAKES TWO OF US, OSBORN.

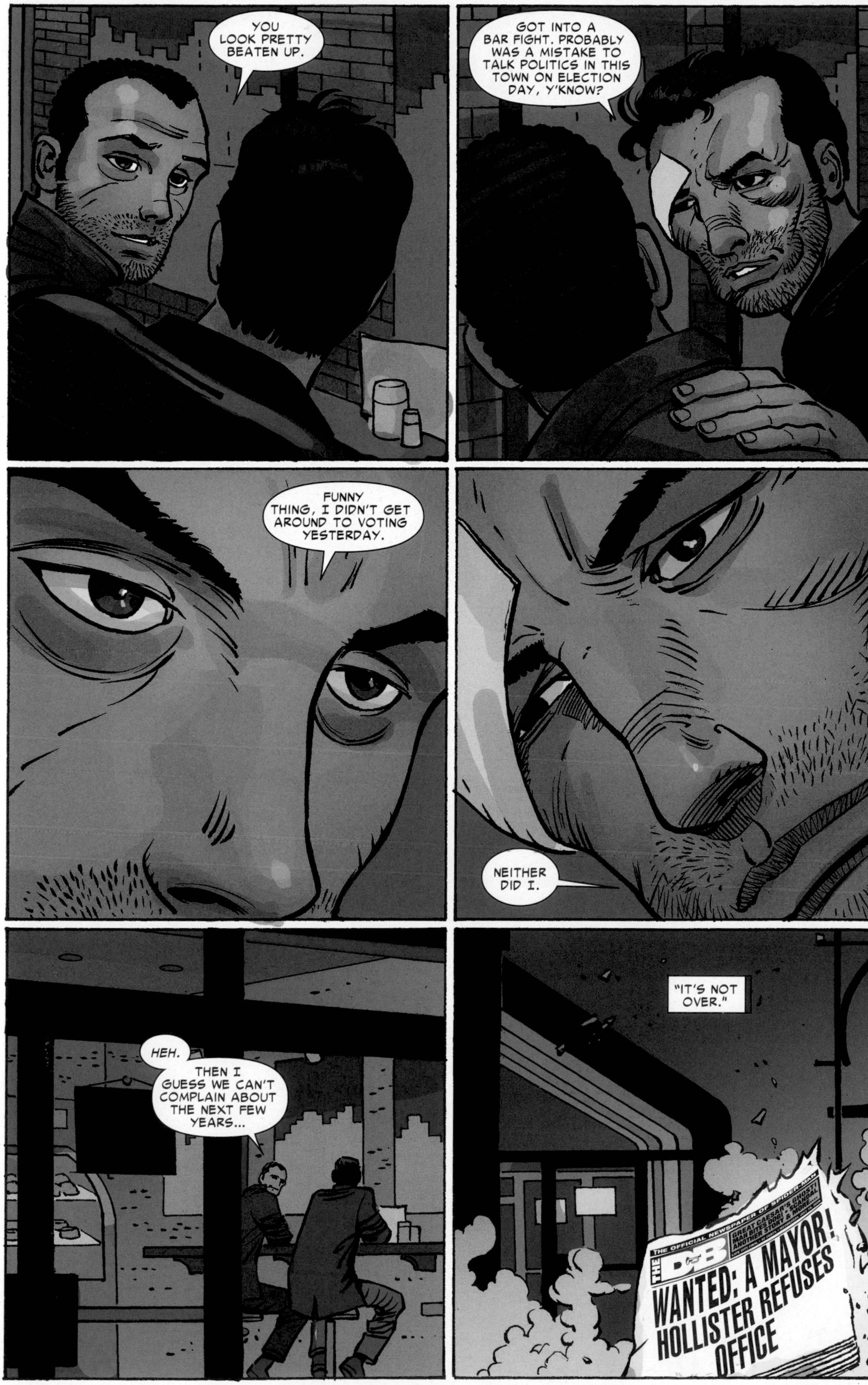
YOU LOOK PRETTY BEATEN UP.
GOT INTO A BAR FIGHT. PROBABLY WAS A MISTAKE TO TALK POLITICS IN THIS TOWN ON ELECTION DAY, Y'KNOW?
FUNNY THING, I DIDN'T GET AROUND TO VOTING YESTERDAY.
NEITHER DID I.
HEH.
THEN I GUESS WE CAN'T COMPLAIN ABOUT THE NEXT FEW YEARS...
"IT'S NOT OVER."
THE OFFICIAL NEWSPAPER OF SPIDER-MAN
THE DB
GREAT CAESAR'S GHOST! MAN BITES DOG! - SCANDAL ANOTHER STORY & MORE...
WANTED: A MAYOR! HOLLISTER REFUSES OFFICE

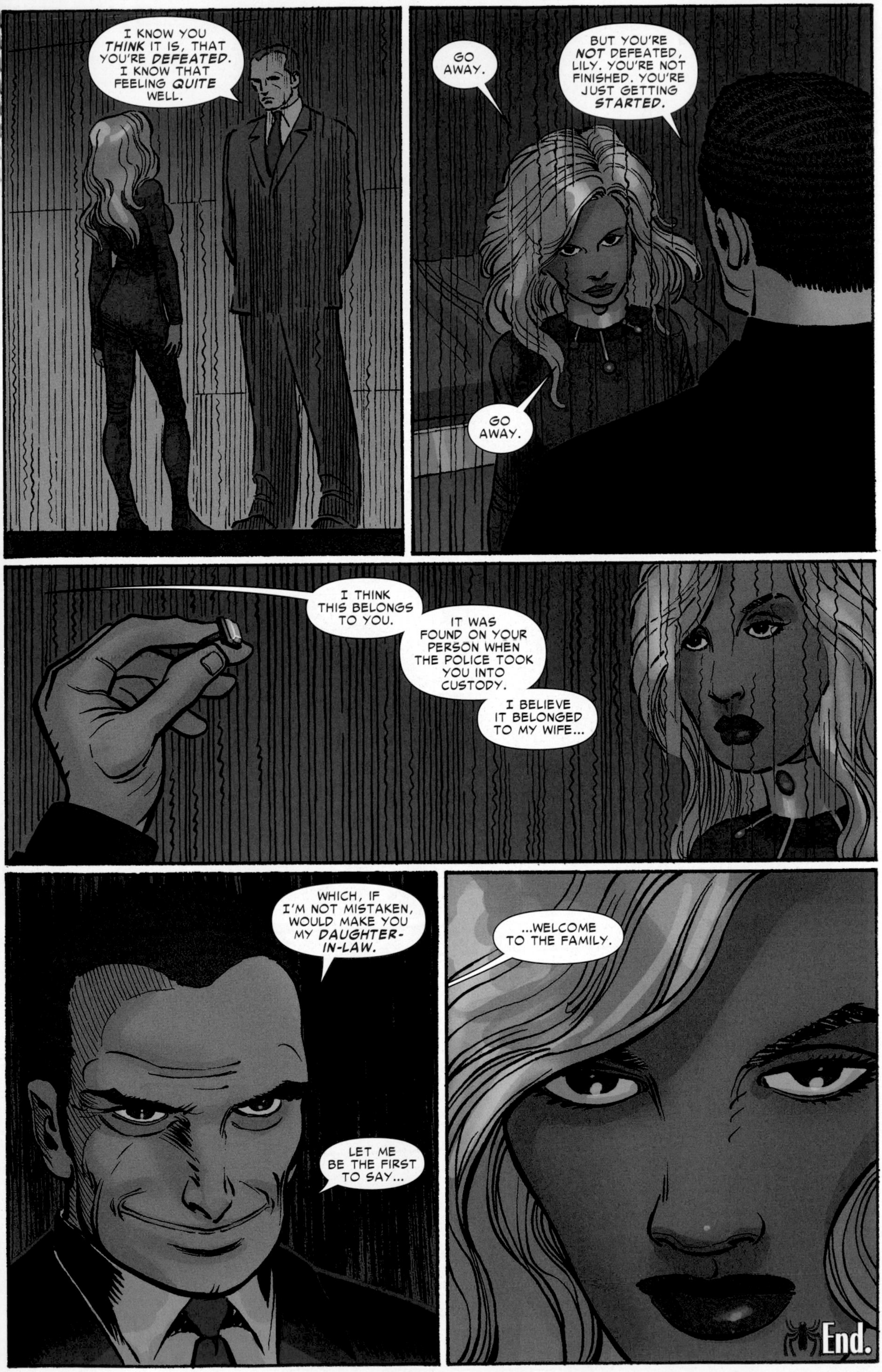

I KNOW YOU THINK IT IS, THAT YOU'RE DEFEATED. I KNOW THAT FEELING QUITE WELL.
GO AWAY.
BUT YOU'RE NOT DEFEATED, LILY. YOU'RE NOT FINISHED. YOU'RE JUST GETTING STARTED.
GO AWAY.
I THINK THIS BELONGS TO YOU.
IT WAS FOUND ON YOUR PERSON WHEN THE POLICE TOOK YOU INTO CUSTODY.
I BELIEVE IT BELONGED TO MY WIFE...
WHICH, IF I'M NOT MISTAKEN, WOULD MAKE YOU MY DAUGHTER-IN-LAW.
LET ME BE THE FIRST TO SAY...
...WELCOME TO THE FAMILY.
End.

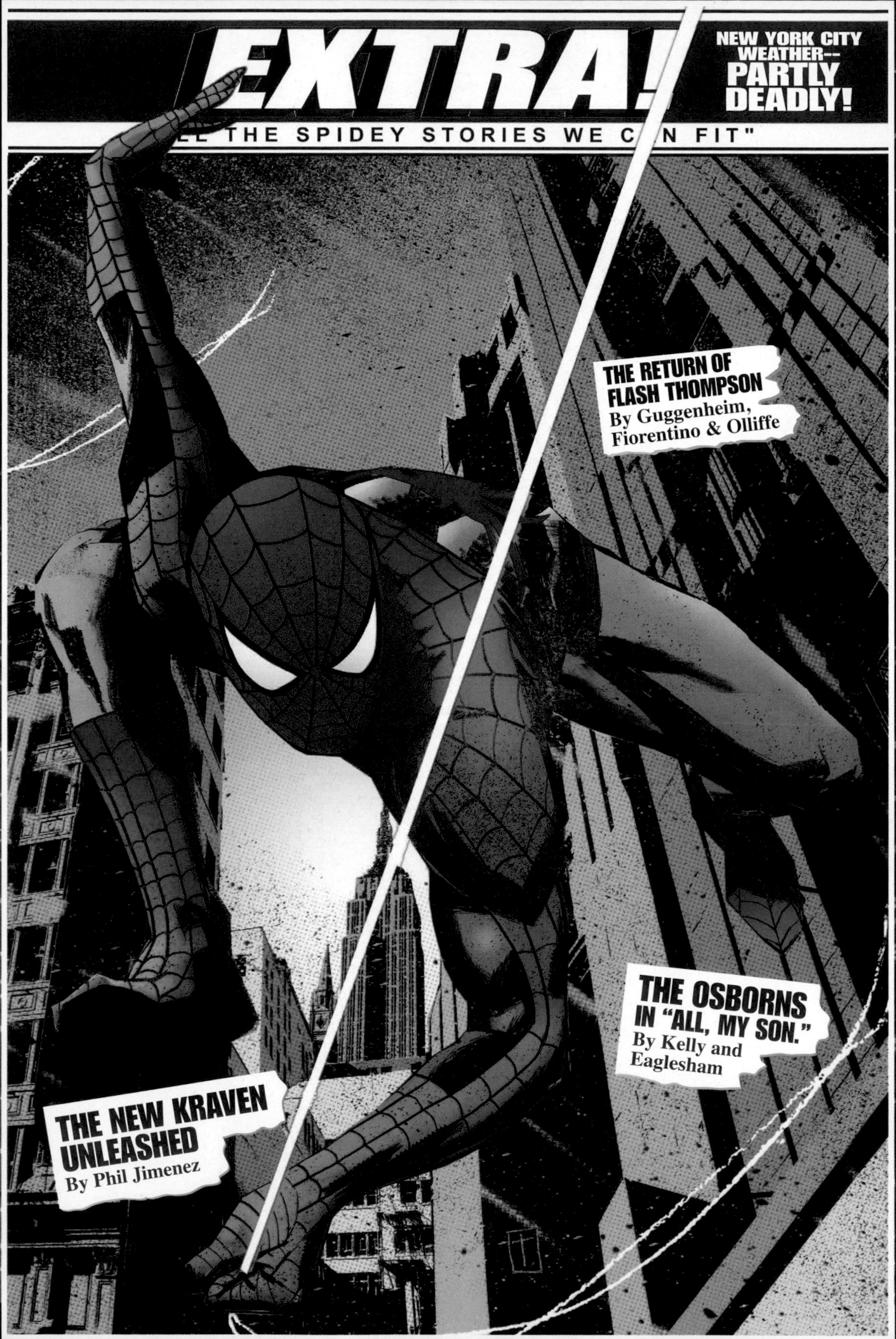
EXTRA!
NEW YORK CITY WEATHER-- PARTLY DEADLY!
"L THE SPIDEY STORIES WE C N FIT"
THE RETURN OF FLASH THOMPSON
By Guggenheim, Fiorentino & Olliffe
THE OSBORNS IN "ALL, MY SON."
By Kelly and Eaglesham
THE NEW KRAVEN UNLEASHED
By Phil Jimenez

AMAZING SPIDER-MAN: EXTRA! #3 – "WITH GREAT RESPONSIBILITY COMES GREAT POWER"

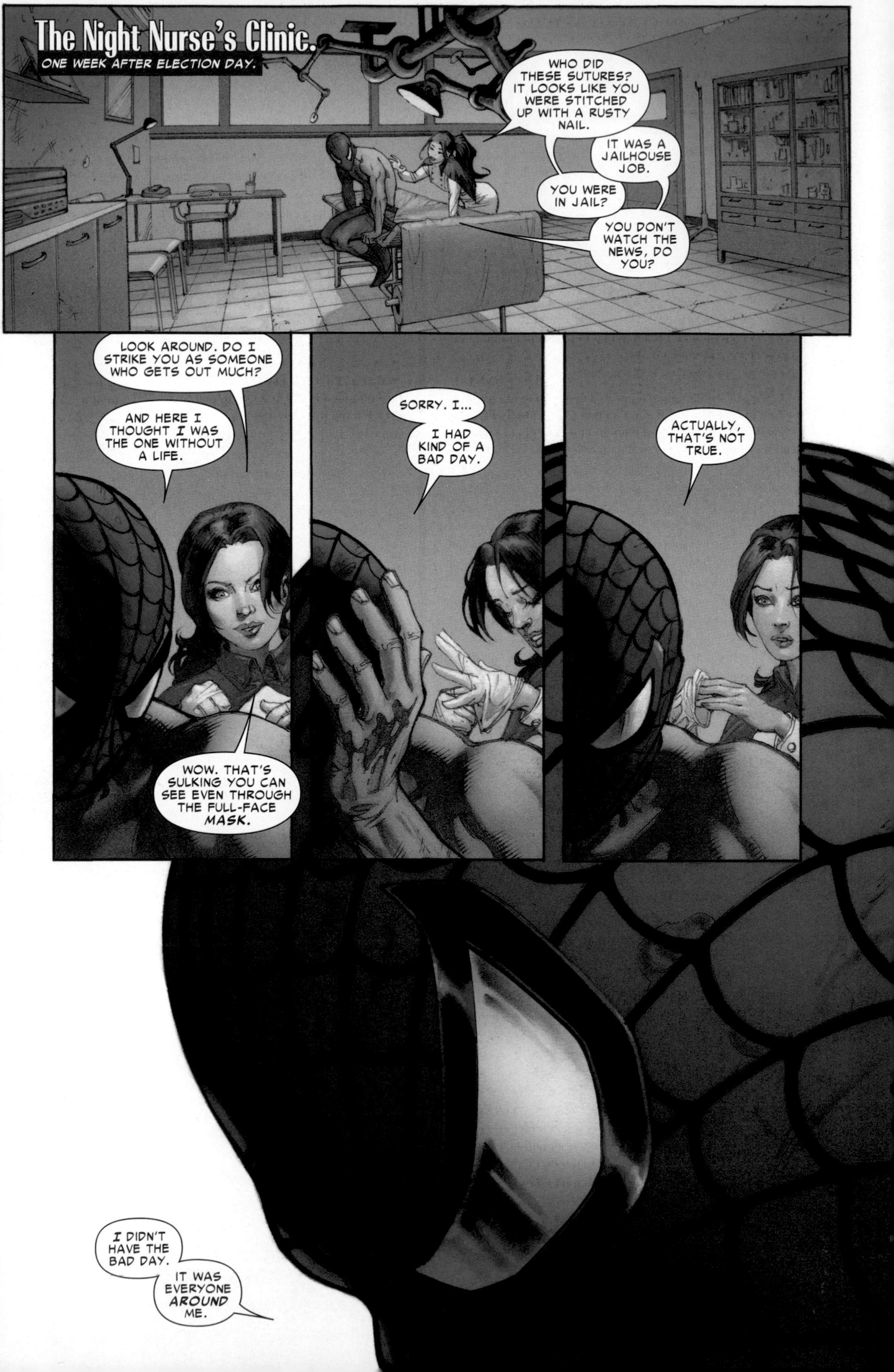
The Night Nurse's Clinic.
ONE WEEK AFTER ELECTION DAY.
WHO DID THESE SUTURES? IT LOOKS LIKE YOU WERE STITCHED UP WITH A RUSTY NAIL.
IT WAS A JAILHOUSE JOB.
YOU WERE IN JAIL?
YOU DON'T WATCH THE NEWS, DO YOU?
LOOK AROUND. DO I STRIKE YOU AS SOMEONE WHO GETS OUT MUCH?
AND HERE I THOUGHT I WAS THE ONE WITHOUT A LIFE.
WOW. THAT'S SULKING YOU CAN SEE EVEN THROUGH THE FULL-FACE MASK.
SORRY. I...
I HAD KIND OF A BAD DAY.
ACTUALLY, THAT'S NOT TRUE.
I DIDN'T HAVE THE BAD DAY.
IT WAS EVERYONE AROUND ME.

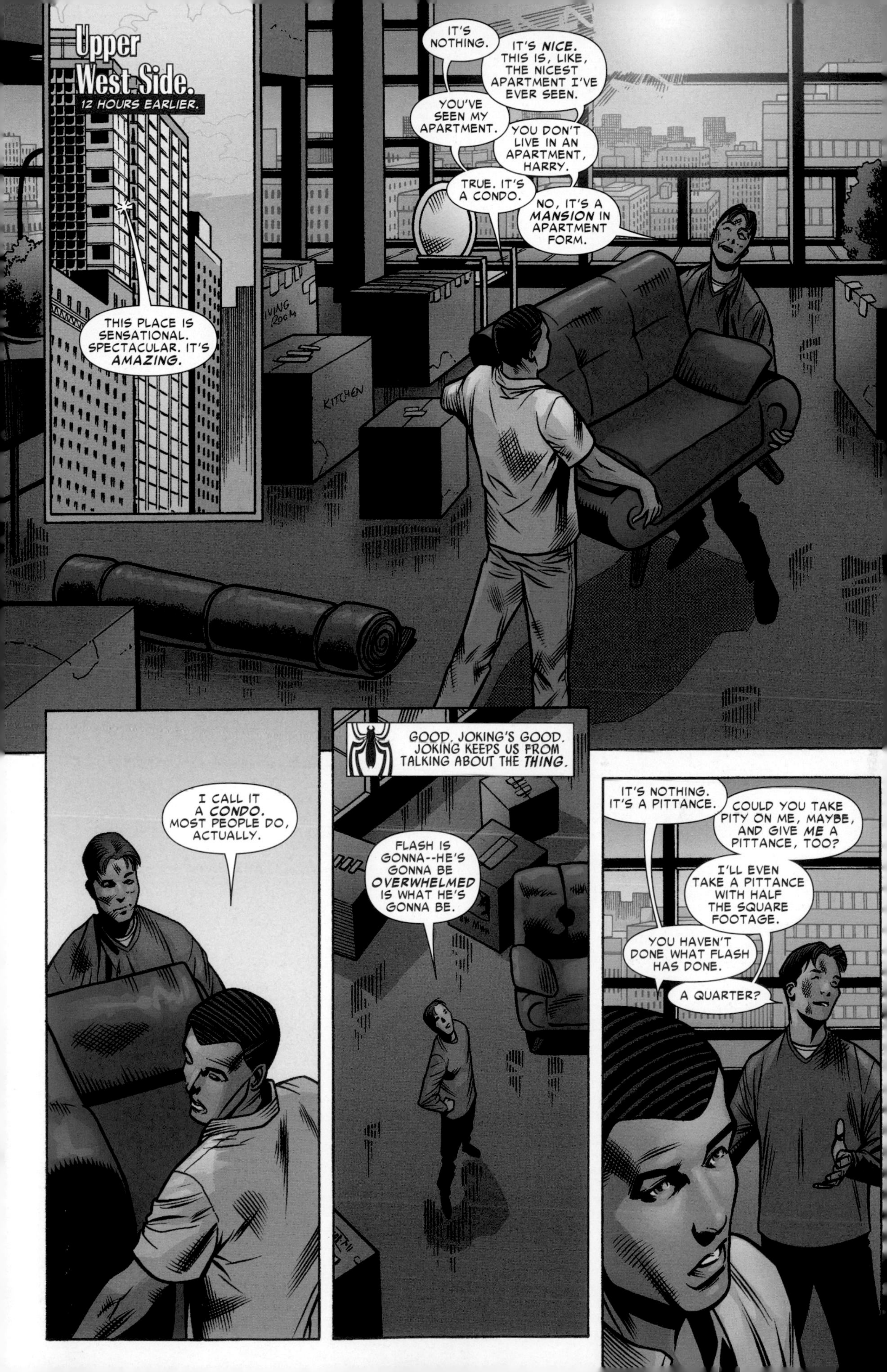
Upper West Side.
12 HOURS EARLIER.
THIS PLACE IS SENSATIONAL. SPECTACULAR. IT'S AMAZING.
IT'S NOTHING.
IT'S NICE. THIS IS, LIKE, THE NICEST APARTMENT I'VE EVER SEEN.
YOU'VE SEEN MY APARTMENT.
YOU DON'T LIVE IN AN APARTMENT, HARRY.
TRUE. IT'S A CONDO.
NO, IT'S A MANSION IN APARTMENT FORM.
LIVING ROOM
KITCHEN
I CALL IT A CONDO. MOST PEOPLE DO, ACTUALLY.
GOOD. JOKING'S GOOD. JOKING KEEPS US FROM TALKING ABOUT THE THING.
FLASH IS GONNA--HE'S GONNA BE OVERWHELMED IS WHAT HE'S GONNA BE.
IT'S NOTHING. IT'S A PITTANCE.
COULD YOU TAKE PITY ON ME, MAYBE, AND GIVE ME A PITTANCE, TOO?
I'LL EVEN TAKE A PITTANCE WITH HALF THE SQUARE FOOTAGE.
YOU HAVEN'T DONE WHAT FLASH HAS DONE.
A QUARTER?

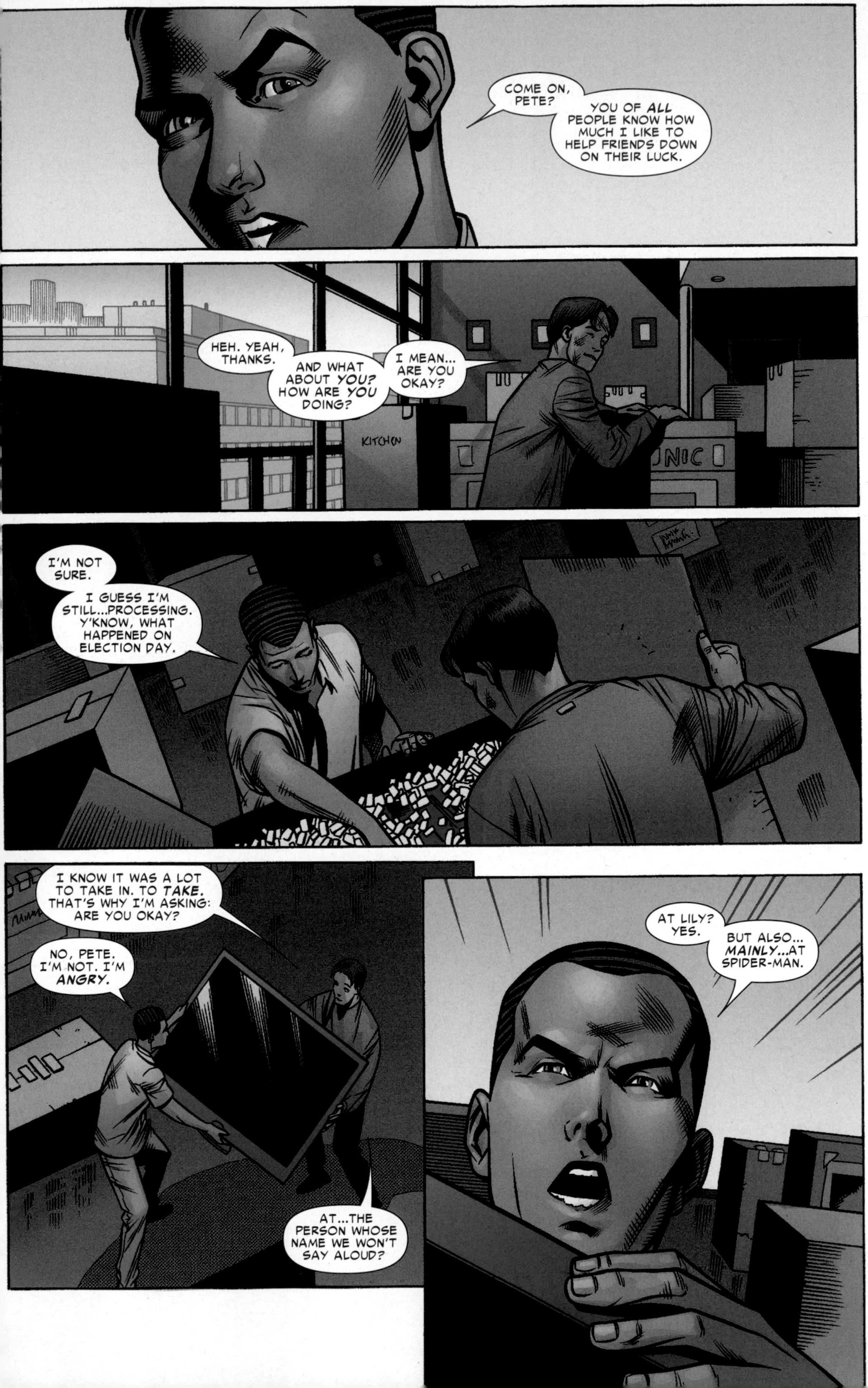

COME ON, PETE?
YOU OF ALL PEOPLE KNOW HOW MUCH I LIKE TO HELP FRIENDS DOWN ON THEIR LUCK.
HEH. YEAH, THANKS.
AND WHAT ABOUT YOU? HOW ARE YOU DOING?
I MEAN... ARE YOU OKAY?
KITCHEN
I'M NOT SURE.
I GUESS I'M STILL...PROCESSING. Y'KNOW, WHAT HAPPENED ON ELECTION DAY.
I KNOW IT WAS A LOT TO TAKE IN. TO TAKE. THAT'S WHY I'M ASKING: ARE YOU OKAY?
NO, PETE. I'M NOT. I'M ANGRY.
AT...THE PERSON WHOSE NAME WE WON'T SAY ALOUD?
AT LILY? YES.
BUT ALSO... MAINLY...AT SPIDER-MAN.

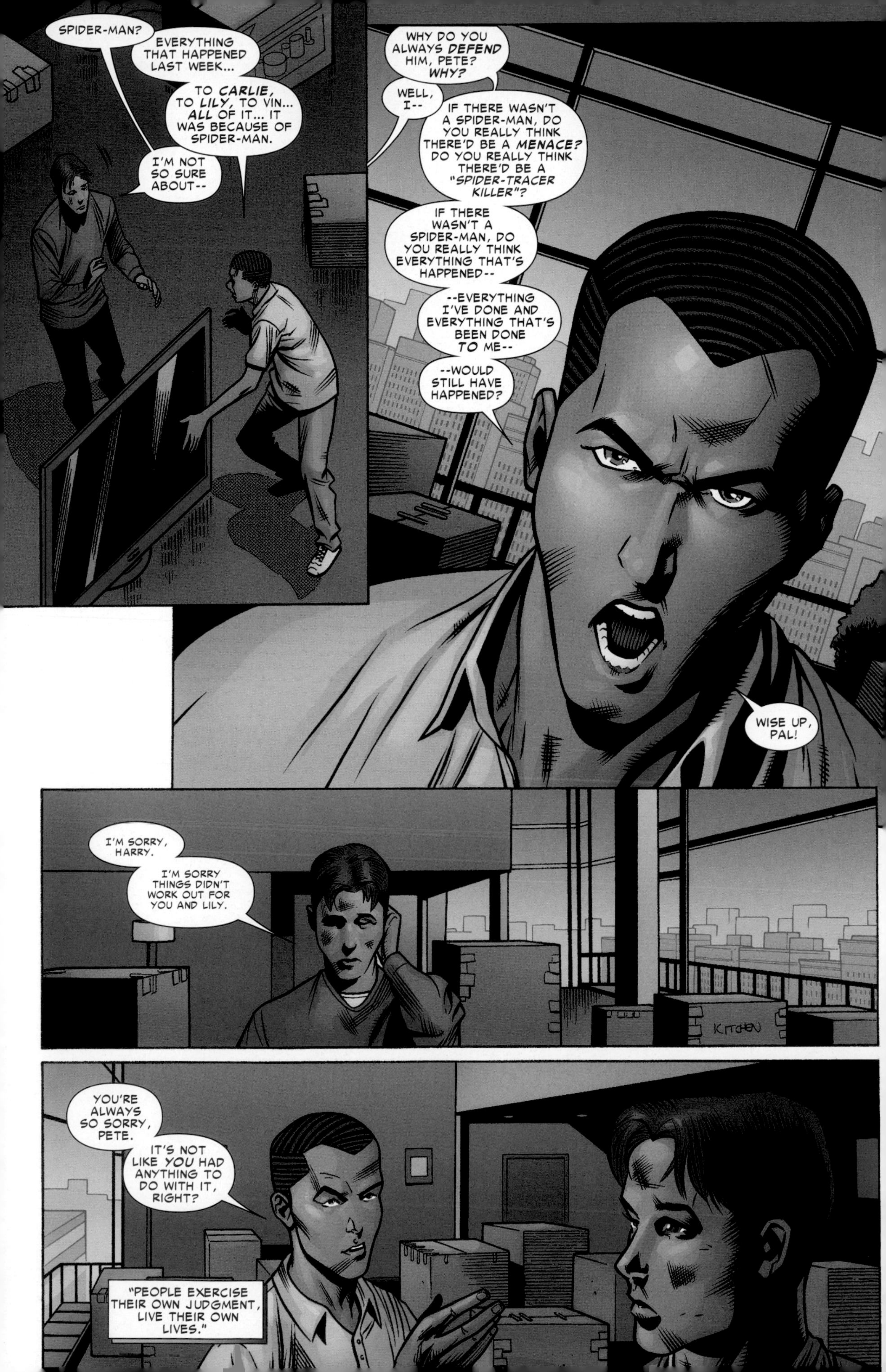
SPIDER-MAN?
EVERYTHING THAT HAPPENED LAST WEEK...
TO CARLIE, TO LILY, TO VIN... ALL OF IT... IT WAS BECAUSE OF SPIDER-MAN.
I'M NOT SO SURE ABOUT--
WHY DO YOU ALWAYS DEFEND HIM, PETE? WHY?
WELL, I--
IF THERE WASN'T A SPIDER-MAN, DO YOU REALLY THINK THERE'D BE A MENACE? DO YOU REALLY THINK THERE'D BE A "SPIDER-TRACER KILLER"?
IF THERE WASN'T A SPIDER-MAN, DO YOU REALLY THINK EVERYTHING THAT'S HAPPENED--
--EVERYTHING I'VE DONE AND EVERYTHING THAT'S BEEN DONE TO ME--
--WOULD STILL HAVE HAPPENED?
WISE UP, PAL!
I'M SORRY, HARRY.
I'M SORRY THINGS DIDN'T WORK OUT FOR YOU AND LILY.
KITCHEN
YOU'RE ALWAYS SO SORRY, PETE.
IT'S NOT LIKE YOU HAD ANYTHING TO DO WITH IT, RIGHT?
"PEOPLE EXERCISE THEIR OWN JUDGMENT, LIVE THEIR OWN LIVES."

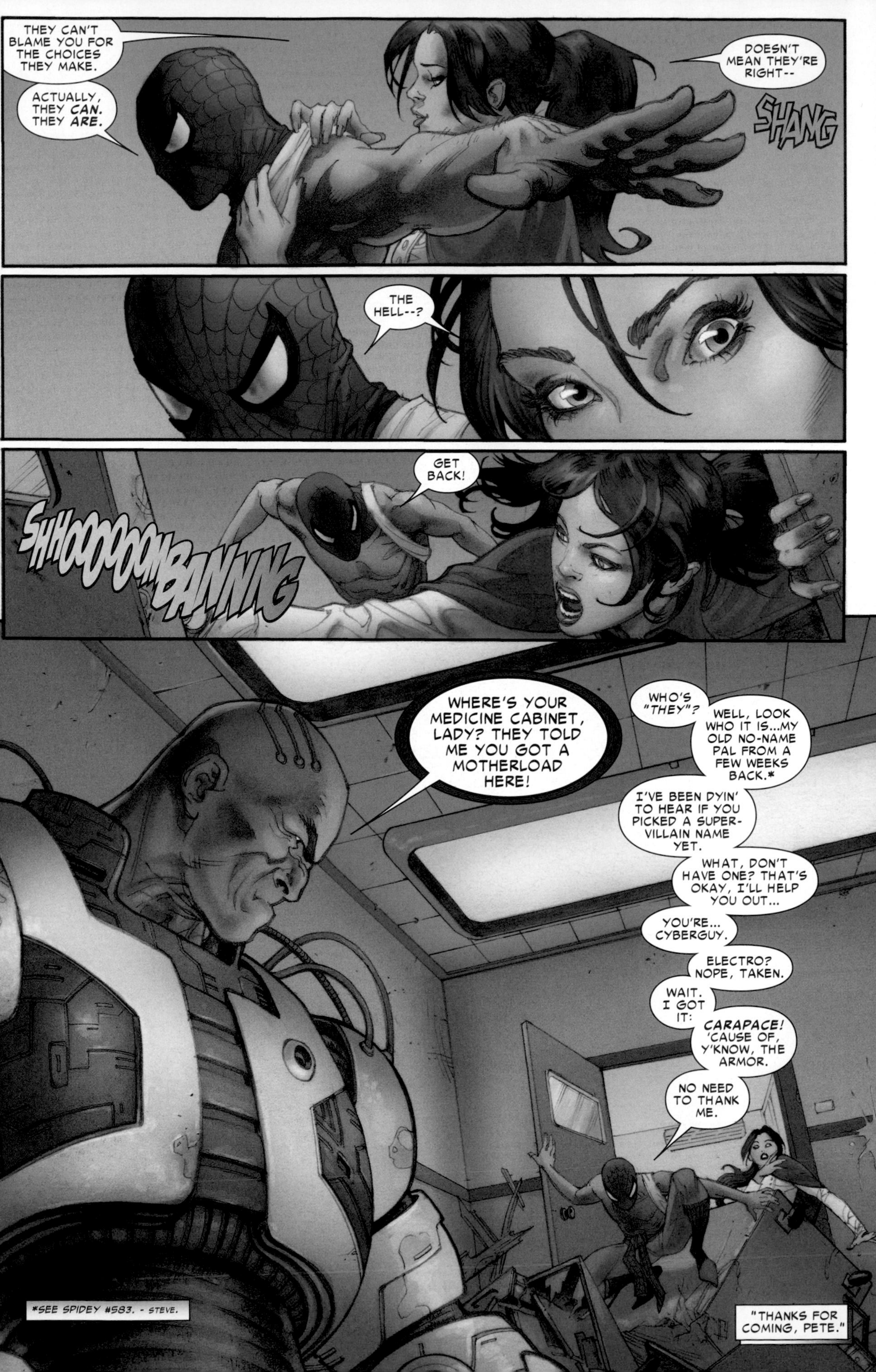
THEY CAN'T BLAME YOU FOR THE CHOICES THEY MAKE.
ACTUALLY, THEY **CAN.** THEY **ARE.**
DOESN'T MEAN THEY'RE RIGHT--
SHANG
THE HELL--?
GET BACK!
SHHOOOOOOMBANNNG
WHERE'S YOUR MEDICINE CABINET, LADY? THEY TOLD ME YOU GOT A MOTHERLOAD HERE!
WHO'S *"THEY"*?
WELL, LOOK WHO IT IS...MY OLD NO-NAME PAL FROM A FEW WEEKS BACK.*
I'VE BEEN DYIN' TO HEAR IF YOU PICKED A SUPER-VILLAIN NAME YET.
WHAT, DON'T HAVE ONE? THAT'S OKAY, I'LL HELP YOU OUT...
YOU'RE... CYBERGUY.
ELECTRO? NOPE, TAKEN.
WAIT. I GOT IT:
CARAPACE! 'CAUSE OF, Y'KNOW, THE ARMOR.
NO NEED TO THANK ME.
*SEE SPIDEY #583. - STEVE.
"THANKS FOR COMING, PETE."

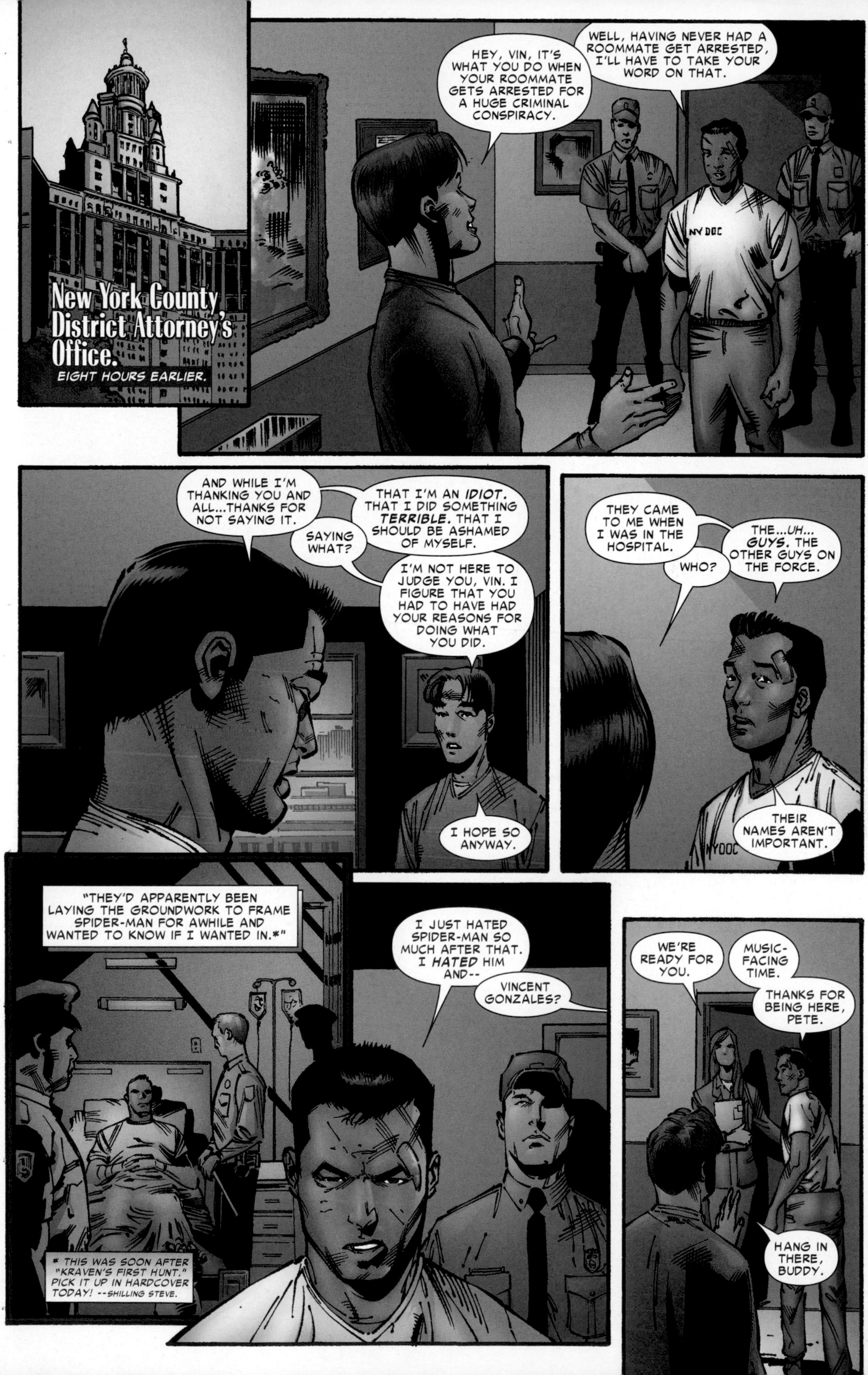
New York County District Attorney's Office.
EIGHT HOURS EARLIER.
HEY, VIN, IT'S WHAT YOU DO WHEN YOUR ROOMMATE GETS ARRESTED FOR A HUGE CRIMINAL CONSPIRACY.
WELL, HAVING NEVER HAD A ROOMMATE GET ARRESTED, I'LL HAVE TO TAKE YOUR WORD ON THAT.
NY DOC
AND WHILE I'M THANKING YOU AND ALL...THANKS FOR NOT SAYING IT.
SAYING WHAT?
THAT I'M AN *IDIOT.* THAT I DID SOMETHING ***TERRIBLE.*** THAT I SHOULD BE ASHAMED OF MYSELF.
I'M NOT HERE TO JUDGE YOU, VIN. I FIGURE THAT YOU HAD TO HAVE HAD YOUR REASONS FOR DOING WHAT YOU DID.
I HOPE SO ANYWAY.
THEY CAME TO ME WHEN I WAS IN THE HOSPITAL.
WHO?
THE...*UH...* ***GUYS.*** THE OTHER GUYS ON THE FORCE.
THEIR NAMES AREN'T IMPORTANT.
NYDOC
"THEY'D APPARENTLY BEEN LAYING THE GROUNDWORK TO FRAME SPIDER-MAN FOR AWHILE AND WANTED TO KNOW IF I WANTED IN.*"
* THIS WAS SOON AFTER "KRAVEN'S FIRST HUNT." PICK IT UP IN HARDCOVER TODAY! --SHILLING STEVE.
I JUST HATED SPIDER-MAN SO MUCH AFTER THAT. I *HATED* HIM AND--
VINCENT GONZALES?
WE'RE READY FOR YOU.
MUSIC-FACING TIME.
THANKS FOR BEING HERE, PETE.
HANG IN THERE, BUDDY.

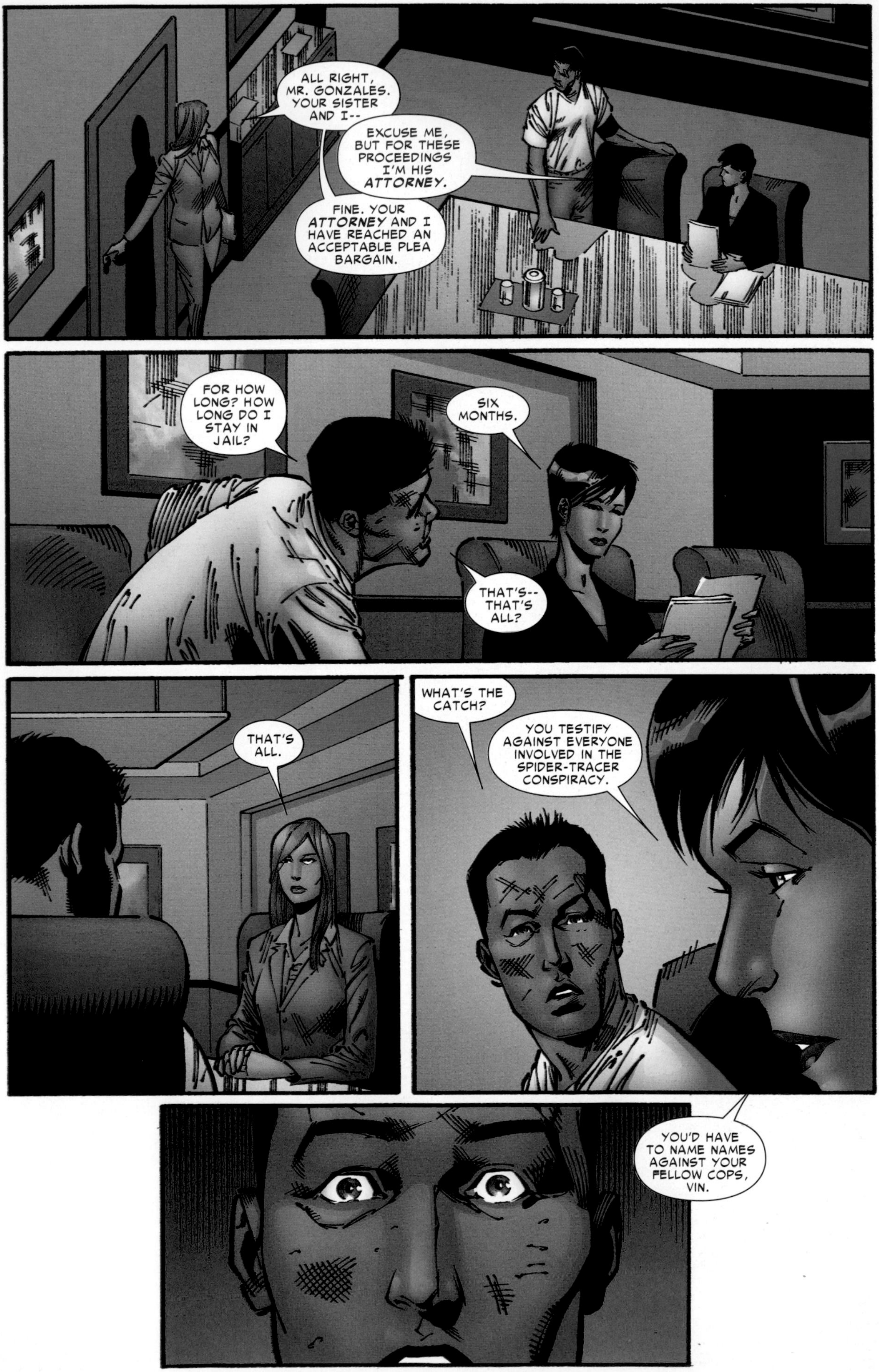
ALL RIGHT, MR. GONZALES. YOUR SISTER AND I--
EXCUSE ME, BUT FOR THESE PROCEEDINGS I'M HIS ATTORNEY.
FINE. YOUR ATTORNEY AND I HAVE REACHED AN ACCEPTABLE PLEA BARGAIN.
FOR HOW LONG? HOW LONG DO I STAY IN JAIL?
SIX MONTHS.
THAT'S-- THAT'S ALL?
THAT'S ALL.
WHAT'S THE CATCH?
YOU TESTIFY AGAINST EVERYONE INVOLVED IN THE SPIDER-TRACER CONSPIRACY.
YOU'D HAVE TO NAME NAMES AGAINST YOUR FELLOW COPS, VIN.

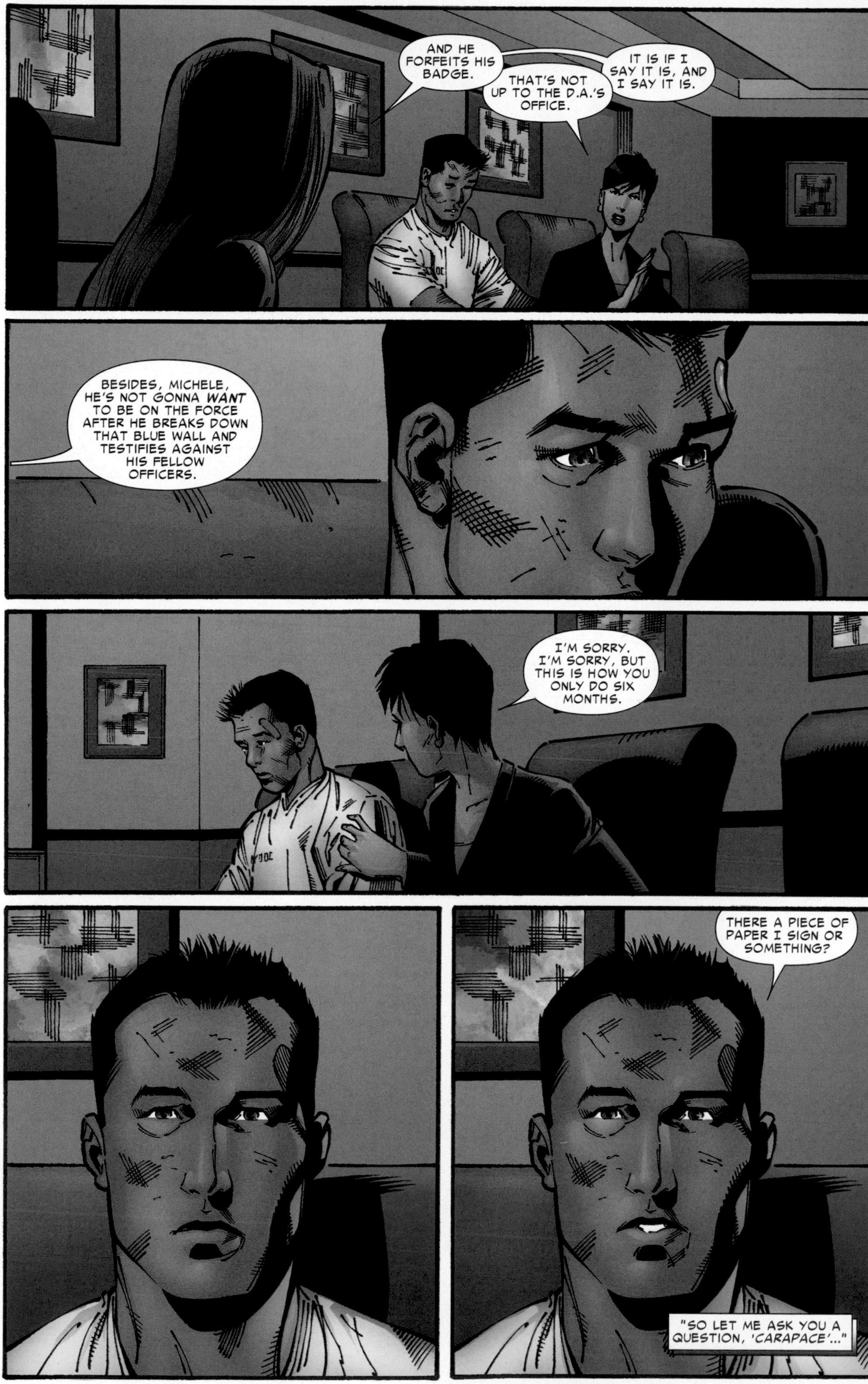
AND HE FORFEITS HIS BADGE.
THAT'S NOT UP TO THE D.A.'S OFFICE.
IT IS IF I SAY IT IS, AND I SAY IT IS.
BESIDES, MICHELE, HE'S NOT GONNA *WANT* TO BE ON THE FORCE AFTER HE BREAKS DOWN THAT BLUE WALL AND TESTIFIES AGAINST HIS FELLOW OFFICERS.
I'M SORRY. I'M SORRY, BUT THIS IS HOW YOU ONLY DO SIX MONTHS.
THERE A PIECE OF PAPER I SIGN OR SOMETHING?
"SO LET ME ASK YOU A QUESTION, *'CARAPACE'*..."

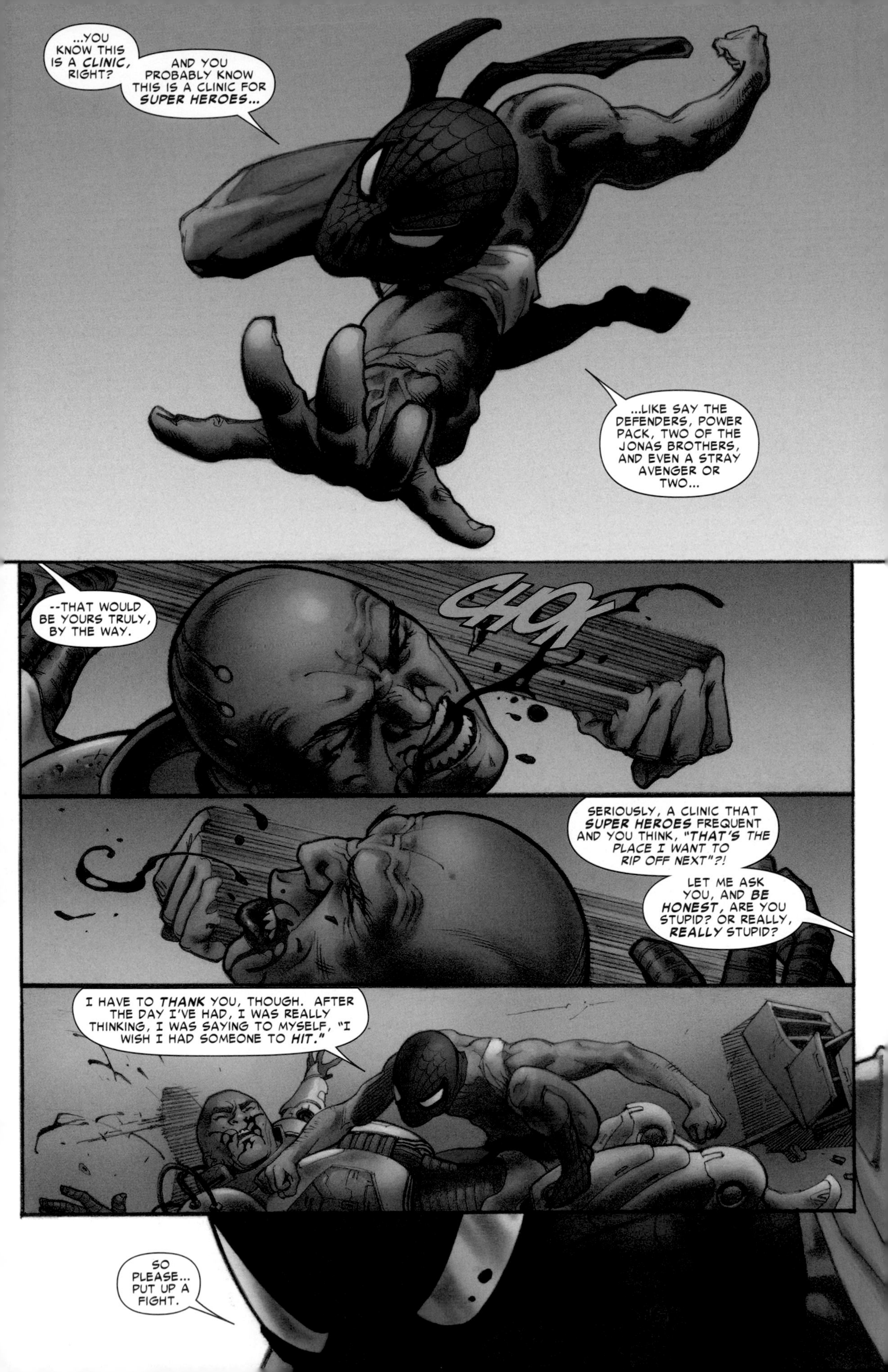
...YOU KNOW THIS IS A CLINIC, RIGHT?
AND YOU PROBABLY KNOW THIS IS A CLINIC FOR SUPER HEROES...
...LIKE SAY THE DEFENDERS, POWER PACK, TWO OF THE JONAS BROTHERS, AND EVEN A STRAY AVENGER OR TWO...
--THAT WOULD BE YOURS TRULY, BY THE WAY.
CHOK
SERIOUSLY, A CLINIC THAT SUPER HEROES FREQUENT AND YOU THINK, "THAT'S THE PLACE I WANT TO RIP OFF NEXT"?!
LET ME ASK YOU, AND BE HONEST, ARE YOU STUPID? OR REALLY, REALLY STUPID?
I HAVE TO THANK YOU, THOUGH. AFTER THE DAY I'VE HAD, I WAS REALLY THINKING, I WAS SAYING TO MYSELF, "I WISH I HAD SOMEONE TO HIT."
SO PLEASE... PUT UP A FIGHT.

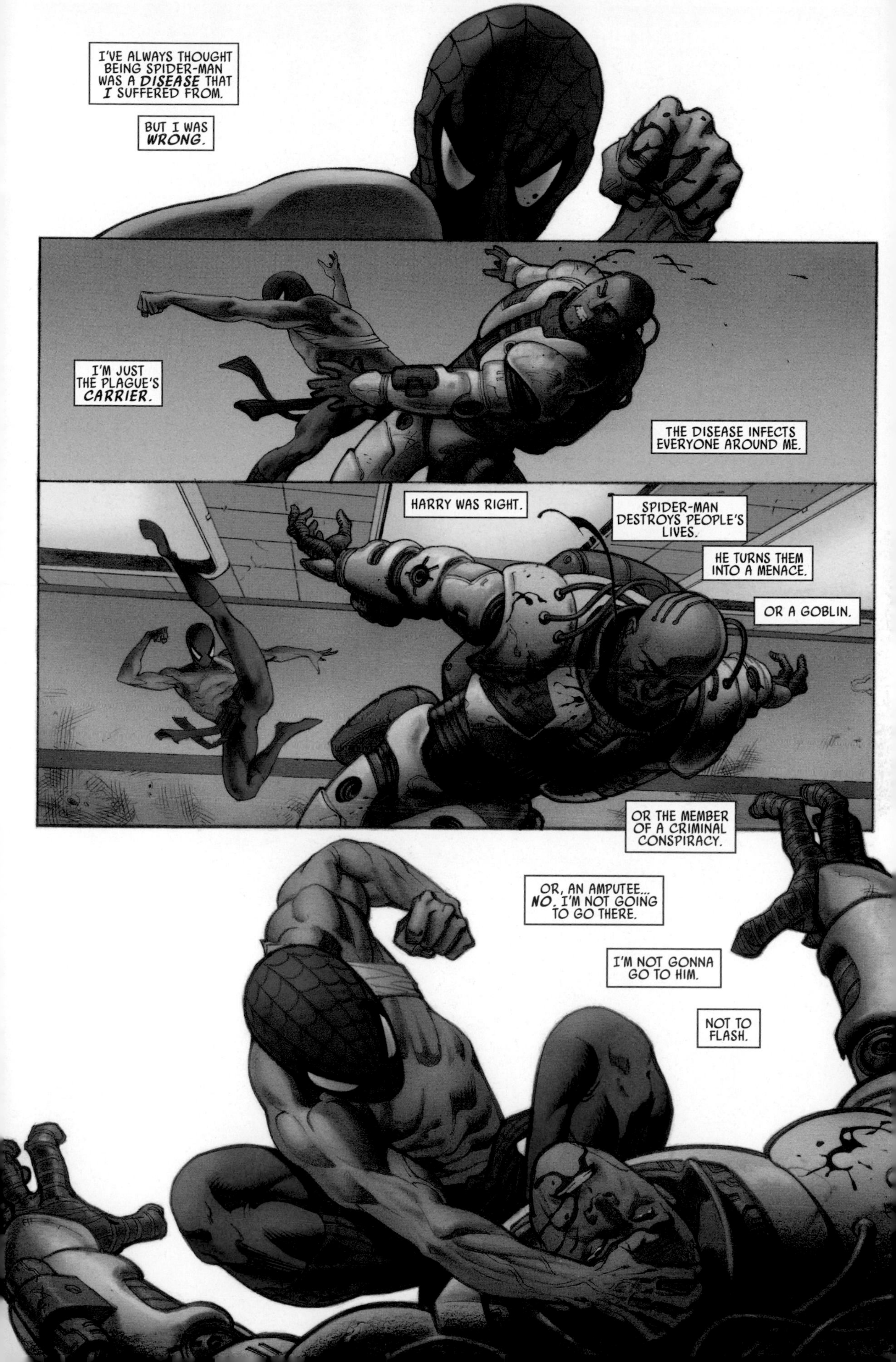
I'VE ALWAYS THOUGHT BEING SPIDER-MAN WAS A DISEASE THAT I SUFFERED FROM.
BUT I WAS WRONG.
I'M JUST THE PLAGUE'S CARRIER.
THE DISEASE INFECTS EVERYONE AROUND ME.
HARRY WAS RIGHT.
SPIDER-MAN DESTROYS PEOPLE'S LIVES.
HE TURNS THEM INTO A MENACE.
OR A GOBLIN.
OR THE MEMBER OF A CRIMINAL CONSPIRACY.
OR, AN AMPUTEE... NO. I'M NOT GOING TO GO THERE.
I'M NOT GONNA GO TO HIM.
NOT TO FLASH.

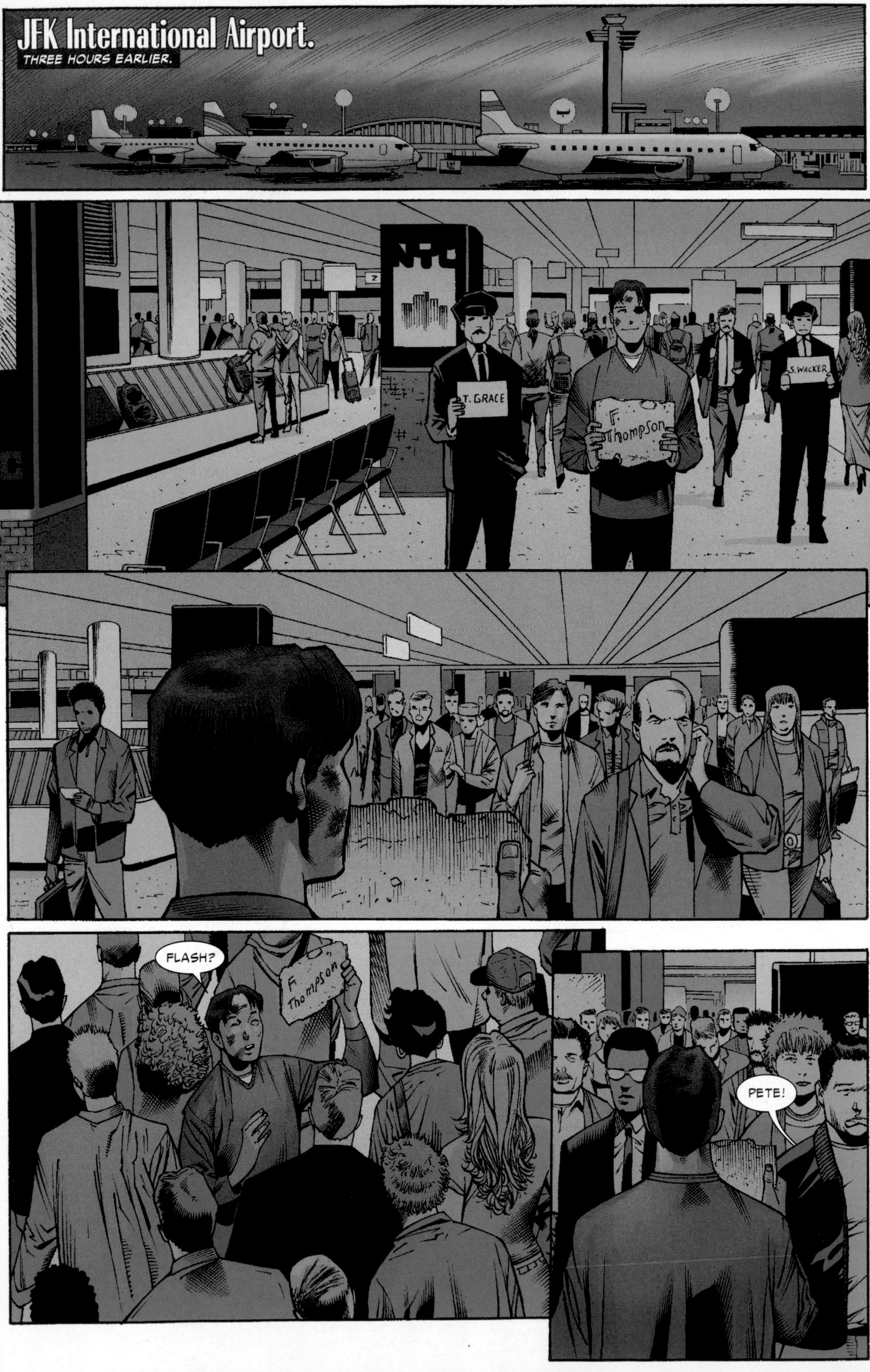
JFK International Airport.
THREE HOURS EARLIER.
T. GRACE
F. Thompson
S. WACKER
FLASH?
F. Thompson
PETE!

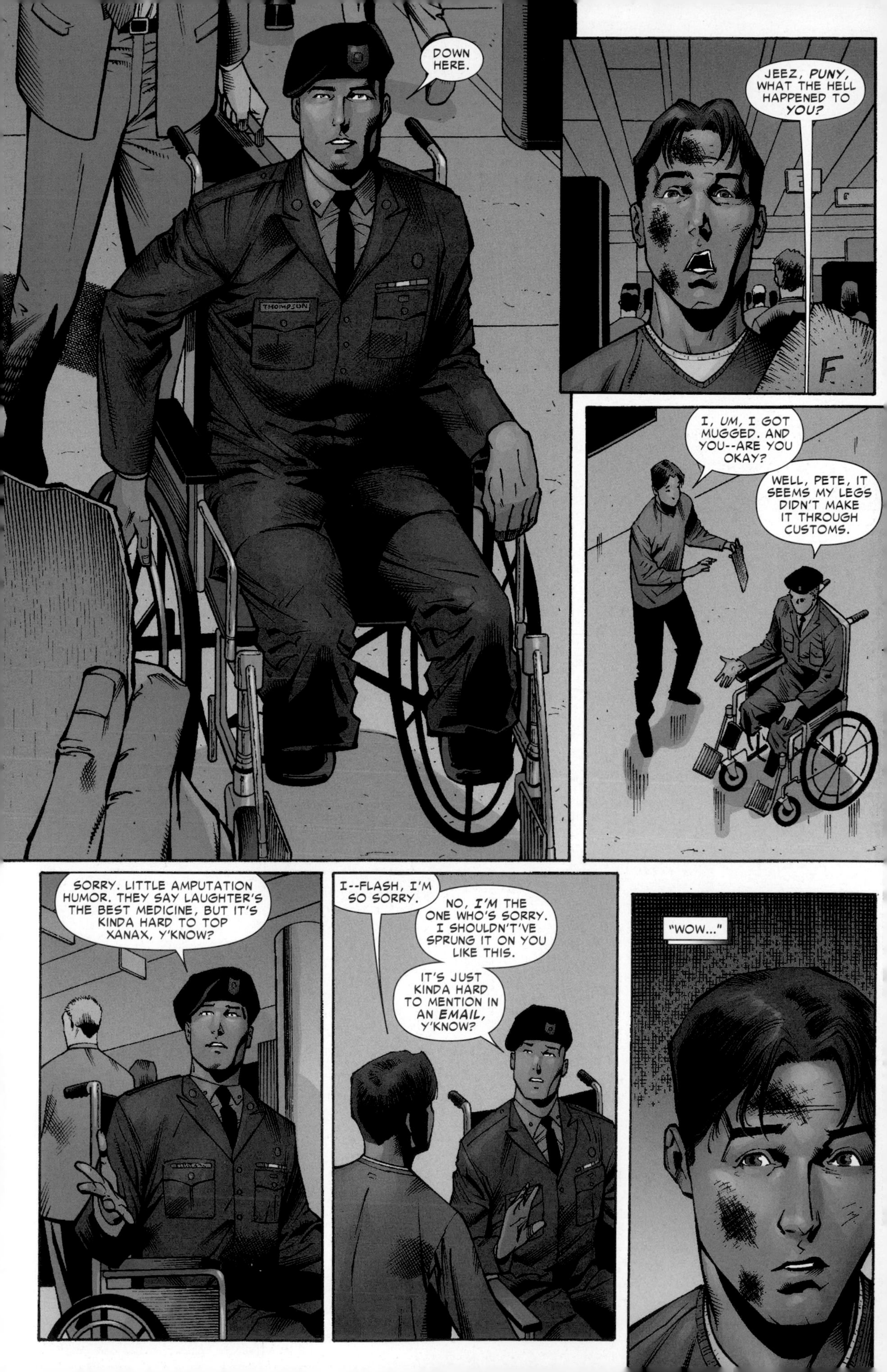
DOWN HERE.
JEEZ, *PUNY*, WHAT THE HELL HAPPENED TO *YOU?*
THOMPSON
I, *UM*, I GOT MUGGED. AND YOU--ARE YOU OKAY?
WELL, PETE, IT SEEMS MY LEGS DIDN'T MAKE IT THROUGH CUSTOMS.
SORRY. LITTLE AMPUTATION HUMOR. THEY SAY LAUGHTER'S THE BEST MEDICINE, BUT IT'S KINDA HARD TO TOP XANAX, Y'KNOW?
I--FLASH, I'M SO SORRY.
NO, *I'M* THE ONE WHO'S SORRY. I SHOULDN'T'VE SPRUNG IT ON YOU LIKE THIS.
IT'S JUST KINDA HARD TO MENTION IN AN *EMAIL*, Y'KNOW?
"WOW..."

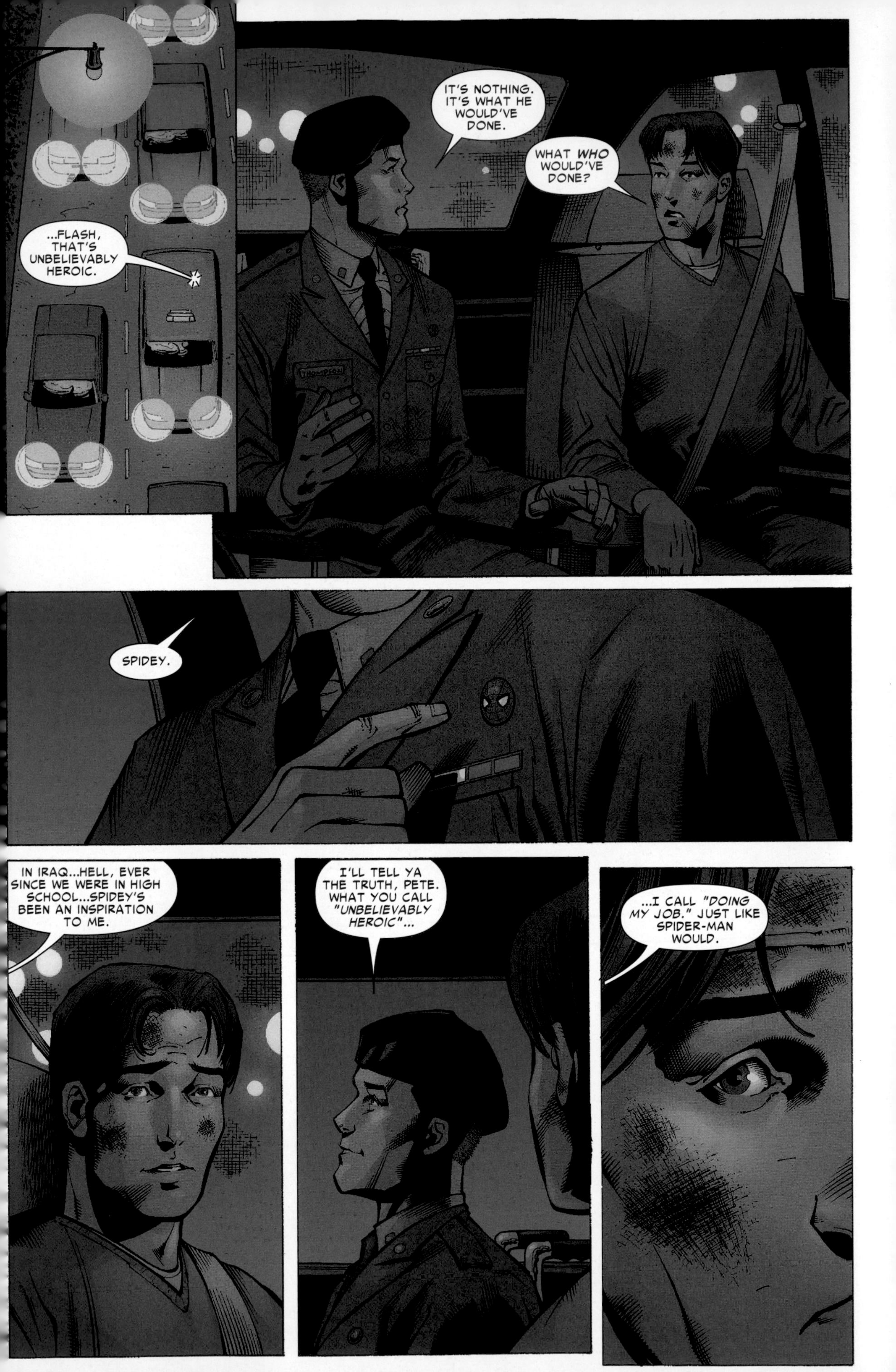
...FLASH, THAT'S UNBELIEVABLY HEROIC.
IT'S NOTHING. IT'S WHAT HE WOULD'VE DONE.
WHAT *WHO* WOULD'VE DONE?
THOMPSON
SPIDEY.
IN IRAQ...HELL, EVER SINCE WE WERE IN HIGH SCHOOL...SPIDEY'S BEEN AN INSPIRATION TO ME.
I'LL TELL YA THE TRUTH, PETE. WHAT YOU CALL "*UNBELIEVABLY HEROIC*"...
...I CALL "*DOING MY JOB.*" JUST LIKE SPIDER-MAN WOULD.

NIGHT NURSE IS *SCREAMING* AT ME TO STOP.

I DON'T LISTEN.

I DON'T *CARE*.

I'M SO ANGRY, SO FILLED WITH *RAGE*...

NO, THAT'S NOT TRUE. IT'S NOT RAGE.

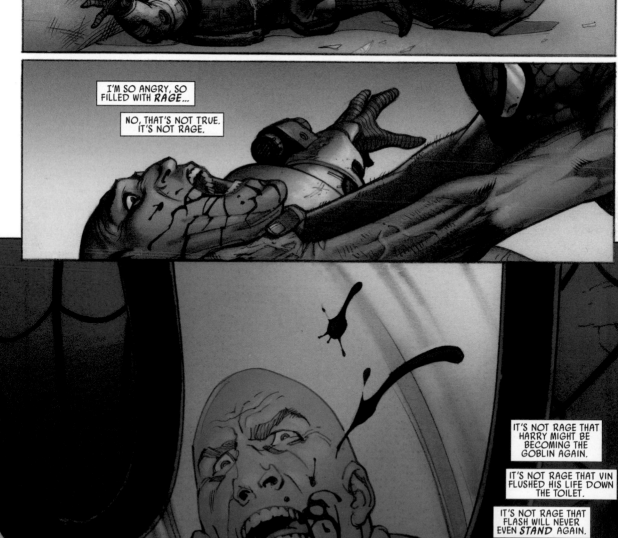

IT'S NOT RAGE THAT HARRY MIGHT BE BECOMING THE GOBLIN AGAIN.

IT'S NOT RAGE THAT VIN FLUSHED HIS LIFE DOWN THE TOILET.

IT'S NOT RAGE THAT FLASH WILL NEVER EVEN *STAND* AGAIN.

(ALL BECAUSE OF SPIDER-MAN.)

IT'S *GUILT*.

(CAN YOU BELIEVE IT?)

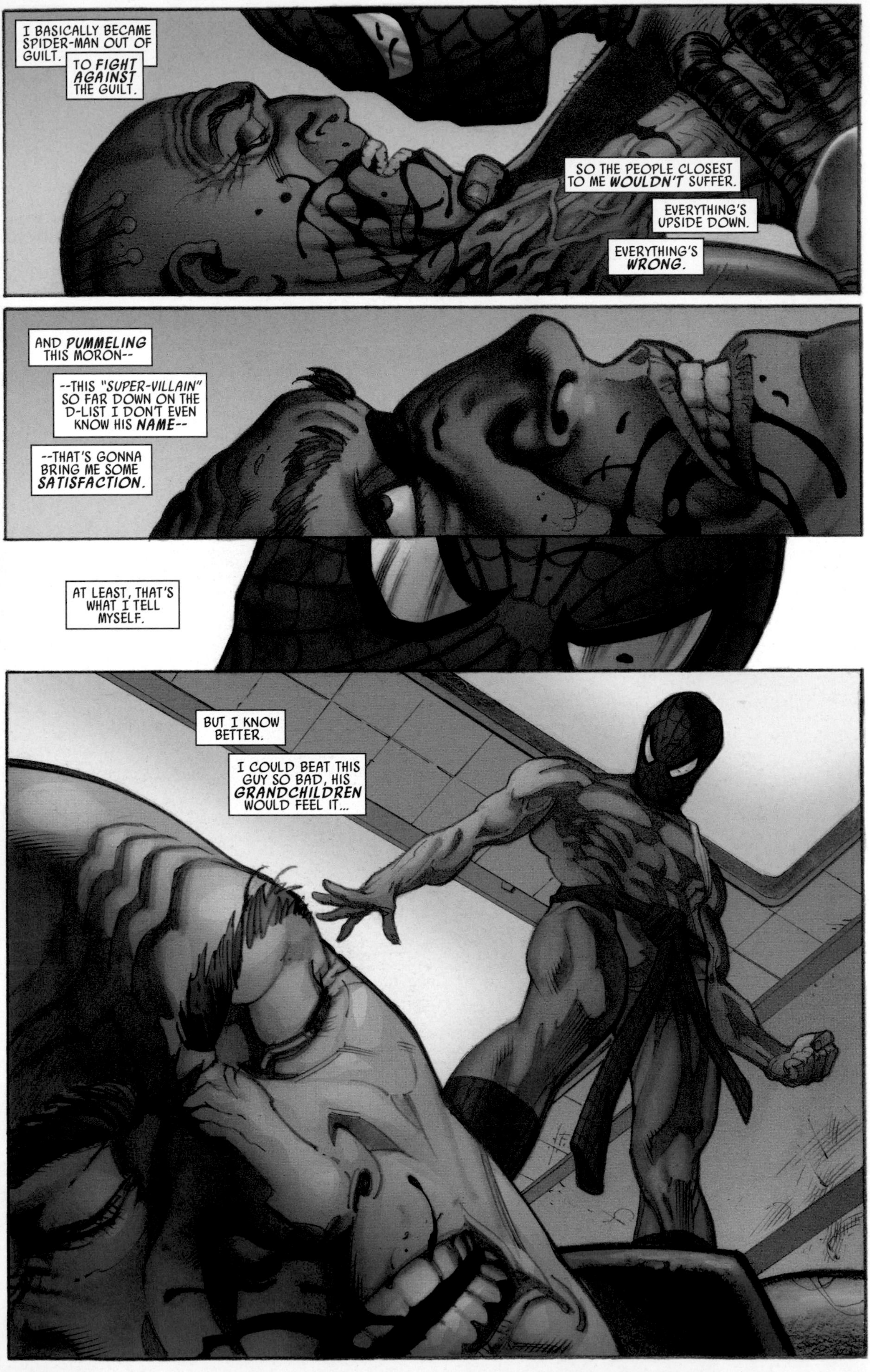

I BASICALLY BECAME SPIDER-MAN OUT OF GUILT.
TO FIGHT AGAINST THE GUILT.
SO THE PEOPLE CLOSEST TO ME WOULDN'T SUFFER.
EVERYTHING'S UPSIDE DOWN.
EVERYTHING'S WRONG.
AND PUMMELING THIS MORON--
--THIS "SUPER-VILLAIN" SO FAR DOWN ON THE D-LIST I DON'T EVEN KNOW HIS NAME--
--THAT'S GONNA BRING ME SOME SATISFACTION.
AT LEAST, THAT'S WHAT I TELL MYSELF.
BUT I KNOW BETTER.
I COULD BEAT THIS GUY SO BAD, HIS GRANDCHILDREN WOULD FEEL IT...

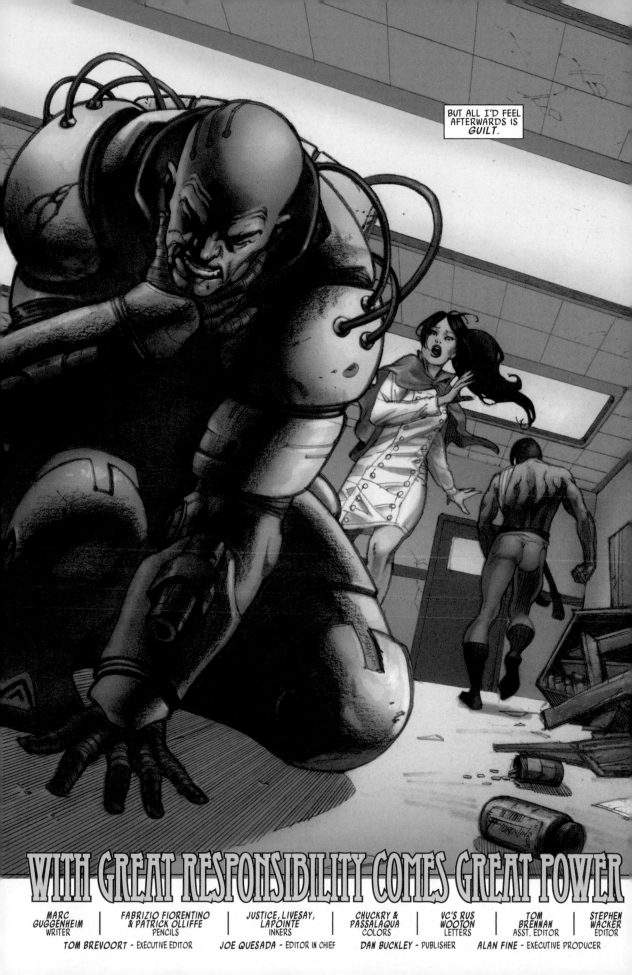

BUT ALL I'D FEEL AFTERWARDS IS *GUILT.*

WITH GREAT RESPONSIBILITY COMES GREAT POWER

MARC GUGGENHEIM
WRITER

FABRIZIO FIORENTINO & PATRICK OLLIFFE
PENCILS

JUSTICE, LIVESAY, LAPOINTE
INKERS

CHUCKRY & PASSALAQUA
COLORS

VC'S RUS WOOTON
LETTERS

TOM BRENNAN
ASST. EDITOR

STEPHEN WACKER
EDITOR

TOM BREVOORT - EXECUTIVE EDITOR

JOE QUESADA - EDITOR IN CHIEF

DAN BUCKLEY - PUBLISHER

ALAN FINE - EXECUTIVE PRODUCER

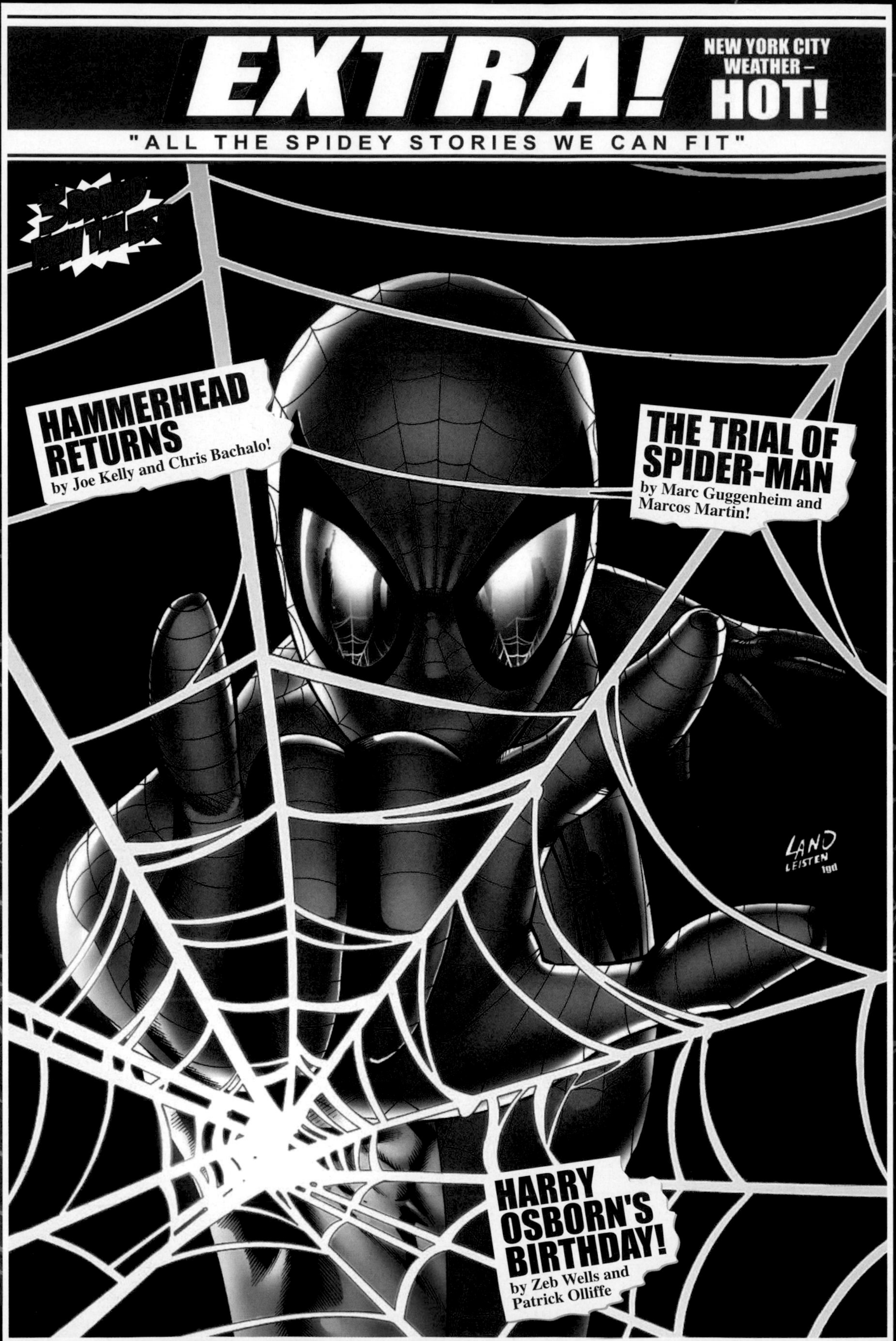

AMAZING SPIDER-MAN: EXTRA #1 – "THE SPARTACUS GAMBIT"

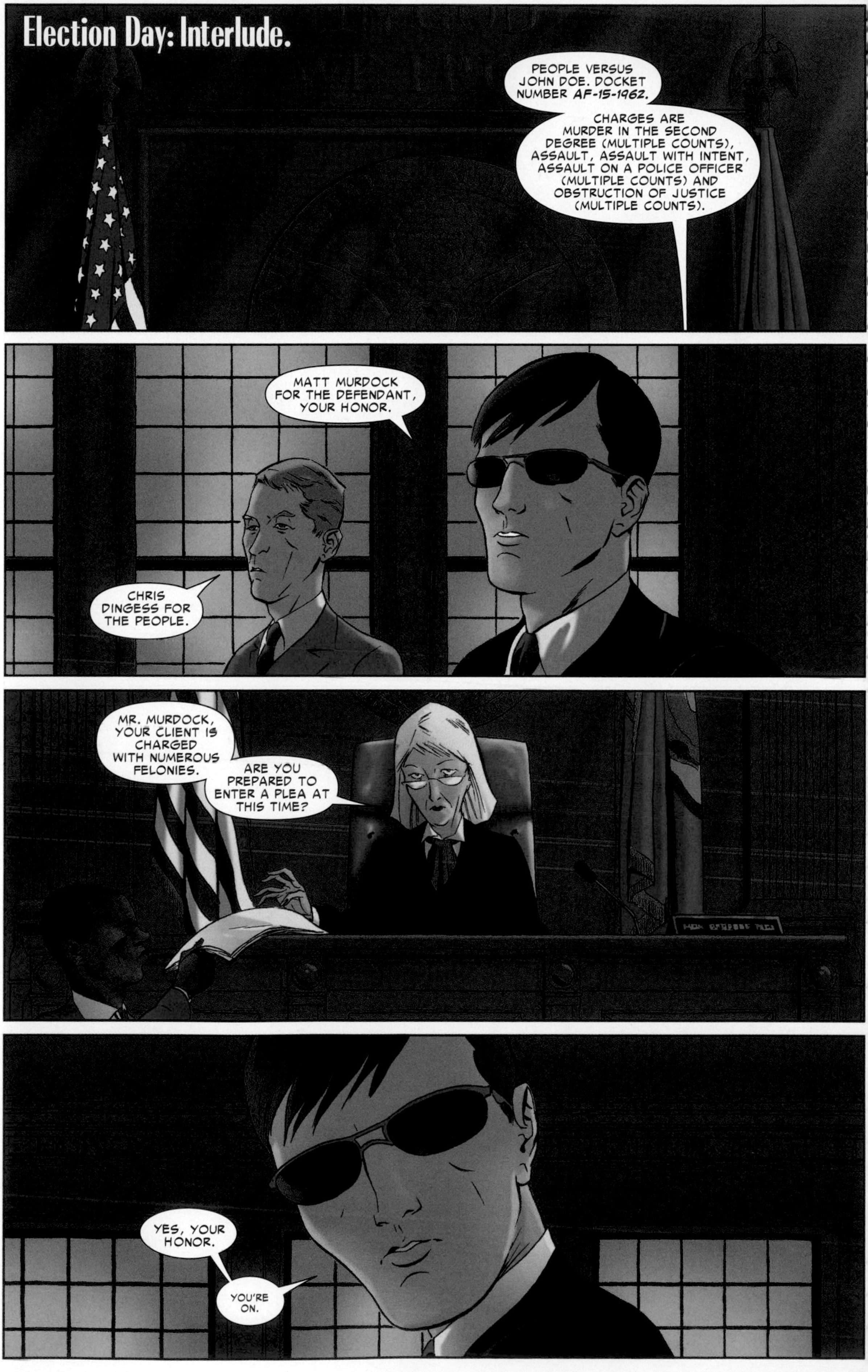
Election Day: Interlude.
PEOPLE VERSUS JOHN DOE. DOCKET NUMBER AF-15-1962.
CHARGES ARE MURDER IN THE SECOND DEGREE (MULTIPLE COUNTS), ASSAULT, ASSAULT WITH INTENT, ASSAULT ON A POLICE OFFICER (MULTIPLE COUNTS) AND OBSTRUCTION OF JUSTICE (MULTIPLE COUNTS).
MATT MURDOCK FOR THE DEFENDANT, YOUR HONOR.
CHRIS DINGESS FOR THE PEOPLE.
MR. MURDOCK, YOUR CLIENT IS CHARGED WITH NUMEROUS FELONIES.
ARE YOU PREPARED TO ENTER A PLEA AT THIS TIME?
YES, YOUR HONOR.
YOU'RE ON.

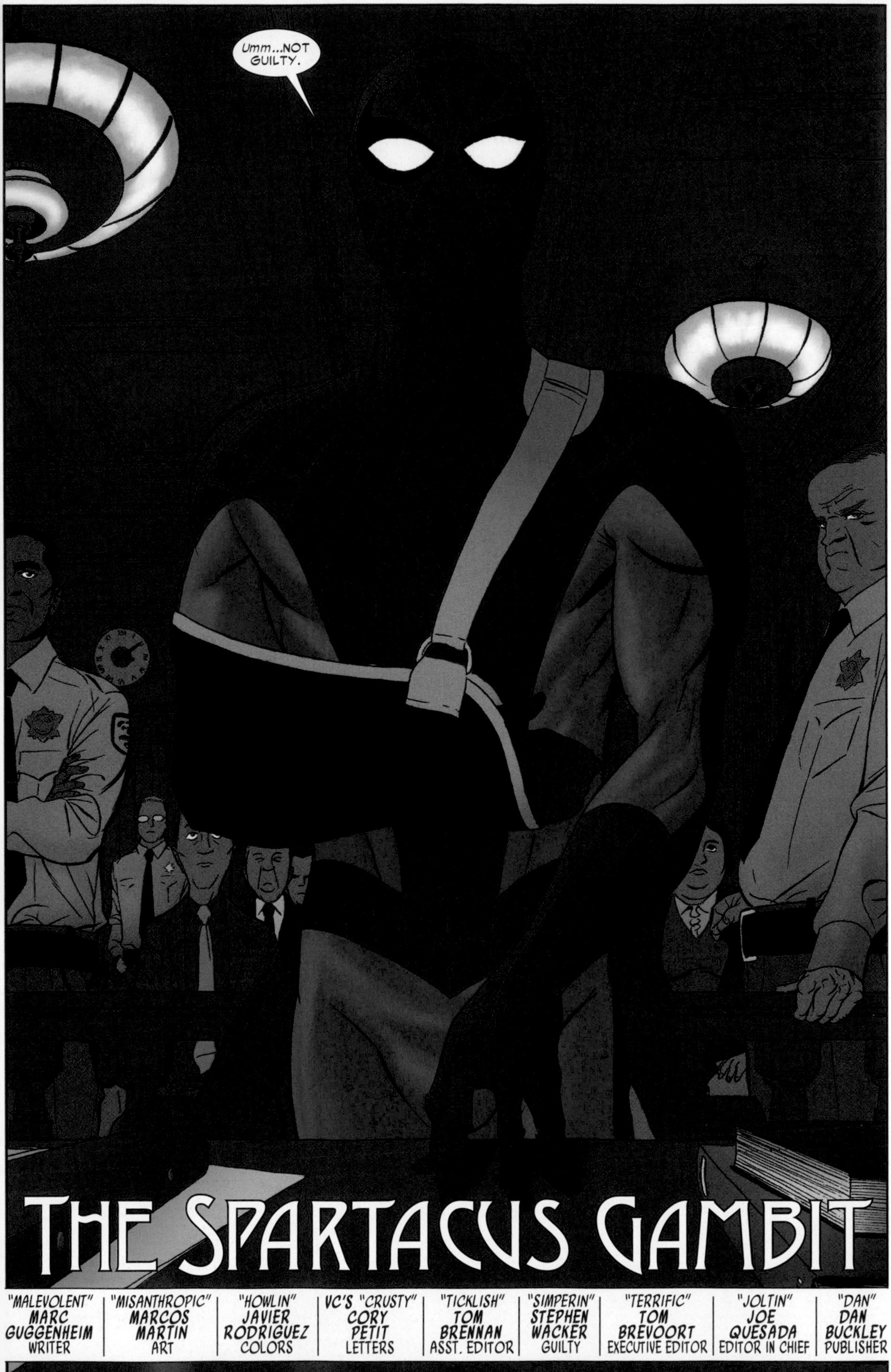

Umm...NOT GUILTY.
THE SPARTACUS GAMBIT
"MALEVOLENT" MARC GUGGENHEIM WRITER
"MISANTHROPIC" MARCOS MARTIN ART
"HOWLIN" JAVIER RODRIGUEZ COLORS
VC'S "CRUSTY" CORY PETIT LETTERS
"TICKLISH" TOM BRENNAN ASST. EDITOR
"SIMPERIN" STEPHEN WACKER GUILTY
"TERRIFIC" TOM BREVOORT EXECUTIVE EDITOR
"JOLTIN" JOE QUESADA EDITOR IN CHIEF
"DAN" DAN BUCKLEY PUBLISHER

QUESTION OF BAIL? DO I EVEN HAVE TO ASK?

NO, YOUR HONOR, I THINK IT GOES WITHOUT SAYING THAT THE DEFENDANT POSES A *SUBSTANTIAL* FLIGHT RISK.

ACTUALLY, I CAN'T FLY.

SPIDER-MAN?

YEAH?

NOT HELPING.

YEAH.

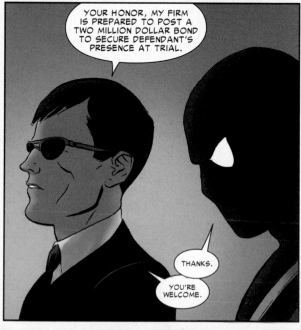

YOUR HONOR, MY FIRM IS PREPARED TO POST A TWO MILLION DOLLAR BOND TO SECURE DEFENDANT'S PRESENCE AT TRIAL.

THANKS.

YOU'RE WELCOME.

AS LONG AS HE'S WEARING THAT MASK, WE DON'T EVEN KNOW WHO YOU'D BE POSTING A BOND *FOR.*

MY REPRESENTATION, AS BOTH THE BONDSMAN AND AN OFFICER OF THE COURT, SHOULD BE SUFFICIENT.

IN ANY CASE, THE DEFENDANT IS *ALLEGEDLY* RESPONSIBLE FOR THE ARREST OF HUNDREDS OF CRIMINALS, BOTH SUPER-POWERED AND OTHERWISE. TO INCARCERATE HIM WITH SAID CRIMINALS PENDING TRIAL IS TANTAMOUNT TO A *DEATH* SENTENCE.

YOU SEEMED TO MANAGE.

MR. DINGESS IS REFERRING TO THE URBAN LEGEND THAT I'M SECRETLY DAREDEVIL, DESPITE THE FACT THAT I'M-- OH, WHAT'S THE PHRASE?-- COMPLETELY BLIND.

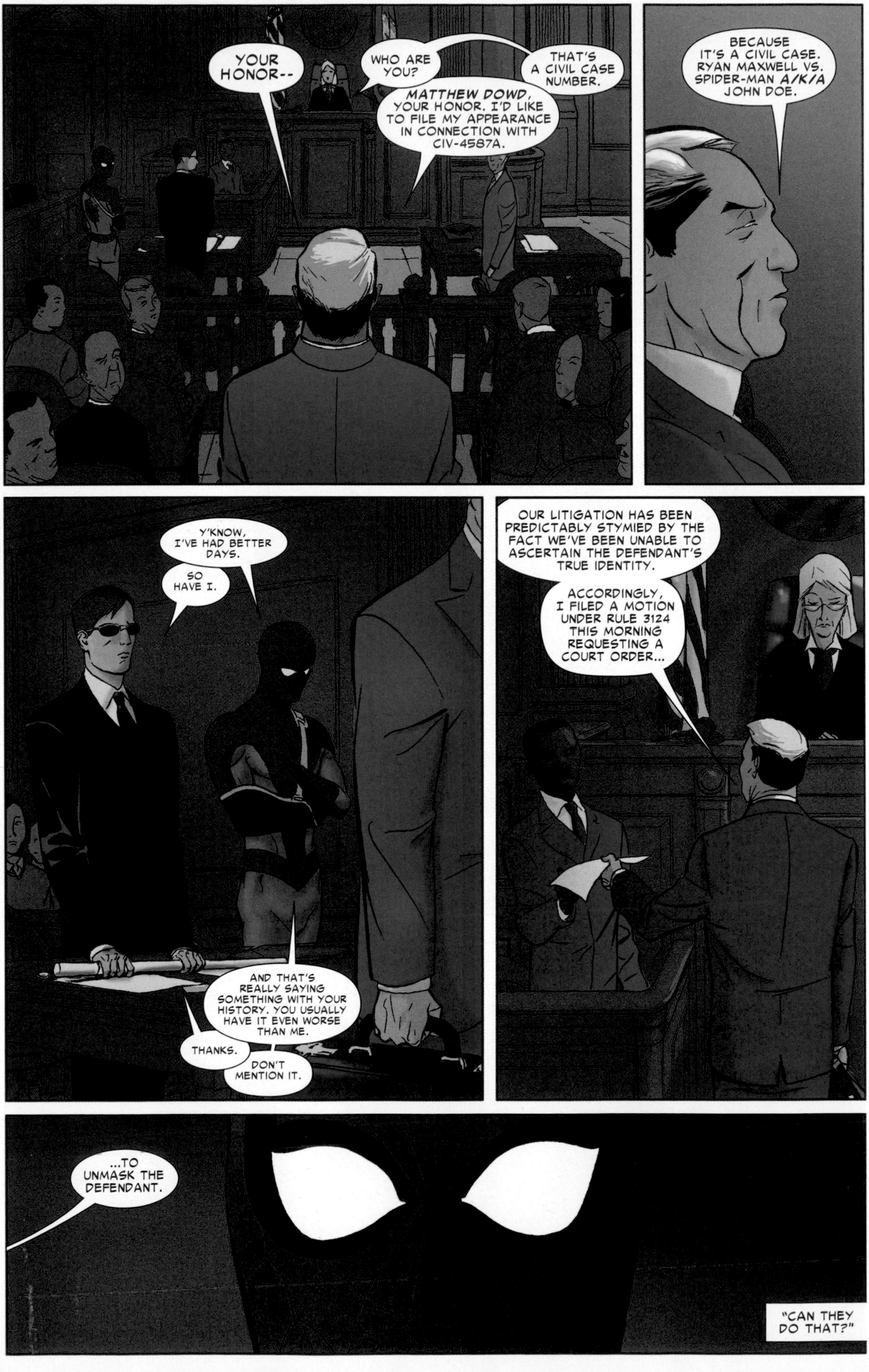
YOUR HONOR--
WHO ARE YOU?
THAT'S A CIVIL CASE NUMBER.
MATTHEW DOWD, YOUR HONOR. I'D LIKE TO FILE MY APPEARANCE IN CONNECTION WITH CIV-4587A.
BECAUSE IT'S A CIVIL CASE. RYAN MAXWELL VS. SPIDER-MAN A/K/A JOHN DOE.
Y'KNOW, I'VE HAD BETTER DAYS.
SO HAVE I.
AND THAT'S REALLY SAYING SOMETHING WITH YOUR HISTORY. YOU USUALLY HAVE IT EVEN WORSE THAN ME.
THANKS.
DON'T MENTION IT.
OUR LITIGATION HAS BEEN PREDICTABLY STYMIED BY THE FACT WE'VE BEEN UNABLE TO ASCERTAIN THE DEFENDANT'S TRUE IDENTITY.
ACCORDINGLY, I FILED A MOTION UNDER RULE 3124 THIS MORNING REQUESTING A COURT ORDER...
...TO UNMASK THE DEFENDANT.
"CAN THEY DO THAT?"

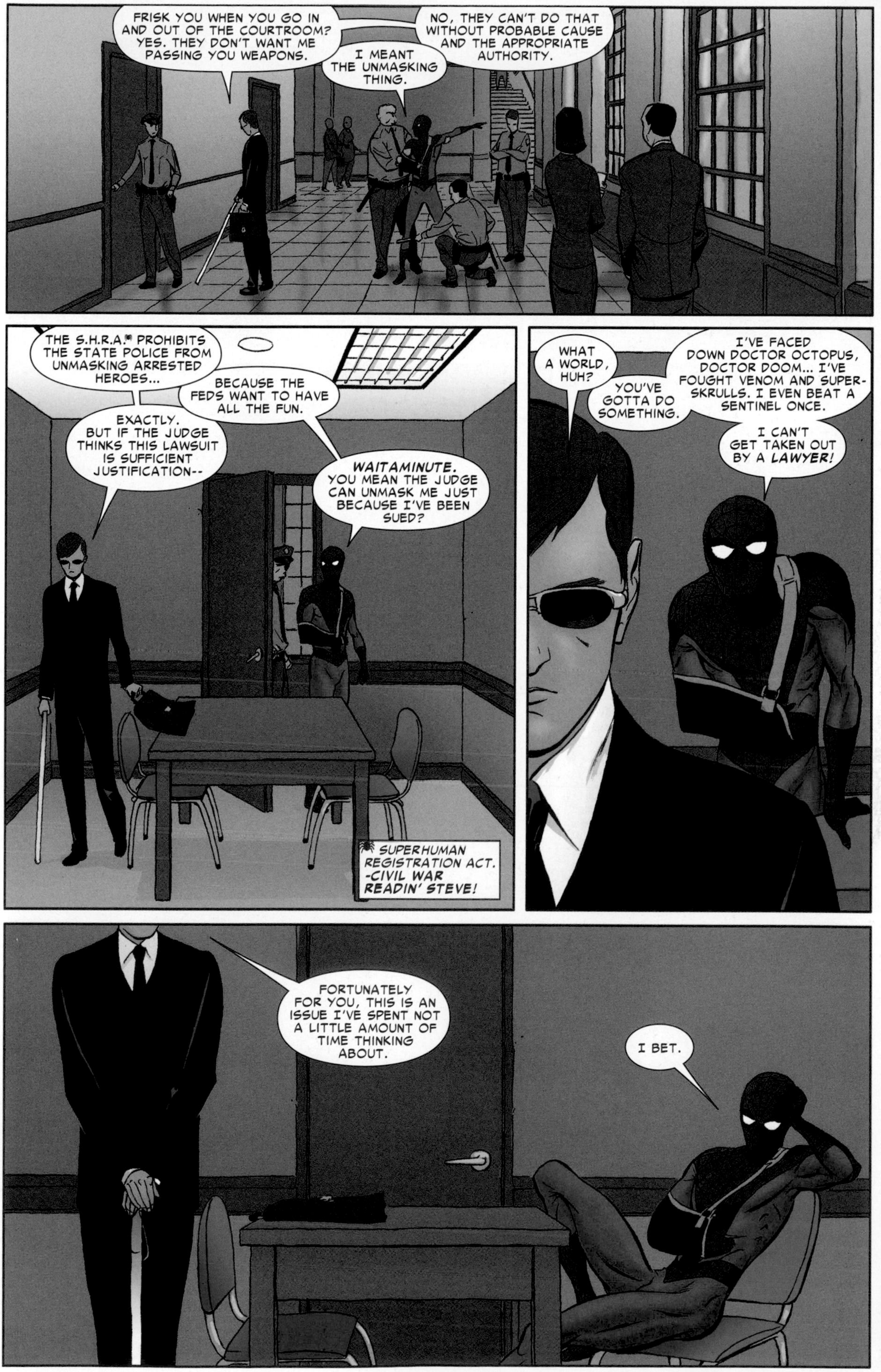

FRISK YOU WHEN YOU GO IN AND OUT OF THE COURTROOM? YES. THEY DON'T WANT ME PASSING YOU WEAPONS.
NO, THEY CAN'T DO THAT WITHOUT PROBABLE CAUSE AND THE APPROPRIATE AUTHORITY.
I MEANT THE UNMASKING THING.
THE S.H.R.A.* PROHIBITS THE STATE POLICE FROM UNMASKING ARRESTED HEROES...
BECAUSE THE FEDS WANT TO HAVE ALL THE FUN.
EXACTLY. BUT IF THE JUDGE THINKS THIS LAWSUIT IS SUFFICIENT JUSTIFICATION--
WAITAMINUTE. YOU MEAN THE JUDGE CAN UNMASK ME JUST BECAUSE I'VE BEEN SUED?
*SUPERHUMAN REGISTRATION ACT. -CIVIL WAR READIN' STEVE!
WHAT A WORLD, HUH?
YOU'VE GOTTA DO SOMETHING.
I'VE FACED DOWN DOCTOR OCTOPUS, DOCTOR DOOM... I'VE FOUGHT VENOM AND SUPER-SKRULLS. I EVEN BEAT A SENTINEL ONCE.
I CAN'T GET TAKEN OUT BY A LAWYER!
FORTUNATELY FOR YOU, THIS IS AN ISSUE I'VE SPENT NOT A LITTLE AMOUNT OF TIME THINKING ABOUT.
I BET.

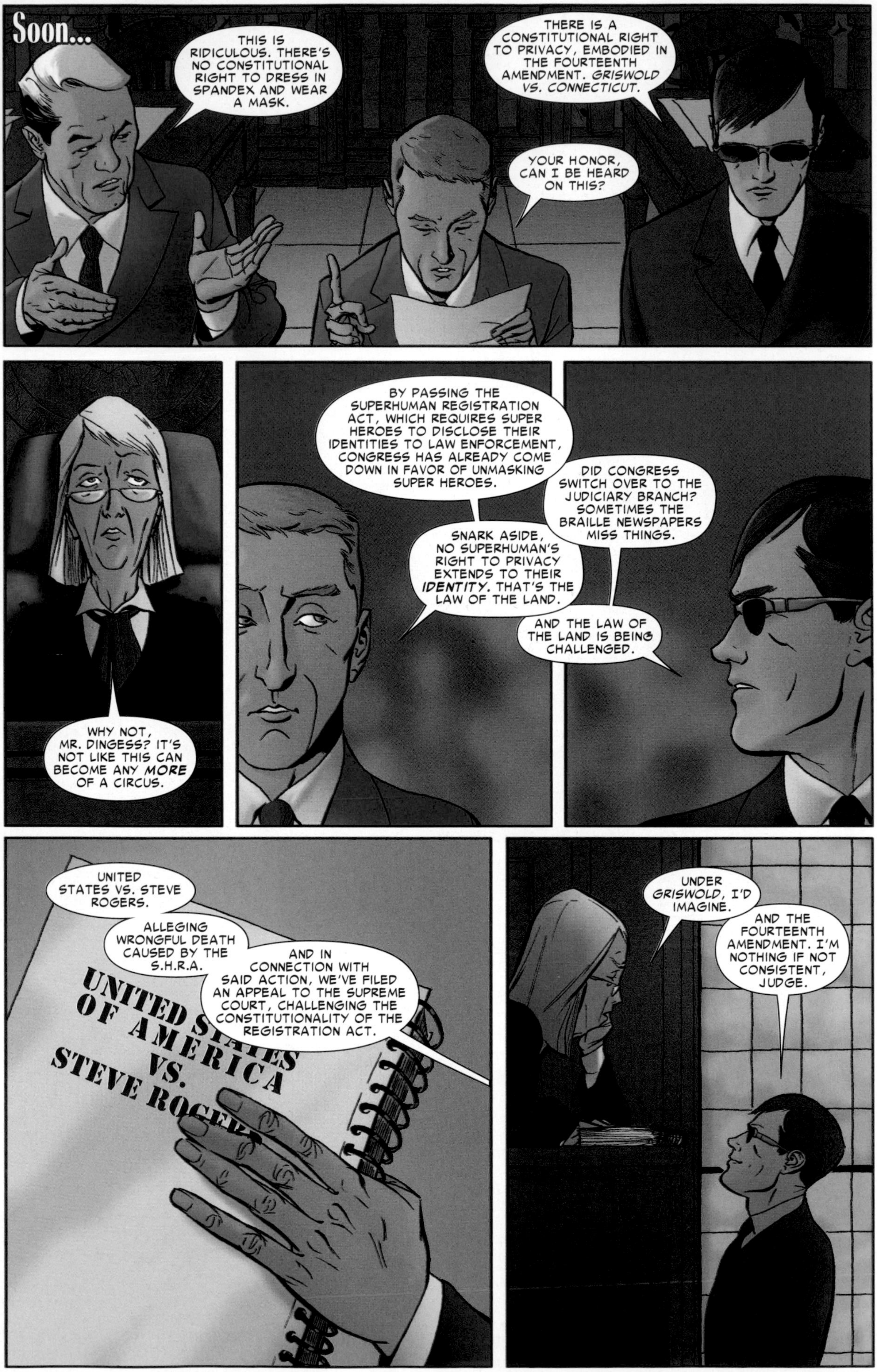
Soon...
THIS IS RIDICULOUS. THERE'S NO CONSTITUTIONAL RIGHT TO DRESS IN SPANDEX AND WEAR A MASK.
THERE IS A CONSTITUTIONAL RIGHT TO PRIVACY, EMBODIED IN THE FOURTEENTH AMENDMENT. GRISWOLD VS. CONNECTICUT.
YOUR HONOR, CAN I BE HEARD ON THIS?
WHY NOT, MR. DINGESS? IT'S NOT LIKE THIS CAN BECOME ANY MORE OF A CIRCUS.
BY PASSING THE SUPERHUMAN REGISTRATION ACT, WHICH REQUIRES SUPER HEROES TO DISCLOSE THEIR IDENTITIES TO LAW ENFORCEMENT, CONGRESS HAS ALREADY COME DOWN IN FAVOR OF UNMASKING SUPER HEROES.
DID CONGRESS SWITCH OVER TO THE JUDICIARY BRANCH? SOMETIMES THE BRAILLE NEWSPAPERS MISS THINGS.
SNARK ASIDE, NO SUPERHUMAN'S RIGHT TO PRIVACY EXTENDS TO THEIR IDENTITY. THAT'S THE LAW OF THE LAND.
AND THE LAW OF THE LAND IS BEING CHALLENGED.
UNITED STATES VS. STEVE ROGERS.
ALLEGING WRONGFUL DEATH CAUSED BY THE S.H.R.A.
AND IN CONNECTION WITH SAID ACTION, WE'VE FILED AN APPEAL TO THE SUPREME COURT, CHALLENGING THE CONSTITUTIONALITY OF THE REGISTRATION ACT.
UNITED STATES OF AMERICA VS. STEVE ROGERS
UNDER GRISWOLD, I'D IMAGINE.
AND THE FOURTEENTH AMENDMENT. I'M NOTHING IF NOT CONSISTENT, JUDGE.

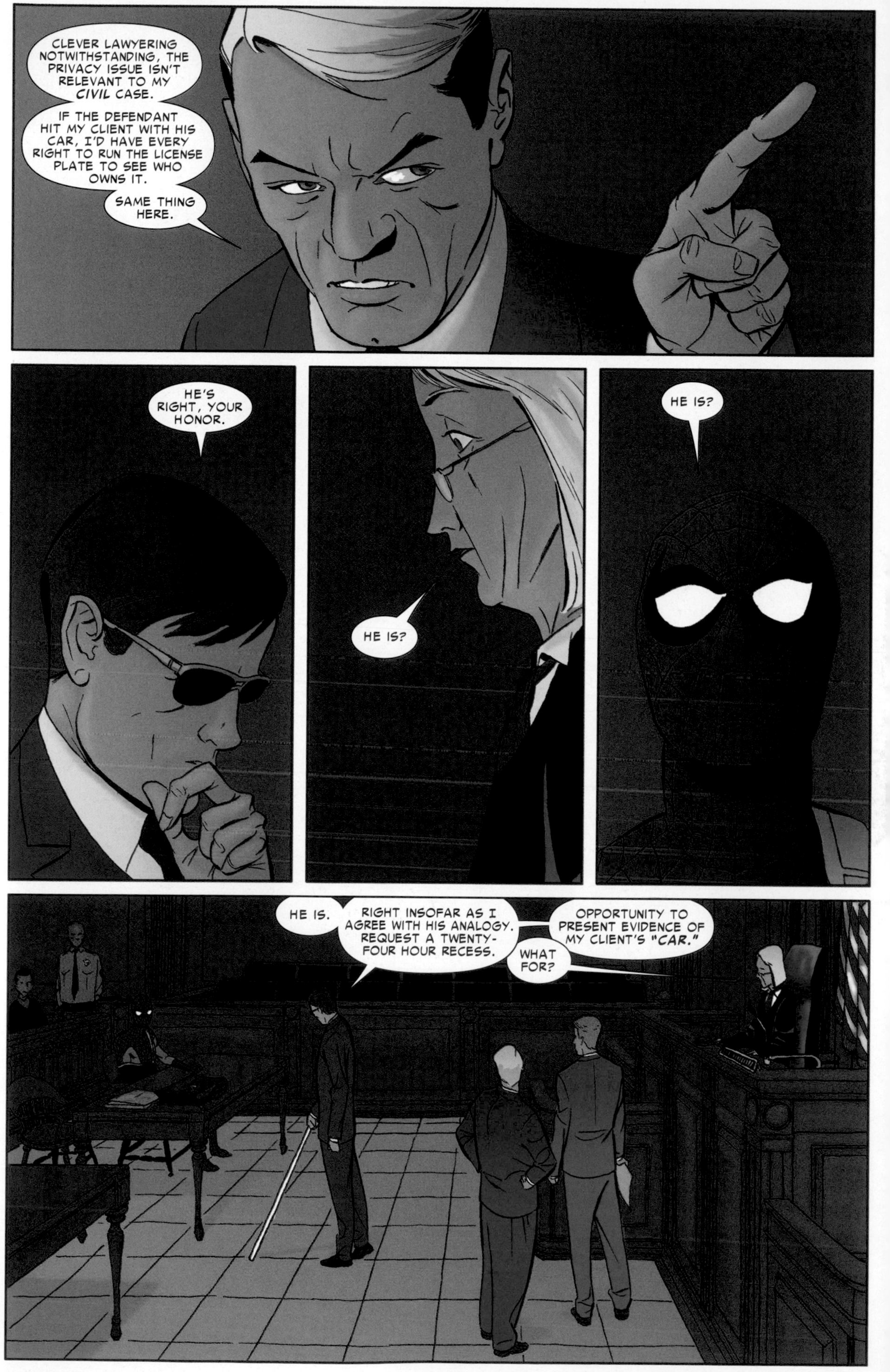
CLEVER LAWYERING NOTWITHSTANDING, THE PRIVACY ISSUE ISN'T RELEVANT TO MY *CIVIL* CASE.
IF THE DEFENDANT HIT MY CLIENT WITH HIS CAR, I'D HAVE EVERY RIGHT TO RUN THE LICENSE PLATE TO SEE WHO OWNS IT.
SAME THING HERE.
HE'S RIGHT, YOUR HONOR.
HE IS?
HE IS?
HE IS.
RIGHT INSOFAR AS I AGREE WITH HIS ANALOGY. REQUEST A TWENTY-FOUR HOUR RECESS.
WHAT FOR?
OPPORTUNITY TO PRESENT EVIDENCE OF MY CLIENT'S "*CAR*."

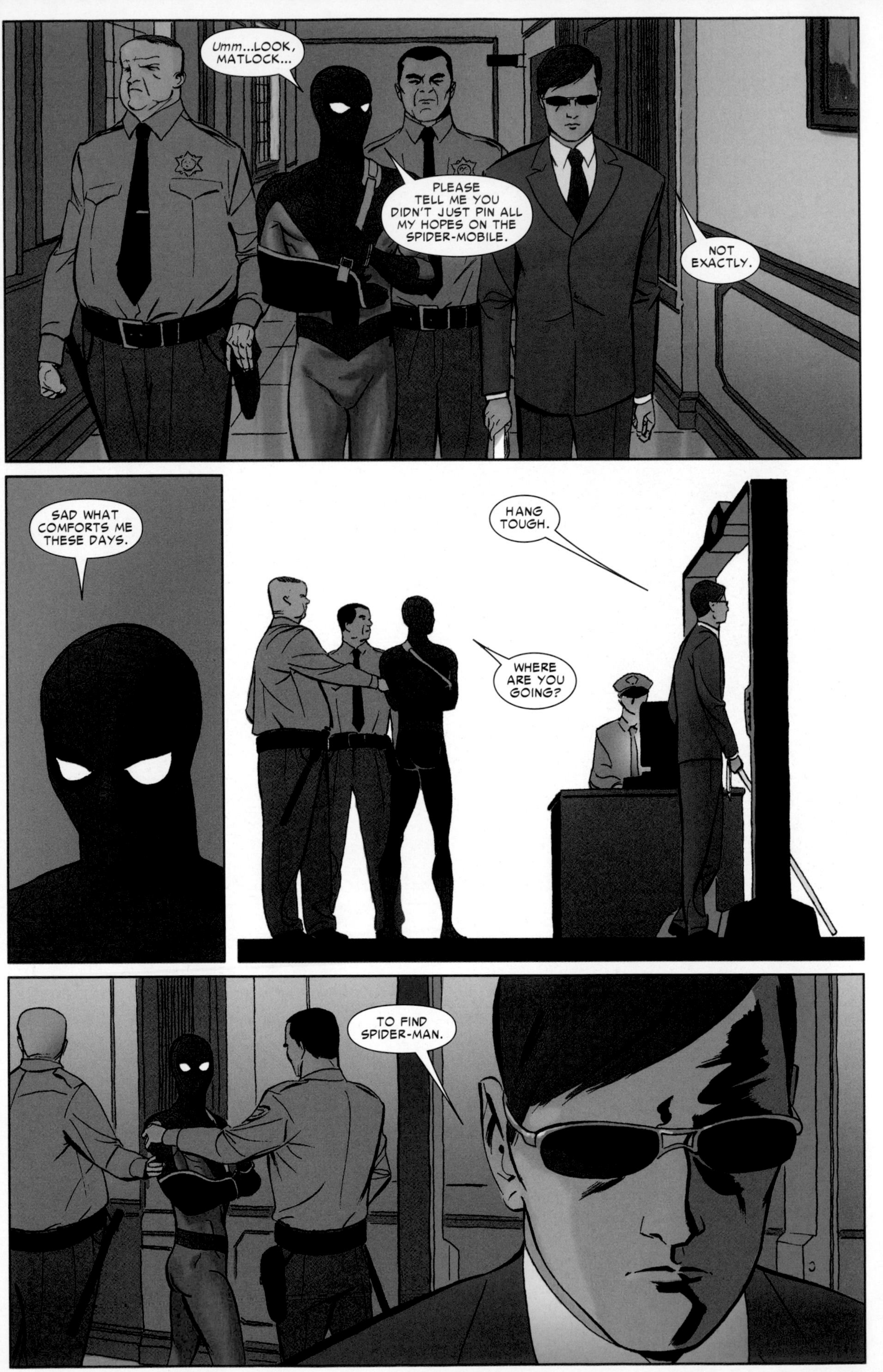
Umm...LOOK, MATLOCK...
PLEASE TELL ME YOU DIDN'T JUST PIN ALL MY HOPES ON THE SPIDER-MOBILE.
NOT EXACTLY.
SAD WHAT COMFORTS ME THESE DAYS.
HANG TOUGH.
WHERE ARE YOU GOING?
TO FIND SPIDER-MAN.

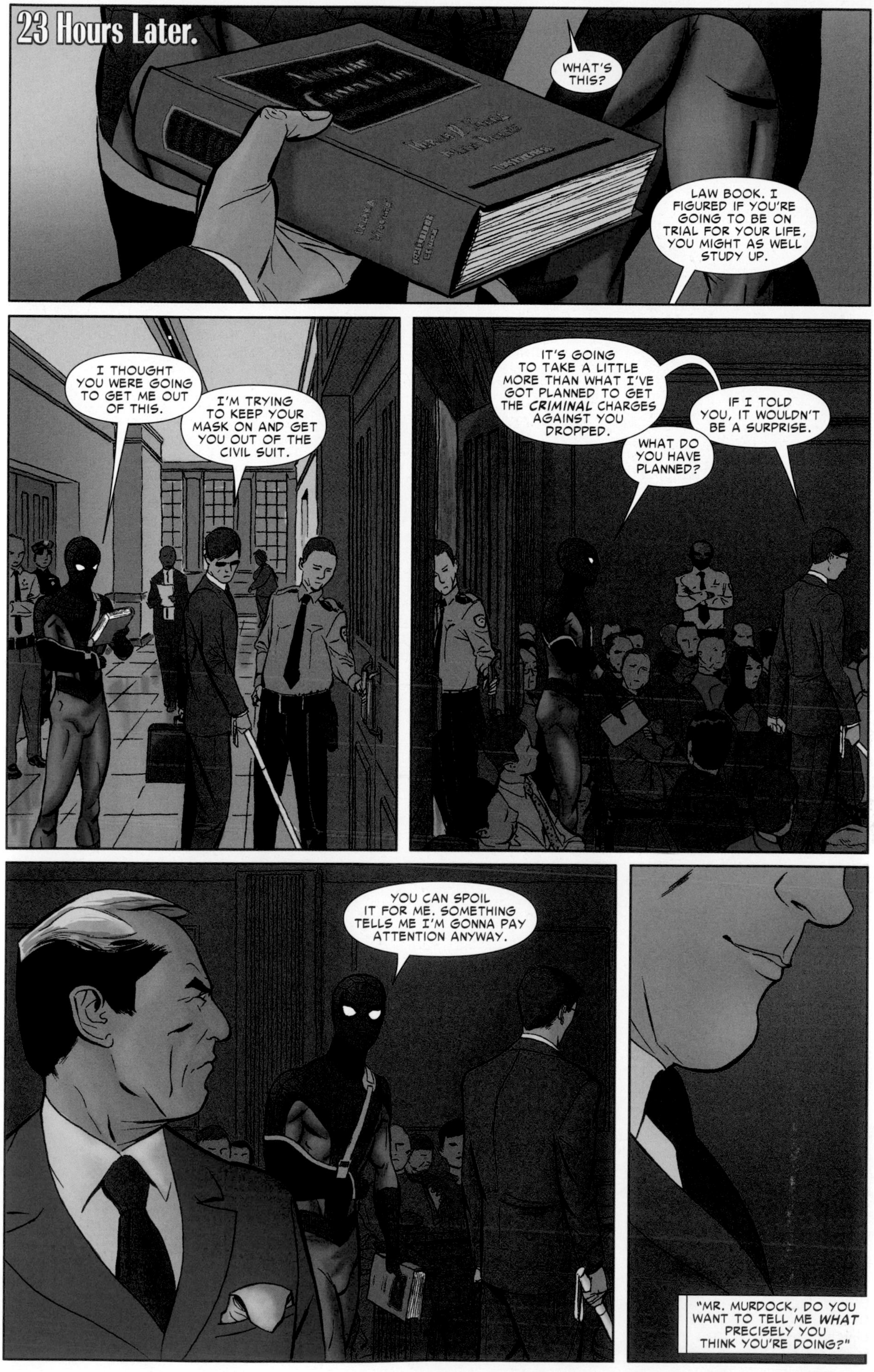
23 Hours Later.
WHAT'S THIS?
LAW BOOK. I FIGURED IF YOU'RE GOING TO BE ON TRIAL FOR YOUR LIFE, YOU MIGHT AS WELL STUDY UP.
I THOUGHT YOU WERE GOING TO GET ME OUT OF THIS.
I'M TRYING TO KEEP YOUR MASK ON AND GET YOU OUT OF THE CIVIL SUIT.
IT'S GOING TO TAKE A LITTLE MORE THAN WHAT I'VE GOT PLANNED TO GET THE *CRIMINAL* CHARGES AGAINST YOU DROPPED.
WHAT DO YOU HAVE PLANNED?
IF I TOLD YOU, IT WOULDN'T BE A SURPRISE.
YOU CAN SPOIL IT FOR ME. SOMETHING TELLS ME I'M GONNA PAY ATTENTION ANYWAY.
"MR. MURDOCK, DO YOU WANT TO TELL ME *WHAT* PRECISELY YOU THINK YOU'RE DOING?"

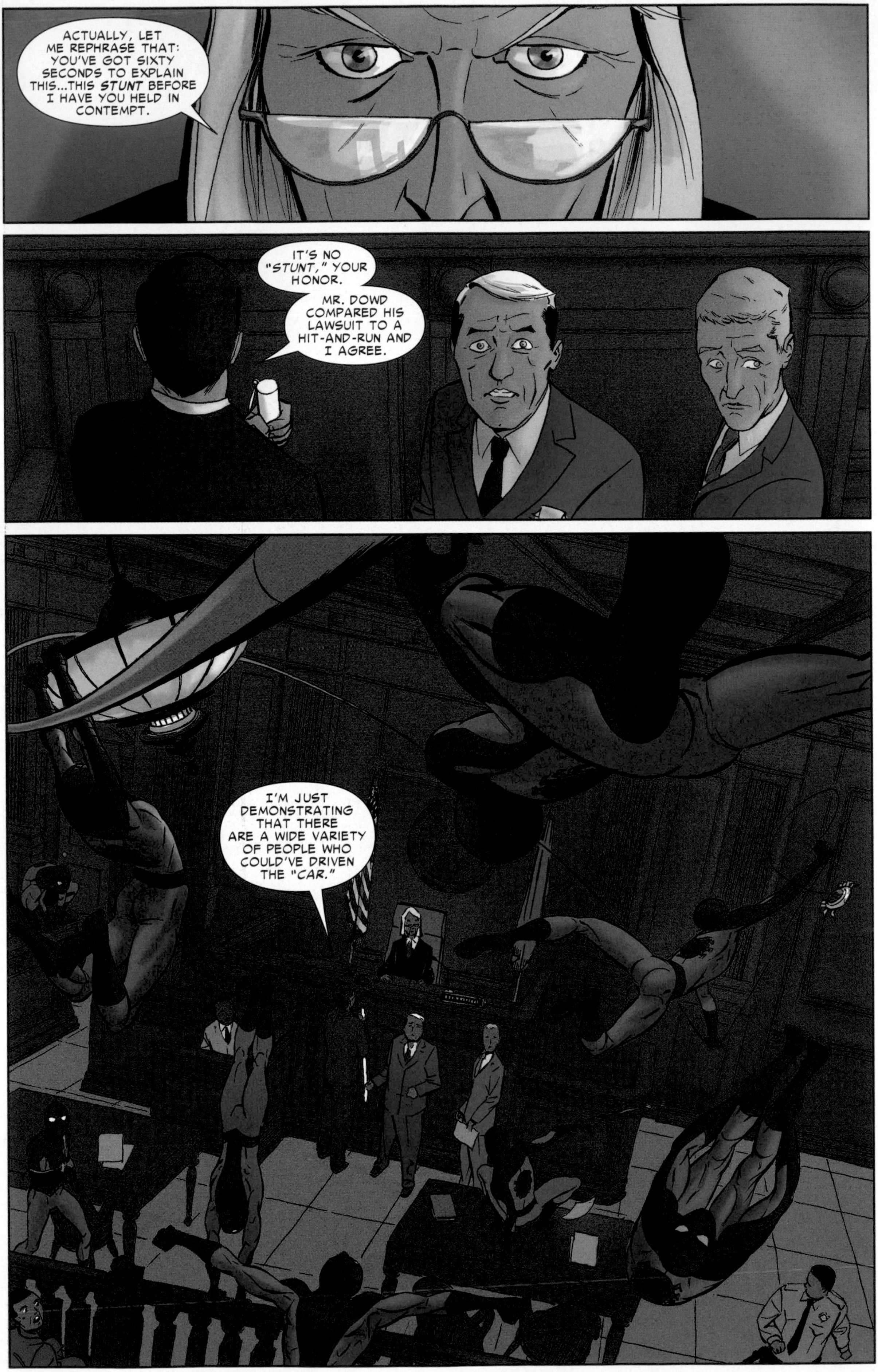
ACTUALLY, LET ME REPHRASE THAT: YOU'VE GOT SIXTY SECONDS TO EXPLAIN THIS...THIS *STUNT* BEFORE I HAVE YOU HELD IN CONTEMPT.
IT'S NO "*STUNT*," YOUR HONOR.
MR. DOWD COMPARED HIS LAWSUIT TO A HIT-AND-RUN AND I AGREE.
I'M JUST DEMONSTRATING THAT THERE ARE A WIDE VARIETY OF PEOPLE WHO COULD'VE DRIVEN THE "*CAR*."

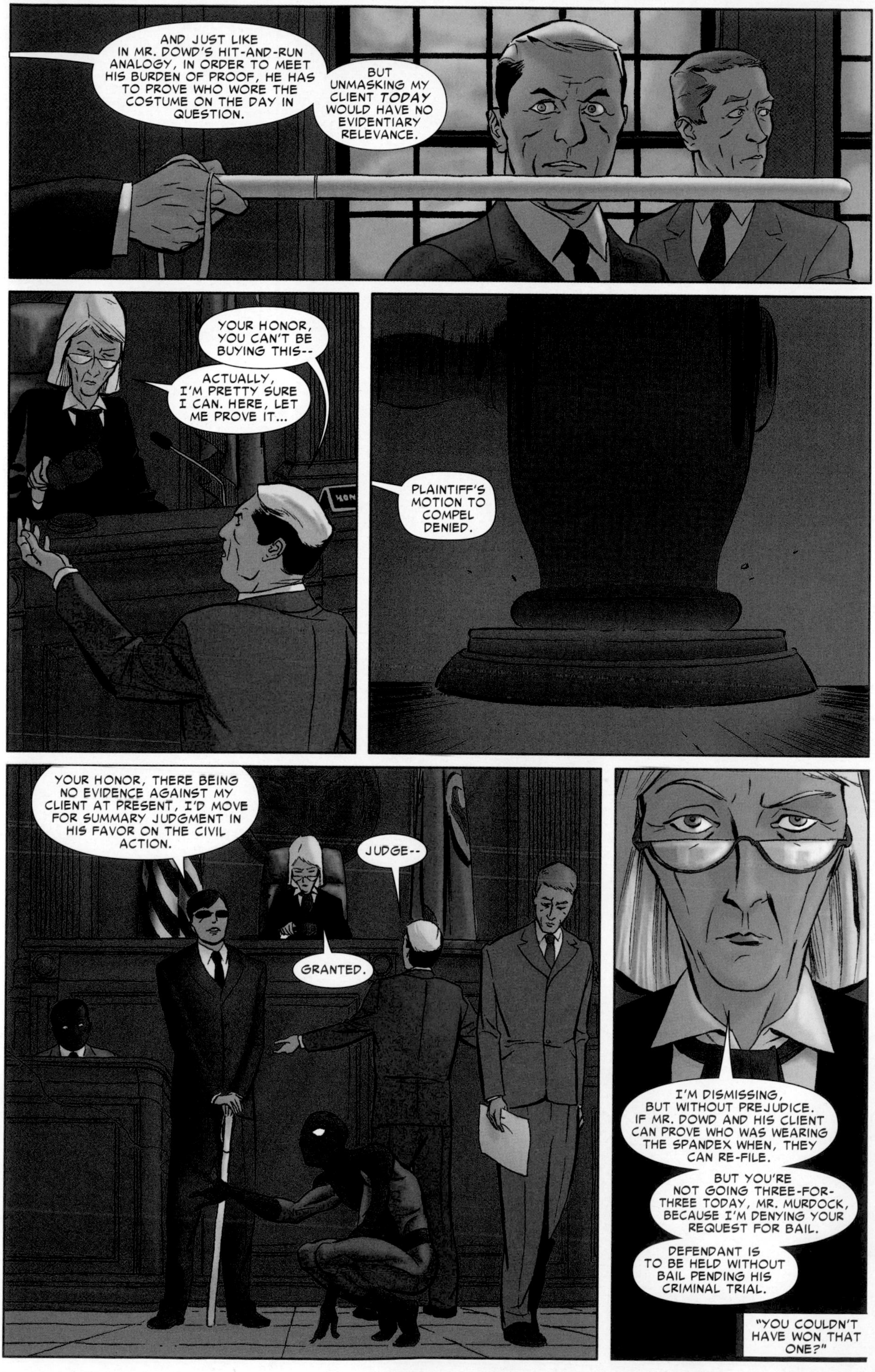
AND JUST LIKE IN MR. DOWD'S HIT-AND-RUN ANALOGY, IN ORDER TO MEET HIS BURDEN OF PROOF, HE HAS TO PROVE WHO WORE THE COSTUME ON THE DAY IN QUESTION.
BUT UNMASKING MY CLIENT TODAY WOULD HAVE NO EVIDENTIARY RELEVANCE.
YOUR HONOR, YOU CAN'T BE BUYING THIS--
ACTUALLY, I'M PRETTY SURE I CAN. HERE, LET ME PROVE IT...
PLAINTIFF'S MOTION TO COMPEL DENIED.
YOUR HONOR, THERE BEING NO EVIDENCE AGAINST MY CLIENT AT PRESENT, I'D MOVE FOR SUMMARY JUDGMENT IN HIS FAVOR ON THE CIVIL ACTION.
JUDGE--
GRANTED.
I'M DISMISSING, BUT WITHOUT PREJUDICE. IF MR. DOWD AND HIS CLIENT CAN PROVE WHO WAS WEARING THE SPANDEX WHEN, THEY CAN RE-FILE.
BUT YOU'RE NOT GOING THREE-FOR-THREE TODAY, MR. MURDOCK, BECAUSE I'M DENYING YOUR REQUEST FOR BAIL.
DEFENDANT IS TO BE HELD WITHOUT BAIL PENDING HIS CRIMINAL TRIAL.
"YOU COULDN'T HAVE WON THAT ONE?"

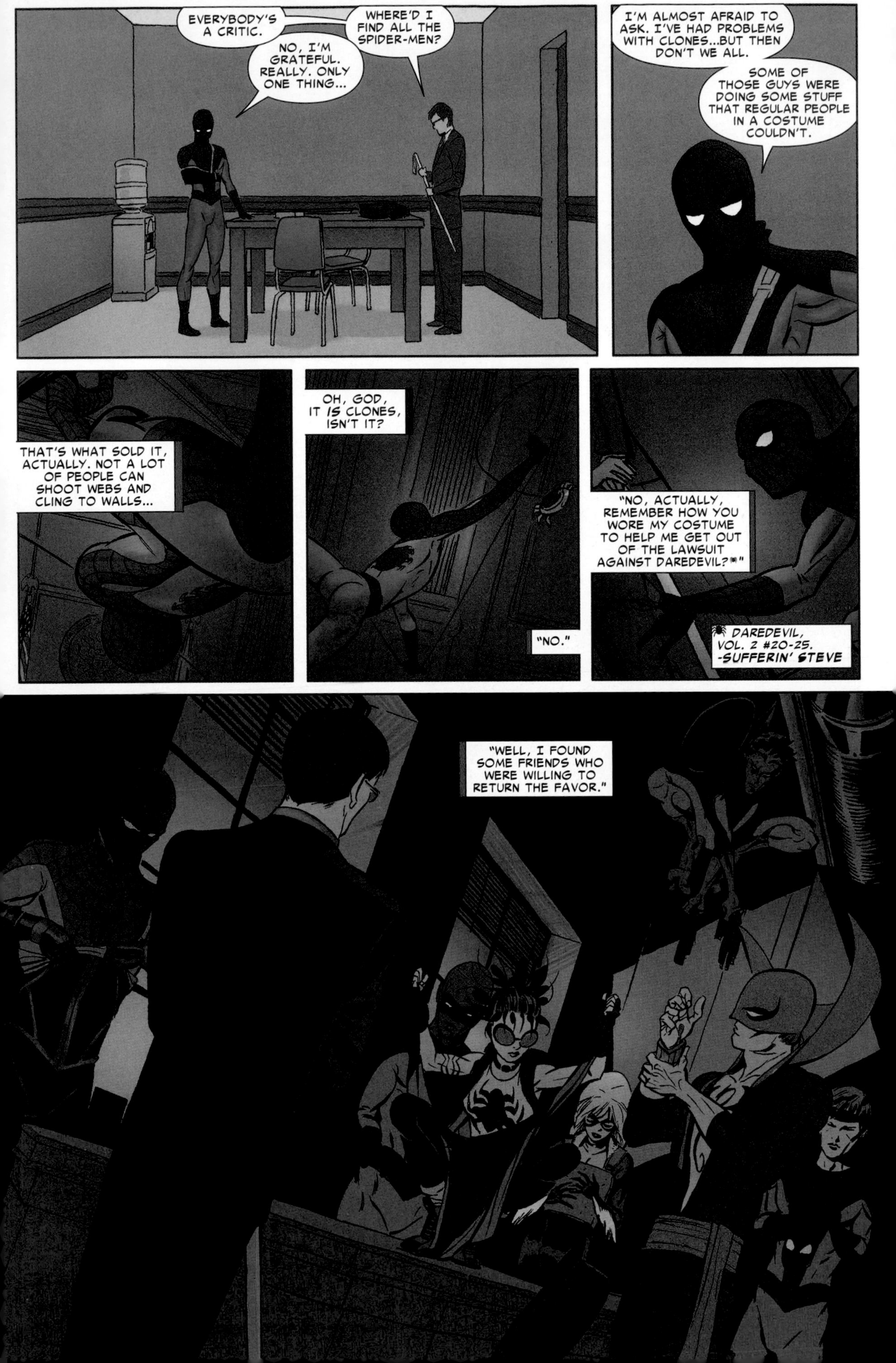

EVERYBODY'S A CRITIC.
WHERE'D I FIND ALL THE SPIDER-MEN?
NO, I'M GRATEFUL. REALLY. ONLY ONE THING...
I'M ALMOST AFRAID TO ASK. I'VE HAD PROBLEMS WITH CLONES...BUT THEN DON'T WE ALL.
SOME OF THOSE GUYS WERE DOING SOME STUFF THAT REGULAR PEOPLE IN A COSTUME COULDN'T.
THAT'S WHAT SOLD IT, ACTUALLY. NOT A LOT OF PEOPLE CAN SHOOT WEBS AND CLING TO WALLS...
OH, GOD, IT *IS* CLONES, ISN'T IT?
"NO."
"NO, ACTUALLY, REMEMBER HOW YOU WORE MY COSTUME TO HELP ME GET OUT OF THE LAWSUIT AGAINST DAREDEVIL?*"
DAREDEVIL, VOL. 2 #20-25. -SUFFERIN' STEVE
"WELL, I FOUND SOME FRIENDS WHO WERE WILLING TO RETURN THE FAVOR."

WHERE'D IRON FIST GET THE WEB-SHOOTER? THEY CONFISCATED MINE AT CENTRAL BOOKING.

APPARENTLY, SOMEONE BROKE INTO THE EVIDENCE LOCKER LAST NIGHT. TRAGIC.

TELL ME YOU DIDN'T BREAK INTO AN N.Y.P.D. EVIDENCE LOCKER.

I DIDN'T. AND I'M OFFENDED YOU THINK I WOULD. THE WEB-SHOOTER JUST... SHOWED UP. I DON'T ASK ANY QUESTIONS.

ON AN UNRELATED POINT, THE BLACK CAT SENDS HER REGARDS.

THANKS FOR ALL THIS.

WAIT 'TIL YOU GET MY BILL.

WHICH INCLUDES ALL THE COSTUMES, BY THE WAY. WEAR 'EM IN GOOD HEALTH.

AND DON'T FORGET TO READ THAT BOOK.

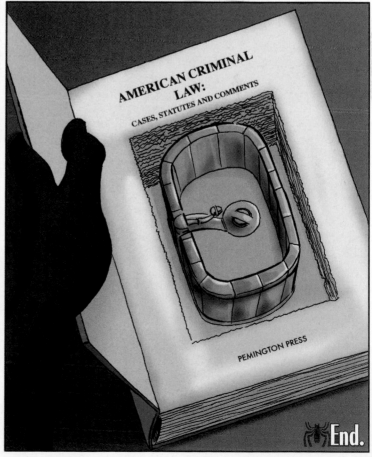

AMERICAN CRIMINAL LAW:
CASES, STATUTES AND COMMENTS

PEMINGTON PRESS

End.

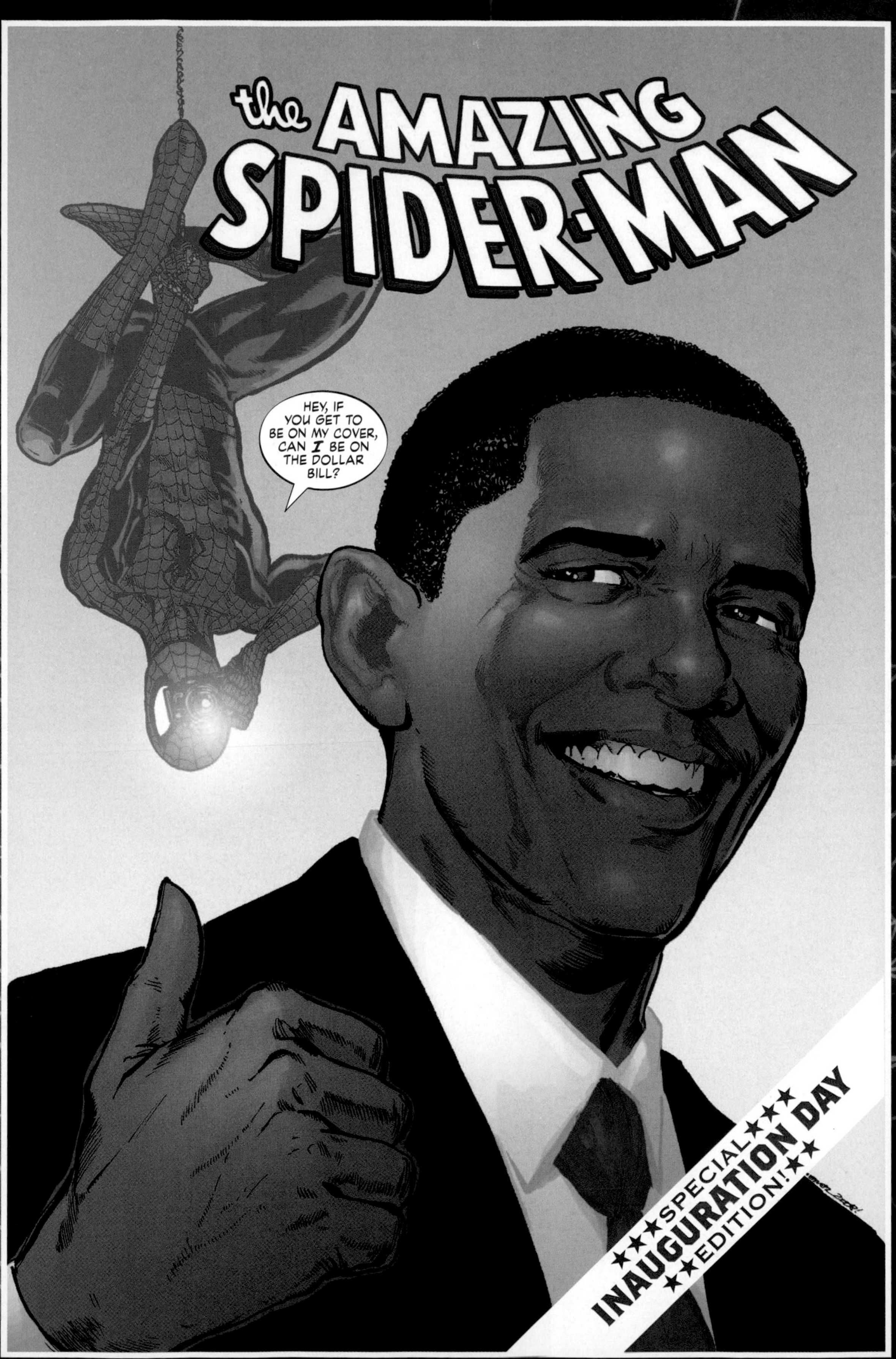
the AMAZING SPIDER-MAN
HEY, IF YOU GET TO BE ON MY COVER, CAN I BE ON THE DOLLAR BILL?
★★★SPECIAL★★★
INAUGURATION DAY
★★EDITION!★★

AMAZING SPIDER-MAN #583 – "SPIDEY MEETS THE PRESIDENT"

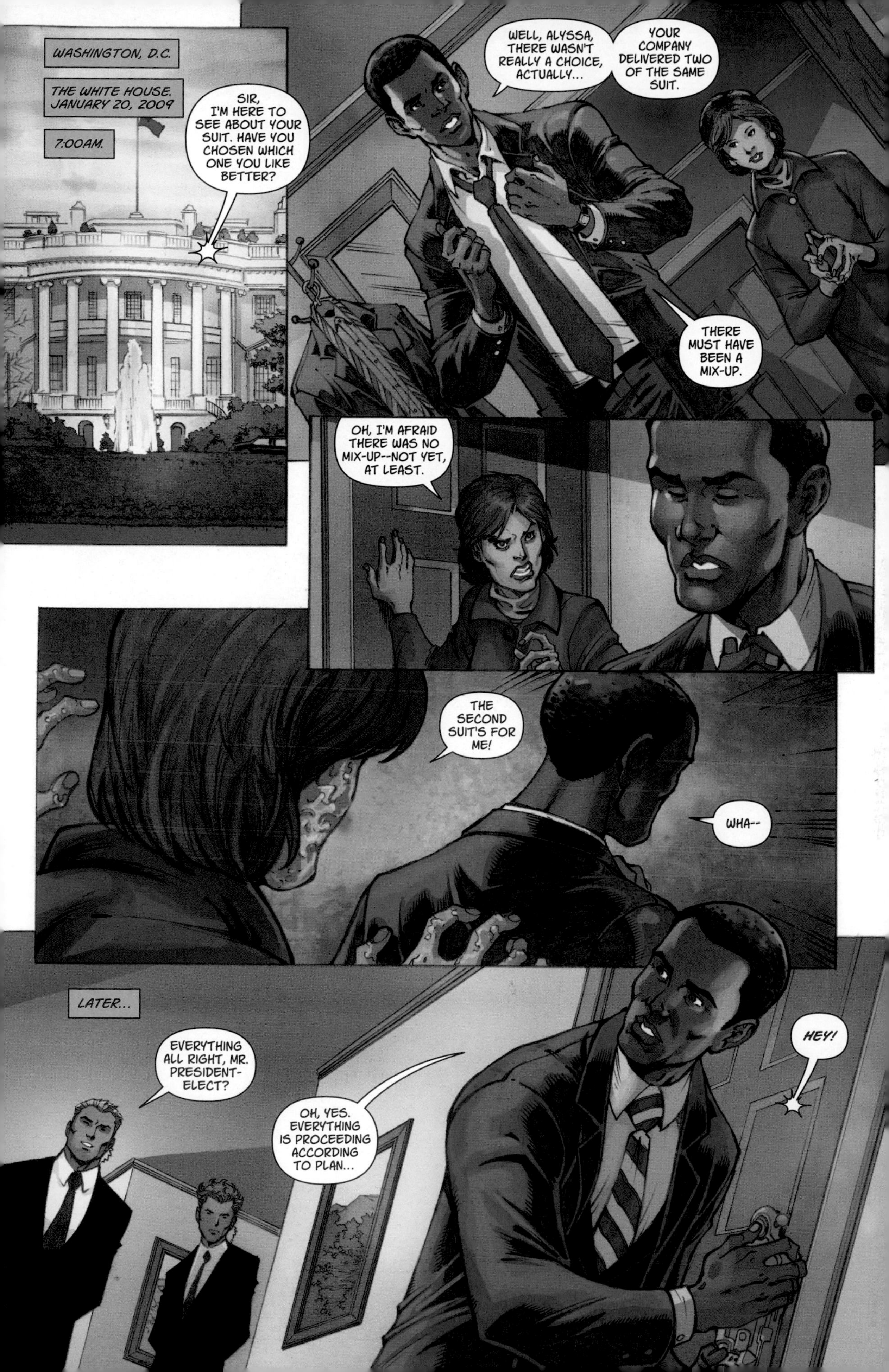
WASHINGTON, D.C.
THE WHITE HOUSE. JANUARY 20, 2009
7:00AM.
SIR, I'M HERE TO SEE ABOUT YOUR SUIT. HAVE YOU CHOSEN WHICH ONE YOU LIKE BETTER?
WELL, ALYSSA, THERE WASN'T REALLY A CHOICE, ACTUALLY...
YOUR COMPANY DELIVERED TWO OF THE SAME SUIT.
THERE MUST HAVE BEEN A MIX-UP.
OH, I'M AFRAID THERE WAS NO MIX-UP--NOT YET, AT LEAST.
THE SECOND SUIT'S FOR ME!
WHA--
LATER...
EVERYTHING ALL RIGHT, MR. PRESIDENT-ELECT?
OH, YES. EVERYTHING IS PROCEEDING ACCORDING TO PLAN...
HEY!

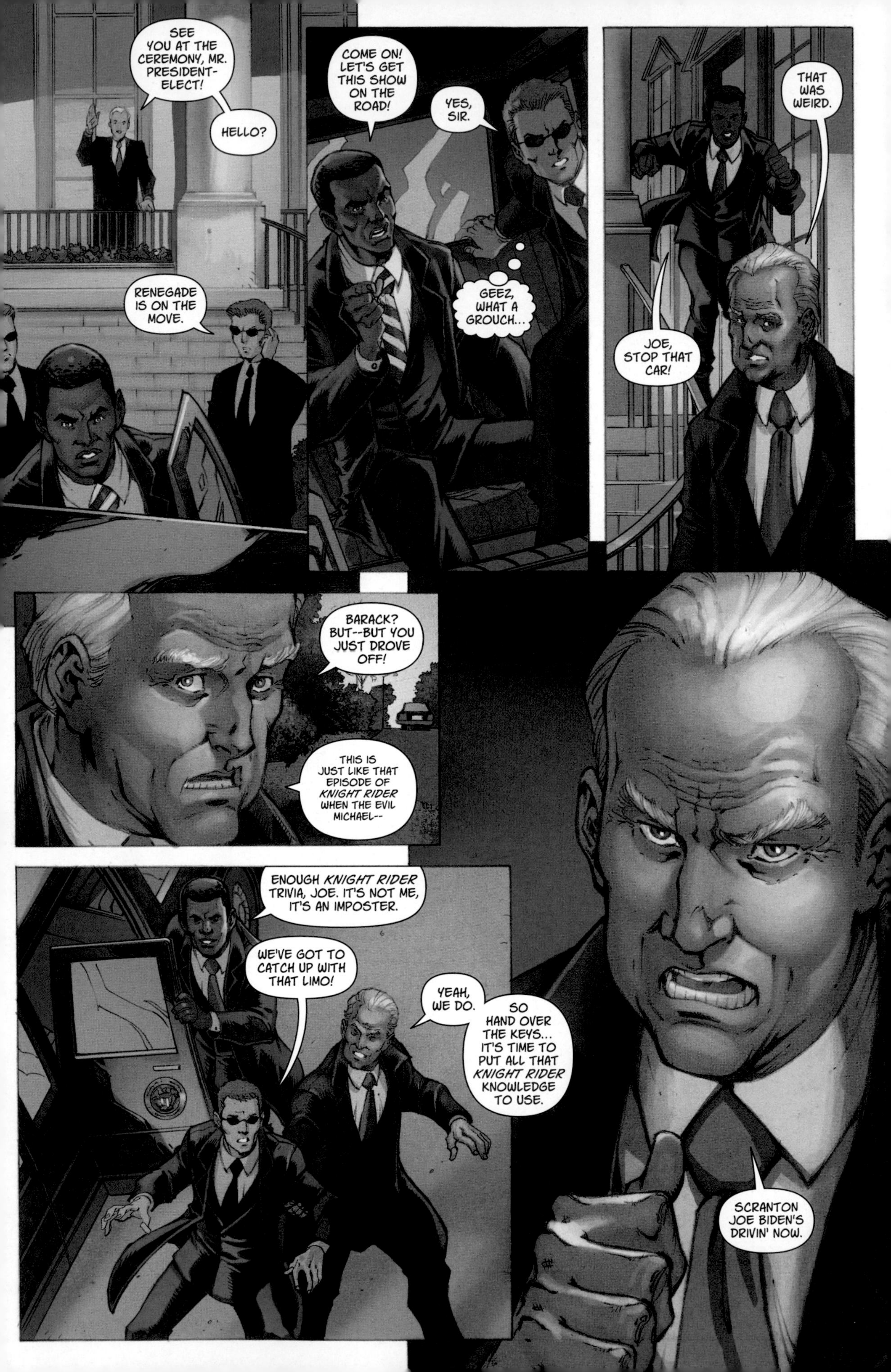

SEE YOU AT THE CEREMONY, MR. PRESIDENT-ELECT!
HELLO?
RENEGADE IS ON THE MOVE.
COME ON! LET'S GET THIS SHOW ON THE ROAD!
YES, SIR.
GEEZ, WHAT A GROUCH...
THAT WAS WEIRD.
JOE, STOP THAT CAR!
BARACK? BUT--BUT YOU JUST DROVE OFF!
THIS IS JUST LIKE THAT EPISODE OF *KNIGHT RIDER* WHEN THE EVIL MICHAEL--
ENOUGH *KNIGHT RIDER* TRIVIA, JOE. IT'S NOT ME, IT'S AN IMPOSTER.
WE'VE GOT TO CATCH UP WITH THAT LIMO!
YEAH, WE DO.
SO HAND OVER THE KEYS... IT'S TIME TO PUT ALL THAT *KNIGHT RIDER* KNOWLEDGE TO USE.
SCRANTON JOE BIDEN'S DRIVIN' NOW.

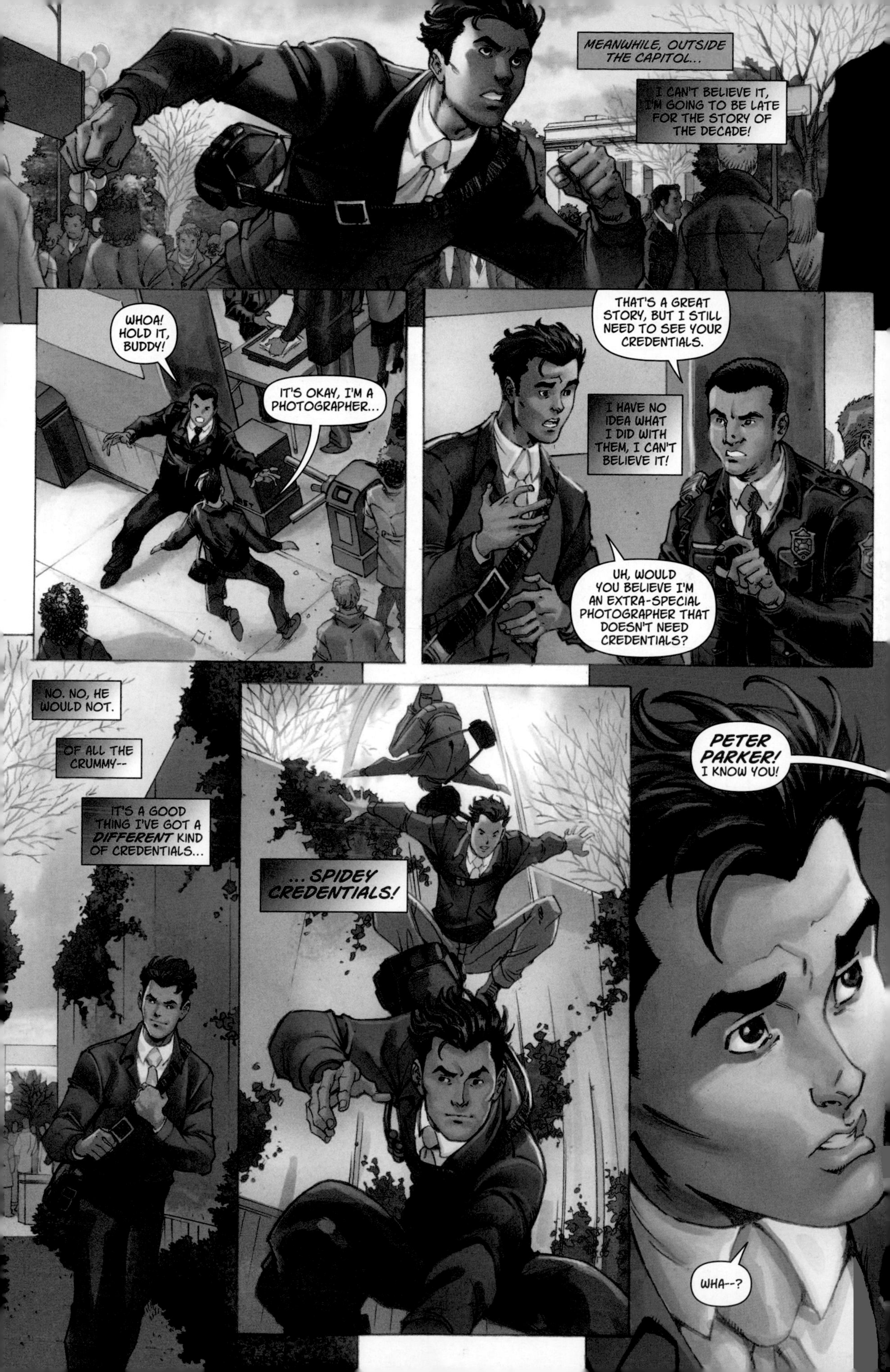
MEANWHILE, OUTSIDE THE CAPITOL...
I CAN'T BELIEVE IT, I'M GOING TO BE LATE FOR THE STORY OF THE DECADE!
WHOA! HOLD IT, BUDDY!
IT'S OKAY, I'M A PHOTOGRAPHER...
THAT'S A GREAT STORY, BUT I STILL NEED TO SEE YOUR CREDENTIALS.
I HAVE NO IDEA WHAT I DID WITH THEM, I CAN'T BELIEVE IT!
UH, WOULD YOU BELIEVE I'M AN EXTRA-SPECIAL PHOTOGRAPHER THAT DOESN'T NEED CREDENTIALS?
NO. NO, HE WOULD NOT.
OF ALL THE CRUMMY--
IT'S A GOOD THING I'VE GOT A *DIFFERENT* KIND OF CREDENTIALS...
...SPIDEY CREDENTIALS!
PETER PARKER! I KNOW YOU!
WHA--?

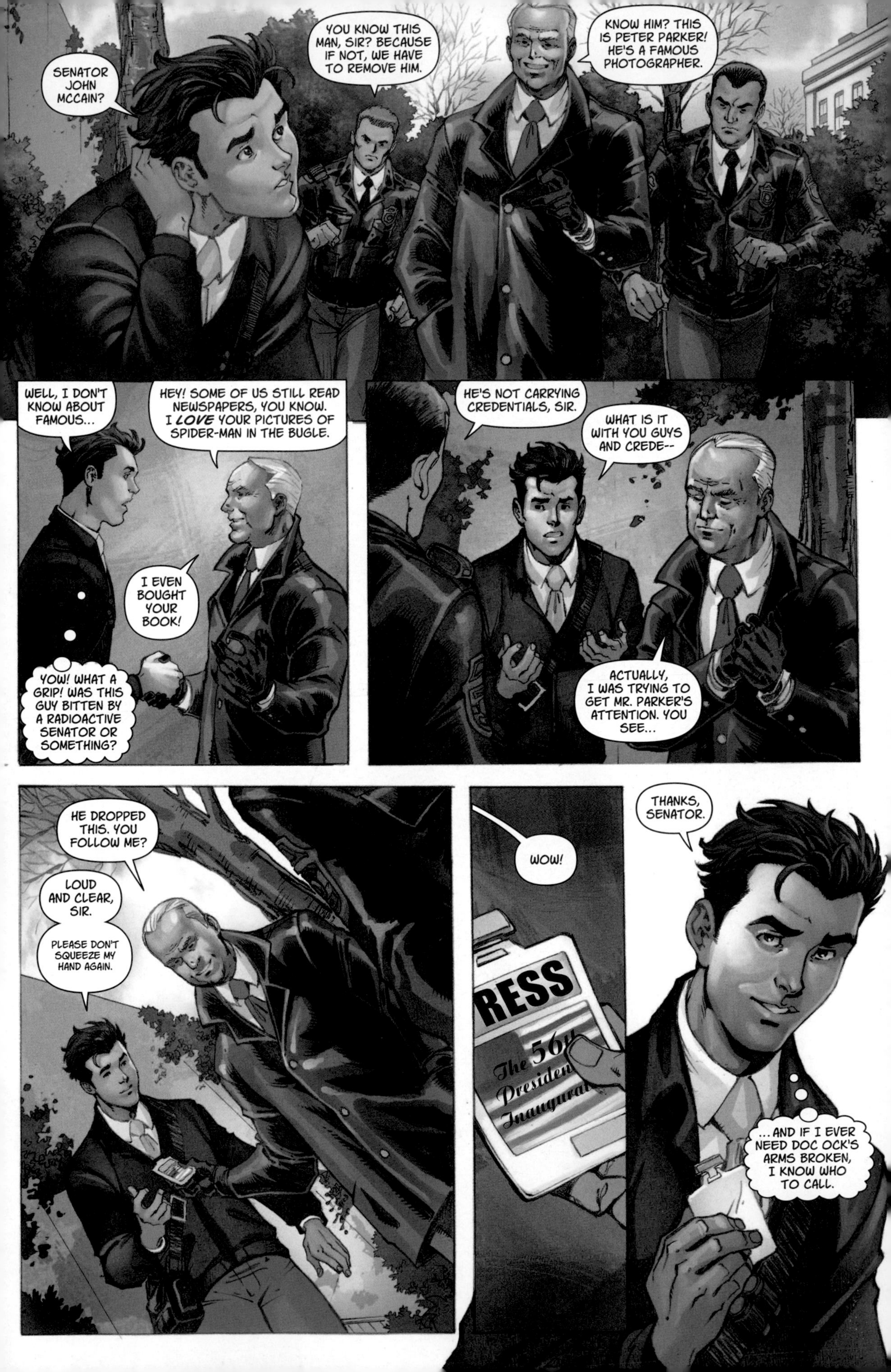
SENATOR JOHN MCCAIN?
YOU KNOW THIS MAN, SIR? BECAUSE IF NOT, WE HAVE TO REMOVE HIM.
KNOW HIM? THIS IS PETER PARKER! HE'S A FAMOUS PHOTOGRAPHER.
WELL, I DON'T KNOW ABOUT FAMOUS...
HEY! SOME OF US STILL READ NEWSPAPERS, YOU KNOW. I *LOVE* YOUR PICTURES OF SPIDER-MAN IN THE BUGLE.
I EVEN BOUGHT YOUR BOOK!
YOW! WHAT A GRIP! WAS THIS GUY BITTEN BY A RADIOACTIVE SENATOR OR SOMETHING?
HE'S NOT CARRYING CREDENTIALS, SIR.
WHAT IS IT WITH YOU GUYS AND CREDE--
ACTUALLY, I WAS TRYING TO GET MR. PARKER'S ATTENTION. YOU SEE...
HE DROPPED THIS. YOU FOLLOW ME?
LOUD AND CLEAR, SIR.
PLEASE DON'T SQUEEZE MY HAND AGAIN.
WOW!
RESS
The 56th Presiden Inaugura
THANKS, SENATOR.
...AND IF I EVER NEED DOC OCK'S ARMS BROKEN, I KNOW WHO TO CALL.

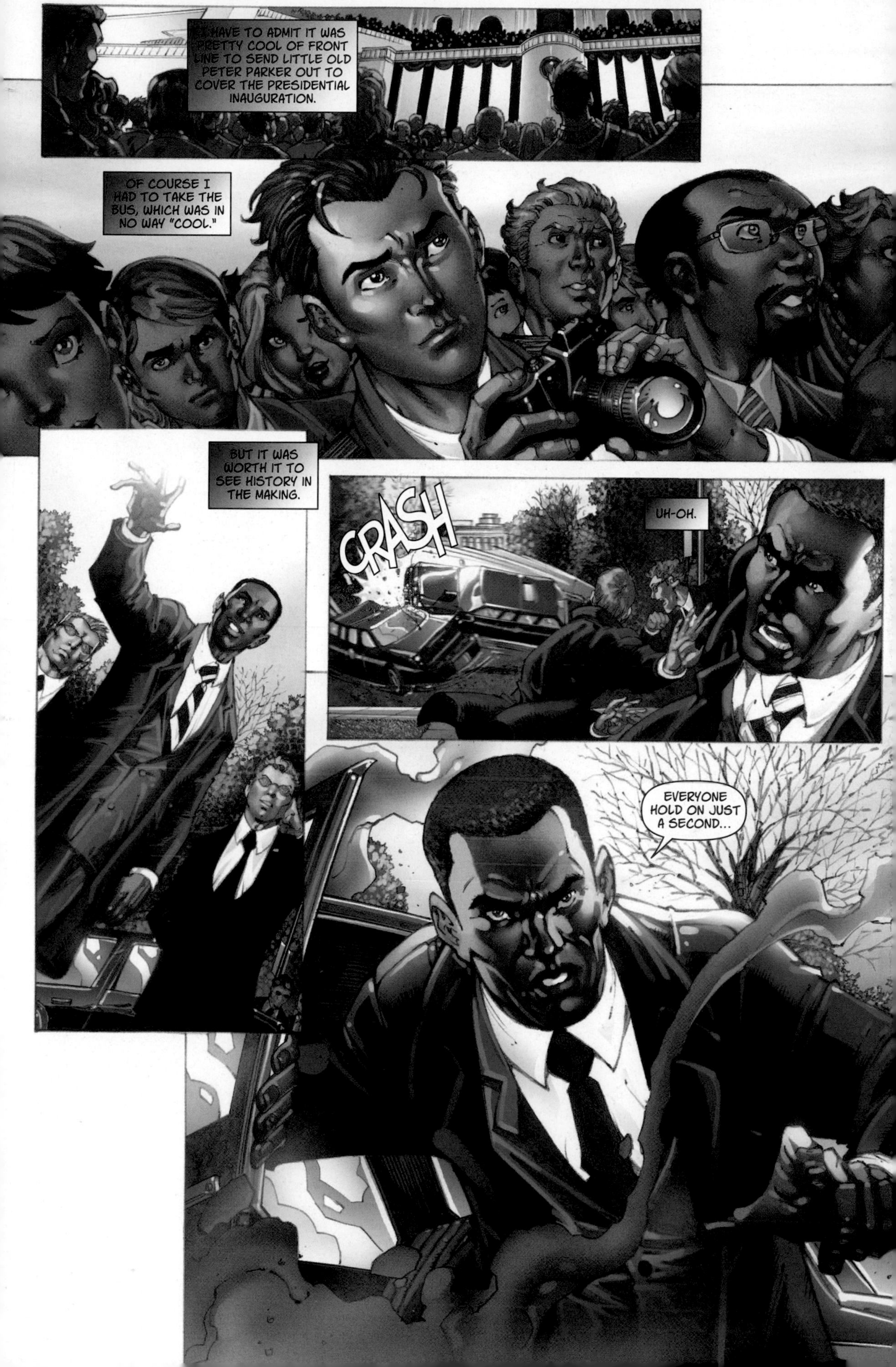
I HAVE TO ADMIT IT WAS PRETTY COOL OF FRONT LINE TO SEND LITTLE OLD PETER PARKER OUT TO COVER THE PRESIDENTIAL INAUGURATION.
OF COURSE I HAD TO TAKE THE BUS, WHICH WAS IN NO WAY "COOL."
BUT IT WAS WORTH IT TO SEE HISTORY IN THE MAKING.
CRASH
UH-OH.
EVERYONE HOLD ON JUST A SECOND...

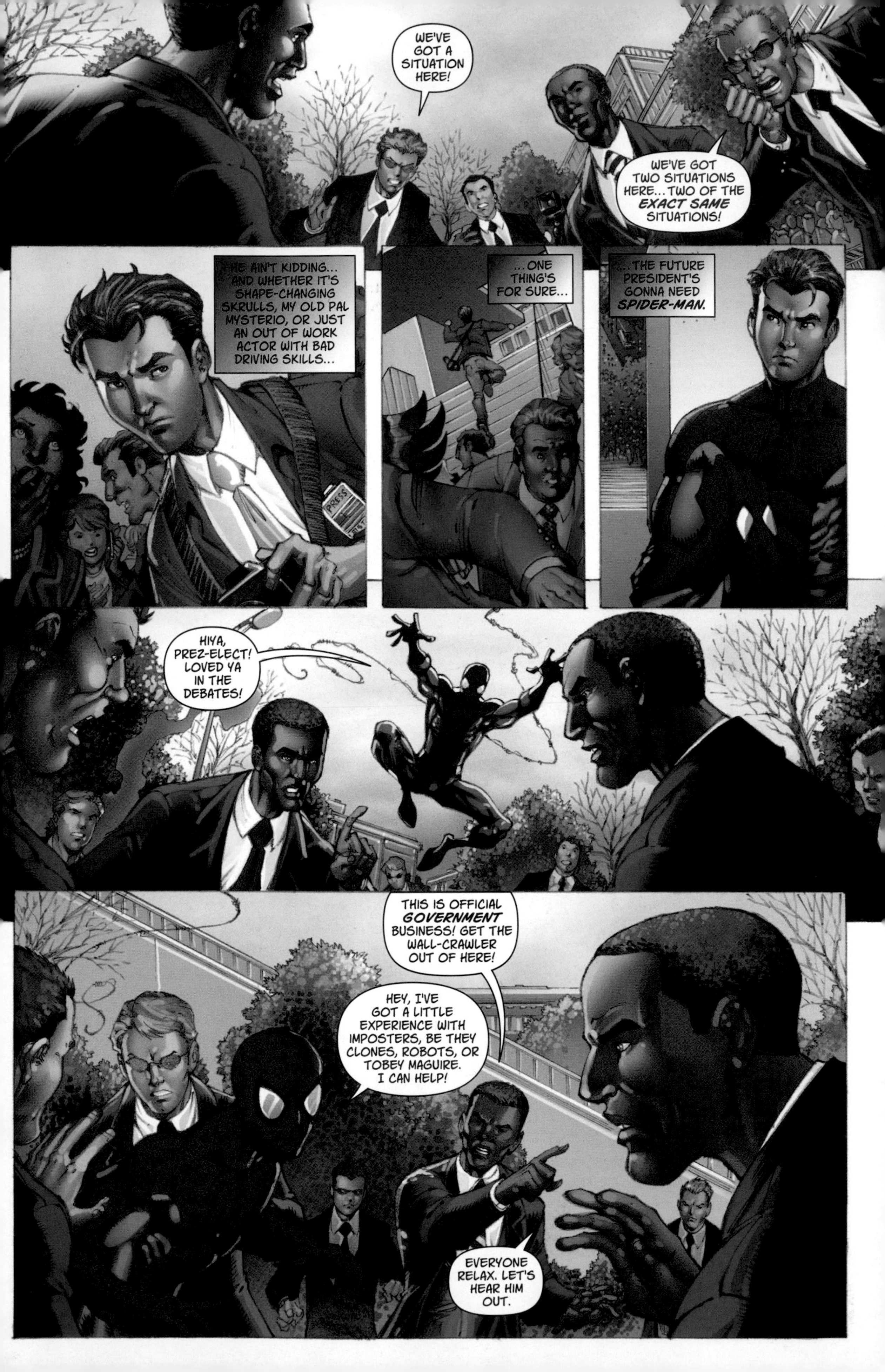
WE'VE GOT A SITUATION HERE!
WE'VE GOT TWO SITUATIONS HERE... TWO OF THE EXACT SAME SITUATIONS!
HE AIN'T KIDDING... AND WHETHER IT'S SHAPE-CHANGING SKRULLS, MY OLD PAL MYSTERIO, OR JUST AN OUT OF WORK ACTOR WITH BAD DRIVING SKILLS...
...ONE THING'S FOR SURE...
...THE FUTURE PRESIDENT'S GONNA NEED SPIDER-MAN.
PRESS
HIYA, PREZ-ELECT! LOVED YA IN THE DEBATES!
THIS IS OFFICIAL GOVERNMENT BUSINESS! GET THE WALL-CRAWLER OUT OF HERE!
HEY, I'VE GOT A LITTLE EXPERIENCE WITH IMPOSTERS, BE THEY CLONES, ROBOTS, OR TOBEY MAGUIRE. I CAN HELP!
EVERYONE RELAX. LET'S HEAR HIM OUT.

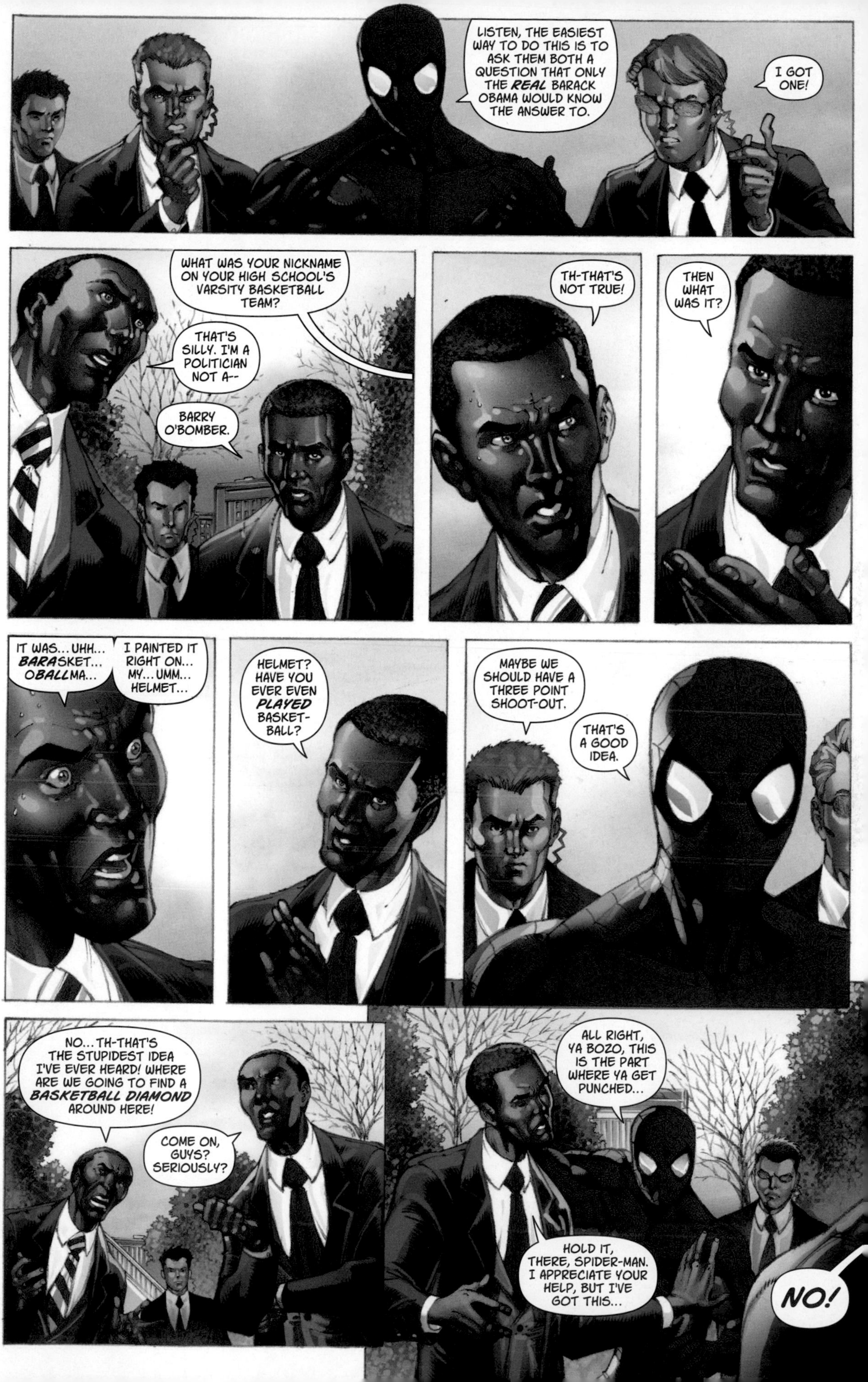
LISTEN, THE EASIEST WAY TO DO THIS IS TO ASK THEM BOTH A QUESTION THAT ONLY THE *REAL* BARACK OBAMA WOULD KNOW THE ANSWER TO.
I GOT ONE!
WHAT WAS YOUR NICKNAME ON YOUR HIGH SCHOOL'S VARSITY BASKETBALL TEAM?
THAT'S SILLY. I'M A POLITICIAN NOT A--
BARRY O'BOMBER.
TH-THAT'S NOT TRUE!
THEN WHAT WAS IT?
IT WAS... UHH... *BARA*SKET... O*BALL*MA...
I PAINTED IT RIGHT ON... MY... UMM... HELMET...
HELMET? HAVE YOU EVER EVEN *PLAYED* BASKET-BALL?
MAYBE WE SHOULD HAVE A THREE POINT SHOOT-OUT.
THAT'S A GOOD IDEA.
NO... TH-THAT'S THE STUPIDEST IDEA I'VE EVER HEARD! WHERE ARE WE GOING TO FIND A *BASKETBALL DIAMOND* AROUND HERE!
COME ON, GUYS? SERIOUSLY?
ALL RIGHT, YA BOZO, THIS IS THE PART WHERE YA GET PUNCHED...
HOLD IT, THERE, SPIDER-MAN. I APPRECIATE YOUR HELP, BUT I'VE GOT THIS...
NO!

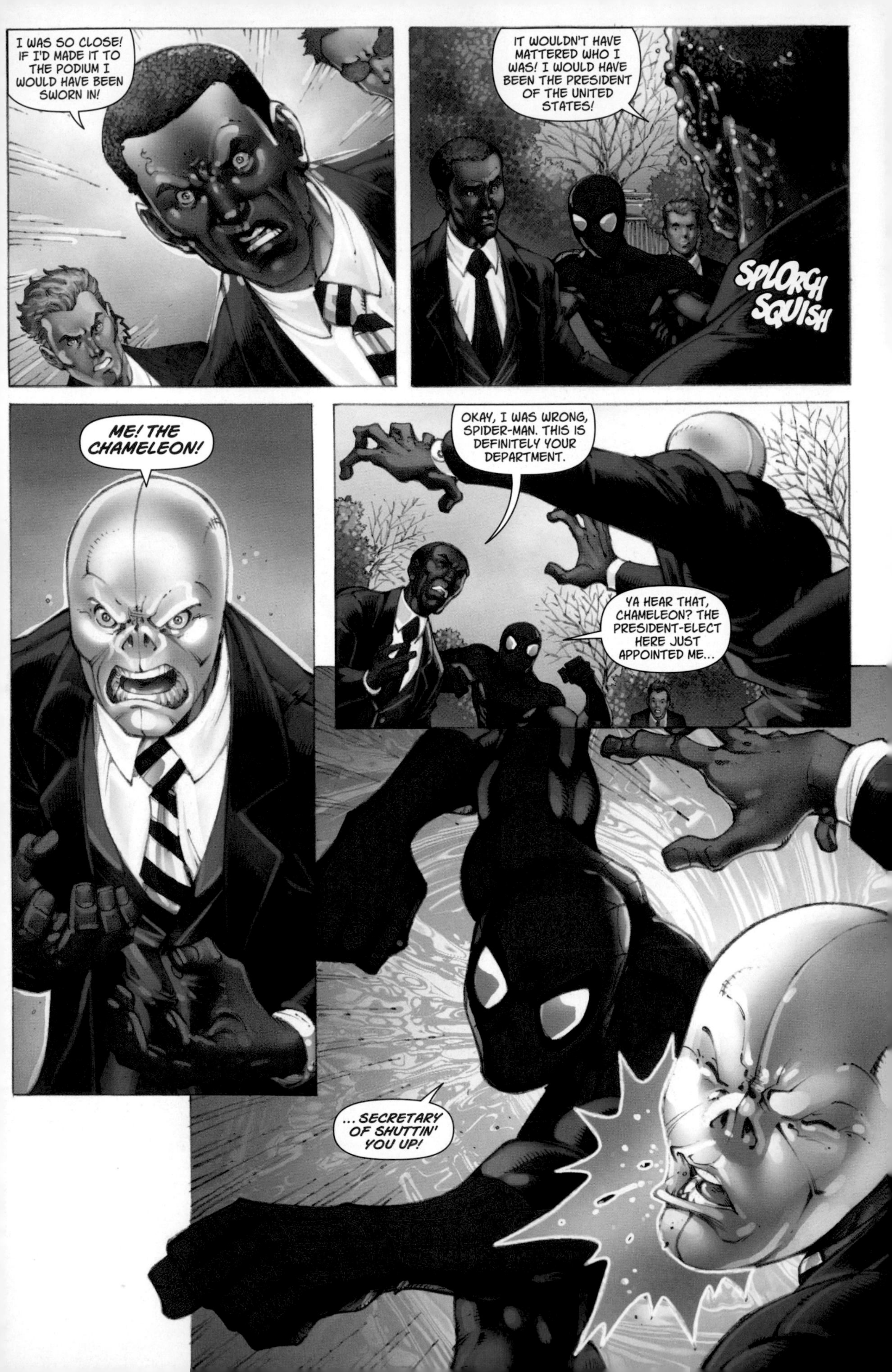
I WAS SO CLOSE! IF I'D MADE IT TO THE PODIUM I WOULD HAVE BEEN SWORN IN!
IT WOULDN'T HAVE MATTERED WHO I WAS! I WOULD HAVE BEEN THE PRESIDENT OF THE UNITED STATES!
SPLORCH
SQUISH
ME! THE CHAMELEON!
OKAY, I WAS WRONG, SPIDER-MAN. THIS IS DEFINITELY YOUR DEPARTMENT.
YA HEAR THAT, CHAMELEON? THE PRESIDENT-ELECT HERE JUST APPOINTED ME...
...SECRETARY OF SHUTTIN' YOU UP!

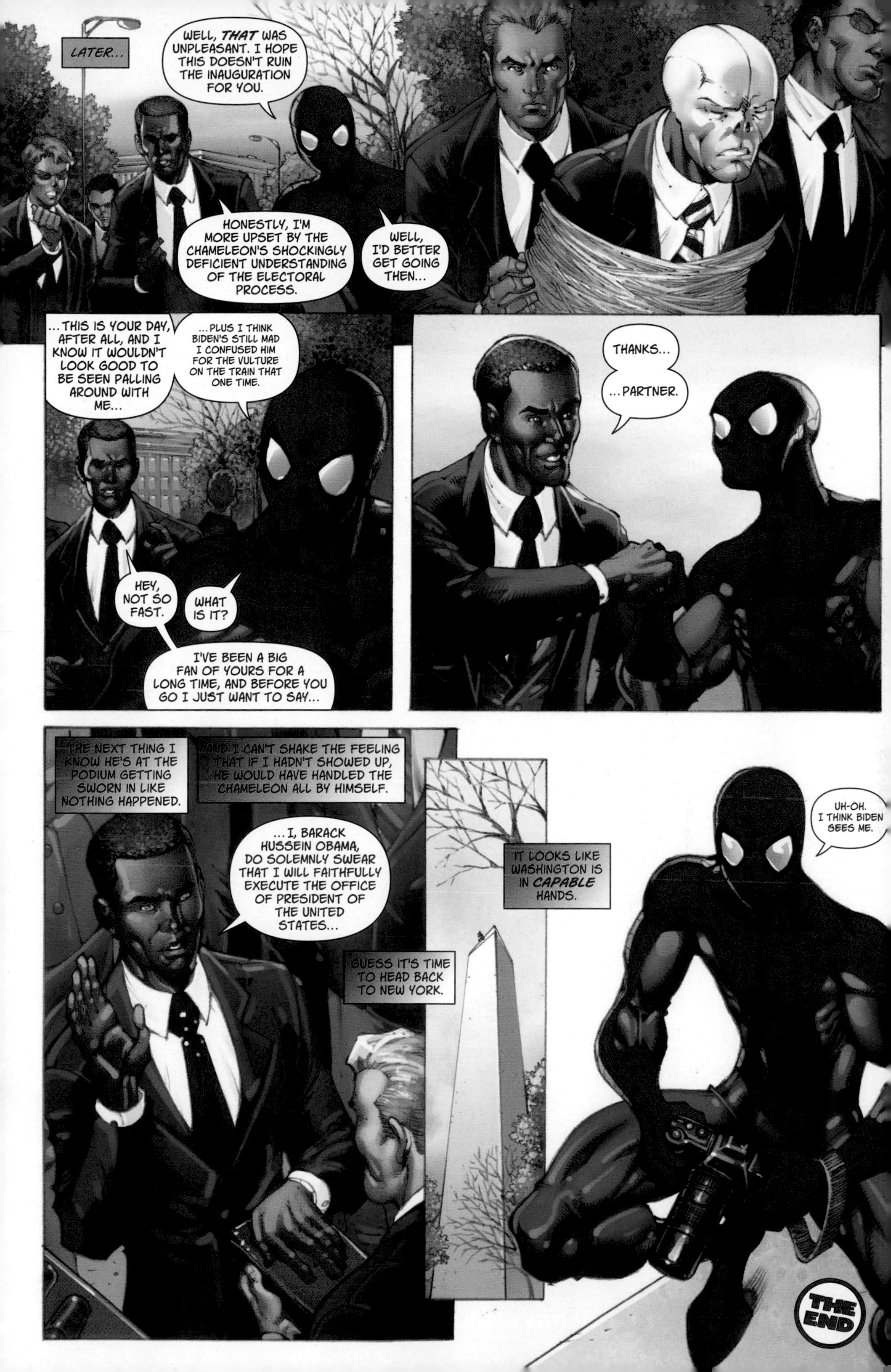
LATER...
WELL, *THAT* WAS UNPLEASANT. I HOPE THIS DOESN'T RUIN THE INAUGURATION FOR YOU.
HONESTLY, I'M MORE UPSET BY THE CHAMELEON'S SHOCKINGLY DEFICIENT UNDERSTANDING OF THE ELECTORAL PROCESS.
WELL, I'D BETTER GET GOING THEN...
...THIS IS YOUR DAY, AFTER ALL, AND I KNOW IT WOULDN'T LOOK GOOD TO BE SEEN PALLING AROUND WITH ME...
...PLUS I THINK BIDEN'S STILL MAD I CONFUSED HIM FOR THE VULTURE ON THE TRAIN THAT ONE TIME.
HEY, NOT SO FAST.
WHAT IS IT?
I'VE BEEN A BIG FAN OF YOURS FOR A LONG TIME, AND BEFORE YOU GO I JUST WANT TO SAY...
THANKS...
...PARTNER.
THE NEXT THING I KNOW HE'S AT THE PODIUM GETTING SWORN IN LIKE NOTHING HAPPENED.
AND I CAN'T SHAKE THE FEELING THAT IF I HADN'T SHOWED UP, HE WOULD HAVE HANDLED THE CHAMELEON ALL BY HIMSELF.
...I, BARACK HUSSEIN OBAMA, DO SOLEMNLY SWEAR THAT I WILL FAITHFULLY EXECUTE THE OFFICE OF PRESIDENT OF THE UNITED STATES...
GUESS IT'S TIME TO HEAD BACK TO NEW YORK.
IT LOOKS LIKE WASHINGTON IS IN *CAPABLE* HANDS.
UH-OH. I THINK BIDEN SEES ME.
THE END

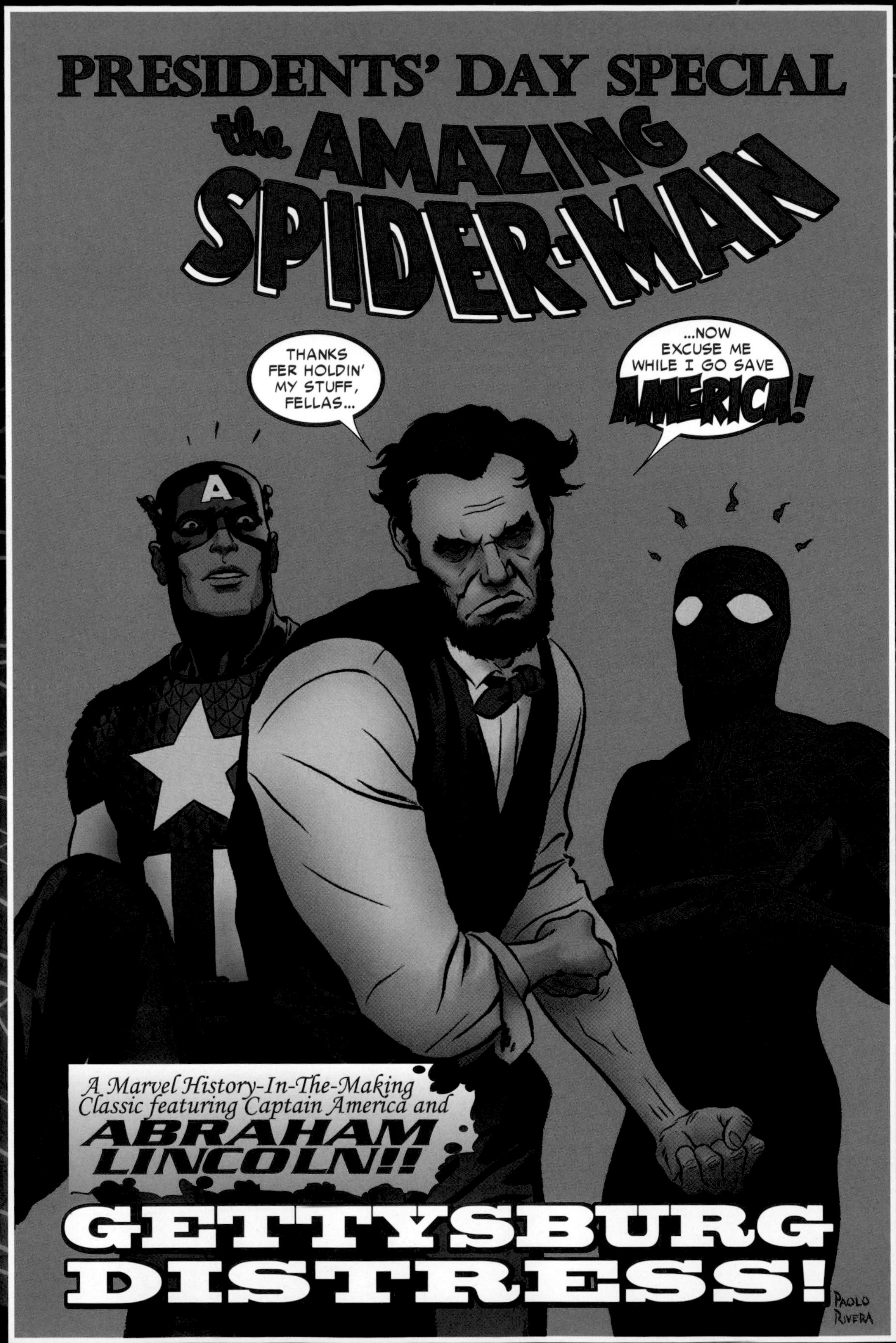
PRESIDENTS' DAY SPECIAL
the AMAZING SPIDER-MAN
THANKS FER HOLDIN' MY STUFF, FELLAS...
...NOW EXCUSE ME WHILE I GO SAVE AMERICA!
A Marvel History-In-The-Making Classic featuring Captain America and
ABRAHAM LINCOLN!!
GETTYSBURG DISTRESS!
PAOLO RIVERA

AMAZING SPIDER-MAN: PRESIDENTS' DAY SPECIAL

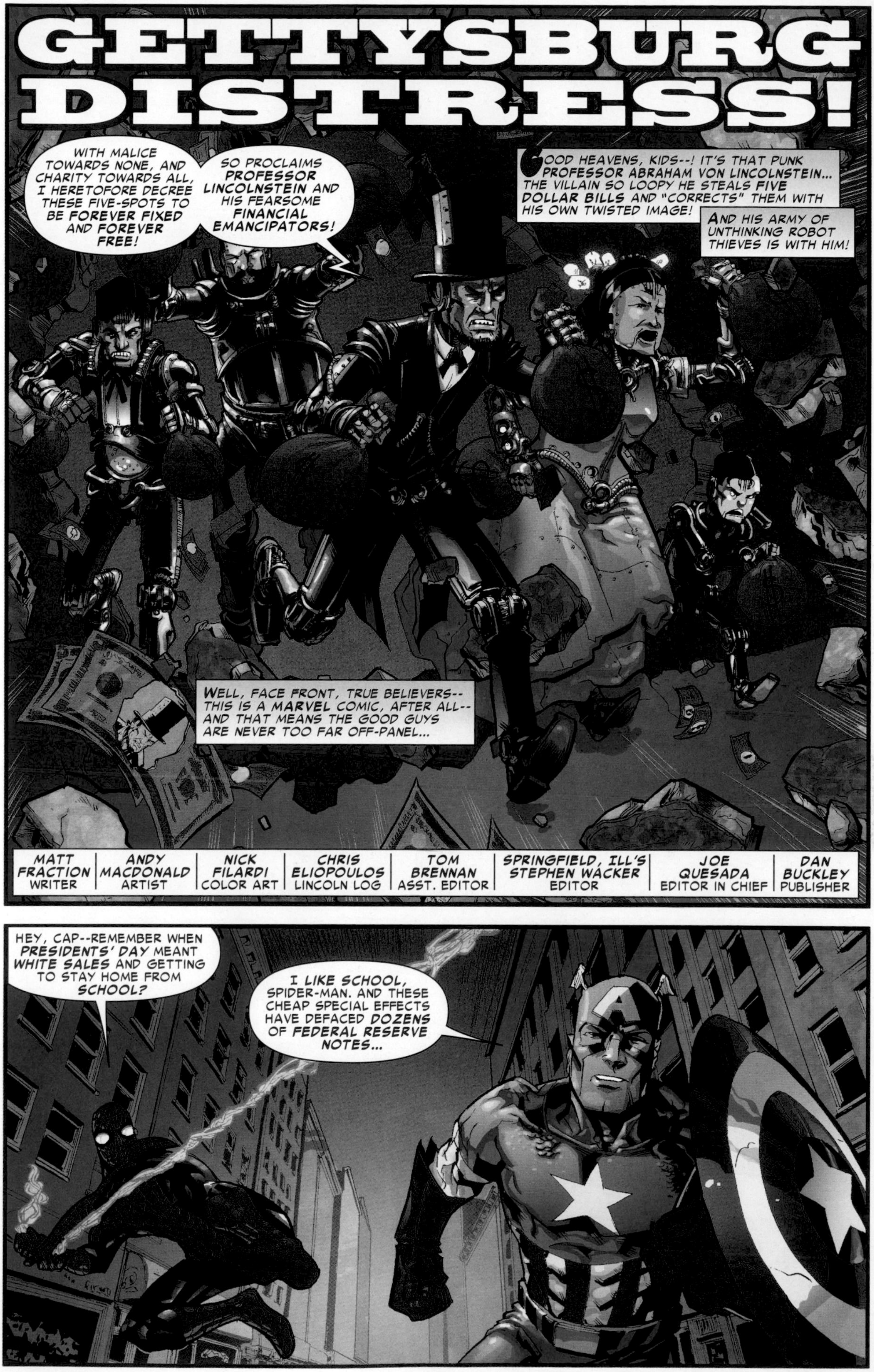
GETTYSBURG DISTRESS!
WITH MALICE TOWARDS NONE, AND CHARITY TOWARDS ALL, I HERETOFORE DECREE THESE FIVE-SPOTS TO BE FOREVER FIXED AND FOREVER FREE!
SO PROCLAIMS PROFESSOR LINCOLNSTEIN AND HIS FEARSOME FINANCIAL EMANCIPATORS!
GOOD HEAVENS, KIDS--! IT'S THAT PUNK PROFESSOR ABRAHAM VON LINCOLNSTEIN... THE VILLAIN SO LOOPY HE STEALS FIVE DOLLAR BILLS AND "CORRECTS" THEM WITH HIS OWN TWISTED IMAGE!
AND HIS ARMY OF UNTHINKING ROBOT THIEVES IS WITH HIM!
WELL, FACE FRONT, TRUE BELIEVERS-- THIS IS A MARVEL COMIC, AFTER ALL-- AND THAT MEANS THE GOOD GUYS ARE NEVER TOO FAR OFF-PANEL...
MATT FRACTION WRITER
ANDY MACDONALD ARTIST
NICK FILARDI COLOR ART
CHRIS ELIOPOULOS LINCOLN LOG
TOM BRENNAN ASST. EDITOR
SPRINGFIELD, ILL'S STEPHEN WACKER EDITOR
JOE QUESADA EDITOR IN CHIEF
DAN BUCKLEY PUBLISHER
HEY, CAP--REMEMBER WHEN PRESIDENTS' DAY MEANT WHITE SALES AND GETTING TO STAY HOME FROM SCHOOL?
I LIKE SCHOOL, SPIDER-MAN. AND THESE CHEAP SPECIAL EFFECTS HAVE DEFACED DOZENS OF FEDERAL RESERVE NOTES...

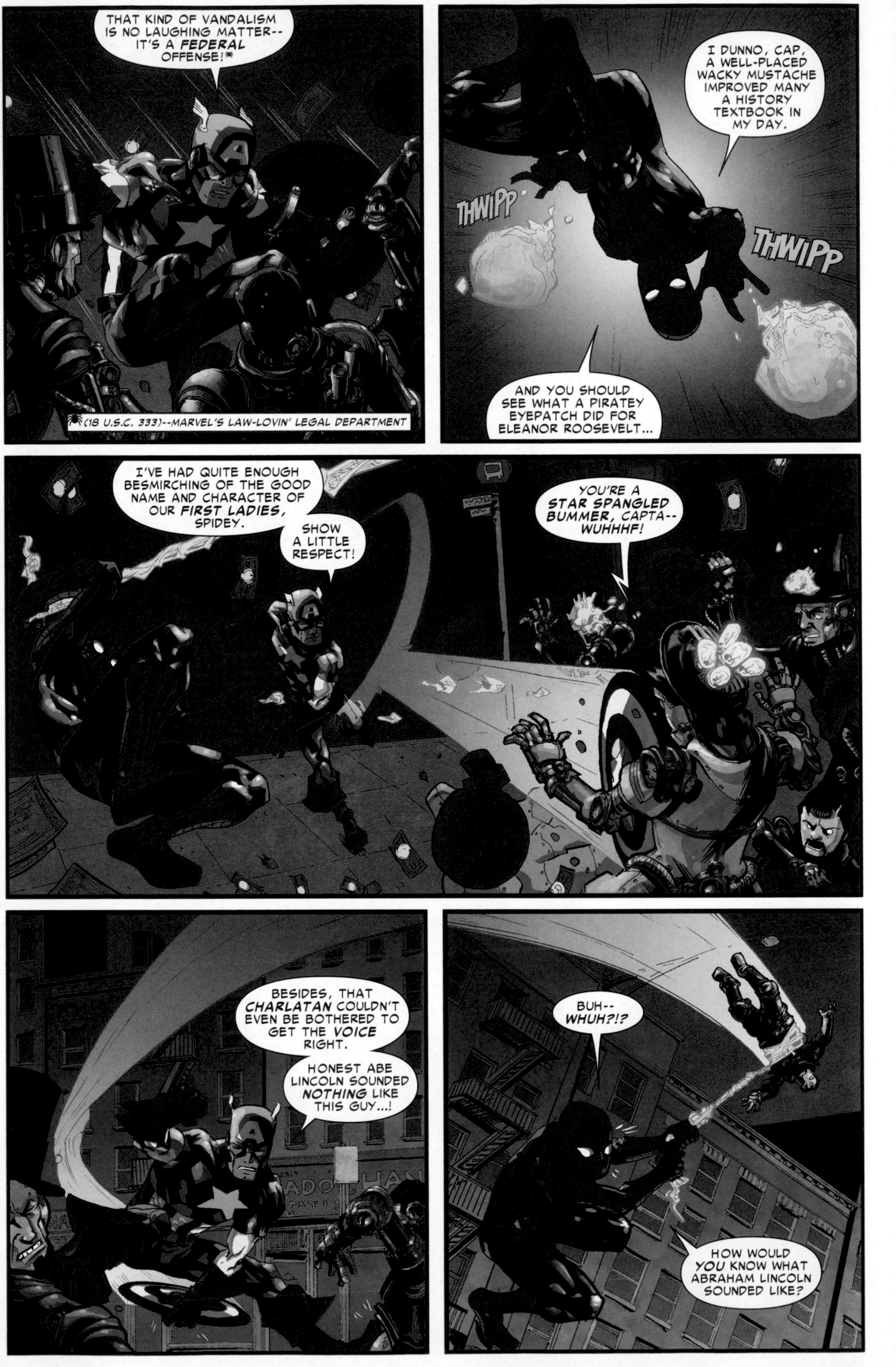
THAT KIND OF VANDALISM IS NO LAUGHING MATTER-- IT'S A FEDERAL OFFENSE!
(18 U.S.C. 333)--MARVEL'S LAW-LOVIN' LEGAL DEPARTMENT
I DUNNO, CAP, A WELL-PLACED WACKY MUSTACHE IMPROVED MANY A HISTORY TEXTBOOK IN MY DAY.
THWIPP
THWIPP
AND YOU SHOULD SEE WHAT A PIRATEY EYEPATCH DID FOR ELEANOR ROOSEVELT...
I'VE HAD QUITE ENOUGH BESMIRCHING OF THE GOOD NAME AND CHARACTER OF OUR FIRST LADIES, SPIDEY.
SHOW A LITTLE RESPECT!
YOU'RE A STAR SPANGLED BUMMER, CAPTA-- WUHHHF!
BESIDES, THAT CHARLATAN COULDN'T EVEN BE BOTHERED TO GET THE VOICE RIGHT.
HONEST ABE LINCOLN SOUNDED NOTHING LIKE THIS GUY...!
BUH-- WHUH?!?
HOW WOULD YOU KNOW WHAT ABRAHAM LINCOLN SOUNDED LIKE?

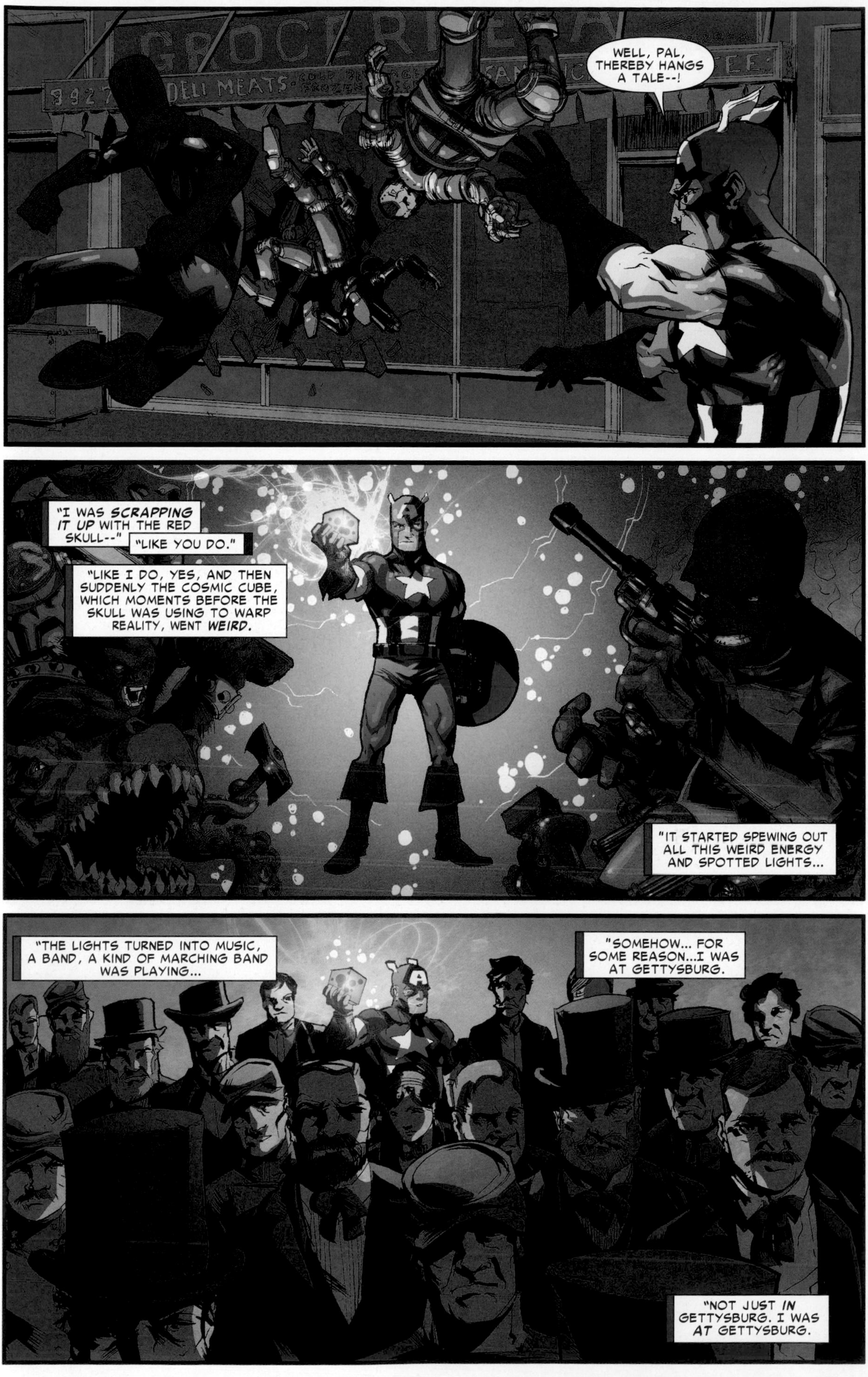
GROCERIES
3927 DELI MEATS
WELL, PAL, THEREBY HANGS A TALE--!
"I WAS SCRAPPING IT UP WITH THE RED SKULL--"
"LIKE YOU DO."
"LIKE I DO, YES, AND THEN SUDDENLY THE COSMIC CUBE, WHICH MOMENTS BEFORE THE SKULL WAS USING TO WARP REALITY, WENT WEIRD.
"IT STARTED SPEWING OUT ALL THIS WEIRD ENERGY AND SPOTTED LIGHTS...
"THE LIGHTS TURNED INTO MUSIC, A BAND, A KIND OF MARCHING BAND WAS PLAYING...
"SOMEHOW... FOR SOME REASON...I WAS AT GETTYSBURG.
"NOT JUST IN GETTYSBURG. I WAS AT GETTYSBURG.

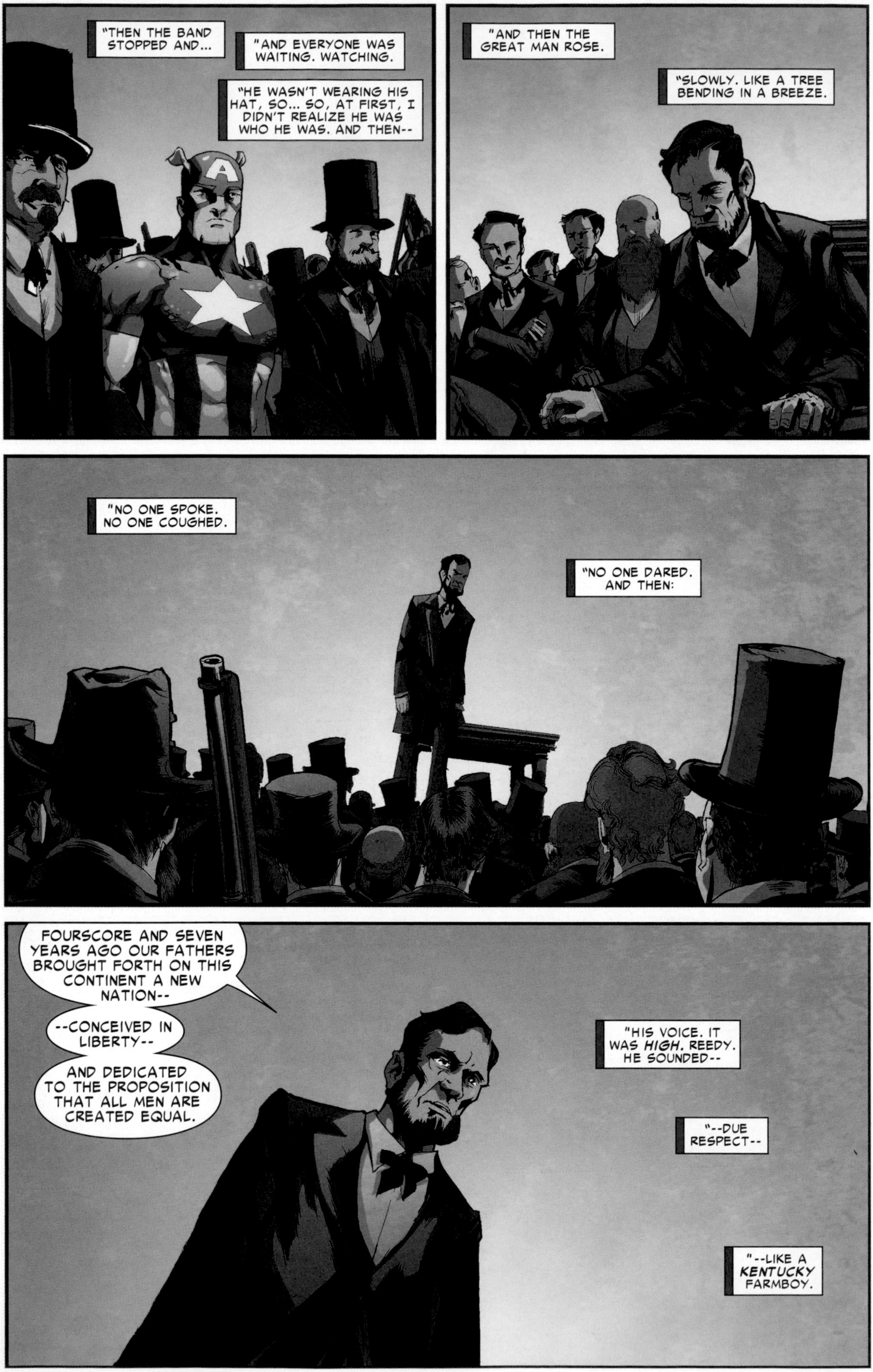
"THEN THE BAND STOPPED AND...
"AND EVERYONE WAS WAITING. WATCHING.
"HE WASN'T WEARING HIS HAT, SO... SO, AT FIRST, I DIDN'T REALIZE HE WAS WHO HE WAS. AND THEN--
"AND THEN THE GREAT MAN ROSE.
"SLOWLY. LIKE A TREE BENDING IN A BREEZE.
"NO ONE SPOKE. NO ONE COUGHED.
"NO ONE DARED. AND THEN:
FOURSCORE AND SEVEN YEARS AGO OUR FATHERS BROUGHT FORTH ON THIS CONTINENT A NEW NATION--
--CONCEIVED IN LIBERTY--
AND DEDICATED TO THE PROPOSITION THAT ALL MEN ARE CREATED EQUAL.
"HIS VOICE. IT WAS *HIGH*. REEDY. HE SOUNDED--
"--DUE RESPECT--
"--LIKE A *KENTUCKY* FARMBOY.

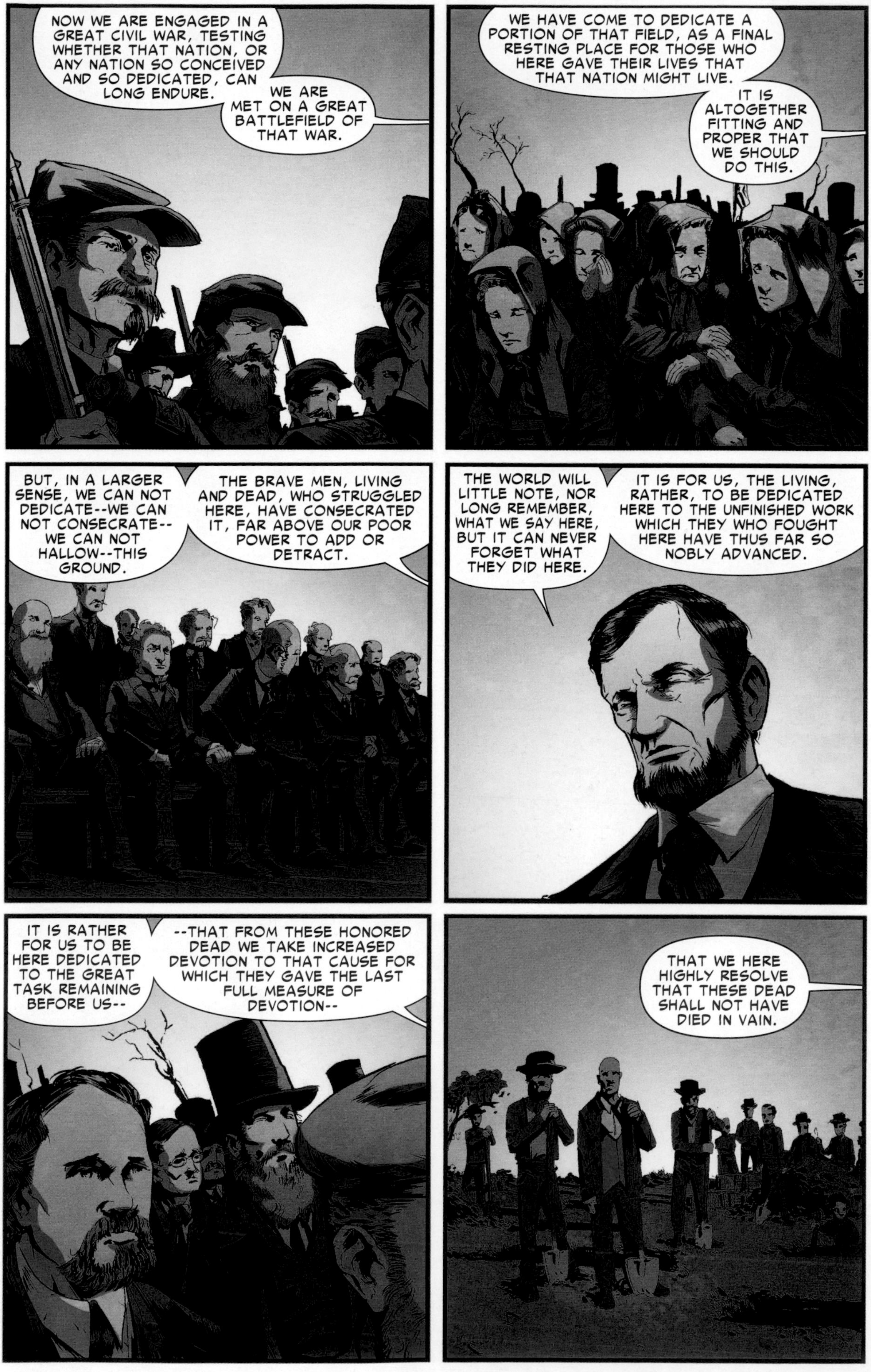
NOW WE ARE ENGAGED IN A GREAT CIVIL WAR, TESTING WHETHER THAT NATION, OR ANY NATION SO CONCEIVED AND SO DEDICATED, CAN LONG ENDURE.
WE ARE MET ON A GREAT BATTLEFIELD OF THAT WAR.
WE HAVE COME TO DEDICATE A PORTION OF THAT FIELD, AS A FINAL RESTING PLACE FOR THOSE WHO HERE GAVE THEIR LIVES THAT THAT NATION MIGHT LIVE.
IT IS ALTOGETHER FITTING AND PROPER THAT WE SHOULD DO THIS.
BUT, IN A LARGER SENSE, WE CAN NOT DEDICATE--WE CAN NOT CONSECRATE--WE CAN NOT HALLOW--THIS GROUND.
THE BRAVE MEN, LIVING AND DEAD, WHO STRUGGLED HERE, HAVE CONSECRATED IT, FAR ABOVE OUR POOR POWER TO ADD OR DETRACT.
THE WORLD WILL LITTLE NOTE, NOR LONG REMEMBER, WHAT WE SAY HERE, BUT IT CAN NEVER FORGET WHAT THEY DID HERE.
IT IS FOR US, THE LIVING, RATHER, TO BE DEDICATED HERE TO THE UNFINISHED WORK WHICH THEY WHO FOUGHT HERE HAVE THUS FAR SO NOBLY ADVANCED.
IT IS RATHER FOR US TO BE HERE DEDICATED TO THE GREAT TASK REMAINING BEFORE US--
--THAT FROM THESE HONORED DEAD WE TAKE INCREASED DEVOTION TO THAT CAUSE FOR WHICH THEY GAVE THE LAST FULL MEASURE OF DEVOTION--
THAT WE HERE HIGHLY RESOLVE THAT THESE DEAD SHALL NOT HAVE DIED IN VAIN.

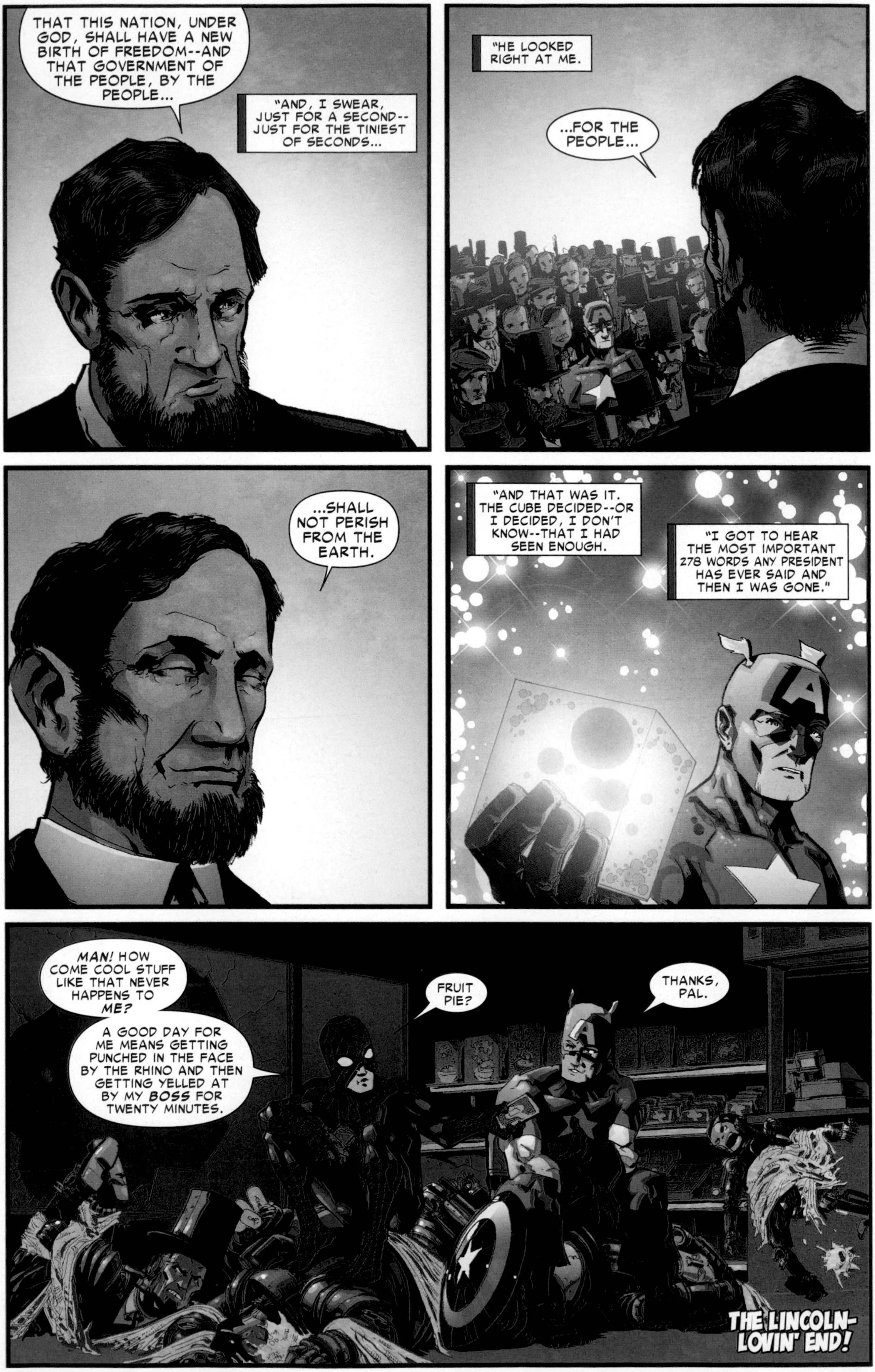
THAT THIS NATION, UNDER GOD, SHALL HAVE A NEW BIRTH OF FREEDOM--AND THAT GOVERNMENT OF THE PEOPLE, BY THE PEOPLE...
"AND, I SWEAR, JUST FOR A SECOND--JUST FOR THE TINIEST OF SECONDS...
"HE LOOKED RIGHT AT ME.
...FOR THE PEOPLE...
...SHALL NOT PERISH FROM THE EARTH.
"AND THAT WAS IT. THE CUBE DECIDED--OR I DECIDED, I DON'T KNOW--THAT I HAD SEEN ENOUGH.
"I GOT TO HEAR THE MOST IMPORTANT 278 WORDS ANY PRESIDENT HAS EVER SAID AND THEN I WAS GONE."
MAN! HOW COME COOL STUFF LIKE THAT NEVER HAPPENS TO ME?
A GOOD DAY FOR ME MEANS GETTING PUNCHED IN THE FACE BY THE RHINO AND THEN GETTING YELLED AT BY MY BOSS FOR TWENTY MINUTES.
FRUIT PIE?
THANKS, PAL.
THE LINCOLN-LOVIN' END!

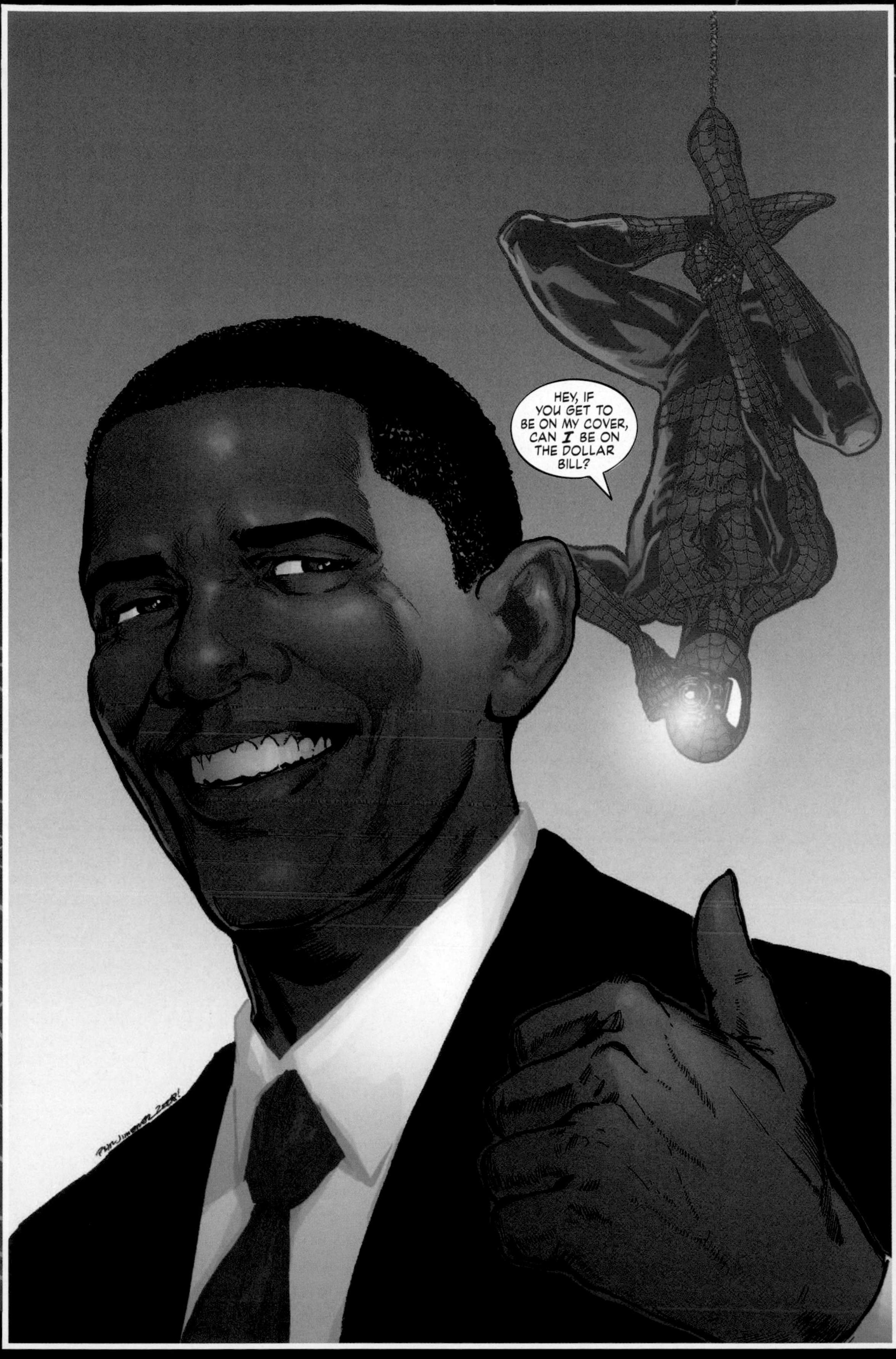
HEY, IF YOU GET TO BE ON MY COVER, CAN I BE ON THE DOLLAR BILL?

AMAZING SPIDER-MAN #583 2ND PRINTING VARIANT

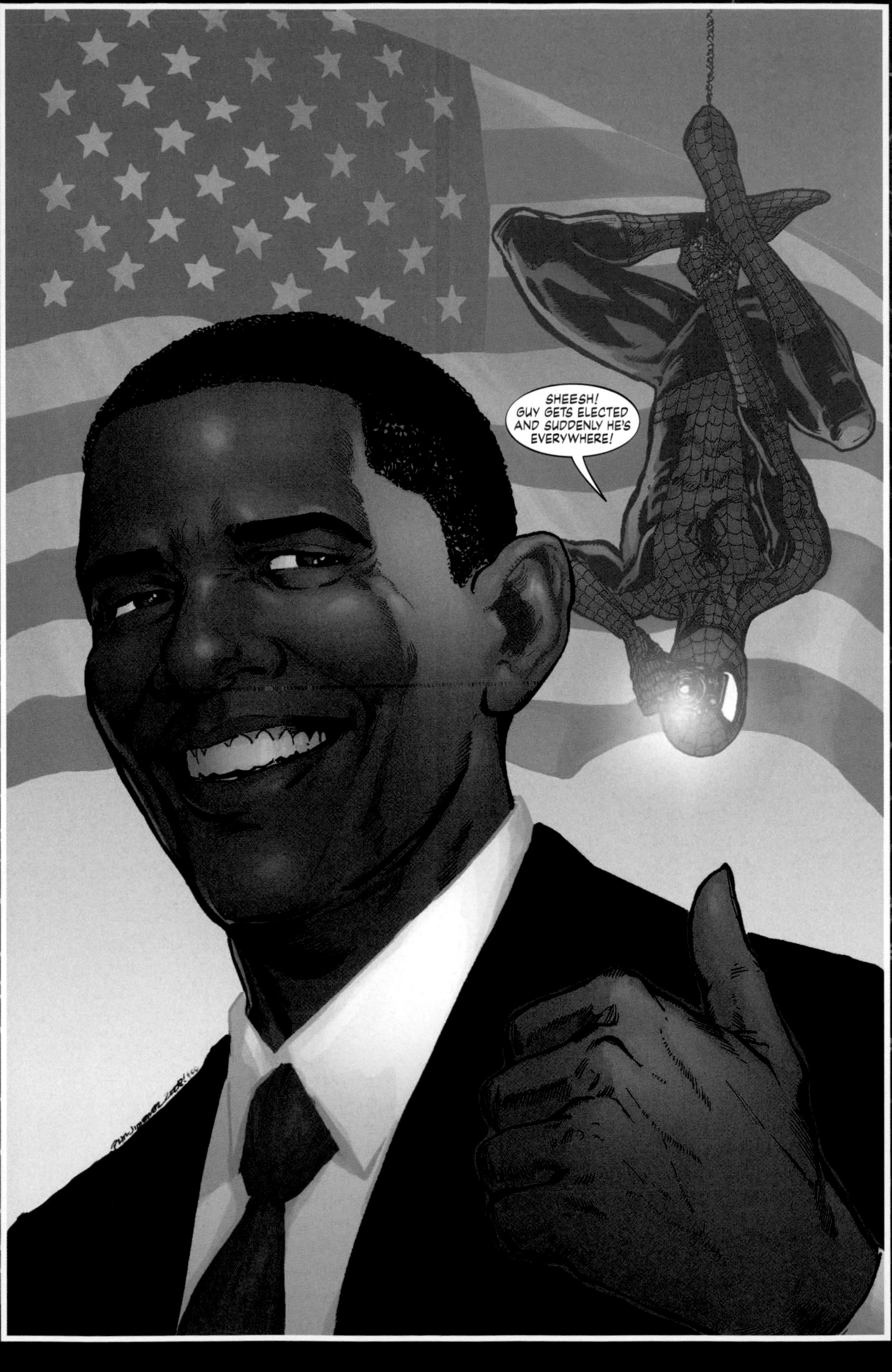
SHEESH! GUY GETS ELECTED AND SUDDENLY HE'S EVERYWHERE!

AMAZING SPIDER-MAN #583 3RD PRINTING VARIANT

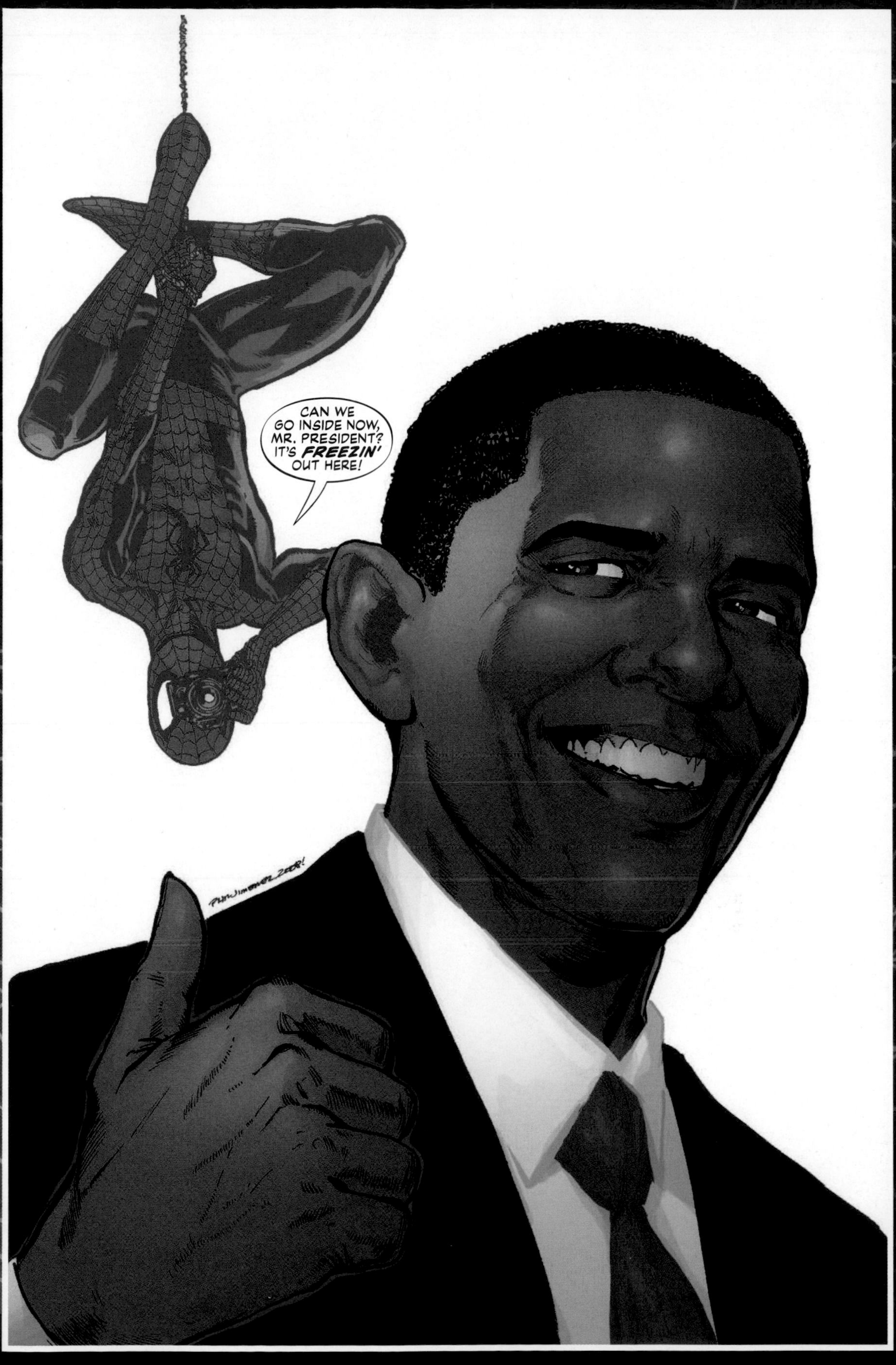
CAN WE GO INSIDE NOW, MR. PRESIDENT? IT'S FREEZIN' OUT HERE!

AMAZING SPIDER-MAN #583 4TH PRINTING VARIANT